THE FORMATION OF THE
SOVIET CENTRAL ASIAN
REPUBLICS

THE FORMATION OF THE SOVIET CENTRAL ASIAN REPUBLICS

A Study in Soviet Nationalities Policy
1917—1936

By
R. VAIDYANATH
Reader, Department of Soviet Studies
Indian School of International Studies, New Delhi

PEOPLE'S PUBLISHING HOUSE

August 1967

Price : Rs. 30.00

Printed by D. P. Sinha at New Age Printing Press, Rani Jhansi
Road, New Delhi, and published by him for People's Publishing
House Private Limited, Rani Jhansi Road, New Delhi 1.

42981

To
Dhanu & Girish

Preface and Acknowledgement

MUCH has been written in recent years on the Soviet nationalities policy in Central Asia, both within the Soviet Union and outside it. It has been examined from different angles and from the standpoint of different theories. Soviet scholars, who have brought out the largest number of books and articles on the subject, have generally tried to show how the implementation of this policy has resulted in the transformation of one of the most backward regions of Tsarist Russia into an economically and culturally developed region. They often hold up the republics of Central Asia as models to the newly independent countries of Asia and Africa which are struggling to modernize themselves. In the works of Soviet writers one does not usually come across the negative aspects of this policy and the failures and frustrations which must have confronted the Soviet authorities at various stages of building the new republics of Central Asia. The need to subscribe to and uphold the "party line" in their writings on the nationalities policy has prevented them, on the one hand, from objectively examining the seamy side of this policy, and, on the other hand, in giving out factual information without which no authentic and comprehensive study on this question could be undertaken. Consequently, an anomalous situation has come to prevail: there is at once too much material but too little information!

Nor is the situation redeemed, to any appreciable degree, by the works of scholars outside the Soviet Union. While the crippling handicaps under which they have to carry on their work on this question (for that matter, on any question pertaining to the Soviet Union) are obvious enough, what is disquieting is the tendency of most scholars to put the Bolsheviks in the dock for whatever they have done. Of course, this is not to deny that among the works which have recently come out from non-Soviet quarters there are indeed some honourable excep-

tions, but the fact remains that the bulk of them are too full of
political and moral overtones. As a result, the essential features
of the Soviet nationalities policy in Central Asia have remained
submerged under a plethora of propaganda of one kind or
another.

The nationalities problem, which the Bolsheviks inherited
from the Tsarist regime in Central Asia, had its roots in the
deep historic past. It was as much a product of Central Asia's
ethnic and socio-economic conditions as of the policies pursued
by its former rulers: the *Amirs* of Bukhara, the *Khans* of Khiva,
and finally, the Tsars of Russia. Any study which seeks to present an objective account of the Soviet nationalities policy in
Central Asia must, first of all, try to unravel the complexity of
the problem and analyse the causes which rendered it so. The
scope of this study, therefore, is not strictly confined to the
period which its title suggests, but covers a fairly extensive
period of the pre-revolutionary history of Central Asia as well.

In the preparation of this book I have set before myself only
two objectives: to endeavour, as best I could, to provide a true
picture of the events and to refrain from making any moral pronouncements. I am fully aware of the many limitations of the
book. In particular, I regret the inadequate treatment given to
the question of economic development in Central Asia in the
early Soviet period. I hope to make amends for this lapse in
the second volume which is under preparation. The other
limitations of the book stem, partly at least, from the type of
material on which it has been based. I had no access to the
bulk of the primary sources which still remain confined to the
confidential sections of the Soviet archives. During my stay in
the Central Asian region in 1960-61, I consulted all available
published sources on this subject. The utility of some of them
is beyond question, but others have wide gaps and they leave
out significant aspects. The difficulties posed by such problems
have been overcome in some measure by an extensive use of
newspapers. In particular, the newspaper *Turkestanskaia
Pravda* was found to be invaluable for this purpose. Thanks
largely to this source, I have been able to provide a great deal
of factual information than hitherto known on many controversial issues. I have also liberally made use of a large number of

books and articles of early and present-day Soviet writers in the preparation of this study.

In transliterating the Russian and russianized Turkic and Persian names the system developed by the Library of Congress has been generally followed. The exceptions are that its tie marks have been omitted and some names like 'Tadjik', 'Djadid', etc., have been transliterated according to their local pronunciations. The names of persons of Central Asian origin have been used in this book in the manner they are employed by Soviet scholars. The method of citation followed is in conformity with the system evolved by the Indian School of International Studies.

I take this opportunity to place on record the deep debt of gratitude I owe to many persons and institutions in India and the USSR for various kinds of help I have received from them in completing this project. I am grateful to the Indian School of International Studies and to its former Director, Dr A. Appadorai, for providing me with the basic research facilities and financial assistance in addition to a generous field trip grant; to Dr M. S. Rajan, the present Director of the School, Dr Anant Rao Baji, Director of Public Relations, The Press Information Bureau, and Mr. M. S. Gurupadaswamy, Minister of State for Food and Agriculture, Government of India, for their unfailing encouragement, help and advice; to Dr K. P. S. Menon, until recently India's Ambassador in Moscow, who made possible my visit to the Soviet Union; to Dr Audray J. Ahmad who willingly shared with me her vast and expert knowledge on Central Asian affairs and to the librarians and members of staff of the Indian Council of World Affairs Library, New Delhi, the Lenin State Public Library, the Fundamental Library of Social Sciences, the Library of the Institute of Oriental Studies, Moscow, the Alisher Navoi State Public Library and the Tashkent State University Library, Tashkent, for all the help they have ungrudgingly extended to me. My thanks are also due to the Director and Members of Staff of the Institute of History and Archaeology, Tashkent, for their kindness and warm hospitality. I very much appreciate the help given by my friend, Mr K. L. K. Rao, who in spite of his busy schedule of work still found time to locate some invaluable materials for me

in the various American libraries. Last but certainly not least, I
recall with gratitude the assistance and help I have received
from my friends, Dr V. M. Reddi, Dr Anirudha Gupta and
Dr N. P. Nair.

R. VAIDYANATH

May, 1967
Department of Soviet Studies,
Indian School of International Studies,
New Delhi.

Contents

GLOSSORY OF NON-ENGLISH WORDS USED IN THIS BOOK

Oblast' (Russian) = Province
Uezd (Russian) = District
Volost (Russian) = Sub-division of a district
Desiatin (Russian) = 2.7 acres
Verst (Russian) = 3,500 feet
Pood (Russian) = 36.113 pounds
Vilaiet (Persian) = Province
Tuman (Persian) = District consisting of one hundred villages
Shuro (Turkish) = District
Kent (Turkish) = Sub-division of a district
Aksakal (Turkish) = Village elder (Literally it means a "grey-beard")
Aksakaldom (Anglicized Turkish) = A group of villages

CHAPTER ONE

The Peoples of Central Asia

THE vast stretch of land mass consisting of deserts, steppes and oases which extends eastward from the Caspian Sea to the western frontier of China, and southward from the Kazakh steppes to the international frontier of the USSR with Iran and Afghanistan was, until recently, known as Russian Turkestan. The term 'Turkestan' means 'the land of Turks', and the adjective 'Russian' got prefixed to it after this region became a part of imperial Russia in the course of the nineteenth century. Thereafter, the expression 'Russian Turkestan' was used in contradistinction to the Chinese and Afghan Turkestans, the latter expressions referring respectively to Sinkiang and Northern Afghanistan which ethnographically are projections of Russian Turkestan. Earlier, the geographic expression *'Māwarān' an-Nahr* or 'Transoxiana' was also used in relation to this region but lately this expression has become largely archaic. Some writers have also employed certain other expressions like 'Tartary,' 'Turan,' 'Russian Central Asia,' etc., to describe this region but none of them seems to be satisfactory. In this study the expression 'Central Asia' has been preferred and it is used in a restrictive sense. It is employed to mean, unless otherwise stated, only those territories which at present are included within the modern Soviet Republics of Uzbekistan, Turkmenistan, Tadjikistan, Kirgizia and the Kara-Kalpak Autonomous Republic. With a view to keep the scope of this study within manageable limits, the Kazakh Republic (excepting its two southern provinces of Syr-Daria and Semirechie) is omitted.

The Central Asian region is situated in the heart of the Asian continent and is completely isolated from the oceans and their influences. In the distant past this region constituted the bed of a large inland sea. The only traces of this sea left today are the Caspian and the Aral Seas. Much of the land surface of Central

Asia is covered with steppes and deserts which are subject to
continental extremes of climate. Life in this arid region is made
possible and pleasanter by the presence of two mighty rivers:
the Amu Daria and the Syr Daria, their tributaries and a few
small rivulets which flow down from the adjoining mountains.
The waters of the relatively small rivers like the Zerafshan, the
Tedzhen and the Murgab are either entirely used up for irrigation or get lost in the sands of the arid deserts or small inland
lakes. Compared to the largeness of the area and the needs of
the population, the water available is too meagre, and that very
meagreness has rendered it precious. The history of Central
Asia, it is said, has been a history of the struggle for water.
There appears to be a great deal of truth in this statement.
While the presence of water enables the arid expanses to bloom
with verdure and life, its absence renders any kind of life impossible. The attempts to own and monopolize the few water
resources of the region had led, in the past, to intermittent
feuds, carnage, devastation of thriving settlements and uprooting
of sedentary populations. It is characteristic of the history of
Central Asia that, while in the scattered oases and river valleys
a rich sedentary culture thrived, the surrounding steppes shelter-
ed restless, warlike and almost semi-wild nomadic tribes who,
at regular intervals, abandoned their traditional occupations in
favour of organizing predatory raids on the neighbouring oases.
In fact, it could almost be said that the location of the nomadic
steppes in the northern and northeastern periphery of the oasis
regions of Central Asia determined, to a large extent, the entire
course of its history. For the steppes of Central Asia were not
only the springboards of many marauding movements, but they
were also the starting points of innumerable waves of migration.
These migrations, invariably occuring in the wake of the
conquering expeditions of steppe nomads over oasis regions,
wrought more radical and lasting changes in the structure of
sedentary societies. The establishment of the nomads' political
supremacy over the conquered territories was followed up by
consolidation of their economic gains. This occurred by way
of settlement of nomadic population in the fertile oases, after
forcibly pushing off their earlier inhabitants. The lawless, warlike and freely-roaming nomads of the steppes, after they
were subjected to different conditions of life in the southern

oasis regions became in course of time, peaceful, law-abiding and sedentary dwellers. Such a transition was of utmost historical significance. For it meant that the nomads had taken that first elementary step, on the foundation of which alone any normal socio-economic life could become possible. Only on the basis of a sedentary mode of life could the movement of any people towards higher forms of civilized living become a reality or could the several disunited and disjointed tribes and clans be fused into a stable union of people.

The change that inevitably resulted from the settlement of the nomadic population in the sedentary regions worked both ways. Though its course was not always smooth, the pattern it followed was invariably the same. The first encounter of two different cultures, languages and ways of living of the conquerors and the conquered led, almost inevitably, to clashes, and to attempts by those who were politically dominant to impose their own culture and language on the subjugated people. However, it soon became clear to the nomads that the culture of the people they had conquered was much superior to their own. This realization led them to abandon all attempts to supress the culture and languages of the sedentary people. What was more significant was the fact that the nomads themselves started taking over the language and culture of the latter and also began enriching them. With this change coming over the conquerors, the assimilating power of the sedentary culture received a fresh stimulus, and in course of time, all differences of race, language and ways of life which at one time existed between the indigenous and the immigrant populations began to disappear. While the nomads accepted the culture of the oasis-dwellers, they, on their part, infused the distinct traits of their own physical type into the population strata of the oases. Such a process of mixing and interbreeding of different racial, ethnic and linguistic groups began occurring on such an extensive scale that ultimately, the Central Asian region was transformed into a vast 'ethnological museum' of mankind.[1]

1. Crossing and interbreeding of peoples of diverse ethnic origins were the inevitable results of the large number of invasions and migrations the Central Asian region has witnessed. Professor V. V. Bartol'd's researches have shown, for instance, that the settlement of the nomadic Oghuz, Karluks, Kipchaks and other Turkic tribes in Semirechie and Khorezm

Against such a background it is but natural that the ethnographic map of Central Asia should appear to be so complex. Nearly two scores of peoples of diverse ethnic origins constitute its population strata. However, out of this ethnic melangé only a few groups stand out preeminently. They are the Uzbeks, Turkmens, Tadjiks, Kirgiz, Kara-Kalpaks and Kazakhs.[2] Apart from being relatively large in number, these peoples inhabit definite territories, possess their own distinct languages, culture and ways of living. Of these, the Tadjiks belong to an Iranian stock-origin, and also continue to speak a language of the Iranian group. The others are of Turco-Mongol origin. Among the latter, however, the community of race has proved as weak as the community of religion, which nominally binds all the peoples of Central Asia except the immigrant European population.[3] Interbreeding and contact with peoples of non-Turkic origins, absence of a common territory, differences of economic

led to the turkification of the physical type and languages of the peoples who earlier inhabited them. In Khorezm, the language of the Oghuz totally supplanted the ancient Khorezmian language.

2. The smaller ethnic groups include the Kipchaks, Kashgaris, Turki, Taranchis, Arabs, Sart-Kalmuks, Dungans, Kurama, etc. The Kipchaks live mainly in the Fergana and the Tashkent regions. In the 1917 census 42,114 persons in the Fergana oblast and 1,627 persons in the Tashkent uezd were registered as Kipchaks. The Kashgaris said to be a turkified Iranian group migrated to this region from Eastern Turkestan (Sinkiang). They live mainly in the Fergana and Semirechie regions. The 1917 census put their strength at 39,528 persons. The Taranchis, an ethnic group of Turkic origin are also immigrants from Eastern Turkestan. The 1917 census registered 55,988 persons in Semirechie as Taranchis. The Arabs, the descendants of the Arab conquerors of Central Asia, live in the Samarkand and Katta-kurgan areas and in 1917 numbered about 7,209 persons. The Sart-Kalmuks also known as 'Mongol Moslems', differ from both the Turkic and Persian groups. In 1917 they constituted about 2,394 persons and lived amidst the Kirgiz population. The Dungans, an ethnic group formed by the fusion of Turks and Chinese are also immigrants from Eastern Turkestan. They live in Semirechie and in parts of the Syr Daria region. In these areas about 18,318 persons were registered as Dungans in 1917. The Kurama, an ethnic group formed as a result of the mixing of Kazakhs and Uzbeks live in the Angren river valley of the Tashkent district. See I. I. Zarubin, 'Spisok narodnosti Turkestanskogo kraia', *Trudy kommissii po izucheniiu plemennogo sostava naseleniia Rossii i sopredel'nykh stran* (Leningrad, 1925) 17-20; *Statisticheskii ezhegodnik 1917-1924 gg* (Tashkent, 1924) I, pt. 3, 3, 45-8.

3. In 1879 Boulger wrote that 'among the subject races (of Central Asia) there is no connecting link save that of religion, which has always in their case proved singularly valueless.' See Demetrius Charles Boulger,

life, etc., have not only weakened the links of race and religion, but also have set each of them on almost independent paths of development.

The facts relating to the ancestry of the present inhabitants of Central Asia are still shrouded in uncertainty. It is rather difficult to trace back their ancestry to any of the ethnic groups of ancient times. However, it is clear that both the ancient aborigines of the land, as well as those who came from outside, have entered, in different proportions, into the composition of the several and sometimes of all the peoples of Central Asia and often of those living beyond its frontiers.[4] Again, it is rather difficult to say with any degree of certainty when each one of these peoples of Central Asia emerged into the portals of history as a distinct people. 'The important task,' writes Professor Tolstov in this connection, 'is to determine that narrow historical moment, and the territorial-social union, when and where the ethnic and glottogonic process of a given people reached a stage near to completion.'[5] No matter at what period the evolution of these people as separate entities occurred, the process of their consolidation was hampered for a long time. Even on the eve of the Russian conquest none of them possessed the traits of a nation. The causes for this puzzling phenomenon must be sought in the peculiar forces which shaped the course of events of Central Asian history.

England and Russia in Central Asia (London, 1879) I, 61. The influence of Islam had been particularly weak among the nomadic peoples of the region.

4. S. P. Tolstov, 'Osnovnye problemy etnogeneza narodov Srednei Azii', *Sovetskaia etnografiia: sbornik statei* (Moscow), VI-VII (1947) 304.

5. Tolstov, n. 4, 304. Professor Tolstov believes, and with him most of the Soviet orientalists agree, that the state of the Karakhanids (IX-XII centuries A.D.) greatly facilitated the evolution of the Uzbeks as a distinct people. Similarly the Samanid state (IX-X centuries A.D.) which preceded the Karakhanids, provided ideal conditions for the Tadjiks to consolidate themselves. The western Oghuz political union (IX-XI centuries A.D.), gave a stimulus to the Turkmens to develop as a separate people. The Kazakhs became unified during the time of the Eastern Kipchak political union (XI-XII centuries) and the Kara-Kalpaks during the time of Pecheneg political union (IX-XI centuries). The Kirgiz perhaps, were the earliest to be consolidated as a distinct group, and they did so during the time of the existence of the Kirgiz state (VI-VIII centuries) and later, during the time of the Kara-Kitais, to which period, evidently, is connected, the settlement of the Kirgiz in Semirechie.

The division of each of the peoples of Central Asia into innumerable tribes, clans and 'bones,' the differences of economic
life manifesting themselves in sharp contrast between the
nomadic economy of the steppes and the agricultural economy
of the sedentary areas, the political dismemberment leading to
the inclusion of different parts of one and the same people
under the rule of different states, the intermittent feudal wars
and oppressions, the religious bigotry of the clergy, the almost
total illiteracy and ignorance of the masses, and the isolation
of the Central Asian region from the more advanced countries
of Asia and Europe, all these, to sum up, were factors which
impeded the political, economic and social progress of the
peoples of the region. As a result of the interplay of such
retrogressive forces, Central Asia, on the eve of the Russian
conquest, remained 'the most backward country in the Moslem
world.'[6]

I. THE TURKMENS

The ancient aborigines of the Turkmen territory belonged
mostly to the Iranian language group. From the sixth century
onwards following the penetration of the Turkic tribes, the
indigenous people were subjected to an unceasing process of
turkification. The formation of the distinct Turkmen group of
people, in the early stages, was closely connected with the west-
ward migration of the Oghuz (also known as Ghuz or Guz)
tribes, and later, with the establishment of the Seldzhuk dynasty
(A.D. 1040-1157).[7] Gradually, the term 'Turkmen' completely replaced the term 'Oghuz' as an appellation of the ancestors of

---

6. See V. V. Bartol'd, *Istoriia kul'turnoi zhizni Turkestana* (Leningrad,
1927) 123.

7. The Ghuz or Oghuz and the Pechenegs were Turkic nomads who
constituted the later waves of migration that swept Central Asia from East
to West. They arrived in Central Asia in the eighth century A.D. and by
the tenth century A.D., the Oghuz and the Pechenegs of the northern
regions started moving westwards through the Ural and the Volga regions.
A century later, the Oghuz-Seldzhuks started their westerly migrations
through Persia and Asia Minor. Those who remained in the Trans-Aral
region became in course of time the chief component element of the
Turkmen group of people. To some extent they also constituted the
ethnic components of the Uzbeks of Khorezm and the Kara-Kalpaks. See
N. A. Baskakov, *Tiurkskie iazyki* (Moscow, 1960) 115.

the modern Turkmens.[8] During the Seldzhuk period, the Turkmens held a special position as kindred clans of the ruling dynasty,[9] and in the favourable conditions which prevailed at the time, they were able to assimilate the other inhabitants of the Transcaspian region. However, it is rather significant to note that the Turkmens themselves were divided, from very early times, into twentyfour tribes.[10] Rashid-ad-Din traces the ancestry of these twentyfour Turkmen tribes to the somewhat mythical Oghuz Khan,[11] which of course, cannot be taken too seriously. The truth is that the mixing of the ancient aborigines of the Transcaspian region with the immigrant Turkic tribes, among whom the Oghuz were preeminent, overlaid by a small, but unmistakably clear Mongoloid element, brought into existence the modern Turkmen people.[12] The Oghuz ancestry of the Turkmens makes them kindred more to the Azerbaidzhanis and to the Anatolian Turks rather than to their Central Asian neighbours. In their physical type, the Turkmens belong to

8. According to Bartol'd, the term 'Oghuz' was employed when these tribes were in Mongolia and the term 'Turkmen' came into existence after the migration of these tribes to the west from the Mongolian region. The term 'Turkmen' first occurred in the writings of Makdisi, an Arab geographer of the tenth century A.D. See V. V. Bartol'd, 'Ocherk istorii Turkmenskogo naroda,' *Turkmeniia* (Leningrad, 1929) I, 5-7.

9. The Vazir Nizam-ul-Mulk who managed the affairs of the Seldzhuk dynasty for nearly thirty years (from A.D. 1064 to 1092) testifies to the special position held by the Turkmens during his life time. The founder of the Seldzhuk dynasty belonged to the *Kynyk* clan which was kindred to the Turkmen tribes. *Ibid.*, 32.

10. Both Rashid-ad-Din and Mohammed Kashgari give detailed accounts of these tribes. Another writer who supplies much useful information on the Turkmens is Abul Ghazi Bahadur Khan, the Uzbek ruler of Khiva. But there is reason to believe that the latter's writings are based more on hearsay than on written records. *Ibid.*, 35-6.

11. According to this legend, Oghuz Khan had six sons and each one of them in turn, had four. Rashid-ad-Din states that the names of the grandsons of Oghuz Khan were taken over by the tribes which sprang from them. Among the twentyfour Turkmen tribes, the important ones in the nineteenth century were the Yomud which inhabited the western regions of modern Turkmen territory and the greater part of the Tashauz district; the *Tekke*, which inhabited the central parts of the Turkmen territory and the Kyzyl-Arvat up to Bairam-Ali; the *Goklen* of the Karakalin region; the *Saryk* which inhabited the Iolotan and Takhta-Bazar regions, and the *Ersar* which had settled down in the eastern parts of the Turkmen territory and the border areas of the Chardzhui and Kerekin districts. Bartol'd, n. 8, 27; also see Baskakov, n. 7, 121-2.

12. The Mongoloid element in the Turkmen physical type is reflected,

the Khorasan type, which is related to the Mediterranean group of anthropological types which extends from India to Morocco.[13]

The Turkmens in the past represented a mere conglomeration of tribes, totally lacking cohesion. Within each tribe, the clan divisions and the authority of the clan patriarchs were preserved intact. Each tribe occupied a definite territory in which its pasture lands were located and fiercely fought the other tribes in defence of its rights. Such inter-tribal feuds were many and intermittent, but any threat from without united for a while all the Turkmen tribes, and gave them a semblance of unity and cohesion. With the disappearance of this threat, however, it was difficult to preserve their unity. It was a well-known boast among the Turkmens that they recognized no authority and each person was his own master.

No uniform social pattern existed among the Turkmens at the time of the Russian conquest. Their social differences largely stemmed from differences in economic pursuits. While a majority of them continued to carry on the traditional occupation of cattlebreeding, some had settled down as agriculturists.[14] There were yet others who pursued neither of these occupations, and made a living out of organizing predatory raids into the Persian territory, and by selling the captured Persians as slaves in the Central Asian markets.[15]

largely, among the Turkmens of the northern and centarl parts of the Transcaspian region. In the south, towards the Persian frontier, it is wholly absent. See, *Ocherki obshchei etnografii: Aziatskaia chast SSSR* (Moscow, 1960) 161; (cited hereafter as *OOE*); also see Arminius Vambery, *Sketches of Central Asia* (London, 1868) 298.

13. *OOE*, n.12, 161.

14. Nature herself by being niggardly, seems to have imposed the nomadic habit of life on most of the inhabitants of the Turkmen region. The harsh climatic conditions, the utter barrenness of terrain, and the scarcity of water, render agriculture almost impossible in most parts, except in the foothill zone of the Kopet-Dag mountains, in the basins of the small steppe rivers on the Persian frontier, and in the oases of larger rivers such as the Tedzhen, the Murgab and the Amu Daria. The smallness of cultivable areas rendered any large scale settlement on land impossible and forced many either to stick on to the traditional occupation of pastoral nomadism, or to take to other professions.

15. The Turkmens held almost a monopoly of trading in slaves. According to the estimates of Von Schwarz, they supplied to the Central Asian markets not less than one million Persian captives who were sold as slaves. See Richard A. Pierce, *Russian Central Asia 1867-1917: A Study in Colonial Rule* (Berkeley, 1960) 312 (notes).

On the eve of the Russian conquest, there were three distinct political groups among the Turkmens. They were:

1. The Turkmen tribes of Transcaspia which inhabited the territory extending eastwards from the Caspian sea to the Amu Daria, and southwards from the Kara-kum desert to the foothills of the Kopet-Dag mountains and the Paropamisus. These tribes were not subject to any centralized political authority, nor did they possess any national unity.

2. The Turkmens of Khiva, most of whom were enrolled in the army of the Uzbek rulers of Khiva. They represented a great force in the turbulent politics of the Khanate, and often held in their hands the fate of the state. By settling these Turkmens on the lower parts of the irrigational canals of the Khivan oasis (mainly in its periphery), the Khans of Khiva, had rendered them economically dependent on themselves and their Uzbek subjects. The clan leaders of Turkmens, largely of the Yomud and the Choudor tribes, were transformed into feudal princelings in service of the Khans.

3. The Turkmens of Bukhara who had come under the influence of the Bukharan clergy and under the economic exploitation of the usurious Uzbek merchants and the feudal dignitaries of the Amirate.

These three groups, largely as a result of the different socio-economic conditions under which they lived, developed somewhat differently and independently of one another. The already existing gulf between them further widened when, after the Russian conquest, only the Transcaspian Turkmens were brought under direct Russian rule, while the Turkmens of Khiva and Bukhara continued to remain, until 1920, under the regime of the Khan and the Amir.[16]

II. THE UZBEKS

The history of the evolution of the term 'Uzbek' has been somewhat different from the history of the people whom it has come to represent. The term seems to have originated in the fourteenth century as an appellation of the nomadic people who

16. E. Shteinberg, *Ocherki istorii Turkmenii* (Leningrad, 1934) 25-6; also see V. Karpych, 'Vozniknovenie Turkmenskoi SSR,' *Turkmenovedenie* (Ashkhabad) 10-11 (1928) 30-40.

inhabited the eastern lands of the Golden Horde and were enrolled in the army of Uzbek Khan (A.D. 1312-42).[17] Following
this historical evidence rather mechanically, some scholars have
come to the conclusion that the modern Uzbeks are the descendants of only the nomadic Uzbek tribes which migrated to
Central Asia towards the close of the fifteenth and the beginning
of the sixteenth centuries. As Professor A. Iu. Iakubovskii has
shown, this view, ignoring as it does the complex nature of the
process of formation of the modern Uzbeks, is obviously incorrect. It assumes that the nomadic Uzbek tribes, on coming
to Central Asia, either did not find any people inhabiting the
region, or that they completely exterminated all of them.[18] The
fact is that neither of these was true. The nomadic Uzbek tribes,
when they arrived in Central Asia, found that the territory of
modern Uzbekistan, or at least parts of it, were densely inhabited by a Turkic-language people. The latter had inhabited this
territory already for a long time, and had almost completely
fused with the descendants of the aborigines of the land. The
nomadic, Uzbek tribes on coming to Central Asia settled down
among these people and after gradually abandoning many of
the traits of their earlier nomadic ways of living, started taking
over almost completely the ways of life, language and culture of
their neighbours. However, the process of settlement of
the nomadic Uzbeks was spread over a long period, and even
at the time of the Russian conquest, they had not yet completely
fused with the original inhabitants of the territory of modern
Uzbekistan. Towards the middle of the nineteenth century
among the people who inhabited the territory of modern Uzbekistan there were three distinct groups. Each of these groups
possessed certain well-marked economic, cultural and linguistic
differences. One of them was the Turkic-language Sarts[19] who

17. *Istoriia narodov Uzbekistana: ot obrazovaniia gosudarstva shaibani-
dov do velikoi oktiabr'skoi sotsialisticheskoi revoliutsii* (Tashkent, 1947) II,
22. (Cited hereafter as *INUZ*).

18. A. Iu. Iakubovskii, *K voprosu ob etnogeneze Uzbekskogo naroda*
(Tashkent, 1941) 3.

19. There is no other term in Central Asian history which is as controversial as the term 'Sart'. While some orientalists, like V. V. Bartol'd,
N. P. Ostroumov and P. I. Pashino, maintained that the Sarts were a
separate ethnic group different from the Uzbeks, Tadjiks, Kirgiz and
Turkmens, others like Vambery, A. Grebenkin and A. P. Khoroshkin

inhabited the Zerafshan valley, and the Fergana, Tashkent and Khorezm oases, and also constituted the bulk of the region's urban population. The second group consisted of several tribes and clans which inhabited the foothills and hilly regions of the territory of modern Uzbekistan. A noted Uzbek writer, Professor M. Vakhabov, calls them the 'Turks of Māwarā 'an-Nahr.' The third group was made up of many large tribes and clans which inhabited the steppes and valleys of the Kashka-Daria, Surkhan-Daria, a part of the Zerafshan valley and the Tashkent and Khorezm oases. These were the Uzbeks proper, the descendants of the nomadic Uzbek tribes which migrated to this region towards the close of the fifteenth and the beginning of the sixteenth centuries.[20] The Turkic-language Sarts were a sedentary people who pursued both agriculture and trade and possessed a relatively developed culture and language. The other two groups, though some of them had started settling down on land, still pursued cattlebreeding as their main occupation. Their semi-nomadic way of life hindered their complete transition to a sedentary living, and was mainly responsible for their social and cultural backwardness. Vestiges of a patriarchal mode of life as well as clan-tribal divisions existed among them.[21]

Thus the Uzbeks do not exhibit a homogeneous ethnic strain, and are a people in whom diverse ethnic components have fused. This has led many scholars to conclude that the Uzbeks are Turkic in language but Iranian in origin, and they claim that this is particularly true of the Sarts[22]. An analysis of the process of evolution of the Uzbeks, however, shows that two distinct trends have operated in levelling all social and cultural differences and dialectical variations among the three groups. On the one hand, the nomadic Uzbek tribes, by going over to a sedentary mode of life, drifted away from their original kinsmen like the Kazakhs, the Nogai tribes, etc., and came

asserted that the Sarts, in fact, were Tadjiks or a part of them. There are yet other theories on this question, all adding to the prevailing confusion.

20. This portion is largely based on Professor M. Vakhabov's work *Formirovanie Uzbekskoi sotsialisticheskoi natsii* (Tashkent, 1961).

21. *Ibid.*, 45-57.

22. Zarubin, n. 2, 14; also see P. P. Ivanov, 'Naselenie: kratkii statistiko-etnograficheskii ocherk,' *Vsia Sredniaia Aziia: spravochnaia kniga na 1926 khoziaistvennyi god* (Tashkent, 1926) 91.

nearer to, and to a considerable extent under the cultural influence of, the Tadjiks. On the other hand, the assimilation by
the Uzbeks of the earlier inhabitants of the territory of modern
Uzbekistan led to the gradual separation of these people from
the Iranian-language Tadjiks. As this process of fusion and assimilation worked itself out, and as the various ethnic strains
crossed and mingled, it became possible to speak of one Uzbek
people. With the growth of national consciousness, the foremost
strata of the Sart community took over the name 'Uzbek' as its
own.[23]

III. THE TADJIKS

The Tadjiks, one of the most cultured peoples of Central
Asia, are the descendants of the ancient aborigines of the land.[24]
They are an Iranian language-group, who belong to the Aryan
branch of the family of Indo-European peoples.[25] In times past,
the ethnographic map of the Tadjiks stretched far beyond the
narrow confines of the hilly region that is Tadjikistan today.
The history of the Tadjiks took shape in the distant past from
the events which occurred in the Central Asian duab (the Amu
Daria and the Syr Daria region), Khorasan and the region of the
western Hindukush.[26] With the beginning of the Turkic invasions and migrations, and later, with the increase of the number
of people abandoning the nomadic way of life in favour of
sedentary living, areas inhabited by the Tadjiks steadily began
to shrink. The Tadjiks were squeezed out of the fertile lands

23. Zarubin, n. 2, 15; also see 'Vtoraia sessiia VTsIK SSSR,' *Narodnoe
khoziaistvo Srednei Azii*, 4 (November, 1924) 201. The Uzbeks are mostly
of European racial extraction. However, certain groups of Uzbeks, like
the Kipchaks of Fergana and the Uzbeks of northern Khorezm, possess
sharp Mongoloid features. The Uzbeks of southern Khorezm (of the Khiva
region) and Fergana, are very much nearer to the Tadjiks. The Soviet
anthropologists include the Uzbeks under the Pamir-Fergana or the *Duab*
anthropological type. *OOE*, n.12, 160-1.
24. Many scholars place the Tadjik culture at a much higher level
than the culture of other inhabitants of Central Asia including the Uzbeks.
See Ivanov, n.22, 102.
25. M. S. Andreev, 'Po etnografii Tadzhikov,' in N. L. Korzhenevskii,
ed., *Tadazhikistan* (Tashkent, 1925) 151.
26. B. G. Gafurov, Istoriia Tadzhikskogo naroda (Moscow, 1949) I, 5;
also see, B. Gafurov and N. Prokhorov, *Tadzhikii narod v bor'be za
svobodu i nezavisimost' svoei rodiny* (Stalinabad, 1944) 3.

and forced to migrate to the barren and mountainous regions.[27] As a result, at the time of the Russian conquest of Central Asia, all that remained in the possession of the Tadjik people was a few hundred square kilometres of hilly region that was known as Eastern Bukhara.[28]

The Tadjiks who escaped to the mountains, which were inaccessible to the Turkic conquerors and settlers, managed to preserve the purity of language and physical type. This group of Tadjiks, until recently, were known as the 'Galcha' or 'mountain' Tadjiks. The 'Galchas' inhabit mainly the upper portion of the Zerafshan and Amu Daria valleys. Even they, however, are not very homogeneous. The 'Galchas' include such diverse ethnic and linguistic groups as the Yagnobis, Roshnanis, Shugnans Wakhanis, etc.[29] Those of the Tadjiks who remained on the plains were swamped by the mighty wave of Turkic immigrants and conquerors, and were turkified to a considerable extent both in language as well as in physical type. The 'Plain Tadjiks', as they come to be known, inhabit mainly the Samarkand, Zerafshan and Fergana regions, and in their way of life, customs and manners, differ little from the surrounding sedentary Uzbek population. Though they continue to speak their old Iranian dialect, as a consequence of their close proximity

27. The coming of the Russians, in a way, was a blessing to the Tadjiks. The establishment of law and order under the aegis of Russian administration put an end to the intermittent marauding raids on the Tadjik settlements by Kirgiz and Uzbek nomads. The last of such raids by the Kirgiz took place in 1865, at the time when Russian soldiers were laying siege to the city of Tashkent. See, V. V. Bartol'd, 'Tadzhiki: istoricheskii ocherk,' in Korzhenevskii, n. 25, 111.

28. Even this region was under the oppressive rule of the Uzbek Amir of Bukhara up to 1920. Uzbek domination in one of its worst forms prevailed in this region right until the end of the Amir's rule in Bukhara. Not only were all the higher offices of administration of Eastern Bukhara manned by Uzbeks of the Mangyt tribe, but no check was ever kept on their activities. As a result, the several *beks* who headed the *bekdoms* of Eastern Bukhara only concerned themselves with self-enrichment, and administrative arbitrariness went to an extent that made the Mangyt rule symbolic of the worst of oriental despotism. The steady infringement of the rights of the Tadjik people, and the continuous encroachment on their lands, brought into existence great national frictions between the Tadjiks and the Uzbeks. See N. A. Kisliakov, *Sem'ia i brak u Tadzhikov* (Moscow, 1959) 16-7.

29. See Bartol'd, n. 27, 100-1; also see Zarubin, n. 2, 6 and Ivanov, n. 22, 102.

with the Uzbeks, many words of Turkic origin have made inroads into it.[30]

The term 'Tadjik' is employed today only in a very restricted sense to connote the majority nation of the Tadjik Republic. In the past the term had a much wider connotation, and it referred to any person of sedentary habits and Muslim culture, irrespective of his linguistic affinities.[31]

The completion of the process of evolution of the Tadjiks as a distinct community is usually assigned to the ninth century A.D. The overthrow of the political supremacy of the Arabs and the subsequent establishment of the Samanid dynasty in the ninth century, symbolized the assertion of independence of the Central Asian region from the tutelage of the Caliphate. The Samanid sultans, who relied on the support of the indigenous population to preserve their dynasty, encouraged the blossoming of the local cultures. By this the Tadjiks, who at the time played an important role in the political, economic and social life of the Samanid empire profited most. They took full advantage of the then existing opportunities to consolidate themselves as a distinct people. The cultural and literary achievements of this period constitute a brilliant chapter in the history of the Tadjiks. The revival of cultural life in both Khorasan and Māwarā'an-Nahr led to the transformation of Merv, Bukhara, Samarkand and Urgench into renowned cultural centres of the time.[32]

The Samanid rule, however, was short-lived. All traces of authority of the Samanid dynasty in Central Asia disappeared

30. The turkification (here it is essentially *Uzbekization*) of the 'Plain Tadjiks' was evident in many places. For instance, Radloff, the famous Russain orientalist, in 1868 found that the inhabitants of Samarkand spoke mainly in the 'Iranian' (Tadjik) language. But within less than forty years the situation had changed radically. Professor Bartol'd, visiting Samarkand in 1904, heard there almost exclusively the Turkic (Uzbek) language. The fact that the inhabitants of the village of Urgut used to complain 'We are Tadjiks but (alas!) our children will be Uzbeks' has been cited as another instance of turkification of the Tadjiks. See Bartol'd, n. 27, 111; Zarubin, n. 2, 8.

31. Bartol'd, n. 27 93-104 and Zarubin, n. 2, 7.

32. Gafurov, n. 26, 174-90; also see M. Ia. Berkovich, 'K voprosu o vozniknovenii Tadzhikskoi natsional'nosti, *Izvestiia Iadzhikskogo filiala akademi nauk SSSR; Istoriia, iazyk i literatura* (Stalinabad, 1946) XII, 86; Tolstoy, n. 4. 304; *Istoriia Uzbekskoi SSR* (Tashkent, 1955) I, pt. 1, 223-37. (Cited hereafter as *IUZSSR*).

by the end of the tenth century. The establishment of the Kara-khanid state, in a sense, marked the reassertion of the hegemony over Māwarā'an-Nahr of the Turkic elements. This resulted in still greater attemps being made to turkify the indigenous population who were mostly Tadjiks. Not only was the progress in all walks of life which was much in evidence among the Tadjiks during the Samanid period arrested, but their survival as a distinct community was also seriously threatened. The forced migrations of the Tadjiks to the hilly regions which started during this period continued unabated until the Russian conquest of Central Asia.

The Tadjiks of the plains are essentially a sedentary people engaged chiefly in agriculture and commerce. The 'Plain Tadjiks' have been famous for a long time for their skill in the field of intensive agriculture. The 'Mountain Tadjiks,' until recently, practised both agriculture and cattlebreeding.

IV. THE KIRGIZ

The Kirgiz[33] are an ancient people of Central Asia whose history stretches beyond the beginnings of the Christian era. In fact, there are no other people in Central Asia who could lay claim to such well known antiquity as the Kirgiz.[34] In the distant past, the ancestors of the Kirgiz inhabited the Altai and Yenisei regions.[35] The date of migration of the Kirgiz to the Tien-Shan region is uncertain and a great deal of controversy surrounds this question.[36]

33. The Kirgiz in the past were called by a bewilderingly large number of names. While the early Chinese sources referred to them first as Kakhas and then as Ki-li-tse, the Dzhungars called them Burut Kirgiz and the Russians 'Diko-Kamenyi Kirgizy' (wild mountain Kirgiz). The Central Asian Muslims referred to them as Kara-Kirgiz (Black Kirgiz). According to Radloff, the name Kara-Kirgiz came into existence as a result of the refusal of the Kirgiz to embrace Islam for a long time. See Bartol'd, n. 9, 210; also see M. A. Czaplicka, *The Turks of Central Asia in History and the Present Day* (Oxford, 1918) 48, 66-7; Eugene Schuyler, *Turkestan: Notes of a journrney in Russian Turkestan, Kokand, Bukhara and Kuldja* (London, 1876) II, 135-6.
34. V. V. Bartol'd, *Kirgizy: istoricheskii ocherk* (Frunze, 1927) 5.
35. *Ibid.,* 10; also see Czaplicka, n.33, 62.
36. A. Bernshtam, the well-known Soviet authority on the Kirgiz, maintains that the Kirgiz migrated to the Tien-shan region in the ninth and the tenth centuries A.D. See his 'K voprosu o proiskhozhdenii Kirgizs-

The history of the Kirgiz falls into two distinct periods: the Yenisei and the Tien-Shan periods. During the former period, the Kirgiz were politically united under one ruler whom the early Chinese sources describe as 'Azho'.[37] Besides having an independent political status, the Kirgiz during this period also possessed their own distinct traits of culture and the so-called Kirgiz runic script. They led a sedentary life based on agriculture and also possessed a relatively developed urban life.

After migrating to the Tien-Shan region, the Kirgiz underwent a great change. Here they came in contact with a culture which was at a higher stage of development than their own. The indigenous population of the Tien-Shan region included the turkified Iranian-language group like the Sogdians. It was only gradually that the Kirgiz were able to assimilate most of them. From the 12th century, however, the population of the Tien-Shan region became largely homogeneous.[38] As a result of the mixing and interbreeding that occurred here, the Kirgiz of the Tien-Shan region sharply differed in their ethnic composition from their ancestors of the Yenisei region. Though the Kirgiz did not participate in the Mongol invasion, still, as a consequence of the inclusion of their territory in the Mongol empire and their subsequent mixing with the Mongols, a considerable Mongoloid element was infused into the physical type of the Kirgiz.[39] In view of the presence of a considerably large Mongo-

kogo naroda,' *Sovetskaia etnografiia*, 2 (1955) 22. For other opinions on this question see Bartol'd, n. 34, 32, 36 and T. R. Ryskulov, *Kirgizistar.* (Moscow, 1935) 22-5.

37. The Kirgiz supremacy was considerably weakened with the rise of the Uigur Turks in Mongolia. The latter defeated the Kirgiz in A.D. 758. What is significant is the fact that the Kirgiz at this time were able to put into the battle-field between 40,000 to 80,000 soldiers. According to the Orkhon inscriptions, the Kirgiz defeated the Uigurs in A.D. 840 and followed it up by invading the Uigur capital on the Orkhon river. The conquest of Mongolia by the Kirgiz was one of the significant events of Central Asian history. Perhaps it was the only conquering movement within the Central Asian region which took place from west to east as against the traditional east to west invasions. See Bartol'd, n. 34, 14-7.

38. Bernshtam, n.36, 22; also see 'Bol'shaia sovetskaia entsiklopediia (Moscow, 1935, 2nd edition) xxi, 76. (Cited hereafter as *BSE*).

39. In view of the presence of a considerably large Mongoloid element in the Kirgiz physical type the assertion of some scholars that the Kirgiz are the truest representatives of the Turkic race appears somewhat odd. For such a view see Vambery, n. 14, 286-7; Czaplicka, n. 35, 50. Charles Warren Hostler, *Turkism and the Soviets: The Turks of the World and*

loid element in their physical type, the Soviet anthropologists include the Kirgiz under the 'South Siberian Anthropological Type.'[40] Though the Kazakhs also come under the same group, they are, however, differentiated from the Kirgiz by the fact of their possessing less Mongoloid, and more European, racial elements.[41]

Until recently, the Kirgiz were divided into two main tribal groups: *On* (right) and *Sol* (left). Each of these groups in turn was divided into a number of tribes, and each tribe into clans and sub-clan divisions.[42] Within each tribe or clan, the patriarchal mode of life remained dominant and the *manaps,* the hereditary clan-feudal dignitaries, exercised great influence and authority. Though in religion the Kirgiz are Sunni Muslims, until recently, they retained many of the survivals of their pre-Islamic religion in their daily life.[43]

On the eve of the Russian conquest, it was found that cattle-breeding was almost the chief occupation among the Kirgiz. However, the known historical evidences indicate that in the distant past the Kirgiz were basically a sedentary agricultural people.[44] The transformation of the Kirgiz from an essentially

their Political Objectives (London, 1957) 71; Robert Shaw, *Visits to High Tartary, Yarkand and Kashgar* (London, 1871) 22 (footnote). For an opposite view see G. Cherdantsev, *Sredne-Aziatskie respubliki* (Moscow, 1928) 67.

40. *OOE*, n.12, 161.

41. N. N. Miklashevskaia, 'K voprosu ob udel'nom vese tsentral'noaziatskogo elementa v obrazovanii antropologicheskogo tipa Kirgizov,' *Trudy Kirgizskoi arkheologo-etnograficheskoi ekspeditsii,* 2 (Moscow, 1959) 371 and 376; Ivanov, n. 22, 101; Schuyler, n. 33, 136. See also 'The Peoples of Central Asia,' *The Central Asian Review* (London), 7 (January 1959) 10.

42. For details of these tribal and clan divisions among the Kirgiz, see K. Usonbaev, 'K voprosu ob obshchnosti territorii Kirgizskogo naroda v dorevoliutsionnyi period,' *Trudy instituta istorii,* Vypusk 2 (Frunze, 1956) 30-1.

43. The Kirgiz were perhaps the last of the Central Asian people to be converted to Islam. Bartol'd is of the opinion that even in the sixteenth century A.D. the Kirgiz had remained 'outside the religion and culture of Islam.' Another curious fact is that even after their conversion to Islam, the Kirgiz often continued to give their children the old Tatar names such as 'Toctamish,' 'Satwaldee' etc. In contrast to them, the sedentary Uzbeks (as also many other peoples of Central Asia), have mostly forgotten their pre-Islamic traditions, and take Muslim names derived from the Arabic. See Bartol'd, n.34, 36; Shaw, n.39, 32-3; also see Czaplicka, n.33, 49.

44. *BSE*, n. 38, 75-6.

agricultural people into pastoral nomads seems to be the handi-work of the Mongols, of the Dzhungars and partly of the Russians.[45]

V. THE KARA-KALPAKS

The ethnic composition of the Kara-Kalpaks is rather com-plex. It includes the ancient tribes which inhabited the territory of modern Kara-Kalpak region, some of whom were of Saka-Massagatai and Sarmatian-Alani origins.[46] The Pachenegs of the tenth and twelfth centuries A.D. also played an important role in the evolution of the Kara-Kalpaks.[47] They emerged as a dis-tinct group in the post-Mongol period, in the process of the break-up of the Golden Horde, the Chagatai *Ulus* and the Hulagu state, which led to the mixing of people of different ethnic strains, and to the evolution and consolidation of new ethnic groups.[48] Ethnically, though the Kara-Kalpaks were closely related to the Golden Horde Uzbeks,[49] in their ways of living they differ from the modern Uzbeks.[50] Though they are nearer to the Kazakhs and the Kirgiz linguistically, in their physical type they are different from these two peoples.[51]

The Kara-Kalpaks lived for a long time in the middle Amu Daria region. Following the occupation of this region by the

45. The trail of destruction left behind by the Mongol invaders remained unerased for a long time in the Kirgiz region. The rich and flourishing cities that were situated on the caravan routes of the east-west trade like Balasagun and Urgench, were razed to the ground by the Mongols. The network of ancient irrigation canals was either totally destroyed, or allowed to decay. And worst of all, the fertile cultivated fields were converted into pastures for grazing cattle. In the upper Yenisei region, where the parent branch of the Kirgiz remained, pastoral nomadism came into being in the wake of the Mongol occupation under Altyn Khan and later, after the Russian conquest in the eighteenth century. *Ibid.*, 76; also see Czap-licka, n. 33, 48; Schuyler, n. 33, 136-7.

46. S. P. Tolstov, 'K voprosu o proiskhozhdenii Kara-Kalpakskogo naroda,' *Kratkie soobshcheniia instituta etnografii*, 2 (1947) 74.

47. See footnote 7 of this chapter.

48. Tolsov, n. 46, 73.

49. *Ibid.*, 75.

50. See Zarubin, n. 2, 17.

51. V. Konovalov, 'Kara-Kalpakskaia avtonomnaia oblast,' *Sovetskoe stroitel'stvo* 1 (66) (1932) 112; also see Ivanov, n. 22, 104; by the same author, 'Kara-Kalpaki,' *Sovetskaia etnografiia*, 4 (1940) 44.

Kazakhs towards the end of the eighteenth century, the Kara-Kalpaks were forced to move into the lower Amu Daria delta.[52] During this period, the Kara-Kalpaks were divided into a number of tribes. Towards the second half of the nineteenth century, however, a process of amalgamation of the smaller tribes had set in, which led to the emergence of two large tribes: *Kongrat* and *Ontort-Uru* (meaning fourteen tribes).[53]

Among the Kara-Kalpaks in the past there prevailed an essentially nomadic cattlebreeding economy. In course of time, it gave place to a mixed economy, in which agriculture also began to play an important role. Gradually, however, agriculture became the chief occupation among the Kara-Kalpaks, and fishing and cattlebreeding were retained only as subsidiary occupations.[54]

Soon after their arrival in the lower Amu Daria delta, the Kara-Kalpaks were subjugated by the Uzbek ruler of the Khanate of Khiva. The territories inhabited by them were transformed into three *bekdoms* of the Khanate. These were Shuman, Kungrad and Kunya-Urgench.[55] Until the middle of the nineteenth century the administrative units in each one of these *bekdoms* were organized in conformity with the clan divisions which were prevalent among the Kara-Kalpaks. In the lower rungs of administration, the clan leaders were allowed to exercise considerable authority. In the fifties of the last century, however, not only were the existing administrative units tampered with, but the little authority enjoyed by the clan leaders was also taken away. All authority in the Kara-Kalpak region came to be vested in the hands of the Uzbek officials of the Khan. These officials, who were concerned only with enriching themselves, became noted for their arbitrary rule and corruption. Driven to despair by the never-ending exactions of the Khan's officials and the oppressive nature of their rule, the leaders of the Kara-Kalpaks of the right bank of the Amu Daria, during the time of the

52. 'Materialy i issledovaniia po etnografii Kara-Kalpakov, in **T. A.** Zhdanko, ed.. *Trudy Khorezemskoi arkheologo-etnograficheskoi ekspeditsii* (Moscow, 1958) 112.

53. See Ivanov, n. 51, 'Kara-Kalpaki,' 37.

54. *Ibid.*, 37-8.

55. R. Kosbergenov, 'Polozhenie Kara-Kalpakskogo naseleniia v Khivinskom khanstve v kontse XIX-nachale XX vekakh,' *Kratkie soobshcheniia instituta etnografii*, 20 (1954) 102.

Khivan expedition, requested on Von Kaufman to accept them as Russian subjects.[56]

VI. THE KAZAKHS

The history of the Kazakhs sheds very little light on their origin. Traditions and legends speak of the Kazakhs as the descendants of an illustrious ancestor, Alash Khan,[57] which of course, cannot be taken seriously. As a recent Soviet work on the history of the Kazakhs states, it is rather difficult and risky to express any definite views on the question of the ethnic origin of the Kazakhs.[58] As such, what follows is at best a sketchy account, tracing the general pattern of evolution of the Kazakh people.

Lying as it does on the route from Asia to Europe, the Kazakh steppe in the course of many centuries experienced a heavy incidence of migration of people belonging to diverse ethnic compositions. Each of them, in different proportions, has left its distinct imprint on the ethnic group which started evolving on the territory of modern Kazakhstan. As a result of this mixed heritage, the modern Kazakhs have come to possess a physical type that is very distinct from the rest of the peoples of Central Asia.

The crystallization of the present connotation of the term 'Kazakh' does not seem to have occurred until the time when the Nogai and the Uzbek tribes had migrated out of the 'Desht-

---

56. *IUzSSR*, n. 34, 93.

57. In the literature of the steppes, Alash Khan figures as the common ancestor of all steppe dwellers. The emotional penumbra surrounding his name is great, and for many Kazakhs, the name of this somewhat mythical hero symbolizes the glorious bygone past, when their ancestors freely roamed over the steppes as an independent people. In view of this, it is not surprising that the nationalist party of the Kazakhs, which for a short while controlled large tracts of the steppe territory soon after the Revolution and during the Civil War, called itself 'Alash Orda' meaning the Horde of Alash.

58. *Istoriia Kazakhskoi SSR* (Alma-Ata, 1957) 132. (Cited hereafter as *IKSSR*).

59. The process of ethnogenesis that worked itself out on the Kazakh territory, in the ancient period, brought into closer contact, and ultimately fused, the several remnants that were left behind by the many migrating tribes which were on their way to the west. Some of the well-known among them were the Huns, Wusuns and Sakas. In course of time, this amalgam was overlaid by a sizable Turkish element and a distinctive Mongoloid racial strain.

i-Kipchak,'[60] the former moving out into the Caucasus, Crimea and the Stavropol steppes, and the latter, into the sedentary regions of the South.[61] In the same century, perhaps somewhat earlier than the Nogais and the Uzbeks started their migration, as a result of the feuds that prevailed in the Uzbek-Kazakh *ulus* of Khan Abul Khair, two princes, Djanibek and Gerei, with considerable following migrated to the Chu river valley of Moghulistan, and built there the nucleus of an independent state. This state, in course of time, became strong and powerful, and from the sixteenth century onwards, came to be known as the Kazakh Khanate.[62]

The Kazakhs, contrary to the popular belief, do not have a homogeneous racial ancestry. Theirs is a mixed racial heritage, and they have 'many Mongoloid characteristics as well as other clearly European racial features.'[63] The Soviet anthropologists include them under the 'South Siberian Anthropological Type.'[64] Notwithstanding the rather sharp Mongoloid features of the Kazakhs, it would be a mistake to consider them as typical representatives of the Mongoloid race.

The fall of the Timurid state and the break-up of the Golden Horde saw the Kazakh Khanate also splitting into three tribal groups: the Great Horde, the Middle Horde and the Little Horde. Following this split, each of them organized itself as a separate and independent state.

The manifestation of the centrifugal tendencies which led to the establishment of the three separate states did not, however, bring about the disintegration of the Kazakh nation. The forces making for unity, though they remained in a dormant state for some time, ultimately asserted themselves, and arrested tendencies on the part of these states to drift further away from one another. At certain times, as it happened in the middle of the eighteenth century, the sense of unity which was still strong among the

60. 'Desh-i-Kipchak' was the earlier name for the territory of modern Kazakhstan.

61. *BSE* (Moscow, 1935, 1st edition) xxx, 588-9.

62. *OOE*, n. 12, 174.

63. Hans A. Findeisen, 'A History of the Kazakh-Russian Relations, *Studies on the Soviet Union* (Munich) 4 (1960) 83.

64. The south Siberian anthropological type was formed as a result of the mixing of the Central Asian Mongols with the indigenous people of Kazakhstan of essentially an European racial extraction, *OOE*, n. 12, 161.

Kazakhs enabled the Middle and the Little Hordes to establish a political union between them. The Great Horde, though it continued to remain outside this union, nevertheless was always concerned about the preservation of the unity and independence of the Kazakh nation. The threat of aggression from without, which is such a powerful factor in forging national unity, also helped the Kazakhs to set aside their differences for a time, and unite to defend themselves against the attack of the Kalmuks. Though ultimately the Russian armed might proved too strong for the Kazakhs to resist, in the hour of national crisis, heroes like Kenesary Kasimov succeeded in uniting large sections of the Kazakh population and offered resistance to the Russians.

The Kazakh social fabric, until recently, had retained many of the survivals of the patriarchal-clan mode of life. The tribal organization of the Kazakh society resembled a pyramid-like structure, with a broad base and a narrow apex. The primary unit of society was the patriarchal family; several such units made up an *aul* (a tribal village consisting of five to ten families). Then came the clan—the highest unit. In the early Kazakh society, the clan seems to have remained the pivotal point around which centred most of the social, economic and political life.[65] However, as a result of the more affluent conditions that were created by the growth of trade with neighbouring regions, an increase in the number of people abandoning their nomadic way of life in favour of agriculture, and finally, the annexation of some of the fertile oasis regions of the south, the rigid clan structure began to disintegrate.[66]

The basic mode of economy that was prevalent among the Kazakhs until recently was nomadic cattlebreeding, which, by its very nature, demanded ownership by the cattlebreeders of extensive grazing grounds. To some extent agriculture was practised in the northern and southern frontier regions, chiefly, under the influence of the Russians and the southern sedentary peoples. But in general, nomadic cattlebreeding was typical of the Kazakh economy.[67]

65. Thomas G. Winner, *The Oral Art and Literature of the Kazakhs of Russian Central Asia* (Durham, N.C., 1958) 5-7.

66. *Ibid.*, 8-9.

67. E. B. Bekmakhanov, *Prisoedinenie Kazakhstana k Rossii* (Moscow, 1957) 26.

VII. LINGUISTIC AFFINITIES AND
DIFFERENCES

The peoples of Central Asia belong to two major language groups. The majority of them (Turkmens, Uzbeks, Kazakhs, Kirgiz and Kara-Kalpaks) belong to the Turkic language group. The Tadjiks, who represent a non-Turkic element in what is otherwise a predominantly Turkic area, belong to the eastern Iranian language group.

The Tadjik language started evolving even before the Arab invasion. By the seventh century A.D. a single spoken language had begun to evolve on the basis of one of the dialects spoken in Tokharistan, Sogdia and Khorasan. This language, in course of time, came to be known as 'Dari.' Towards the ninth century A.D., a period which witnessed the assertion of the independence of the Central Asian region from the Caliphate, Dari became a literary language chiefly under the patronage of the Samanid sultans. Until the fourteenth century Dari remained a common literary language both for the Tadjiks of Central Asia and for the Persians. Only after this century a differentiation began to manifest itself which ultimately led to the birth of the separate Tadjik and Persian literary languages.[68] Although from the time of the fall of the Samanid dynasty to the period of the formation of the Tadjik Republic, there did not exist any independent Tadjik state, the Tadjik language managed to remain the language of state and culture of the Amirate of Bukhara.[69] Even after the fall of the Amirate, the Tadjik language continued to remain predominant for some time in Bukhara.

Though the Turkic languages of the peoples of Central Asia belong to the same family of Turkic languages, there are significant differences not only between them and the ancient Turkic language, but also between one another. Although the languages of the early Turks served as the common source for all of them,

68. *OOE*, n.12, 159; also see Gafurov, n.26, 189.
69. Of the three Uzbek Khanates of Khiva, Bukhara and Kokand, the Tadjik language had least influence only in the Khanate of Khiva. In comparison to Khiva the Tadjik element in Bukhara was so great that it led a Khivan historian to describe even the Bukharan army as consisting mostly of Tadjiks, whereas the truth was that the Uzbeks remained dominant in the Amirate and especially so in the army. Bartol'd, n. 27, 110; also see Serge A. Zenkovsky, *Pan-Turkism and Islam in Russia* (Cambridge, Mass., 1960) 74.

none of the modern Turkic languages, including those spoken
in Central Asia, could be said to be in the direct line of descent
from the parent group. Not only do the modern Turkic languages differ from their parent group in their lexical, morpholo-
gical and phonetical subtleties, but many of the ancient
Turkic words and usages have entirely gone out of circluation.
The ever-increasing needs of life, and contacts with people belonging to non-Turkic language groups (mostly Persian and
Arabic) led not only to the incorporation of many words which
are distinctly of non-Turkic origin, but to the coining of entirely
new words. The factors which led to the evolution of the different ethnic groups also led to the formation of their distinct
dialects. Though in the initial period, the differences among the
various dialects were small and insignificant, with the passage of
time, they tended to assume an importance. After a certain stage
the different ethnic groups were no longer able to understand
the dialects other than their own. However, out of the numerous
dialects which had come into existence, only a few emerged
preeminent. These were the dialects of the Turkmens, Uzbeks,
Kazakhs, Kirgiz and the Kara-Kalpaks which today enjoy the
status of full-fledged languages.

The Turkmen language (like the languages of the Azerbaid-
zanis, the Osmanli Turks and the Turkic language tribes of
Persia) belongs to the southwestern or Oghuz branch of the
Turkic languages.[70] Though it evolved on the basis of the dialects
of the Oghuz tribes, the Turkmen language, in the course of
its development, absorbed certain elements of the languages of
the ancient aborigines of Central Asia. During the thirteenth
and fourteenth centuries the Turkmen language came under the
influence of the Kipchak language. Between the fifteenth to the
eighteenth centuries the influence of the Chagatai language remained predominant on it. However, from the eighteenth century onwards, it steered an independent course and paved the
way for the emergence of the modern Turkmen literary
language.[71]

The several dialects of the Turkmen tribes, on the basis of

70. *OOE*, n.12, 159. According to another classification, it is related to
the Oghuz-Turkmen subgroup of the Oghuz group of the western branch
of the Turkic languages. See Baskakov, n.7, 117.

71. Hostler, n.39, 69.

which the Turkmen language was formed, were unified into two rather unequal groups. While the first group brought together the dialects of the *Yomud, Tekke, Salyr* and *Ersar* tribes, the second group united the dialects spoken by the Turkmen tribes living in the regions adjoining the Uzbek and Persian frontiers.[72]

The Uzbek language belongs to the southeastern or Chagatai branch[73] of the Turkic languages. It first came into existence as a result of the turkification of the languages of the aborigines, mostly the Iranian-language Sogdians and Khorezmians. Subsequently, the Uzbek language passed through three broadly clearcut periods of evolution. The earliest literary creations of the old Uzbek languages were the writings of the Muslim saint of twelfth century, Ahmed Yasavi. The second and perhaps, the most brilliant period of the Uzbek literary language belongs to the fifteenth and the sixteenth centuries, when it came to be employed as the literary medium of the works of Alisher Navoi (1441-1501), Zahir-ed-Din Babur (1483-1530), Mohamed Salikh (A.D. 1535 *d.*) and others. With the advent of the Uzbek supremacy, it became the literary language of the states of Khiva and Kokand.[74] Its third and final stage belongs to the post-revolutionary period.

The formation of the spoken Uzbek language belongs to the fifteenth century. Several dialects and languages, including the languages of the ancient Khorezmians, Tadjiks and other Iranian language groups, and the dialects of the ancient Uigurs, Tirgesh, Karluk, Oghuz and Kipchaks, have contributed considerably to its formation.[75]

The Kirgiz, Kazakh and Kara-Kalpak languages belong to the northwestern or Kipchak branch of the Turkic languages.[76] Of these, the Kirgiz language was the earliest to evolve; it took shape on the basis of the languages of the eastern Turkic people. Its substratum was the ancient Kirgiz language spoken by the Yenisei Kirgiz. In its earlier stages of evolution, the Kirgiz language developed in close proximity with the Mongolian,

---

72. Baskakov, n.7, 121-2.
73. *OOE*, n.12, 159.
74. Baskakov, n.7, 178-9.
75. *Ibid.*, 180.
76. *OOE*, n.12, 159.

Tunguso-Manchurian and Paleo-Asiatic languages.[77] In the later stages of its development, the Kirgiz language came under the influence of the language of the Kipchaks.

The Kazakh and the Kara-Kalpak languages evolved considerably later. Their evolution is usually ascribed to the period of the break-up of the Golden Horde (14-15th centuries A.D.). Though they originated mainly on the basis of the Kipchak language, the Kazakh as well as the Kara-Kalpak languages owe much to the languages of the Pechenegs and the Bulgars.[78]

The Kazakh language, though spoken over a large territory and by relatively numerous people, has not given rise to any dialects. In the past, there was a sharp contrast between the conversational language of the Kazakh elite and the masses; the language of the former had a higher percentage of words of alien origin like Arabic, Persian, Chagatai and the language of the Volga Tartars.[79]

Although the Kazakh languages with a rich vocabulary and a perfected grammatical structure came into existence as early as the fifteenth century, the formation of the literary language was slow of growth. Until the seventeenth century the Kazakhs did not produce any outstanding literary works.[80]

The Kara-Kalpak langauge, until recently, was divided into two main dialects: the northeastern and the southwestern dialects. While the former was spoken in the Karauziak, Takhtakupyr and Muinak areas, the latter was widely spoken in the Chimbai, Kegeilin, Kuibyshev, Kungrad, Khodzheili, Kypchak, Shabbaz and Turtkul regions.[81]

VIII. LITERATURE

As in other spheres, so also in the field of literature of the peoples of Central Asia, there are certain fundamental differences. The clear-cut dichotomy which until recently existed in

---

77. Perhaps as a result of this close proximity, the Kirgiz language, as compared to the other Central Asian languages of the western branch of the Turkic languages, contains a larger percentage of Mongolian words and a very low percentage of words of Persian and Arabic origin. See Baskakov, n.7, 210-11.

78. *OOE*, n.12, 159; also see Baskakov, n. 7, 216.

79. *BSE*, n.61, 604.

80. *IKSSR*, n. 58, 216.

81. Baskakov, n. 7, 167.

the economy, social life and culture of the peoples of the steppe and oasis regions, also to a large extent reflected in the literature of these two regions. While the nomads chiefly concerned themselves with the creation of oral traditions (the heroic epochs) and folklore themes, the oasis inhabitants developed a written literature which often became noted for its grandeur, artistic skill, sublimity of themes and perfection of form. In addition to these distinctions which arose from the differences of economic and social life, certain other distinctions of a national character started manifesting in the literature of the people of Central Asia. While it is largely true that all steppe nomads developed mostly oral traditions, it would, however, be wrong to presume that all these oral traditions were alike. In fact the oral traditions of the various nomadic peoples of Central Asia exhibited certain unique national distinctions. Thus, for instance, while both the Kazakhs and the Kirgiz preserved and cultivated certain pre-Islamic traditions in their literary creations, the Turkmens, on the other hand, cultivated chiefly the spirit of Muslim mysticism in most of their literary works of the past.[82]

The Uzbek language developed under different circumstances. After overthrowing the Timurid dynasty and settling down to a sedentary mode of life, the Uzbeks became the inheritors and purveyors of the cultural and literary traditions of the Chagatai and Timurid epochs. This culture, unlike its counterpart among the nomads, grew on the basis of a sedentary economy which, besides agriculture, also possessed indigenous industries, a prosperous commerce and a thriving urban life. There were also a considerably large number of educated people among the Uzbeks, who, after having accepted the traditions of the Chagatai period of Central Asiatic Turkic literature, began to develop a literature of a highly educated class. On the territory of modern Uzbekistan, throughout the nineteenth century the Fergana valley and Khorezm were particularly noted for such literary creations. Similar developments could not have taken place among the relatively backward Kazakhs, Kirgiz and Turkmens.[83]

82. A. N. Samoilovich, 'Ocherki po istorii Turkmenskoi literatury,' in *Turkmeniia* (Leningrad, 1929) 131.

83. *Ibd.*, 132.

From the foregoing analysis it becomes clear that there were —and there still are—significant differences not only between the Iranian (mainly the Tadjiks) and the Turkic language groups of people of Central Asia, but among the members of the Turkic group itself. Thus, the Turkmens, in origin as well as in language, are closer to the Azerbaidzhanis, the Turkic language tribes of Persia and the Osmanlies, than to their Central Asian neighbours. The Uzbeks, though they are kindred in origin to the Kazakhs and the Nogai Mangyts, have subsequently drifted away from them and have come much nearer to, and under the cultural influence of, the Tadjiks. The Kirgiz, who have a great deal of Mongoloid blood in their veins, contrary to the popular belief have little in common with the Kazakhs,[84] and they are oriented more towards the Siberian Turks. These differences are significant and they stem not only from distinct origins of these people, but also extend to the spheres of language, literature, traditions, economic pursuits, and general ways of living.

---

84. Except for a very brief period of common political life, there was nothing in common between the Kazakhs and the Kirgiz from the beginning. After the death of Khok-Nazar, even this political union broke down and they were never again brought under a single state. Even during the time of this political Union, the Kirgiz had not accepted Islam, at least not to the extent it was accepted by the Kazakhs. See Bartol'd, n.34, 37-9.

CHAPTER TWO

The Colonial Background

I. THE RUSSIAN CONQUEST OF CENTRAL ASIA

ALTHOUGH Russia had sporadic contacts with Central Asia for several centuries, and fairly regular ones from the seventeenth century, the Russian conquest of Central Asia did not commence until the second quarter of the nineteenth century. While Russia in successive strides went on to conquer Kazan (1552), Astrakhan (1554) and Siberia (from 1552 to 1647), it did not for a long time exhibit any great interest in annexing the Central Asian region. Ignorance of geography and of the economic potential of Central Asia, coupled with the remoteness of the region from European Russia, conspired in keeping out Russia's interest for a long time from Central Asia. However, towards the second quarter of the nineteenth century, Russia not only cast away its indifferent attitude towards Central Asia, but became alive to its obvious economic, military and political importance. The necessity of containing the commercial and political expansion of Great Britain in the region became as important to Russia as securing the region's cotton for its textile industry and opening the Central Asian market for its manufactured articles.[1] Besides, Russia also became aware of the

1. The economic aspects of the Central Asian campaign were of considerable importance and they rendered it popular among an influential section of the Russian society. The newspaper *Golos* (Voice) called upon the government to transform the Caspian Sea into a Russian lake. Another influential news organ, *Moskovskie vedomosti* (Moscow News) pleaded for energetic measures on the Central Asian front. Blaranburg, a noted figure of his day and a person who held several important assignments in the Ministry of Finance, wrote that the 'European market is closed to the Russian manufactured articles due to the competition of almost every state in this region, as such willy-nilly Russia has to turn to the Asian countries for marketing its products.' Professor A. Lobanov-Rostovsky writes that the 'economic reasons in themselves were sufficient to warrant Russian penetration' into Central Asia. See N. A. Khalfin, *Politika Rossii v*

enormous political prestige that would accrue to it from annexing the vast Central Asian region and of the possibility of apply-
ing pressure on Britain from one of the most sensitive parts of
the latter's far-flung empire.[2]

These factors proved decisive in inducing the imperial government to decide to annex the Central Asian region. Preparations for realizing this objective were afoot as early as 1839.
But the attempts which were made until 1856 were half-hearted
and they failed to achieve any significant results. But soon after
the termination of the Crimean War (1853-58), in an attempt
to bolster up national prestige and also to gain compensation
for its losses in the war, the Tsarist government ordered its
forces to move deep into the Central Asian region. Soon afterwards, two Russian armies started closing on the decadent
Khanates of Central Asia from different directions.

The city of Aulie-Ata was captured on 4 June 1864, Turkestan
on 12 June and Chimkent on 22 September the same year. On
17 June 1865 Tashkent, one of the most important cities of
the region, was in Russian possession. In the following year the
Russian armies captured Khodzhent, Ura-Tube, Dzhizak and
Yangi-Kurgan. On 2 May 1868 the famous city of Samarkand was
taken. The Khivan campaign, commenced in 1873, resulted in
the humbling of that state and annexation of large tracts of
territory lying on the right bank of the Amu Daria. The Transcaspian region passed into Russian hands following the defeat
of the Turkmen tribes in the battle of Goek-Tepe on 12 January
1881. On 6 May 1881 this region was formally annexed to the
empire. The Russian conquest of the Central Asian region was
completed with the capture of Merv (January 1884) and Kushka
(March 1885).[3]

The Russian advance in Central Asia, which began in 1839,

Srednei Azii (Moscow, 1960) 62-71; also see *Istoriia Uzbekskoi SSR*
(Tashkent, 1956) I, pt. 2, 81-2. (Cited hereafter as *IUzSSR*); A. Lobanov-
Rostovsky, *Russia and Asia* (Michigan, 1951) 150-1.

2. The Russian Foreign Secretary, Count Nesselrode, was even reported
to have declared in a cabinet meeting in 1816 that 'as long as Central
Asia is not ours, we cannot by any means think of conquering the whole
of Asia.' See Baymirza Hayit, *Turkestan im XX Jahrhundert* (Darmstadt,
1956) 17.

3. See Louis E. Frechtling, 'Anglo-Russian Rivalry in Eastern Turkestan 1863-1881', *Journal of Royal Central Asian Society* (London) 26
(July 1939) 482-3; also see Khalfin, n.1, 191-233.

in the course of less than half a century resulted in the reduction of the Amirate of Bukhara and the Khanate of Khiva to vassal status and the total annexation of the territories of the Kokand Khanate. The present southern frontiers of the USSR in the region indicate the limit beyond which Russia possibly could not have advanced unless it was prepared to risk a major war with Great Britain which, from its base in India, suspiciously viewed every move of Russia southward as a potential threat to its 'crown's brightest jewel.'[4] Russia's frontier with Afghanistan was demarcated in 1895 by an Anglo-Russian Frontier Commission as a result of which Russia secured a part of the Pamir region.[5]

II. RUSSIAN ADMINISTRATION

With the acquisition of new territories in Central Asia, there arose the need to organize their administration. During the initial stages of the conquest, when only a small portion of the Central Asian territory was in Russian possession, an *ad hoc* arrangement was made by which this territory was constituted into a separate oblast (province) with a military governor at its head. This arrangement, however, proved inadequate as larger tracts of territory were being brought under Russian control. In view of this, an imperial ukase, on the basis of the recommendations of the Giers Commission, was issued on 11 July 1867, constituting a separate Governor-Generalship of Turkestan.[6] The new Governor-Generalship consisted of the erstwhile Turkestan oblast and a part of the Semipalatinsk oblast lying to the south of the Tarbagatai range.[7] Following the gradual accretion of territory, the jurisdiction of the Governor-Generalship was extended over the newly created administrative divisions. The Fergana oblast was brought under the administrative control of

4. W. K. Fraser-Tytler, *Afghanistan: A Study of Political Developments in Central and Southern Asia* (London, 1950, 2nd edition, 1953) 129.

5. Olaf Caroe, *The Soviet Empire: The Turks of Central Asia and Stalinism* (London, 1953) 82-3.

6. For a full text of this ukase see Demetrius Charles Boulger, *England And Russia in Central Asia* (London, 1879) I, 315-7 (appendix).

7. The detachment of the Turkestan oblast from the Governor-Generalship of Orenburg had rather dire consequences for the Kazakh population. A large number of them who inhabited the northern portion of

the Turkestan Governor-Generalship in 1876, the Amu Daria division was added to it in 1873, the Transcaspian oblast and the Pamir region in 1897.[8] In addition to these oblasts which were under the direct administrative jurisdiction of the Governor-Generalship of Turkestan, the Amirate of Bukhara and the Khanate of Khiva also remained within its overall setup

this oblast were administratively separated from their kinsmen and placed under the new administration of Turkestan Governor-Generalship. Attention to this fact was drawn by the Governor-General of Orenburg, but the military authorities who scrutinized the Giers Commission's proposals did not think that this problem was important enough to merit consideration. See Eugene Schuyler, *Turkestan: Notes of a Journey in Russian Turkestan, Kokand, Bukhara and Kuldja* (London, 1876) II, 202.

8. The Turkestan Governor-Generalship originally consisted of the Syr Daria and the Semirechie oblasts. The former comprised the uezds of Kazalinsk, Perovsk, Chimkent, Aulie-Ata, Kuraminsk, Khodzhent and Dzhizak. In 1887 the Kuraminsk uezd was transferred to the Samarkand oblast and the Amu Daria Military Division was incorporated into the Syr Daria oblast as a separate uezd. The Semirechie oblast formed in 1867 consisted of the uezds of Sergiopol, Kopal, Issyk-kul, Tokmak and Vernyi. In 1893 the Dzharkent uezd was formed from parts of the Issyk-kul and Kopal uezds. The Semirechie oblast was transferred to the new Governor-Generalship of the Steppes in 1882 and was re-transferred to the Turkestan Governor-Generalship in 1899. The Zerafshan district was formed in 1868 consisting of the territories ceded by the Amir of Bukhara. It comprised three uezds: Samarkand, Katta-Kurgan and Pendzhikent. In 1887 the Zerafshan district was renamed Samarkand oblast and it also came to incorporate the Khodzhent and Dzhizak uezds which were formerly under the administrative jurisdiction of the Syr Daria oblast. In 1873 the Amu Daria Division was formed from the territories ceded by the Khan of Khiva. It functioned as an independent administrative unit until 1887 when it was incorporated into the Syr Daria oblast. In 1876, after the annexation of the Khanate of Kokand to Russia, the Fergana oblast was formed consisting of the uezds: Namangan, Andizhan, Osh, Maregelan and Kokand. The Transcaspian oblast formed in 1882 consisted of the uezds: Mangishlak, Krasnovodsk and Akhal-Teke. In 1890 when the Transcaspian oblast was detached from the Governor-Generalship of the Caucasus, the Merv and Tedzhen districts were reorganized into uezds. In 1897, following the extensive administrative reforms introduced in the Turkestan region, the Transcaspian oblast finally became a part of the Governor-Generalship of Turkestan. In the same year the Pamir region was added to the Fergana oblast and administratively it came under the jurisdiction of both the governor of Fergana and the headquarters of the Turkestan military district. See 'Administrativnoe delenie Turkestana v proshlom i nastoiashchem,' *Materialy po raionirovaniiu Turkestana* (Tashkent, 1924) vypusk I, 20-1. (Cited hereafter as *MRT*.); also see N. A. Kisliakov, *Sem'ia i brak u Tadzhikov* (Moscow, 1959) 7.

but outside its direct administrative jurisdiction.[9]

In its final form the Governor-Generalship of Turkestan consisted of an extensive territory which exceeded in size England, France, Italy, Denmark, Switzerland and Belgium put together. It had an area of 1,616,158 square *versts* and a population of 5,280,983 persons in 1897. Mostly as a result of large-scale immigration of Cossacks and Russian peasant settlers, the population of the Turkestan region went up by almost a million within the course of next twelve years. In 1909 its population was placed in the neighbourhood of 6,243,422 persons.[10]

Formed on the basis of the proposals of a special committee which scrutinized the recommendations of the Giers Commission, the Turkestan administration was modelled to facilitate the fulfilment of Russia's colonial policies in Central Asia.[11] Its dominant feature was the overwhelming preponderance of the military element. Not only were the offices of the Governor-General of the Turkestan region and the governors of its oblasts were staffed with military officers, but the entire Turkestan administration itself was placed under the charge of the Ministry of War.[12] The borderland position of the Turkestan and the alleged

9. According to the treaties of capitulation signed by the rulers of these states with Russia, they renounced the right to enter into relations with foreign powers directly and agreed to the stationing of Russian political agents in their territories. Their continued existence as semi-independent states was more a matter of sufferance on the part of Russia than of any recognized treaty rights. However, the imperial government until 1917 adopted a policy of strict non-interference in the internal affairs of these states and thereby allowed the medieval, despotic and almost anachronistic regimes of the Khan and the Amir to continue unchecked. Like most Indian princely states during the British rule, these two native states remained backward while the neighbouring provinces made rapid progress.

10. *Materialy k istorii sovetskogo gosudarstya i prava Uzbekistana* (Tashkent, 1958) 20. (Cited hereafter as *MISGPUz*). One *verst* is equal to 3,500 metres.

11. According to the opinion of one of the ablest senators of the imperial regime, the Turkestan region was conquered by Russia to serve a twofold objective. On the one hand, the Turkestan region was to provide revenue to the imperial government and a market for Russian manufactured articles. On the other, the region was to absorb a part of the surplus population of the central *gubernias* of the Russian empire. See *Materialy k kharakteristike narodnogo khoziaistva v Turkestane: revizii Gr. Palena* (St. Petersburg, 1911) 3.

12. In the 'Regulations for the Administration of the Turkestan Region' it was specifically stated that the incumbent of the office of governor of

'hostile character' of its population towards the Russians were
cited as excuses to justify the delegation of almost extraordinary
powers to the Governor-General of the region and for retaining,
until the end, the essentials of a militarized administration.[13]

In organizing the oblast, uezd, and volost divisions of the
Turkestan region the Tsarist officials gave importance not so
much to cool thinking and systematic planning as to the military, political and administrative exigencies of the moment. In
organizing these administrative units they sought, on the one
hand, to maximize the scope for the continuity of the interests
of the Russian autocracy and, on the other hand, to provide for
filling up of the vacuum created by the suppression of the former
Khanates.

The new régime also enjoined upon the peoples of the Turkestan region to place their loyalty to the Russian Tsar over and
above their regional, dynastic and tribal loyalties. By creating
new administrative units whose frontiers cut across and physi-
cally erased altogether the frontiers which existed earlier in
Central Asia, the Turkestan administration sought to obliterate
the remnants of all traditional loyalties in the consciousness of
the local people. That in achieving this objective, the newly
demarcated administrative frontiers were also cutting across
areas of homogeneous populations ignoring their natural affinities and common economic interests was only obvious. But to
the Tsarist officials, the 'guardians of the imperial interests on
the spot,' these factors either did not count, or, in comparison

an oblast must necessarily be a military officer. The military governors
enjoyed wide powers and like the Governor-General of the region combined in their office the civil and military authority in their respective
oblasts. See *MISGPUz*, n. 10, 22.

13. The Governor-General of the Turkestan region was vested with
powers which his counterparts elsewhere in the empire did not possess.
In addition to the general administrative powers and prerogatives he
enjoyed, he was given the authority to suspend or to make qualification to any regulations. As the head of the military district of Turkestan, he enjoyed supreme military powers and possessed the authority to
commence, wage and suspend a war within the region without the previous sanction of the authorities in St. Petersburg. Besides, he enjoyed
the rank of a minister plenipotentiary in relation to the neighbouring
regions and could carry on diplomatic relations with them. In short, he
was the personal nominee of the emperor charged with the task of ensuring the fulfilment of the supreme law of autocracy and the interests of the
empire. See *ibid.*, 21.

with the 'paramountcy of imperial interests,' did not deserve to be taken note of.

In the organization of the lower units of administration again, attempts to safeguard Russian interests resulted in ignoring the obvious distinctions which existed in the ways of life among the sedentary, nomadic and semi-nomadic peoples of the region. Neither in law nor in administrative practice did these basic differences find adequate reflection.[14] Attempts to herd together in composite administrative units peoples who sharply differed from one another in their ways of life, levels of culture and language led, almost inevitably, to the general backwardness of all. In particular it led to the exploitation of the economically weak and culturally less developed nomadic people by the more advanced sedentary population.

The haphazard manner in which the boundaries of the various administrative units were drawn without taking into consideration the pattern of ethnographic distribution of the people resulted in the long run in yet another great handicap to the local population. When the peoples of Central Asia became politically conscious and started organizing national liberation movements, they found that they were effectively balkanized. This made it extremely difficult for them to build any large, well-knit and cohesive political organization which alone was capable of challenging the domination of Russia in Central Asia. Writing on this issue an American scholar remarks:

> In addition to the dividing up of the territory of Central Asia into 'native states' and Russian Turkestan, the native people were rendered still less able to organize themselves for independence by a gerrymandering of boundary lines which split every local nationality into a number of groups each with a different type of government to face.[15]

The result of this policy was that some of the regions of Central Asia which possessed a compact population structure lost their homogeneity and were transformed into administrative units with a highly heterogeneous population. For instance the population of Turkestan was composed of 35.77 per cent

---

14. *MRT*, n.8, 26.
15. See William Mandel, *The Soviet Far East And Central Asia* (New York, 1944) 100; for an opposite view see Richard A. Pierce, *Russian Central Asia 1867-1917 : A Study in Colonial Rule* (Berkeley, 1960) 59-63.

Uzbeks, 44.36 per cent Kazakhs and Kirgiz, 4.98 per cent Turkmens, 6.73 per cent Tadjiks, 2.2 per cent Kara-Kalpaks, 3.75 per cent Russians and 2.15 per cent others.[16] The population structure of the Amirate of Bukhara and the Khanate of Khiva also reflected a similar heterogeneity since these two states were inhabited by the same national groups which lived in Turkestan. Within each of these three major political units, in turn, every national group was torn into petty segments among their several oblasts, uezds, volosts, *bekdoms* and *shuros*.[17] Thus, the Uzbeks were divided not only among Russian Turkestan, Bukhara and Khiva, but within Russian Turkestan, they were administratively split among Samarkand, Fergana and the Syr Daria oblasts. Similarly, the Tadjiks were divided between the Turkestan Governor-Generalship and the Amirate of Bukhara, and within the former they were split between the Samarkand and the Fergana oblasts. The Kirgiz within Russian Turkestan were administratively split up among the Fergana, Semirechie and Syr Daria oblasts. Though a predominant portion of the Turkmens lived within Russian Turkestan a considerable part of them languished under the feudal oppression of the Amir of Bukhara and the Khan of Khiva. The Kazakhs perhaps suffered most. Not only were they administratively divided between the Syr Daria and Semirechie oblasts within Russian Turkestan, but in the steppe region, they were divided among no less than three separate Governor-Generalships! It might be true that gerrymandering is a distinct product of American political history, but the Tsarist régime though it failed to conceptualize its practices showed that gerrymandering was not a monopoly of American politicians.

The officials of the imperial regime did not exhibit any great concern for safeguarding the interests of the indigenous population of Turkestan. Without least concern to the wishes and aspirations of the local population, they bandied various administrative units from one Governor-Generalship to another. While they set aside valuable recommendations made by the various imperial commissions, they often undertook major and far-reaching administrative reforms in the Turkestan region in order to reward the favourites of the Ministry of War. Among a number of reforms which were introduced in Turkestan, as a result of such bureaucratic revolutions,' the territorial regroupings which were undertaken in 1882 and 1898 stand out pre-eminently not only for the large-scale change they brought about but also for the motives which impelled their introduction. In 1882 the 'Semirechie oblast' was detached from the Governor-Generalship of Turkestan and merged with the newly-created Governor-Generalship of the Steppe. The intention behind this reform was not to carve out a homogeneous Kazakh region as it appears on the surface but only to resolve the rivalry between General G. A. Kolpakovski and General Cherniaev for the post of Governor-General of Turkestan. Again in 1897, the Semirechie oblast was reincorporated in the Governor-Generalship of Turkestan along with the Transcaspian oblast, not for any administrative or economic reasons, but to provide a big enough Governor-Generalship to suit the eminence of General A. N. Kuropatkin.[18] Such practices do not look so strange against the background of administrative corruption and arbitrariness which were so vividly described by Eugene Schuyler after his travels in the Central Asian region. Schuyler testified that the virus of corruption had spread from top to bottom in the Turkestan administration and that the army of the region 'had become a refuge for the scum of the military society.'[19] During the period of General Kaufman's rule in Central Asia, all attempts to eradicate the evils of corruption were discouraged because the Governor-General believed that any large-scale probe into this matter was bound to discredit the Russian administration in the eyes of the natives. At last in 1908 the Palen Commission succeeded in subjecting the entire Turkestan administration to a systematic and thoroughgoing investigation. The facts brought to light by this commission shocked everyone in both Tashkent and St. Petersburg. In the Transcaspian oblast, in particular, the commission found a corrupt military clique running the administration to suit itself. No less than two-thirds of the officials of the oblast were suspended by the commission and subsequent-

18. Pierce, n.15, 54-5, 86
19. Schuyler, n.7, 220.

ly almost all of them were convicted.[20]

III. COLONIZATION OF TURKESTAN

Soon after the military conquest of Central Asia was completed, the region which came under direct Russian administration was thrown open for colonization by Russians, first to the Don and Ural Cossacks and later to peasant settlers. By colonization the imperial government sought to achieve a two-fold objective. Firstly, colonization was encouraged in order to relieve the rural part of central Russia of its surplus population which had become economically impoverished and politically restive.[21] Secondly, it was favoured as a means of consolidating Russia's gains in Turkestan which was inhabited mainly by a non-Russian population. The advantages of settling amidst the newly-conquered and hostile peoples of the region settlers belonging to the Russian nation and loyal to the imperial regime were obvious. These settlements in course of time became not only the bastions of Russia's strength but also the disseminating centres of Slavic culture and civilization. In short, colonization became a panacea for containing both revolutionary and national movements within the empire.

During the initial stages of the conquest, dictated by the exigencies of strategy and security, the Cossacks were settled along the Syr Daria and in the Semirechie oblast as early as 1847.[22] Following the emancipation of the serfs in 1861, the

20. Pierce, n.15, 88-9.
21. The uneconomic nature of peasant holdings and the prevalence of large-scale rural unemployment had brought about a great crisis in the central regions of Russia. To overcome this explosive situation the government revised its colonization policies and began to encourage the peasants to undertake colonization. For a graphic description of the conditions of the Russian peasants in the post-emancipation period, see John Maynard, *Russia in Flux* (London, 1941) 29-56; also see *Istoriia narodov Uzbekistana* (Tashkent, 1947) II, 339. (Cited hereafter as *INUz*).
22. The first Cossack settlements sprang up in the lower Syr Daria region soon after the formation of the Syr Daria line in 1847. In Semirechie, the Cossack colonization took place by way of organization by the authorities of two Cossack divisions with instruction to settle down in certain specified regions. In 1847, the first of such settlements sprang up in Sergiopol and Kopal. By 1867 there were 14 Cossack *stanitsas* (large Cossack villages) and hamlets in Semirechie with a population of 14,413 persons. By the close of the nineteenth century, the Cossack population in Semirechie rose to 29,323 persons and by 1906 to 34,468 persons. See V. V. Bartol'd, *Istoriia kul'turnoi zhizni Turkestana* (Leningrad, 1927) 147.

colonization movement underwent a change both in its size and character. Henceforth, it became essentially a peasant movement.[23]

With the beginning of the Stolypin Reaction, the policy governing the colonization question came in for a thorough reappraisal. The government, feeling more secure after the suppression of the revolution of 1905-07, sought to create for itself a reliable basis of support in the rural areas of the empire and particularly in the borderland regions. It endeavoured to achieve this objective by attempting to strengthen the position of the *kulak* elements and by making them instrumental in 'strengthening Russian domination' and also in 'spreading Slavic culture in the midst of the Turco-Mongol peoples.'[24] The policy of the government thus orientated, attempts were made to create in Turkestan 'an economically sturdy and politically reliable' Russian population. Henceforth, even peasants who were in more affluent circumstances were induced to trek out from the central regions of Russia to colonize the borderlands.[25]

In Turkestan, the colonization policies of the government encountered serious opposition from the native population. But in the nomadic areas, the government easily overcame the opposition of the Kazakhs and the Kirgiz and went ahead with its projects of land confiscation. In the southern sedentary regions, however, the prospects for colonization were relatively meagre in view of the non-availability of surplus land as also due to the seriousness of opposition of native peasants.[26] Prevented thus

23. The first peasant settlers, some 242 families from the Voronezh *gubernia*, arrived in Semirechie in 1868. By 1882 the peasant settlements in the oblast had risen to 29 with a population of 15,000 persons. By 1889 the number of settlers rose from 15,000 to 38,000 persons. Between 1891 and 1892 another 1,791 families arrived in the oblast. In July, 1903 certain specified areas in Syr Daria and the Fergana oblasts were opened to settlers. In 1906, the Syr Daria resettlement district was opened. See *INUz*, n. 21, 342-3.

24. *Ibid.*, 343.

25. *Ibid.*, 343-4. In the Syr Daria oblast, the first Russian peasant settlements appeared in the Kazalinsk area. Settlements of Russian emigres sprang up in the Aulie-Ata area in 1875. In this area, besides the Russian colonies there were five settlements of the Volga Germans. By 1890 settlers began to make their way even into the Tashkent uezd where soon nearly one-third of the total newly-irrigated land was allocated to them. See Bartol'd, n. 22, 151.

26. There existed only one Russian settlement along the Zerafshan

from entering the rural areas in the southern region, the Russian settlers started flooding the cities and towns, thereby giving to Russian colonization in this region an urban character.[27] By 1911, the total Russian population in the Turkestan region had risen to as much as 400,000 persons or six per cent of the total population of the region.[28] It ranged from two per cent of the population of the Samarkand and Fergana oblasts to as much as seventeen per cent of the population of the Semirechie oblast. The Transcaspian and the Syr Daria oblasts came in between with eleven per cent and six per cent respectively.[29] Though in its size the Russian population of the Turkestan region was considerably less than that of the steppe region, it was not altogether insignificant.[30]

river in 1911 with a population of 307 persons. In the Fergana oblast, the first Russian settlement came into existence in 1893 (in the Osh area). In 1901 another hamlet sprang up here and in 1908 three more. In the Namangan uezd, the first Russian settlement was established in 1907 with fifteen families having 69 persons. In the Andizhan uezd until 1901 there existed only three Russian settlements which after 1908 rose to eleven. A Russian settlement was founded in Margelen uezd in 1899. *Ibid.*, 157.

27. The Russians constituted as many as 54,000 persons of the population of Tashkent city, one-fifth of the population of Samarkand city, a little more than one-sixth of the population of Andizhan, one-third of the population of old Margelan and constituted an absolute majority in Novyi Margelan. In Ashkabad the Russian population was about 9,000 out of its total population of 44,000. Their number was less in cities like Kokand (only 4,000 out of its total population of 113,000), and Namangan (1,900 persons out of its population of 74,000 persons). See *INUz*, n.21, 350-1; also see Bartol'd, n.22, 168.

28. *Aziatskaia Rossiia* (St. Petersburg, 1914) I, 67-9; also see Frank Lorimer, *The Population of the Soviet Union: History and Prospects* (Geneva, 1946) 27. According to the estimates of General N. A. Kuropatkin, the last Governor-General of Turkestan Region, the number of Russians living in Turkestan in 1916 was 540,000 and they constituted as much as 7.5 per cent of the total population of that region. See A. N. Piaskovskii, ed., *Vosstanie 1916 goda v Srednei Azii i Kazakhstane: sbornik dokumentov* (Moscow, 1960) 97.

29. The Russian settlements in the Transcaspian oblast had grown up rapidly. By 1896 there were already ten settlements in the region and during the course of the next two years they were nearly trebled (27 settlements with a population of 5,000 persons). By 1911, in Ashkhabad city alone, the Russians constituted as much as one-fifth of its total population (9,000 out of its total population of 44,000 persons). See Bartol'd, n. 22, 156, 168.

30. The Russian population in the Kazakh steppe, for the corresponding period was in the neighbourhood of 1,500,000 persons. The Russians constituted 37 per cent of the population of the Uralsk oblast, 33 per cent

The influx of the Russian immigrants into Turkestan inevitably led to large-scale confiscation of land from the indigenous population. By 1908 the government had alloted for the utilization of 60,350 peasant settlers 231,250 *desiatins* of land[31] and 610,484 *desiatins* to the Cossack settlers (34,468 persons) in the Semirechie oblast.[32] With the arrival of new settlers, the size of land confiscations began to swell and by 1915 it reached the record figure of 3,963,000 *desiatins*.[33] In many places, the seizure of land from the nomadic population was almost complete. Consequently, thousands of nomads and cattle began to die out of sheer starvation. For instance, it was said that between 1902-07 almost twentyseven per cent of the Kirgiz cattle perished and between 1903-13 the Kirgiz population itself fell by seven to ten per cent.[34]

IV. ECONOMIC DEVELOPMENT OF TURKESTAN UNDER COLONIAL RULE

Russia's interests in Turkestan were not limited to mere military occupation and colonization. The desire to secure the region's raw materials and to open its markets to Russian manufactured articles had been important factors which led to the Russian conquest of Turkestan.[35] After rounding off the conquest, Russia itself became interested in developing and exploiting the resources of the Turkestan region and in transforming Central Asia into a sort of raw-material appendage of the metro-

---

of the population of the Turgai oblast, 58 per cent of the population of Akmolinsk and 20 per cent of the population of Semipalatinsk oblasts. See *Aziatskaia Rossiia*, n.28, 67-8; also see Lorimer, n.28, 27.

31. One *desiatin* is equal to 2.7 acres.

32. Georgi Safarov, *Kolonial'naia revoliutsiia: opyt Turkestana* (Moscow, 1921) 43; also see P. G. Galuzo, *Turkestan—koloniia: ocherki istorii kolonial'noi politiki Russkogo tsarizma v Srednei Azii* (Tashkent, 2nd edition, 1935) 162.

33. The data available for 1915 indicates that the Russian settlers also owned a greater portion of the available irrigated land in Semirechie which amounted to about 485,000 *desiatins*. See *Turkestanskaia Pravda* (Tashkent) 28 (39), 8 Februray 1923.

34. According to Ryskulov, the Kirgiz cattle during this period fell by about 35.9 per cent and the Kirgiz population itself by 8 to 9 per cent. See T. R. Ryskulov, *Kirgizstan* (Moscow, 1935) 46; also see *BSE* (Moscow, 1st edition, 1936) XXXII, 377.

35. See footnotes 1 and 11 of this chapter.

politan industrial regions.[36] But before this could be achieved,
formidable difficulties needed overcoming. Until then the
Central Asian region was completely isolated from the rest of
the world largely owing to the absence of modern means of
communication and also by the near-anarchic conditions which
prevailed there. The peoples of Central Asia who still used the
slow-moving camel and the donkey in their transit trade had
not even heard about the railways. Until Central Asia was linked with the other parts of Russia by modern means of communication, it was a foregone conclusion that most of its riches
was bound to remain beyond the reach of Russia.

The introduction of railways in Central Asia required great
enterprise and capital. Russian private capital was as yet un-
prepared to shoulder major risks in the region. The initiative
in railroad building therefore was taken by the government
itself. The initial attempts towards railroad construction were
governed chiefly by military considerations, and the railroads
first came into existence in the region lying on the eastern shore
of the Caspian Sea. The Transcaspian Railway, as this line subsequently came to be called, was completed between 1881-86. It
linked Kyzyl-Arvat, Mikhailovskii Bay, Ashkhabad, Merv and
Chardzhui and extended up to the Amu Daria.[37] After the construction of a bridge over the Amu Daria, Samarkand was connected by railway in 1888. The 'Samarkand-Andizhan Railway',
with its offshoots stretching as far as Tashkent and Novyi
Margelan, was completed in 1899. The length of the trunk route
of the Central Asiatic Railway from Krasnovodsk to Tashkent
was 1,748 versts. In 1905 another railway line connected Tash-

---

36. The economic importance of Central Asia to Russia was considerable. Prior to the conquest, the region had carried on with Russia a
flourishing trade and both its textiles and raw materials were in demand
all over Russia. Central Asian silk had gone as far as Marseilles. Between
1827-37 the Central Asian exports to Russia exceeded imports from Russia
by two million rubles. In 1855 Central Asian exports to Russia exceeded
imports by 1,599,999 rubles and in 1860 by 3,100,000 rubles. See
'Nationalism And Progress,' *The Central Asian Review* 5 (1957) 3; also see
Galuzo, n.32, 25; V. I. Masal'skii, *Turkestanskii krai* (St. Petersburg, 1913)
507.

37. B. G. Gafurov, *Istoriia Tadzhikskogo naroda* (Moscow, 1949) I,
414-5; also see M. G. Vakhabov, *Formirovanie Uzbekskoi sotsialisticheskoi
natsii* (Tashkent, 1961) 98.

kent city with Orenburg.[38]

Towards the beginning of the nineties of the last century, Russian private enterprise, which until then had shown a reluctance to participate in any major ventures in distant Central Asia, started evincing a keen interest in the development of the resources of the region.[39] The Fergana and Bukharan railways were constructed mainly by Russian private enterprise. By 1915 railroad building within the region had gone to such an extent as to make possible the linking of almost all the important cities by railways. Of special importance was railroad construction in the Fergana valley, facilitating the linking of this densely populated area and one of the richest cotton growing areas of the region, not only with its neighbouring regions but also with European Russia.[40]

One of the main objectives in building up the Central Asian Railway had been to facilitate quick and regular transport of Central Asian cotton to the industrial regions of Russia. The cotton crop grown in the region assumed such an importance in the economic life of the empire that Central Asia henceforth came to be known as the 'land of the white gold.' Within

---

38. *IUzSSR*, n.1, 120-1.

39. The noted Tadjik orientalist and historian B. G. Gafurov divided Russia's colonial policies in Central Asia into two periods. The first one, beginning from the time of the conquest is said to have lasted until the nineties of the last century. This period was characterized by the relatively small role played by Russian private enterprise in the development and exploitation of the resources of Central Asia. Much of the export and import trade between Russia and Central Asia during this period was carried mainly through the medium of the local merchants and export of Russian capital into the region, as a rule, did not take place. The second period commenced from the nineties of the last century and lasted until the outbreak of the Revolution of 1917. The characteristic feature of this period was the active participation of Russian private enterprise in almost all fields of economic activity in Central Asia. Particular attention was given to the extension of the cotton crop over larger areas and ensuring its regular transport to Russia. See Gafurov, n.37, 412-3. Between 1914-16 Russian industrialists and financiers invested over 313,000,000 rubles in Central Asia. See Serge A. Zenkovsky, *Pan-Turkism and Islam in Russia* (Cambridge, Mass., 1960) 22.

40. Of the several branches of railroads constructed by 1915, the Gorchakovo-Skobelev, Andizhan-Grunchimar, Kokand-Namangan, Andizhan I-Andizhan II, Grunchimar-Dzalal-Abad, Kagan-Bukhara, Kagan-Karshi, Karshi-Amirabad, Karshi-Samsonovo and Karshi-Guzar-Kitab were notable ones See *IUzSSR*, n. 1, 230.

Central Asia itself almost all other economic activities came to be centred around the cotton crop.[41]

Following the shrinkage of cotton imports from the United States, Russia began to develop Central Asia as one of the major cotton-growing regions of the empire. Initial successes attained in the growing of the American variety of cotton in the region led to its extension over larger areas.[42] First successfully sown on a modest scale of only 300 *desiatins* in 1884, the American type of cotton claimed more than 14,000 *desiatins* in 1887, 50,000 *desiatins* in 1889 and 110,000 *desiatins* by 1895.[43] Only 8 years after its introduction in the region, three million poods of American variety of cotton were exported from Central Asia to Russia. The American type of cotton proved so popular that soon everywhere in the region it had almost completely supplanted the old indigenous variety.[44]

According to the estimates of the Central Statistical Committee of the imperial government, the total area under cotton in Central Asia by 1911 had risen to 320,081 *desiatins*.[45] This estimate took into account only the cotton growing areas of Russian Turkestan and excluded the cotton growing areas in Bukhara and Khiva. It was estimated that in Bukhara and Khiva for the corresponding period, the cotton crop occupied at least 150,000 *desiatins* of land. The total area under cotton in Central Asia was estimated to be 550,000 *desiatins* in 1913 and

41. Cotton though not an indigenous crop of Central Asia, was grown there from a remote past. Until the coming of the Russians, the Central Asian cotton had only a local significance and only a small portion of it was exported. Being mainly of the short-staple rough variety, it was said to be limited in its utility for large-scale textile manufacturing.

42. Soon after the conquest, Russian industrialists tried to establish in Central Asia, cotton growing plantations on the American model. A few of such cotton plantations appeared in Tashkent, Fergana and Samarkand oblasts. However, it was soon discovered that economically they were not feasible which led to their closure. See Gafurov, n.37, 413.

43. *Aziatskaia Rossiia* (St. Petersburg, 1914) II, 276.

44. By 1888 the American type of cotton had claimed 35,000 *desiatins* in Fergana, 26,000 *desiatins* in Syr-Daria and 8,000 *desiatins* in Samarkand oblasts. *Ibid.*, 276-7.

45. The oblastwise distribution of this figure was Syr Daria 52,059 *desiatins*, Fergana 186,415 *desiatins*, Samarkand 46,936 *desiatins* and Transcaspia 34,617 *desiatins*. *Ibid.*, 272-3.

658,000 *desiatins* in 1915.[46] The Fergana oblast alone claimed nearly half of the entire cotton growing areas of Central Asia[47] and within this oblast more than two-thirds of its entire irrigated land was under the cotton crop.[48] Fergana's gross output of cotton was 1,015,687 poods in 1892, 1,800,000 poods in 1894 and 3,896,000 poods in 1900. The cotton output of this one oblast alone equalled nearly 80 per cent of the entire cotton production of Central Asia.[49]

Within Central Asia not only did the cotton crop begin to claim larger areas of land each year but cotton-growing itself began to assume a highly developed commercial character.[50] A large number of cotton firms, exchanges, banks and other credit institutions sprang up in Central Asia; they endeavoured to stimulate a further expansion of cotton growing and to secure the entire cotton output of the region for the textile mills of Russia. These credit institutions and a large number of Russian and native middlemen competed with one another to buy in advance the cotton crop raised by the local *dekkhans* (peasants). This system of advance buying of the cotton crop proved quite disadvantageous to the peasants.[51]

46. Kh. Sh. Inoiatov, *Oktiabr'skaia revoliutsiia v Uzbekistane* (Moscow, 1958) 15; also see N. Tiuriakulov, 'Turkestanskaia avtonomnaia respublika,' *Zhizn' natsional' nostei,* 1 (January, 1923) 86.

47. Within the Fergana oblast, the cotton crop claimed nearly 34.9 per cent of the total irrigated land in the Andizhan uezd, 34.9 per cent in the Kokand uezd, 30.6 per cent in the Skobelev (not Fergana) uezd and 25.1 per cent in the Namangan uezd. See M. G. Vakhabov, 'K voprosu o formirovanii Uzbekskoi burzhuaznoi natsii', *Materialy ob'edinennoi nauchnoi sessii posviashchennoi k istorii Srednei Azii i Kazakhstana v dooktiabr'skii period* (Tashkent, 1955) 151.

48. P. I. Liashchenko, *Istoriia narodnogo khoziaistva SSSR* (Moscow, 4th edition, 1956) II, 542; also see *MISGPUz*, n.10, 14.

49. Cotton exports from Central Asia to Russia were in the order of 15 million *poods* in 1905, 25 million *poods* in 1910 and 33,918,000 *poods* in 1915. Liashchenko, n.48, 546.

50. To the peasants also cotton growing proved lucrative. The rise in price of cotton from 40 kopeks a pood to 4 roubles and 15 kopeks rendered cotton more profitable than other crops. As against 6 rubles 74 kopeks the peasants obtained from growing wheat and 16 rubles 24 kopeks by growing rice in one *desiatin* of land, they were able to get as much as 70 to 80 rubles by growing cotton in the same area. See *MISGPUz*, n.10, 14; also see *IUzSSR*, n.1, 115.

51. As a result of the destruction of the local textile industry and the newly-evolved system of buying the cotton crop in advance, the native peasants came increasingly under the mercy of the Russian cotton buyers

The cotton crop, owing to the endeavour made by the government, the industrialists, merchants and the local beys, started assuming the character of a mono-culture in many parts of Central Asia. Consequently, cotton exports to Russia began to swell year after year. Even a somewhat conservative estimate made by the Central Statistical Committee of the imperial government admits that within a span of twentyfive years (from 1888 to 1920), the cotton exports from Central Asia to Russia rose from 873,000 poods to 1,369,700 poods.[52] By 1912 the Central Asian region had started supplying about four-fifths of the entire cotton requirements of the Russian empire.[53]

The extensive development of cotton growing in Central Asia and the flourishing cotton export trade, in turn, brought into existence a large number of industrial enterprises. These industrial establishments were engaged mainly in the initial processing of cotton and in the manufacturing of its byproducts. In 1908, out of the 220 cotton-processing plants which Russia possessed, 204 were located in the Turkestan region alone.[54] Besides cotton-processing and cotton-ginning industries, a large number of industrial enterprises engaged in the manufacture of a variety of articles also came into existence. The total number of such industrial establishments by 1913 had risen to 706.[55] Nearly half of them were located in Fergana which, in its industrial development, had overtaken not only the neighbouring regions but also some of the highly industrial-

and the native middlemen. The credit advanced to the peasants by them carried with it an interest of more than four per cent per month. Consequently, the peasants became heavily indebted and lost their freedom of raising in their fields the crop of their own choice. The moneylenders brought a great deal of pressure on the peasants to grow only cotton. Although the nature of the economy of the region was changing rapidly, the *Bay-dekkhan* relationship remained the same. The usurious terms of credit often robbed the peasants of their lands and reduced them to the rank of either sharecroppers or agricultural workers. See Mandel, n.15, 79; also see Tiuriakulov, n.46, 87.

52. *Aziatskaia Rossiia*, n.43, 278.

53. The trade balance for 1914 indicated that out of the articles exported from Central Asia to Russia, 51 per cent consisted of articles of cotton industry (fibres, oilcakes, seeds, etc.,) which claimed 75 per cent of the value of the articles exported. See Inoiatov, n.46, 16.

54. Liashchenko, n.48, 546-7.

55. *Ibid.*, 546; also see A. M. Aminov, *Ekonomicheskoe razvitie Srednei Azii: kolonial'noi period* (Tashkent, 1959) 71.

ized regions of central Russia like the Ekaterinoslav gubernia.[56] By 1917 the industrial establishments in Turkestan had risen to nearly 869.[57] The rate of growth of these enterprises was considerably higher after 1905. Between 1880-1900 the average annual increase was about 7 enterprises, between 1900-10 22 enterprises and between 1910-14 as many as 45 enterprises.[58]

An inevitable consequence of industrialization and growth of commercial activities of the Turkestan region was the growth of its urban population. Between 1897 and 1907 the urban population of Turkestan rose by 30.51 per cent as against 15.78 per cent rise in its rural population. The rise in the ratio of urban and rural population oblast-wise was as follows: Semirachie 45.30 per cent and 5.55 per cent; Transcaspia 26.32 per cent and 4.62 per cent; Samarkand 30.90 per cent and 22.54 per cent; Syr Daria 23.28 per cent and 21.30 per cent and Fergana 49.27 per cent and 10.90 per cent. While the rural population fell relatively, the urban population between 1897 and 1907 increased almost by one-third.[59] The rise of the urban population was particularly impressive in some of the cities located on the territory of modern Uzbekistan. Between 1897 and 1910 the population of Tashkent rose from 155,673 to 201,191, of Kokand from 81,354 to 113,636, of Andizhan from 47,627 to 76,367 and of Samarkand from 55,128 to 89,693.[60] Within a short span of only thirteen years, the population of these cities increased by nearly fifty per cent.

In the rural areas of Turkestan, though the feudal order remained dominant, certain changes began to make themselves felt. The most important of them was the steadily increasing number of nomads settling on land. In 1867 the nomadic population of the region constituted as much as 84 per cent of its *total* population but by 1877 it had already come down to 47

---

56. I. Khodorov, 'K probleme raionirovaniia promyshlennostei Srednei Azii,' *Planovoe khoziaistvo* 1 (1927) 189.

57. Vakhabov, n.47, 151-3.

58. Vakhabov, n.37, 100; also see *IUzSSR*, n.1, 224.

59. Safarov, n. 32, 30. This rise was impressive in view of the fact that on the eve of Russian conquest of Central Asia, it was estimated that 95 per cent of the population of Khiva, 82 per cent population of Bukhara and 80 per cent of the population of Turkestan consisted of rural population. See *Turkestanskaia Pravda*, 60 (351), 21 March 1923.

60. Vakhabov, n. 37, 102.

per cent and by 1917, it was estimated that it was not more than 30 per cent of its rural population.[61] This transition from nomadism to sedentary living proceeded at a faster pace among the Uzbek population of the region. By the beginning of the twentieth century, only 1.72 per cent remained nomads among the Uzbeks in the Syr Daria oblast as against 69.04 per cent engaged in agriculture and 29.24 per cent engaged in handicrafts. In the Fergana oblast, among the Uzbeks, the nomadic way of life had almost totally disappeared and in the Samarkand oblast only 2.16 per cent of them remained nomads. As a result of the bulk of the Uzbek population taking to sedentary living, some of the sharp differences noticed earlier among the different sections of the Uzbeks completely disappeared. An almost uniform way of life, both economic and cultural, came to exist among all Uzbeks. Though the same cannot be said of the Turkmens, Kazakhs and Kirgiz, the increasing tempo of settlement on land even among them was discernible. The Tadjiks already for a long time had been basically a sedentary agricultural people.[62]

Along with these changes which were taking place in the urban and rural areas of Central Asia came yet another change. Under the impact of the economic changes, the traditional clan and tribal divisions which were so characteristic of the peoples of Central Asia began to crumble down, leading to a new social stratification based on occupation. New social divisions like artisans, officials, traders and peasants began to arise even in the more backward societies of the Kirgiz and Turkmens.[63] One of the more significant results of such a stratification was the

61. Bartol'd, n. 22, 121.

62. Even in the Amirate of Bukhara and the Khanate of Khiva similar changes were taking place. Within the former, except among the Kazakh population of the Kenimekh area and among a small part of the inhabitants of Kungrad, Takhta-Bazar, Baisun and Shirabad, the bulk of the people (mainly Uzbeks and Tadjiks) pursued agriculture. In Khiva most of the Uzbek population and a considerable portion of the Turkmen population also pursued a sedentary agricultural occupation. See *Materialy po raionirovaniiu Srednei Azii*, vypusk I (Tashkent, 1926) 7; also see G. Skalov, 'Khivinskaia revoliutsiia 1920 goda,' *Novyi vostok*, 3 (1923) 241-3.

63. Ryskulov, n. 34, 41; also see 'Zasedanie vtoroi sessii TsIK SSSR 24 Oktiabria 1924g,' *Narodnoe khoziaistvo Srednei Azii*, 4 (November 1924) 201.

emergence of a class of moneyed aristocracy.[64] Though this class for a long time confined its activities to usury, with the increase in the commercial activities of Central Asia it began to venture into other fields. Consequently, in cotton export trade, cotton-processing and ginning, leather tanning, silk reeling and other industries, the native bourgeoisie began to have a large share. For instance, out of the 157 cotton processing enterprises which were located in the Fergana valley, about 109 belonged to native industrialists. By the beginning of the twentieth century, in other parts of Central Asia also, the newly-evolved class of native bourgeoisie had emerged into prominence. Commenting on this phenomenon, the governor of the Fergana oblast' in one of his despatches, declared that 'in the Russian period such a phenomenon has begun to make its appearance as the concentration of as much as 14,000,000 rubles in the hands of the illiterate Mirkamil Muminbaev.'[65] Besides Muminbaev, other natives also came into prominence by the size of their wealth such as Ubaidullah Arifkhodzhaev, Allakul'bek Dzhurabek in the Tashkent uezd and Rakhimbaev in Merv.[66] Outstanding among the industrial and commercial enterprises owned by the natives were the Bukharan firm of Khodzhaev and Arabov, the cotton-ginning enterprises of Sali Iagachi, the leather tanning industries of Tiuriakhodzhaev and the cotton-processing industries of Vad'iaev brothers.[67] Even in the more backward Bukharan and Khivan regions, millionaires and multimillionaires began to emerge.[68]

---

64. Bartol'd, n.22, 171.

65. *MISGPUz*, n.10, 82.

66. P. A. Kovalev, *Mobilizatsiia na tylovve raboty naseleniia Turkestana vosstaniie 1916 goda* (Manuscript) 82.

67. S. I. Iakubovskaia, 'Likvidatsiia fakticheskogo neravenstva natsii na primere istorii narodov Srednei Azii i Kazakhstana,' *Istoricheskie zapiski*, 48 (Moscow, 1954) 159.

68. The evolution of the new class of native bourgeoisie occurred in Central Asia in its own distinct form. In the cotton growing regions, the former feudal *Beys* by virtue of their privileged and affluent position were better equipped than others to take advantage of the new economic opportunities and quickly transformed themselves into merchants and industrialists. In the nomadic regions the former *Khans*, *manaps* and other feudal dignitories were said to have been 'reborn as capitalists.' See E. Steinberg, *Ocherki istorii Turkmenii* (Leningrad, 1934) 64-5; also see G. I. Karpov, *Vosstanie Tedzhenskikh Turkmen v 1916g* (Ashkabad, 1935) 64-5; M. Nemchenko, 'Natsional'noe razmezhevanie Srednei Azii,' *Mezhdunarodnaia zhizn'*, 4-5 (1924) 72-3; Dervish, 'Bukharskaia sovetskaia

V. CULTURAL AND POLITICAL AWAKENING

The attempts made to throw open the Central Asian region for systematic ·economic exploitation set in motion a chain reaction in the native society and brought into existence many things which the Russians never consciously encouraged.[69] As the structure of the native society started changing, traditional patterns of life began to alter.[70] Some of the more outstanding of these developments were the development of agriculture, particularly, the enormous increase in cotton growing, the quickening of the pace of settlement of the nomads to sedentary life, the crumbling of traditional clan-tribal divisions, the growth of trade and industry, the establishment of modern means of communication like the railways, posts and telegraphs, the beginning of the new social stratification which led to the emergence of a class of moneyed aristocracy and industrial workers, etc. These developments exercised a profound influence on the culture of the indigenous people and set a new tone to their

narodnaia respublika,' *Zhizn' natsional'nostei,* I (1923) 196; Skalov, n.62, 241-3; Ryskulov, n.34, 36-7. Also see General Kuropatkin's report to Tsar Nicholas II on the causes and course of the 1916 rebellion in Piaskovskii, n.28, 94.

69. It is interesting to note that while the changes which accompanied the process of opening up of the Central Asian region to systematic economic exploitation began to shake the native society in a big way, thereby forcing it to abandon traditional patterns of life and adjust itself to the altering circumstances, Russian official policy in this respect remained altogether passive. Russian policy with regard to social, religious and cultural issues in Central Asia lacked a positive content largely because of the conservatism of the bureaucracy and the army officials. As a result, many traditional institutions of the natives which had become wholly anachronistic instead of disappearing became revitalized. Thus, the courts of the *Kazi* and the *Bii,* the laws of the *Shariat* and the *Adat,* the outdated religious education of the *maktabs* and the *madrasas,* the feudal political institutions of the amirs, khans, *beys* and *aksakals,* the dominant position of the bigoted clergy and, in short, all those things which symbolized social, political and cultural retrogression in the native society, not only gained a fresh lease of life but in some spheres, were even strengthened. Though the somewhat restrained attitude of the Russian administration towards the social, religious, cultural and·political institutions of the indigenous population is praiseworthy, it must not be forgotten that largely on account of this negative policy which Russia pursued in Central Asia, the latter remained, even in the twentieth century, one of the most backward regions in the Móslem world.

70. See Galuzo, n.32, 202-3.

social life.[71] In particular, the urban population of the region among whom all creative social and cultural activities had become static, now began to throb with a new life. The intelligentsia of the cities began to vie with one another in establishing public libraries, museums, clubs, scientific societies and other cultural institutions and also began to publish journals and newspapers.[72]

It would be a mistake to think that such cultural activities were confined only to the immigrant population—the Russians, Tatars and Azerbaidjanis. There is every indication that a considerable number of indigenous people had also begun to participate in such activities. Among them, the Uzbeks took the lead. In Central Asia, the Uzbeks were the first to develop not only an urban commercial bourgeoisie but also a middle class intelligentsia. The Uzbeks learnt the Russian language earlier than others, many of them became teachers and officials, some found places even in the army. They greatly profited from the attempts made by the Russians to develop the region economically and amassed great wealth by venturing into trade and industry. When facilities for travel became available, many Uzbeks started travelling to European countries and some went as far as London.[73] Among the other peoples of the region, except among the Kazakhs, similar developments did not take place for a long time. Among the Kazakhs in the steppe region, an intelligentsia came into existence very early and began to wield considerable influence not only on their own kinsmen within Central Asia but also on their neighbours. By the time cultural awakening came to the Tadjiks, the Kirgiz and the Turkmens, they found that not only were they left far behind by the Uzbeks, but their own progress was considerably hindered by Uzbek chauvinism.[74]

71. Bartol'd, n.22, 168; also see G. I. Broido, 'Nasha turkestanskaia politika i angliiskaia zhurnalistika,' *Novyi vostok*, 2 (1923) 76.
72. Bartol'd, *ibid.*, 169.
73. *Ibid.*, 170.
74. Like the Tatars of the Volga region, the Uzbeks in Central Asia sought to utilize local reform and national movements to consolidate their own position. As the adherents of the regional Muslim movement which sought for the establishment of a Muslim state, the Uzbek intelligentsia fought against the separatist movements of the less advanced peoples of the region and subordinated their cultural, economic and political interests to their own. *Source?*

Thus towards the close of the nineteenth and the beginning of the twentieth centuries, as in all other former colonies of European powers, in Central Asia also a newly-born native intelligentsia had started gathering strength and influence. Its size, of course, remained small but like its counterparts in all other former colonies, the Central Asian intelligentsia became extremely vocal and started exercising an influence which was out of proportion to its numerical strength. The intelligentsia among the indigenous population of the region was divided, broadly, into three main groups:

1. The intellectuals on whom the impact of the Russian cultural influence was great and who worked for 'drawing nearer' the Russians and natives. Foremost among them were scholars and writers like Furkat, Gurbat, Nodim, Mukhimi and Hamza Hakimzade Niazi among the Uzbeks; Said Akumed Adzhizi, Akhmed Donish and Tashkodzha Asiri among the Tadjiks; Chokan Valikanov, Ibragim Altynsarin and Abai Kununbaev among the Kazakhs. They sought to make known and interpret the Russian cultural and literary legacies through their writings to their own peoples. They favoured the opening of the Russian-native schools among the natives and endeavoured to popularize them. Though their role in bringing about the cultural awakening among their own peoples was of considerable importance, these intellectuals did not have any great following among the natives except among a small number of men who had come under similar influences.[75]

2. The intellectuals who hailed from the ranks of the *Khadimists* (traditionalists). These stood for the preservation of Islamic orthodoxy and the unity of the *Islamiat* and opposed all reforms which sought to modernize the native society on European lines. The *Khadimists* controlled all educational, religious and cultural institutions.

75. The Russian-native schools, though their number began to increase after 1900, did not become popular among the indigenous population. In 1896 there were 28 Russian-native schools which rose to 83 in 1906 and to 89 in 1911. See Bartol'd, n.22, 137; also see *INUz*, n.21, 330; Gafurov, n.37, 451-2; Kovalev, n.66, 69.

Their supporters came from among the Muslim clergy, landlords, wealthy merchants and also from the vast hinterland of peasant masses. The *Khadimists* worked against the other two groups and sought to isolate the indigenous population from all European influences. They had a long tradition of militant resistance to the Russian rule in Central Asia.[76]

3. The intellectuals who were under the Tatar cultural influence.[77] These stood for fighting the religious fanaticism

76. The conservative and orthodox elements of the native society who were shocked and annoyed at young natives flocking to the Russian restaurants, clubs, drinking and public houses and attributed the slackening of morals, manners and growing indifference to religion among the younger generation to the influence of the 'foreign culture of the infidels' were the enthusiastic supporters of this group. Stirring up the deep-seated religious antipathy of the indigenous population against the Russians, this group organized a series of armed rebellions in Central Asia. In the eighties and nineties of the last century, the *Khadimists* organized no less than 250 rebellions against the Russians out of which the uprising of 1885 in the Fergana valley under Darvish-Khan Tiuria, the Tashkent Cholera Riot of 1892 and the Andizhan rebellion of 1898 under Ishan Madali were the notable ones. In Fergana particularly, it was said, such rebellions had become almost an annual feature. After 1900, though such open and organized rebellions became steadily rarer, the tradition of militant resistance to the Russian rule was continued in a different form. It took the form of small-dimensional attacks on Russian settlers and officials and the so-called 'crimes against law and order.' Between 1899-1916 there were no less than 4,922 attacks on Russians in the region; the oblast-wise breakdown of this figure was Fergana 2,249, Samarkand 1,215, Transcaspia 775, Syr Daria 398 and Semirechie 285. The 'crimes against law and order' in the Fergana oblast between 1900-13 rose from 16 to 316; in the Samarkand oblast between 1900-10 from 120 to 379; in the Syr Daria oblast between 1906-13 from 255 to 2,766 and in the Transcaspian oblast between 1902-11, from 492 to 1,141. It is significant to note that such incidents took place almost always in the rural areas. This indicates that while a somewhat sophisticated nationalist movement began to evolve in the urban parts of the region, the rural areas remained strongholds of less enlightened but more militant anti-Russian elements. The *Khadimist* activities in Central Asia, in a way, were to be the precursors of the great uprising of the natives in 1916 and the later Basmachi movement. See P. G. Baluzo, 'Dva etapa natsional'no-osvoboditel'nogo dvizheniia v Srednei Azii,' *Pravda Vostoka*, 172 (1665), 30 July 1928; A. Arsharuni and Kh. Gabidullin, *Ocherki panislamizma i panturkizma v Rossii* (Moscow, 1931) 13-4; INUz, n.21, 357-70; Piaskovskii, n.68, 95.

77. The Tatars of the Volga region who developed at an early date an urban bourgeoisie, a large group of intellectuals and a well developed economy, took the lead in stimulating the cultural awakening not only among their kinsmen in Crimea and the Caucasus but also among the

and obscurantism of the masses by spreading new secular literature, developing European type of schools and replacing the purely religious and scholastic system of education by a system of secular education which was more in keeping with the needs of modern times.[78] They advocated the relaxation of the rigour of censorship and the development of a free native press, lowering of taxes and regularisation of the tax structure. In Bukhara and Khiva, in addition to these things, they demanded the limitation of the autocratic powers of the Khan and the Amir, fixation of taxes and their proper management and granting of legal guarantees for the security of life and property. Their supporters hailed from diverse occupations like teachers, advocates, students, officials, petty bourgeois elements etc. While they enjoyed a relatively large-scale support from among such urban professional classes, they had no following whatsoever in the rural areas. Confining their activi-

other Moslem populations of the Russian empire. In Central Asia a covert competition took place for a long time between the Russian and Tatar cultures for establishing their influence on the indigenous population and the latter, more often than not, emerged more successful. To check the growing influence of the Tatars in the region a ban was imposed on their entering into the teaching profession and acquiring property, etc. Within Central Asia, the Tatar immigrants started the 'new method' schools, publication of journals and newspapers and other cultural activities and began to draw many indigenous peoples into such activities. Towards the close of the nineteenth century, the newspaper *Tardjuman* (Interpreter) edited by the well-known Crimean Tatar, Ismail Bay Gaspirali, began to have a large circulation among the indigenous peoples of Central Asia. This newspaper played an important role in stimulating the cultural awakening among the peoples of Central Asia. See Bartol'd, n.22, 165-6; Safarov, n.32, 53; L. M. Uyazebek, 'The Political Status of the Tatar Autonomous Republic, *Studies on the Soviet Union* (Munich) 1 (1), new series (1961) 15-16; Zenkovsky, n. 39, 12-23.

78. The *maktabs* and *madrasas* which imparted only a religious education to their students were controlled by the *Khadimists* and had become strongholds of reaction. The entire education pattern of these religious schools was outmoded and needed drastic changes. The extent to which these schools had failed in disseminating knowledge had become clear from the fact that although there functioned nearly 7,000 schools with a student population exceeding 75,000, the bulk of the population of the region remained basically illiterate. In 1897, when the first census in the region was taken, it was found that the literate part of the population of Central Asia was proportionally lower than even that of the Yakut region. See *Turkestanskaia Pravda*, 24 (35), 3 February 1923; also see Kovalev, n.66, 69.

ties mainly to cultural activities in the initial stages, after the revolution of 1905 the members of this group began to give a political colour to their movement.[79]

Of these, the intellectuals who belonged to the last group, in spite of all the opposition they encountered from both their own kinsmen and the Russian authorities, succeeded to a considerable extent in reviving the cultural and political awakening of the indigenous peoples. They began their activities first in the field of education and proposed a radical reorganization of the old educational system. They sought to do this by agitating for the adoption of a comprehensive school curriculum which provided for the teaching of arithmetic, geography and science subjects. More significant was their advocacy of the phonetical method of study (*usul-i-djadid*) which brought to them the appellation 'Djadidists' (meaning the adherents of the 'new method' of study).

The attempts made by the Djadidists to persuade the authorities of the old *maktabs* and *madrasas* to switch over to the phonetical method of study ended in failure. Following this the Djadidists themselves started opening a number of the 'new method' schools in many of the cities of the Central Asian region. Besides, they also began compiling new alphabets and special text books to suit the new methods of study.[80] By 1910-11 there had come into existence sixteen 'new method' schools in Tashkent, seventeen in Semirechie, thirty in Fergana, two in Samarkand, five in Bukhara, two in the city of Turkestan and one in Perovsk. By 1917 the total number of 'new method' schools had risen to ninetytwo.[81] The rate of growth of the

79. Faizulla Khodzhaev, *K istorii revoliutsii v Bukhare* (Tashkent, 1926) 3-4, 12-13; also see the same writer's 'O Mlado-Bukhartsakh,' *Istorik marksist*, 1 (1926) 127-9; Arsharuni and Gabidullin, n. 76, 114; Safarov, n.32, 54; Galuzo, n.32, 200.

80. Abdul Rasul, a resident of Tashkent, compiled the first alphabet in the Uzbek language in conformity with the phonetic method and also wrote the first primer. Published first in 1900, this work subsequently ran into seventeen editions. Another work written by Munnever Kary, *Edib-i-Evvel* (meannig the 'first master') proved equally popular. Certain modifications were made in the Arabic alphabet with a view to simplify it. A dictionary of six languages was compiled by Ishak Khan of Tiuria-Kurgan. See Vakhabov, n.37, 206; also see Hayit, n.2, 41.

81. Bartol'd, n.22, 136-7; also see Baluzo, n.32, 199.

'new method' schools was not spectacular and their number remained small. Nevertheless, these schools became the crucibles of the cultural revolution in Central Asia. An entire generation of men who were subsequently to play an important role in the political life of the region was trained in these schools.[82]

The Djadidist movement, however, did not remain for long confined to mere educational and cultural activities. These, no doubt, constituted its basic work in the initial stages and continued to remain important items in its programme. But under the impact of the political developments which were taking place in Russia and in other Muslim countries, Djadidism gradually began to transform itself into a political movement. The Russo-Japanese War and the following Russian Revolution of 1905 were events of utmost importance in stimulating the political awakening among the innumerable nationalities which were herded together in the multi-national Russian Empire. The slogans of liberty and self-determination which the revolutionaries carried throughout the length and breadth of the empire reached even the distant Central Asian region.[83] Closely following on the heels of the 1905 Revolution came the Persian revolution of 1906, which forced Shah Muzaffar-ud-Din to grant his people a constitution and agree to the summoning of the National Assembly. This event which occurred in the neighbouring Muslim country exercised a powerful influence on the

---

82. Faizulla Khodzhaev, T. Fedorov and others, *Ocherki revoliutsionnogo dvizheniia v Srednei Azii* (Moscow, 1926) 6-7.

83. A great deal of controversy surrounds the question of the attitude of the indigenous population to the 1905 revolution. While earlier Soviet writers like Georgi Safarov, Muraveiskii, D. I. Manzhara and others almost categorically deny any participation of the indigenous population in the 1905 revolution later Soviet writers, assert that the local population took an active part in it. While it is true that the role of the indigenous populaion in the events of 1905 was passive, however, it cannot be denied that the revolution was a great event which profoundly influenced the political thinking of a considerable section of the native population. See Safarov, n. 32, 7; S. Muraveiskii, *Ocherki po istorii revoliutsionnogo dvizheniia v Srednei Azii* (Tashkent, 1926) 11; D. I. Manzhara, *Revoliutsionnoe dvizhenie v Srednei Azii 1905-1920*: vospominaniia (Tashkent, 1934); Kh. Sh. Inoiatov, 'Protiv falsifikatsii istorii sovetskoi Srednti Azii,' *Obshchestvennykh nauk,* (Uzb. AN) 1 (1961); Iu.N. Aleskerov, 'Pervaia Russkaia revoliutsiia i osvoboditel'naia bor'ba narodov Srednei Azii,' *Trudy Tadzhikskoga uchitel'skogo instituta imeni S. S. Aini* (Samarkand, 1955) IV, 5.

peoples of the region. Only two years later, Turkey, which always had exercised such profound religious and cultural influence on the peoples of Central Asia, was itself in the throes of the 'Young Turk' revolution. The slogan of 'unity and progress' raised by the Young Turks reverberated throughout the Central Asian region and parties modelled on the Young Turks Party came into existence in Russian Turkestan, Bukhara and Khiva.[84]

During the time of the revolution of 1905 and in the years which followed it, the Djadidists began to publish a number of books, journals and newspapers, and sought to propagate their views through them. Until 1905 there existed only one newspaper which was published in the Uzbek language under the editorship of O. P. Ostroumov. The 'Turkestan Native Newspaper' as it was called, usually expressed only official views and opinions and did not provide a forum for discussing and propagating the reforms advocated by the Djadidists. After the proclamation of the Tsar's Manifesto of 17 October 1905, the Djadidists started pleading with the Governor-General to lift the ban on the publication of newspapers by the natives and to allow them to bring out their own papers. After repeated refusals, the Governor-General finally gave in but on the condition that the editor of the proposed newspaper was to be appointed by him. Subsequently, the newspaper *Urta Aziening Umr Guzorligi—Taraqqi* (The Central Asiatic Commentator—Progress) came to existence under the editorship of the Governor-General's nominee, Ivan Grigor'iev.[85] Though it published many articles written by Djadidist leaders on issues like the reformation of the schools, changing the method of utilization of the income from the *wakf* lands, etc., this paper was far from being an organ of the Djadidist movement. The 'impartiality' of its editor enabled the opponents of the Djadidists to make use of the paper to frustrate the reforms advocated by the latter. Soon the Djadidists themselves turned away from this 'wholly impartial, spineless and voiceless' paper.[86]

84. Khodzhaev, 'K istorii revoliutsii v Bukhare,' n.79, 3; also see A. V. Piaskovskii, 'Revoliutsiia 1905-1907gg v Turkestane,' *Revoliutsiia 1905-1907 gg v natsional'nykh raionakh Rossii* (Moscow, 1949) 538.

85. M. Vakhabov, *Tashkent v period trekh revoliutsii* (Tashkent, 1957) 96-7.

86. *Ibid.*, 97.

Towards the beginning of 1906, the Djadidists succeeded in bringing out another newspaper *Taraqqi* (Progress) under the editorship of Gabitov. This paper gave much attention to the question of stimulating the national consciousness among the indigenous population of the region. When certain articles which were critical of the Turkestan administration appeared in this paper, the censors closed it down in August 1906. Following the closure of *Taraqqi*, Munnever Kary, the foremost Djadidist leader of Tashkent, under his own editorship began the publication of the paper *Khurshid* (Sun) in September 1906. Like its predecessor, this paper also began to publish many articles intended to arouse the national consciousness of the natives. On 11 October 1906, it published an article by Mohemmed Khodzha Bek-budi,[87] which outlined the programme and tactics of the Djadidists of Turkestan. Fearing the closure of the paper by the authorities, the Djadidists considerably toned down their criticism of the administration. Nevertheless, *Khurshid* was closed down in November 1906. The newspaper *Sohrat* (Fame) was started towards the end of 1907. In its first two numbers, a lengthy article by Bek-budi entitled 'On the problems facing the nation' was published. In this article Bek-budi asserted that so long the cultural backwardness of the people persisted, it was difficult to rouse their national consciousness. He insisted that the Djadidists must give greater attention to the question of providing the physical and spiritual basis to the emerging nation. For this purpose, he advocated the training of a large cadre of engineers, doctors, jurists, economists, administrators and other experts in cities like Moscow and St. Petersburg and a large number of priests in the centres of Islamic culture like Istanbul and Alexandria. For strengthening the economic foundation of the nation, Bek-budi enjoined upon the indigenous people to boycott the Indian, Jewish and other foreign traders and to buy goods only from the local Muslim merchants.[88]

87. Mohammad Khodzha Bek-budi, who was a Mufti before he was drawn into the Djadidist movement, was in many ways a remarkable personality. He was a poet, scholar, journalist, teacher and social reformer. He edited the journal *Aina* (Mirror) from 1913 and was considered to be the chief theoretician of the Djadidist movement.

88. Vakhabov, n.37, 211-2.

After the paper *Sohrat* was also closed down by the authorities, the Djadidists began the publication of the paper *Asiya* (Asia). Even this paper was unable to publish more than five issues. During this time the Tashkent millionaire Said Karim Said Azimbaev began the publication of the paper *Tudzhar* (Trader) which, after a time, ceased to exist owing to its failure to secure any subscribers. None of the Djadidist papers which were published from Tashkent survived for more than a year because of official intransigence. However, during their short span of life each one of them did much to popularize the Djadidist ideology and to stimulate the cultural awakening and national consciousness among the indigenous population.[89]

By 1912 the Djadidists once again began their publishing activities. This time their papers began to appear from many other cities of the region besides Tashkent. In 1913 Bek-budi started publishing his journal *Aina* (Mirror) from Samarkand. In 1914 the publication of the paper *Sadoi Turkestan* (Voice of Turkestan) was begun in Tashkent. Another journal *Al-Isok* (Reform) began its publication from 1915. The Djadidists of Bukhara started publishing the newspaper *Bukhara-i-Sharif* (Bukhara the Noble) and *Turan*.[90] Other newspapers like *Samarkand*, *Yurt* (Homeland), *Sadoi Fergana* (Voice of Fergana), *Tirik Suz* (Living Word) also made their appearance during this time.[91]

While some of the Djadidists sought to limit the activities of their movement to the cultural sphere alone, a great majority of them, however, believed that the cultural revival was not an end in itself but a means to a larger end. Writing in this connection, Munnever Kary, the editor of *Khurshid* and a leader of the Djadidist movement, stated:

... our ideas of reform do not restrict themselves to a revival

89. Besides the Djadidist papers, a number of Russian language newspapers were published in Tashkent between 1907-12. Apart from the official newspaper, *Turkestanskii Vedomosti* (Turkestan News), papers like *Turkestanskii Kur'er* (Turkestan Courier), *Turkestanskaia Torgovo-Promyshlennaia Gazeta* (The Turkestan Trade and Industrial Gazette), *Turkestanskaia Zhizn'* (Life of Turkestan), *Vecherniaia Zaria* (the Evening Dawn), *Na Rubezhe* (on the Frontier), *Tashkentskii Golos* (Voice of Tashkent, *Tashkentskoe Utro* (The Morning of Tashkent) were published from Tashkent. See Vakhabov, n. 85, 105.
90. *Ibid.*, 122.
91. Vakhabov, n.37, 110, 212-3.

of our spiritual life in the present day, but they endeavour to achieve national freedom, yes, they go still further and seek for the resurgence of the nation in which the new way of thinking and the old spiritual culture should be linked together, the cultural and spiritual life should regain their former position and an absolute national consciousness should come to prevail.[92]

Thus, the reorganization of the educational system and other cultural reforms which the Djadidists advocated were directed towards the achievement of the ultimate goal: the awakening of national consciousness and the achievement of national freedom. This change in emphasis from cultural to political issues was an important milestone in the development of the Djadidist movement in Central Asia.

In their political activities, the Djadidists were drawn towards the Russian Cadets (Constitutional Democrats) and almost wholly endorsed their demands for the establishment of a constitutional monarchy. Outlining the policies of the Djadidists, Mohammed Khodzha Bek-budi wrote in the newspaper *Khurshid* that the policies of the socialists and the party of 'Bureaucrats and Monarchists' were unacceptable to the Djadidists. Bek-budi reasoned that while the objectives of the former violated the spirit of Islam and ran counter to the laws of the *Shariat*, the latter were largely responsible for the continued backwardness of the Muslims of Russia. While supporting the Cadets on political issues, Bek-budi called upon the peoples of Central Asia to endorse the decisions of the Muslim Congresses on economic, ideological and scientific issues. On the national question again, Bek-budi declared that the Djadidists stood for cultural nationalism, which was endorsed both by the Cadets and by the Muslim Congresses.[93]

92. Cited in Hayit, n.2, 38.
93. Vakhabov, n.87, 208-9. Delegates from Turkestan, Crimea, Caucasus, Kazan, the Ural region, Siberia and other Moslem borderlands of Russia met in three Muslim Congresses in 1905 and 1906. These Congresses adopted resolutions which favoured closer contacts among the different Muslim regions of Russia; focussing attention on the common problems confronting Russian Muslims; on adopting a programme for the guidance of the Moslem members of the State Duma and on forming a Muslim Union. *Ittifak-ul-Muslimin*, as this organization came to be called. was intended to be the common political organization for all Muslims of Russia. The objectives of the Muslim Union, however, remained ill-

In the organizational sphere, the Djadidist movement remained extremely weak and ineffective. Before 1917, the Djadidists were not able to develop a unified and integrated political organization in Central Asia. They functioned as independent groups scattered over many cities of the region; these groups had little or no contact with one another. After 1910 the cities of Tashkent, Kokand and Bukhara became the centre of Djadidist activities. In Tashkent the Djadidists were active in the 'Progressive Giab' under the leadership of Mennever Kary, the Khodzhaev brothers, Mulla Abdulla Auliamov and Sarymsanov. In Kokand the 'Young Party' rallied around it all the Djadidists and carried on its activities openly. In Bukhara, owing to the prevalence of the Amir's autocratic regime, the prospects for Djadidist activities were limited. Functioning as a secret organization for a long time, the Djadidists of Bukhara later transformed themselves into the 'Young Bukharan Party.' They were led by Mirza Abdul Vahid, Hamid Khodzha and Ahmedjan Ma'zum Hamid. In Khiva the Djadidists became active considerably later and functioned more or less on the same lines as the Djadidists of Bukhara. In later years they organized the 'Young Khivan Party'.

The leanings of the Djadidist intellectuals towards pan-Islamic and pan-Turkic ideologies were well known from the beginning of the Djadidist movement in Russia. Ismail Bey Gaspirali and his Tatar associates, who wielded great influence on the Central Asian Djadidist intellectuals, were strongly drawn towards Turkey. That the Djadidist intellectuals of Central Asia also shared the Tatars' sympathies for Turkey became clear from their reaction to the Balkan wars (1912-13). Soon after the outbreak of the Balkan wars, several secret pan-Islamic societies

defined and little known. Though the third Muslim Congress, held in August 1906, favoured the introduction of regional autonomy into Russia, it remained vague whether this autonomy should have a national or a religious basis. Largely dominated by Tatar intellectuals of decidedly pan-Turkic persuasions, the *Ittifak* always minimized the social, cultural, economic, ethnic and linguistic differences which prevailed among the various Muslim populations of Russia and endeavoured to herd them together on the basis of a community of race and religion. See Arsharuni and Gabidullin, n.76, 23-7; also see Richard Pipes, *The Formation of the Soviet Union: Communism and Nationalism 1917-1923* (Cambridge, Mass., 1954) 13-5.

came into existence in the Central Asian region. The pro-Turkish propaganda these societies began to carry among the peoples of Central Asia alarmed the authorities considerably in view of the fact that Russia's own relations with Turkey were extremely strained during this period. Only six days after Germany declared war on Russia, martial law was imposed upon the entire Turkestan region. The Governor-General and the governors of the Turkestan region were empowered with special powers to deal with any emergency that might arise in the region. The head of the Turkestan administration was instructed to forbid the 'public divulgence or circulation of any false alarms or excitement on the events of the war under the threat of penalty extending to 1,000 rubles or imprisonment.' After the entrance of Turkey into the war, the fine was increased to 3,000 rubles and the term of imprisonment to not less than three months.[94] The governors and the uezd commandants were given strict orders not to relax surveillance on noted intellectuals who could stir up 'patriotic feelings' among the people. Further, they were instructed to ban the entrance of any immigrant Asiatics to cities and *auls* and to exile foreign subjects to their states on 'least suspicion.'[95] The Governor-General of Turkestan at a largely-attended parade of soldiers warned the peoples of Turkestan that the Chirchik river would flow with the blood of their families, of their sons and daughters, if they dared to indulge in pro-Turkish activities.[96]

Soon several natives were arrested for alleged pro-Turkish activities. Not all these natives, however, were guilty of the charges that were levelled against them, and subsequent investigations revealed that the officials had acted arbitrarily in many instances.[97] The arrest of the noted Fergana millionarie, Mir Kamil Kuminbaev and several others on similar charges created a lot of public excitement. Muminbaev after a short term of imprisonment was exiled from Turkestan for one year. But on

94. Kovalev, n.66, 152.
95. *Ibid.*, 153.
96. *Turkestanskaia Pravda*, 164 (441), 29 July 1924.
97. A notable instance of such official arbitrariness was the arrest and subsequent imprisonment of a native youth, Alimov Nasredin, on the flimsy charge that he had refused to buy a telegram containing the news of some victory won by Russian soldiers against Turkey. See Kovalev, n.66, 156.

the birthday of the Tsar in 1916 he was granted an amnesty and was allowed to return to Turkestan. Muminbaev on his return was given a rousing welcome and was hailed as a national hero.[98]

VI. THE REBELLION OF 1916

The Tsarist government's relation with the peoples of Central Asia which was never too cordial, started further deteriorating after Turkey entered World War I against the Allies. After this event the Turkestan administration found it increasingly difficult to secure the willing cooperation of the indigenous people of Central Asia to Russia's war efforts. When voluntary contributions started dwindling, the administration began resorting to forced exactions. Forced requisitions of raw materials, foodstuffs, cattle, and the collection of cash contributions under duress became the order of the day. The government taxes in the Turkestan region which were already between 50 to 150 per cent higher than those levied upon the population of European Russia[99] were further increased. This rise in the tax burden coming in the wake of crop failures, depletion of cattle stock, and general rise in prices of essential commodities created an explosive situation.[100] The Kazakhs and Kirgiz who had been squeezed out of their fertile lands under the Stolypin regime now found themselves in a state of famine.[101] The general discontentment was so acute that everywhere the law and order situation steadily began to deteriorate. Towards the close of 1915 and the beginning of 1916 food riots were reported all over the Turkestan region.[102] Attacks against Russians and the so-called 'crimes against law and order,' which were on the increase since

98. *Ibid.*, 157.

99. Mandel, n.15, 100.

100. Piaskovskii, n.28, 7.

101. By 1914 in Semirechie alone the government had distributed among Russian settlers 4,200,000 *desiatins* of land confiscated from the natives. See A. N. Zorin, *Revoliutsionnoe dvizhenie v Kirgizii* (Frunze, 1931) 15; also see Galuzo, n.32, 204.

102. The governor of the Fergana oblast, in June 1915, complained that the native officials instead of cooperating with the administration in enforcing law and order, were often found to encourage its violation themselves. See *Pravda Vostoka*, 172 (1665) 30 July 1928.

1900, reached their apogee towards the end of 1915.[103] The situation became so explosive that it needed only a spark to set off a general conflagration. This spark soon came in the form of the Tsarist ukase of 25 June 1916, 'On the mobilization of the *Inorodets* population of the Astrakhan gubernia, Siberia and Central Asia for services behind the front'.[104]

Russia's strategic and military considerations had dictated in the past the total exemption of the people of the Turkestan region from compulsory military service. But in 1916, following the heavy losses of men in the war, the Tsarist government decided to break with its old policy, and ordered that the Turkestan region should furnish 220,000 men of the age group 19-43 for services behind the front.[105] The absence of any records of date of births of the indigenous population rendered the methods of calling up men for service on the age group basis impossible. In view of this difficulty, the Turkestan administration decided to raise the required number of men by alloting a quota for each oblast.[106] Instructions were sent to volost heads and village elders that while drafting men for service, care should be taken to exclude all *kazis, mullahs* and other influential men among the indigenous population. As a result, the burden of the drafting fell mostly on the poorer sections of the population.

News about the proposed mobilization started spreading even before the official announcement on it was made. To many natives, the real purport of mobilization appeared different from what they were officially informed about it. They believed that the real motive behind the mobilization was to get a large num-

---

103. *Ibid.*

104. The text of the ukase is given in Piaskovskii, n.28, 25-6. The term *Inorodets* (alien by origin) was used with reference to all the non-Russian population of Asiatic Russia who were viewed as a people belonging to an inferior race.

105. *Ibid.*, 48.

106. The quota for each oblast was as follows: Syr Daria 60,000 persons, Samarkand 32,407 persons, Fergana 51,233 persons, Semirechie 43,000 persons and Transcaspia 13,830 persons. The quota was allocated in this manner in order to ensure that the cotton production of the region whose military and economic importance was immense did not suffer. Thus the Fergana and Transcaspian oblasts, which were the main cotton growing areas, were asked to contribute less men than they would otherwise have had to contribute if the drafting had been done on a population basis. See document 30, *ibid.*, 50.

ber of natives killed at the front so that their lands could be allotted to Russian settlers.[107] When bitter memories of the forced colonization of previous years still lingered in people's memory, such a view looked natural enough. The outcome was a spontaneous outburst of all the accumulated fury which enveloped the region in the form of mighty rebellion.[108]

The Khodzhent incident[109] was the signal for the outburst of the rebellion all over Turkestan. On 11 July two persons lost their lives in Tashkent following a clash between Russian soldiers and natives. On 13 July in the Dzhizak uezd the rebels killed eightythree Russians including the uezd commandant and destroyed property worth more than a million rubles.[110] On 24 July the Kazakhs of the Amu Daria Division attacked and killed the Russian prefect and his wife. Between 9—25 July a series of outbreaks of violence were reported from Kokand, Namangan, Andizhan and the Margelan uezds of the Fergana oblast.

The rebellion did not spread to Semirechie before August. But when it did begin there, it soon took such a serious turn as to completely overshadow the events elsewhere in the Turkestan region. The reason for this was obvious enough. Semirechie more than any other part of the Turkestan region had borne the brunt of Russian colonization, and its famine-stricken nomadic population was seething with hatred against both the Russian settlers and the government. The Kazakhs and the Kirgiz nomads saw in the events of 1916 an excellent opportunity to settle their long-standing scores with the Russian immigrants. The main centres of rebellion in Semirechie were the Przhevalsk, Dzharkent and Pishpek uezds. In Przhevalsk uezd alone, the

107. Document 49, *ibid.*, 93.
108. The character of the rebellion soon made it clear that the mobilization order was not after all such an important cause for the uprising. Its real causes lay in the smouldering discontent of the indigenous population against the colonial policies of Russia. The flooding of the region with Russian settlers, and the attendant land confiscations which had brought the nomads to the verge of starvation, the proclamation of martial law, the arbitrary arrests, increase in taxes, and the war time extortions, all served to incite the people to take recourse to arms.
109. On 4 July two persons were killed in Khodzhent following a clash between soldiers and the natives. See S. Radzhabov, 'Etapy razvitiia sovetskogo gosudarstvennogo stroia v Srednei Azii,' *Sovetskoe gosudarstvo i pravo* (Moscow) 11 (1948) 339-41.
110. See document no. 49, Piaskovskii, n.28, 87-8.

official estimates put the losses at 2,179 Russians killed and properties of 6,024 Russian families destroyed. The total number
of Russians killed in Semirechie was estimated at 3,839 persons.
Losses in property exceeded several million rubles.[111]

In Transcaspia, the Yomuds of the Atrek region (Krasnovodsk
uezd) took up arms against the Russian administration towards
the middle of August. Until the beginning of December 1916
they successfully resisted all attempts on the part of the
authorities to put them down. Their main targets of
attacks were the Russian settlements situated in the Girgiun region. The Russian losses in life and property were heavy. Only
towards the beginning of December 1916 was the Turkestan
administration able to organize an expedition under Lieutenant-
General Madritov, to put down the rebellion of the *Yomuds*.[112]

In spite of the disorganized character of the 1916 rebellion
and the primitive type of weapons employed by the rebels, the
suppression of the rebellion did not prove an easy task. The
police and armed forces which were at the disposal of the Turkestan administration proved inadequate to quell the rebellion.
To overcome this inadequacy, the administration organized
several armed divisions consisting mainly of Russian settlers and
gave them a free hand to deal with the rebels. The Russian
settlers took this opportunity to avenge the losses they had
suffered in the initial 'period of the uprising. In Semirechie,
with the connivance of the authorities, the Russian settlers organized punitive expeditions and hunted down the natives mer-
cilessly. They not only destroyed hundreds of Kazakh and Kirgiz
settlements, but confiscated all their lands and cattle. Finding
themselves unable to defend against the organized attack of
Russian settlers, the Kazakh and Kirgiz population of thirtynine
volosts of Przhevalsk, Dzhakent and Pishpek uezds fled to China.
Thousands of them died on the way from starvation and expo-
sure to the cold. Their cattle also met with a similar fate.[113] In the
Transcaspian oblast, following the expedition of Madritov, more

---

111. Document no. 49, *ibid.*, 90. In the Issyk-kul region and in the
Tekes valley, the Kirgiz were reported to have killed nearly 2,000 Russian
settlers and destroyed more than 1,000 Russian houses. See document 488,
ibid., 685.

112. See documents 49, 498 and 499, *ibid.*, 90-2 and 698-706.

113. See document 494, *ibid.*, 692-5, 743.

than 2,000 Yomud-Turkmen families fled to Persia, abandoning
to the Russians their land and cattle.[114] After an extensive tour
of the Turkestan region, Kerensky, who was later to become the
head of the Provisional Government, reported to the State Duma
that in putting down the rebellion, the Russian soldiers and
settlers showed utmost cruelty and killed the natives indiscriminately without regard to age and sex.[115] General Kuropatkin,
the head of the Turkestan administration, was not content in
merely putting down the rebellion. He believed that the task
of his administration consisted in teaching the indigenous peoples of Central Asia a permanent lesson for daring to take up
arms against their Russian masters. On 22 February 1917 he
wrote to Tsar Nicholas II:

> It is essential for the native population to know well that
> shedding of Russian blood is visited upon not only by punish-
> ing those who are guilty but also by confiscation of lands of
> all natives living in the area where the crime has been per-
> petrated... This principle must be strictly adhered to in all
> cases of trouble resulting in the shedding of Russian blood
> and it is the only way of impressing upon all natives the need
> to prevent the unreasonable elements among them from taking
> up arms against the Russian authorities.[116]

Kuropatkin proposed to undertake a series of measures for implementing this 'principle'. He ordered the confiscation of 2,000
desiatins of land from the inhabitants of the Dzhizak uezd, and
their distribution among the Russian settlers. On 31 December
1916 he ordered A. S. Madritov to undertake 'special measures
for strengthening the Russian elements' in the Atrek and
Girgiun regions and to make them an important basis of support
for Russian authority and influence. These special measures
consisted simply in the confiscation of the land of the Yomud-
Turkmens and its allocation to the Russian settlers.[117] In Semirechie Kuropatkin sought to establish several purely Russian-
inhabited uezds by forcibly removing all the Kazakh and Kirgiz
populations from the Issyk-kul region, the Chu river valley and
the Przhevalsk, Dzharkent and Pishpek uezds. He planned to

114. See documents 49 and 501, *ibid.*, 91, 707-8.
115. See document 496, *ibid.*, 696-7.
116. See document 49, *ibid.*, 97.
117. *Ibid.*, 743.

settle the displaced Kirgiz population in the Naryn uezd. By implementing this scheme, it was estimated that an area of 2,510,361 *desiatins* of land would become available in the Przhevalsk, Dzharkent and Pishpek uezds for fresh colonization.[118] But before General Kuropatkin could fully implement this grandiose scheme, the imperial regime itself collapsed. The revolution was soon to consign to limbo not only Kuropatkin's ambitious plans of land confiscation but the very system of which he was such an ardent and devoted adherent.

118. See document 44, *ibid.*, 684-7; also see Ryskulov, n.34, 59.

CHAPTER THREE

The Revolution and the Aftermath

1. THE FEBRUARY REVOLUTION AND THE DEMAND FOR AUTONOMY

TOWARDS the beginning of 1917 when the authority of the imperial regime started crumbling down all over Russia, the situation in Central Asia had become highly explosive. By then, a number of factors such as the loss of large areas of land by the natives, the wartime levies and extortions, the high-handed manner in which the rebellion of 1916 was suppressed, the semi-famine conditions, etc., led the indigenous population to work for emancipating itself from the Russian tutelage. On the other hand, the immigrant Russian population, which thrived on the lands seized from the natives, on the privileged positions offered by the Russian colonial administration and on the trade and industrial monopoly it held in the region, stoutly contested the right of the natives to self-rule. This sharp divergence of interests and objectives of the two communities was bound to have its deep impact on all the subsequent events which took place in Turkestan, and it also rendered the national question the outstanding issue. In Khiva and Bukhara the discontent against the autocratic rule of the Khan and the Amir was mounting. The situation in these two native states, in fact, had so much deteriorated that the Khan and the Amir in 1916-17 were forced to seek the help of the Russian armies to suppress popular uprisings against their regimes.

Following the abdication of Tsar Nicholas II on 17 February 1917 (o.s.) and the formation of the Provisional Government at St. Petersburg, a system of dual authority came into existence in Turkestan. A short time before these events occurred, General Kuropatkin, the last imperial Governor-General, had sought to preserve the old order of things in Turkestan by raising before the Russian community the bogey of an impending native re-

bellion. But neither he nor the Turkestan Committee of the
Provisional Government which soon replaced him, was able to
prevent the coming into existence of a radical Soviet of Workers' and Soldiers' Deputies which soon made a bid for power.[1]

The passing of control over the regional administration from
the former Tsarist officialdom to the Turkestan Committee and
the Soviet of Workers' and Soldiers' Deputies meant only a
shifting of power from one section of the Russian community
to another, since both these new bodies were almost exclusively
Russian in composition. Neither of them made any attempt to
enlist the support of the indigenous population for their organizations. The Djadidists, who constituted the politically conscious
and active part of the local population, however, did not choose
to remain merely the impassive observers of the manoeuvrings
which were going on among the different sections of the Russian
community. On 13 March 1917, the local Djadidists met in a
conference and proclaimed the formation of the *Shuro-i-islamie*
(the Council). Within a short period branches of this organization were established in all the main cities of the Turkestan
region. Of these the Tashkent, Kokand and Andizhan organizations soon became very active.[2] The adherents of the *Shuro-i-
islamie* organized conferences and meetings, issued manifestos
which outlined their aims and objectives, and sought to enlist
the support of the native population for the realization of their
programme.[3] In April 1917 a conference convoked by the local
Tatars provided an excellent opportunity for the Djadidists to

1. On March 1917 the Tashkent Soviet of Workers' and Soldiers'
Deputies was established under the chairmanship of the Menshevik G.I.
Broido. Out of the fifteen members who composed it there were only
three Bolsheviks. Soon after, similar organizations sprang up in most of
the important centres of the Turkestan region. All of them were under the
predominant influence of either the Mensheviks or the Socialist Revolutionaries. The Tashkent Soviet of Workers' and Soldiers' Deputies occupied a central position in all events which followed the February revolution. See I. Dodonov, 'Burzhuazno-demokraticheskaia revoliutsiia 1917
goda v Turkestane,' *Pravda Vostoka,* 66 (7194), 1 April 1927.

2. S. Muraveiskii, *Ocherki po istorii revoliutsionnogo* dvizheniia v Srednei Azii (Tashkent, 1926) 13-14; also see *Istoriia narodov Uzbekistana*
(Tashkent, 1947) II, 444 (cited hereafter as INUz).

3. Representatives of the various Djadidist organizations of the Fergana
region met in a conference in May 1917 in Kokand and discussed many
political and economic problems. The conference debated such issues as
the election to the Constituent Assembly, the establishment of a special

focus attention on the outstanding issues of the Central Asian region. This conference, which met between 13–20 April 1917, expressed itself in favour of the establishment of a federal democratic republic in Russia, the granting of equal rights to the Muslims of Russia and the formation of a responsible government in Bukhara under the aegis of the Young Bukharan Party.[4]

The April days also witnessed the organization of the conservative Muslim clergy into the *Jamait-i-Ulema* (the Society of Clerics) with Sher Ali Lapin as its head. On 26 April the *Jamait* established its permanent executive organ, the *Turkestan Mussalman Merkezi-Surasi* (The Turkestan Central Muslim Council).[5] A few native workers' organizations like the *Ittifak* (Union of the Toiling Mussalmans) also made their appearances in cities like Khodzhent, Samarkand and Kokand. Following the establishment of political organizations of the different sections of the indigenous population, the political, economic and social problems of the Turkestan region were discussed in a number of party conferences. Of the various groups which became politically active in the post-February period in Turkestan, the Djadidists were preeminent. They were better equipped than the other political groups to propagate their views and objectives effectively and to influence the thinking of a considerable section of the local population. Their newspapers like *Uluk Turkestan, Kenegash, Turk-eli* and the Orenburg Djadidist paper *Vakht* were widely read among the peoples of Turkestan.[6] Out of this growing political awareness emerged the demand for the autonomy of the Turkestan region.

A factor which considerably influenced the thinking of the politically conscious part of the local population in favour of autonomy was the decision of the First All-Russian Muslim

bureau in Petrograd for assisting the Fergana delegates to the Constituent Assembly to voice effectively the needs of their region, the development of a vigorous native press, the resolution of the food crisis etc. See S. M. Dimanshtein, ed., *Revoliutsiia i natsional'nyi vopros: dokumenty i materialy po istorii natsional'nogo voprosa v Rossii i SSSR v XX veke* (Moscow, 1927) III, 346-7.

4. *Ibid.*, 345-6.
5. Baymirza Hayit, *Turkestan im XX Jahrhudert* (Darmstadt, 1956) 24.
6. Georgi Safarov, *Kolonial'naia revoliutsiia: opyt Turkestana* (Moscow, 1921) 57.

Congress held in May 1917. In the deliberations of this Congress the question of introducing political autonomy on national, territorial and federative principles in the various Muslim regions of Russia gained immense popularity and also figured in the final recommendations which were forwarded by the Congress for implementation by the Provisional Government.[7] The Central Asian region in this Congress was represented among others by Abdullah Khodzhaev and Zaki Validov Togan. While supporting the motion on national-territorial autonomy in the Congress, Togan exploded the myth of the existence of the so-called 'Muslim nation' in Russia and argued that the Russian Muslims were not racially and linguistically homogeneous. The Russian Muslims, stated Togan, consisted of Turks and non-Turks and further.

the former (i.e., the Turks) are themselves divided into eastern, central and southern Turkic groups, each with its distinct language, culture and history... In some parts of Russia, as, for instance, Central Asia, Turks form from 61 to 96 per cent of the total population of the province. These provinces should unquestionably be granted national territorial autonomy, and even form a federation within Russian frontiers.... *If we want national autonomy, and not merely a national fiction, we must organize our self-governments on historical and ethnic bases bearing in mind the national-geographic boundaries of these Turkic peoples.*[8]

The fact that the resolution on national-territorial autonomy was supported by an overwhelming majority of delegates in the Congress in spite of the warning of the Tatar delegates that the implementation of this resolution was bound to lead to the establishment of fortyeight autonomous republics in the Caucasus and twelve in Central Asia, was indicative of the waning of the popularity of pan-Islamic and pan-Turkic ideologies and along with it of the Tatar leadership.[9] The awakening of the

7. Dimanshtein, n.3, 294-305.

8. From the proceedings of the All-Russian Moslem Congress. As cited in Serge A. *Zenkovsky, Pan-Turkism and Islam in Russia* (Cambridge, Mass., 1960) 149. (emphasis added).

9. In fact, the speeches of some delegates in this Congress clearly indicated this. The Kazakh delegate, Dosmuhammedov, expressed his fellow-delegates' apprehension of Tatar ambitions for spiritual and political dominance over the other Turkic peoples of Russia. He bluntly ques-

national consciousness of the Azerbaizhanis, Bashkirs, Kazakhs, Uzbeks and others led them to stress the primacy of their national interests over those which were supposed to be common to all Russian Muslims. In Central Asia, as yet, only the Uzbeks voiced the demand on autonomy, and in doing so they identified the ideals of Uzbek nationalism with the interests and aspirations of all other national groups which inhabited the region. This, in turn, was bound to further complicate the already complex national tangle in the region and create fresh problems.

The events which took place in the post-February days, however, did not change in any way the political climate of Central Asia. The local Russian community continued to believe that the 'new order' had meaning only to the 'progressive Russian society' and that it meant hardly anything to the politically immature and socially backward native population. A group of advocates from Tashkent warned Prime Minister Kerensky that 'if the Muslims are granted the right of self-determination at present, the future presents a picture of grim struggle for power among the various tribes resulting ultimately in a bloody carnage.'[10] The Provisional Government also was averse to the idea of changing the *status quo* in Central Asia.[11] A semi-official conference which examined the feasibility of introducing autonomy in the Turkestan region pointed out that

> the exceptional situation which prevails in the Turkestan region renders the introduction of full political autonomy impossible. As a colony Turkestan must be developed towards

tioned the Dagestani delegate (Tsalikov) who had sided with the Tatars, 'Do you have any idea what a nationality is? It is the unity of blood, spirit, culture, traditions, language, customs and territory. You cannot create a "Muslim nation" on the basis of a non-territorial, centralized autonomy. Are you not, incidentally, a pan-Islamist? We know that behind pan-Islamism there are concealed machinations of one nationality to dominate others' (here is the clearest hint at Tatar ambitions to dominate other Muslim populations of Russia). *Ibid.*, 147-8.

10. Cited in P. Alekseenov, 'Natsional'naia politika vremennogo pravitel'stva v Turkestane v 1917 goda,' *proletarskaia revoliutsiia*, LXXIX (1928).

11. A clear indication that the Provisional Government did not envisage any radical departure from the policies of the previous regime in Central Asia was its attitude to Bukhara and Khiva. In these two vassal states of Russia, the Provisional Government not only allowed the old Tsarist Residents to continue, but also did not renounce the extra-territorial rights enjoyed by Russia.

self-rule on the same lines as the British and the French
colonies. However, in this connection, the vast difference
which prevails between the culturally advanced peoples of
Canada and Australia and the cultural backwardness of the
peoples of Turkestan must be borne in mind.[12]

The local Social Democratic organizations also refused to
recognize the validity of the claims of the natives for self-rule.
Though a regional conference of the Social Democrats held in
June 1917 favoured the establishment of 'a politically autonomous Turkestan', it took care to point out that it was to be
based 'on the cultural-national autonomy for the various
nationalities inhabiting the region.'[13] By restricting the
rights of the various local national groups to the cultural sphere,
the Social Democrats, in effect, sought to perpetuate the
dominance of the Russian element in political, economic and
administrative matters of the Turkestan region.

This uncompromising attitude of both the liberals and the
Social Democrats to the issue of autonomy only helped in
forcing the relatively progressive Djadidists into the company
of the rabidly conservative *Ulema*. On 3 September 1917 on the
initiative of the *Shuro-i-Islamie* and the *Jamait-i-Ulema* the second Extraordinary Regional Muslim Congress was summoned
to chalk out the course of campaign for the attainment of the
autonomy of Turkestan. The Congress, however, did more than
this. It provided what, in fact, was a virtual blueprint of the
autonomy of Turkestan. The Congress declared that it was its
intention to establish an 'Autonomous Turkestan Federated Republic' as an integral part of the Democratic Republic of
Russia. Elaborating this scheme, the Congress proposed that the
Turkestan Autonomous Republic should compose of the
Fergana, Syr Daria, Samarkand, Transcaspian and Semirechie
oblasts,[14] and that it should have a bicameral legislative organ

12. Cited in S. Radzhabov, 'Etapy razvitiia sovetskogo gosudarstvennogo storia v Srednei Azii,' *Sovetskoe gosudarstvo i pravo* (Moscow) 11
(1948) 61-2.
13. Justifying this resolution, the Conference went on to say that 'until
the destruction of capitalism, it is possible only to moderate national
oppression and in the modern conditions, only cultural national autonomy
could be defended as the right of a national minority.' See Safarov, n.6,
55.
14. Because of the absence of delegates from Semirechie, the Congress
omitted the name of this oblast from the composition of the proposed

consisting of a Central Asian Parliament and a Clerical Senate. The Congress proposed that the Central Asian Parliament should be elected every five years on a universal franchise and on the proportional representation system, and that the *Makhami Shariia* (Senate) should be the representative organ of the clergy presided over by the *Sheikh-ul-Islam* (Guardian of Islamic Orthodoxy). The Congress declared that the Central Asian Parliament should have competence to legislate on all matters which came within the jurisdiction of the Autonomous Turkestan Republic. The Congress empowered the Senate to scrutinize all the laws passed by the Parliament and to see that they conformed to the tenets of the *Shariat*. The Senate was also empowered to act as the highest judicial tribunal.[15] The Congress adopted certain other resolutions which favoured the introduction of the *zemstvo* type of self-rule in the various oblasts of Turkestan, a wide measure of native participation not only in the Turkestan Committee of the Provisional Government but also in the oblast', uezd and volost administrations,[16] suspension of cotton growing and switching over to grain cultivation, etc.[17] Before winding up its sessions, the Congress resolved to amalgamate all the existing Muslim organizations of Turkestan region in a single political organization, the *Ittifak-ul-Muslimin*, which was charged with the task of securing the realization of the programme adopted by the Congress.

II. THE OCTOBER REVOLUTION IN TURKESTAN

While the slogan 'autonomy for Turkestan' steadily gained popularity among the indigenous population the revolutionary situation in Turkestan deepened. In September, 1917, in response to the call of the Central Committee of the Russian Social Democratic Workers' Party (RSDRP) to effect the transfer of 'all power to the Soviets,' the Bolshevik faction of the Tashkent

Turkestan Autonomous Republic. However, it expressed a desire that Semirechie should also join it.

15. *Turkestanskii Kur'er*, 11 November 1917 as cited by Safarov, n.6, 63-4.

16. *Turkestanskii Vestnik*, 14 November 1917 as cited by Safarov, *ibid.*, 64.

17. *Ibid.*, 65.

Soviet of Workers' and Soldiers' Deputies made an attempt to capture power in Turkestan. Though this move was frustrated by the Provisional Government, the defection of a large number of soldiers of the Tashkent garrison to the Soviet side finally brought about the collapse of the authority of the Provisional Government in Turkestan towards the end of October 1917. Following this event the system of dual authority which had persisted in the Turkestan region ever since February 1917 came to an end.[18] Soon afterwards, with the outbreak of the Civil War in Russia, Central Asia was completely cut off from the central regions of Russia.

The Third Congress of Soviets of Workers', Peasants', and Soldiers' Deputies, which met in Tashkent between 15–22 November, proclaimed the formation of a Soviet government in Turkestan.[19] The Congress favoured the formation of the new government by the 'victors alone.'[20] In view of this, a proposal made by the Congress of the *Ulema* to establish the government on a broad base by ensuring in it the participation of representatives of the indigenous population was rejected on the ground that

> the inclusion of the Mussalmans in the higher organs of the regional revolutionary government is not possible in view of the uncertainty of attitude of the indigenous population towards the Soviets of Soldiers', Workers' and Peasants' Deputies and (also) because of the absence of class proletarian organizations among the native population which the faction could welcome into the organs of the higher regional Government.[21]

The Congress of Soviets after thus having brushed aside the

18. *Istoriia Uzbekskoi SSR* (Tashkent, 1958) II, 10-48. (*Cited* hereafter as *IUzSSR*). Also see Z. Urazaev, *Turkestanskaia ASSR i ee gosudarst-venno-pravovye osobennosti* (Tashkent, 1958) 42-6.

19. Commenting on the composition of this Congress, Mustafa Chokaev wrote that 'one of the strangest peculiarities of this Congress was the fact that no representative of the native population of Turkestan took part in its deliberations. The soldiers sent thither from the interior province of Russia, the peasants settled therein on the lands confiscated from our people, and the workers accustomed to regard us haughtily from above— these were the people who were to decide at this moment the fate of Turkestan.' See Mustafa Chokaev, 'Turkestan and the Soviet Regime', *Journal of Royal Central Asian Society*, XVIII (1931) 406.

20. Safarov, n.6, 68.

21. *Pobeda velikoi oktiabr'skoi sotsialisticheskoi revoliutsii v Turkes-tane: sbornik dokumentov* (Tashkent, 1947) 93. (Cited hereafter as

claims of the indigenous people, elected the *Sovnarkom* (Council of People's Commissars) composed exclusively of persons of European origin. Though there were only four Bolsheviks in the *Sovnarkom* as against eight Left Socialist Revolutionaries and two Right Socialist Revolutionaries, the Bolshevik leader, F. Kolesov, was elected its chairman.[22] In the initial stages of the Soviet rule in Turkestan it was difficult to distinguish the attitude of the Bolsheviks from that of the other Russian political parties to the question of the participation of the natives in the Tashkent Soviet. In other words, the Bolshevik attitude to this question was wholly negative.[23] This rather hostile attitude of the local Bolshevik faction towards the natives, largely arose from its peculiar composition.

Before the October revolution in Central Asia, there did not exist an independent Bolshevik party. In little isolated groups the Bolsheviks were scattered all over the Turkestan Region. In particular, in Tashkent, Samarkand, Perovsk, Kagan and other cities the Bolsheviks functioned as a part of the Social Democratic organizations which were under the predominant influence of the Mensheviks and the Socialist Revolutionaries. Only towards June 1918 an independent Communist Party of Turkestan was formed.[24] Soviet writers usually assert that ever since the 1905 revolution, a separate, independent and well integrated Bolshevik faction existed in Turkestan and played an important role in the revolutionary movement in the region. Facts, however, do not wholly corroborate this view. Moreover, there appears to be some truth in Safarov's statement that 'it was not the Bolshevik party that created the Bolshevik power in Turkestan; it was the Bolshevik power which created the Bolshevik party.'[25] The Bolsheviks in the

PVOSRT). It is interesting to note that a recent official history of the Turkestan Communist Party does not touch upon this issue at all. On the other hand, it goes on to emphasize the significance of the Third Regional Congress for proclaiming the Soviet authority in Central Asia. See *Ocherki istorii kommunisticheskoi partii Turkestana* (Tashkent, 1959) II, 106. (cited hereafter as OIKPT)

22. D. I. Manzhara, *Revoliutsionnoe dvizhenie v Srednei Azii* (1905-1920): *vospominaniia* (Tashkent, 1934) 80.

23. *Ibid.*, 81-2.

24. R. Golubeva, 'Velikaia oktiabr'skaia revoliutsiia v Uzbekistane', *Istoricheskii zhurnal* (Moscow) II (1939) 81.

25. Safarov, n.6, 71.

region hailed mostly from among the railway workers, and being secluded in a remote corner of Russia, they had lost touch both with the central Bolshevik organization and with the main revolutionary currents which were then sweeping the European part of Russia. They lacked the revolutionary tradition, experience and organization, and what was worse, they had fallen victims to the sinister influence of the colonial mentality which characterized the immigrant Russian community in the region. Soon after the October events, the lack of a clear-cut Bolshevik policy helped a large number of 'adventurers, careerists and even simple criminal elements' to infiltrate their ranks.[26] These elements had no interests either in the revolution or in emancipating the poor, and utilized the vantage positions they had gained in the Bolshevik party to serve their own interests.[27] As a result, 'the proletarian dictatorship in Central Asia right from its inception put on a typically colonizing cloak.'[28] Later, with the clarity and thoroughness which were characteristic of communist self-analysis of the time, the Fifth Regional Congress of the Communist Party of Turkestan set to diagnose the ills which had beset the Bolsheviks during this time. Without mincing words the Congress pointed out:

> Unacquaintance with experience of class war in the international context, absence of revolutionary traditions in the past, the chronic situation of colonial oppression and na-

26. *Ibid.*, 71.

27. M. V. *Frunze na frontakh grazhdanskoi voiny: sbornik dokumentov* (Moscow, 1941) 310. The Tashkent Soviet government in which the Bolsheviks and the Socialist Revolutionaries hobnobbed with the Russian *kulaks* of Semirechie and with the former Tsarist officials not unnaturally appeared as a hostile force to the native population. All these discordant elements by flocking under the Bolshevik banner rendered the new regime a defender of the *status quo*. In Semirechie the Russian settlers, who were on inimical terms with the Kazakh and Kirgiz nomads, utilized the October Revolution in Turkestan for grabbing the land, property and cattle of the natives. In the Syr Daria oblast, a small group of Russian settlers and officials adopted similar policies. In the Transcaspian oblast too those who profited from the Revolution were the Russian settlers. The existence of the Soviet regime in Tashkent did not in any way alter the old agrarian relations in the two predominantly sedentary oblasts of Samarkand and Fergana nor did the native handicraftsmen stand to gain from the new regime. The existing trade unions served the interests of the Russian labour aristocracy. The indigenous workers were rated as second class citizens. See Safarov, n.6, 86, 115-18 and Muraveiskii, n.2, 20-1.

28. Safarov, n.6, 71.

tional inequality conditioned the peculiar course which the revolution in Central Asia took. Having taken a leading position in the revolution for the first time, the small group of the Russian workers... being torn away from the proletarian Centre and deprived of its ideological guidance, let the events to take their own course...[29]

A noted Soviet writer of the time who subjected the policies of the Tashkent Soviet to searching criticism stated:

A large number of officials who have remained in the borderlands as well as the proletariat who support the revolution belong to the Russian nationality. The Russian railway workers in Turkestan thought that the newly established dictatorship of the proletariat should serve their interests and completely ignore the interests of the indigenous population... The Soviet régime has not brought about any changes; instead of the former Russian official there now sits the Russian proletariat who although he speaks of the equality of all only cares for himself. The native masses, not having found support from the Russian proletariat, have once again come under the influence of their bourgeois nationalists, *mullahs* and others who only goad them on to a fight against the Soviet régime.[30]

The company of the Socialist Revolutionaries led the Bolsheviks to further misadventures. Apprehensive of the growing power of the Bolsheviks at the Centre, the Socialist Revolutionaries forced the Tashkent Soviet to pursue an independent course. This resulted in either completely ignoring the directives of the Centre or perverting its policies. The Tashkent Soviet, in fact, soon became so much independent of the Centre that the Socialist Revolutionary leader, Cherneskii, was able to boast: 'we already have autonomy since we do not communicate with Petersburg on the work of administration of Turkestan, we administer it ourselves.'[31] Stalin, keeping this attitude of the Tashkent Soviet in mind, was to point out later to Lenin, 'I have no doubt that if only our policies in Turkestan had been implemented as they are done now, there would not have been in our midst tens of thousands of Basmachis.'[32] Against such a back-

29. *Rezoliutsii V kraevogo partiinogo s'ezda o zadachakh kommunistiche-skoi partii v Turkestane* (Tashkent, 1920) 35.
30. I. Trainin, 'Postanovka natsional'nogo voprosa,' *Vlast' sovetov* (Moscow) 5 (1923) 29.
31. *Svobodnyi Turkestan*, 24 January 1918 as cited in Safarov, n.6, 76.
32. *Leninskii sbornik* (Moscow) xxxiv, 373.

ground it was not surprising that the Soviets in the region emerged as the defenders of the privileges of the Russian workers and the Russian settlers against the pretensions of the local population.[33]

III. THE AUTONOMOUS GOVERNMENT OF TURKESTAN

The refusal of the Soviet to allow the natives to participate in the Tashkent Soviet led the *Ulema* and the *Shuro-i-islamie* to convoke the Fourth Extraordinary Muslim Congress in Kokand towards the beginning of December 1917 and to proclaim the formation of the Autonomous Government of Turkestan. On the eve of the meeting of this Congress two broad tendencies were discernible among the native intelligentsia: some favoured the declaration of independence of Turkestan and its inclusion in the Dutov-sponsored anti-Communist South-Eastern Union; others stood for the proclamation of a provisional autonomous government of Turkestan. The latter view emerged dominant in the Congress and obtained its concurrence. The attempt to create an impression that the Congress represented all the regions and national groups of Turkestan, however, did not materialize. While the Kazakh and Kirgiz-inhabited region of Semirechie went altogether unrepresented in the Congress, only a solitary delegate represented the Turkmen region of Trans-caspia. The Uzbek regions were represented better with 150 delegates from Fergana, 23 from Samarkand and 22 from Syr Daria.[34] Notwithstanding this great imbalance in its representation, the Congress claimed that it represented 'the will of the peoples of Turkestan' and adopted a resolution which stated:

> The Fourth Extraordinary Congress, expressing the will of the peoples of Turkestan to self-determination in accordance with the principles proclaimed by the Great Russian Revolu-

33. Chokaev, n.19, 406.
34. Also present in the Congress were the representatives of General Dutov, the Russian elements opposed to the Soviets like the Right Socialist Revolutionaries, the Kazakh Djadidists like Tanyshbaev, Mustafa Chokaev and others, the Bashkir nationalist, Zaki Validov Togan, the Uzbek merchants and bankers like Isuf Davydov, the Vadiaev brothers, Mirkamil Mir Muminbaev, Akhmetzhan Khodzhaev, Temirbekov, Said Akhmed Khodzhaev etc. The Uzbek Djadidists led by Munnever Kary and Abdurashidov were fairly well represented. Soviet writers allege that nearly

tion, proclaims Turkestan territorially autonomous in union with the Federal Democratic Republic of Russia.[35] The elaboration of the form of autonomy of Turkestan is entrusted to the Constituent Assembly of Turkestan which must be convened as soon as possible. The Congress solemnly declares herewith that the rights of the national minorities will be fully safeguarded.[36]

In addition to proclaiming the *Turkestanskii Mukhtoriat* (the autonomy of Turkestan) on 11 December 1917, the Congress elected a 32-member delegation to the Constituent Assembly, the executive and the legislative organs of the new government. It also elected a twelve-member Council of Ministers headed by the Kazakh leader, Tanyshbaev.[37] On 13 December 1917 (the birth anniversary of Mohammed the Prophet), the formation of the Autonomous Government of Turkestan was proclaimed with great ceremony in Tashkent. This event was followed by mass demonstrations by the inhabitants of the native part of the Tashkent city.

With the establishment of the Turkestan Autonomous Government, the system of dual authority which had come to an end in Turkestan after the October Revolution, now once again came into existence. The authority of the Tashkent Soviet extended over a number of cities including Kokand, the seat of the Autonomous Government of Turkestan. The jurisdiction of the Autonomous Government of Turkestan was confined to the Fergana valley. Of the two rival governments which began to compete with one another for authority in Turkestan region, the Kokand government was the weaker having in its possession neither funds nor arms. The Kokand government was aware that with its meagre resources it was almost impossible to dislodge its rival power which was securely entrenched in Tashkent. Hence it decided to seek the assistance of the Central Bolshevik government to remove from the Turkestan scene the local

43 per cent of the delegates who attended this Congress were Tatars. See Manzhara, n.22, 82-3; also see P. Alekseenov, 'Kokandskaia avtonomiia,' *Revoliutsiia v Srednei Azii* (Tashkent, 1928).

35. With the Bolsheviks virtually in power at the Centre, this reference to the Federal Democratic Republic of Russia looked rather odd.

36. Cited by Chokaev, n.19, 407.

37. In January 1918 Mustafa Chokaev succeeded Tanyshbaev as the head of the Autonomous Government of Turkestan. For the allocation of the portfolios of the new government see Safarov, n.6, 72.

Bolshevik regime. By a subtle diplomatic move the Kokand government sought to persuade the Centre on this issue. In January 1918, the Kokand government summoned a 'Turkestan Congress of workers and peasants' and prevailed upon this Congress to make an appeal to the Central Soviet government to dissolve the Tashkent Soviet which 'leaned on the foreign elements hostile to the native population of the country contrary to the principles proclaimed by the October Revolution of self-determination of peoples.'[38]

The Central government, before replying to this appeal, took stock of its own position vis-a-vis the Tashkent Soviet. It was fully aware that the latter was far from being the genuine workers' and peasants' government it claimed to be. But because of its own preoccupations in the European part of Russia and also in view of the blockade imposed on Central Asia by Dutov and other 'White generals,' the Central government was unable to undertake any energetic measures. These considerations weighed heavily on the Centre while replying to the appeal of the Kokand government. The People's Commissar for Nationality Affairs, Stalin, on behalf of the Central government sent a non-committal reply which read:

> The Soviets are autonomous in their internal affairs and discharge their duties by leaning upon their own actual resources. The native proletariat of Turkestan, therefore, should not appeal to the Central Soviet power with the request to dissolve the Turkestan *Sovnarkom*, which in their opinion is leaning upon the non-Muslim army elements, but should themselves dissolve it by force, if such a force is available to the native proletariat and peasants.[39]

In the meantime, the Fourth Regional Congress of Soviets of Workers' and Soldiers' Deputies assembled in Tashkent in January 1918. The Congress adopted a resolution which asserted

38. Chokaev, n.19, 408. After the fall of the Autonomous Government of Turkestan, Mustafa Chokaev from Ashkhabad was reported to have sent cables addressed to the Central and Regional Soviet governments in Moscow and Tashkent, to Woodrow Wilson, Clemenceau and other leading personalities and organizations in the West pleading for the recognition of the sovereign existence of the Turkestan region. In the appeal sent to Woodrow Wilson it was alleged that Chokaev stated, 'we hope to liberate eight million peoples of Turkestan with your help from the Bolshevik annexationists.' *Zvezda vostoka*, 8 (1952) 143; also see Safarov, n.6, 96.

39 As cited in Chokaev, n.19, 408.

that 'the self-determination of the people only means the self-determination of the toiling strata,'[40] and declared that the Soviets alone should be the undisputed masters of the Turkestan region.[41] This resolution, in effect, was a call for action against the Autonomous Government of Turkestan. Armed with the approval of the Fourth Regional Congress of Soviets, the Tashkent Soviet set about disbanding its rival power in Kokand. On 19 February 1918 the Kokand government was destroyed. In the process of disbanding of the Kokand autonomous government, the Soviets indulged in a great deal of violence and pillage.[42] The fall of the Kokand autonomy, however, did not put an end to the opposition of the natives to the Soviet régime in Turkestan. On the contrary, it only hardened their will to resist. Out of the ashes of the Kokand autonomy rose the Basmachi Movement which, in different regions of Central Asia and in different forms, fought against the Soviets until 1927. The Basmachi rebellion, more than anything else, brought home to the Soviets the need to accommodate the interests of the indigenous population in any government which sought to wield power in Central Asia.

Soon after disbanding the autonomous government at Kokand, the Tashkent Soviet was forced to pay attention to the steadily deteriorating situation in the Transcaspian region. Here, following the October events in Tashkent, the Turkmen Djadidists, collaborating with the army officers who were drawn into the fold of Turkmen nationalism and with the conservative strata of the Turkmen society, had set up the Turkmen National Executive Committee. This organization headed by a well-known Turkmen army officer, Colonel Oraz Sardar, had become a stronghold of Turkmen nationalism.[43] The ostensible

40. See *OIKPT*, n.21, 147. In a predominantly agrarian region like Turkestan where the proletarian element among the indigenous population was almost non-existent, the slogan 'self-determination for the proletariat' only meant the continued dominance of the Russian workers over the native population. See Safarov, n.6, 78.

41. *IUzSSR*, n.18, 58.

42. G. Skalov, 'Sotsial'naia priroda basmachestva v Turkestane,' *Zhizn' natsional'nostei* (Moscow) 3-4 (1923) 56.

43. The demand for autonomy began to be voiced among the Turkmens by 1917. As elsewhere in Central Asia, the Turkmen nationalists drew inspiration from the Young Turks Movement. The appearance of the

aim of this organization was to undertake relief measures in the
famine-stricken areas of the Transcaspian oblast. But it soon
became clear that its real aim was to set up an anti-Soviet front
analogous to that of the Turkestan autonomous government.
Towards February 1918 the National Committee began organizing a Turkmen national army with the Turkmen cavalry
stationed at Keshi as its nucleus. Though this attempt was
thwarted by the timely intervention of Kolesov, the head of the
Tashkent Soviet, the Bolshevik rule did not survive for long in
Transcaspia.[44] Following the abortive attempt of Kolesov on
Bukhara, widespread rebellions occurred in Kizyl-Arvat, Ashka-
bad, and other areas of the Transcaspian oblast against the
Soviet régime. A large section of the railway workers led by the
Mensheviks and the Socialist Revolutionaries overthrew the
authority of the Soviets in Transcaspia. The new government
which came into existence here enjoyed the support of the
Turkmen nationalists and the British troops stationed in
Meshed under General Malleson.[45]

IV. FORMATION OF THE TURKESTAN ASSR

The destruction of the Autonomous Government of Turkestan, and the disbanding of the Turkmen National Committee
and the Turkmen National Army did not, however, resolve the
issue of autonomy. The peculiar composition of the Tashkent
Soviet and its pronounced hostile attitude towards the question
of native participation precluded any possibility of solving the
question of autonomy on a satisfactory basis. The Fourth Extra-

German and Turkish armies in the Caucasus in 1918 gave an impetus to
the Turkmen nationalist movement. See V. Karpych, 'Vozniknovenie Turkmenskoi SSR,' *Turkmenovedenie* (Ashkhabad) 10-11 (1928) 40.

44. E. L. Shteinberg, *Ocherki istorii Turkmenii* (Moscow, 1934) 71-2;
also see *Istoriia Turkmenskoi SSR* (Ashkhabad, 1957) II, 84-5.

45. The newly-formed Transcaspian Provisional Government soon alienated the Turkmen Djadidists. The Russian elements, which held a dominant position in the government, were averse to the Djadidist programme
which aimed at realizing native self-rule. Though the Turkmen National
Committee composed of Turkmen national intellectuals like Ovezbaev,
Khadzi-Murat, Kokadzhan Berdyev, Bekki Berdyev and others continued
to exist, it hardly enjoyed any power under the new setup. Dissatisfied, the
Turkmen Djadidist leaders became the active collaborators of the Soviets
when Tashkent's dominance was once again restored on Transcaspia in
August 1919. See Shteinberg, *ibid.*, 72-3 and 78-87.

ordinary Congress of Soviets which met in Tashkent in January 1918 also failed to resolve this question. Though the Congress devoted considerable time to the discussion on the question of autonomy, it took no concrete measures to realize it. Its discussions only brought to the surface the incompatibility of interests of the indigenous and immigrant European populations of the region and the anti-native phobia of the members of the Tashkent Soviet. The resolution adopted by this Congress, in fact, reduced the issue of autonomy into a farce and barred the door for any compromise on the question of the participation of the natives in the administration. The narrow and distorted interpretation the Congress gave to the Bolshevik doctrine of national self-determination as a right exclusively of the toiling strata, in effect, was nothing but an apology for the continued dominance of a small group of Russian workers in a region which possessed a predominantly agricultural population.[46] Tobolin, a prominent Bolshevik, even declared, 'one should not talk of introducing autonomy immediately, since autonomy entails the withdrawal of the Russian soldiers from the region.'[47]

Towards the beginning of April 1918, on the initiative of the Central government, the question of autonomy once again came to the forefront. In a well-known circular addressed, among others, to the Council of People's Commissars of Turkestan, Stalin pointed to the necessity of organizing an autonomous government in Turkestan. In this circular Stalin disapproved the negative attitude which the local Bolsheviks had taken on the issue of autonomy and insisted that the organization of an autonomous government in Turkestan was the only way to raise the masses to the level of Soviet authority and to draw into the fold of the Soviets their best representatives. Further he declared:

Not the denial of autonomy, but its recognition—this is the immediate task of the Soviet government. But it is imperative to build autonomy on the basis of local soviets because only under such conditions can the government become national and close to the masses. In other words, it is essential to see that this autonomy ensures the power of the lower stratum

46. See *OIKPT*, n.21, 147.
47. Cited in *Materialy k istorii sovetskogo gosudarstva i prava Uzbekistana* (Tashkent, 1958) 167. (Cited hereafter as *MISGPUz*)

of the population and not the upper one. This is the essence
of the matter and in view of this the Soviet government...
intends to declare autonomy...for the Turkestan region.[48]
The People's Commissar for Nationality Affairs also enjoined
upon the local Bolsheviks to abandon their hostile attitude towards the natives and to establish appropriate institutions to
enable the representatives of the indigenous population to participate in the regional administration.[49] The instructions contained in this circular had a moderating influence on the working of the Tashkent Soviet in its relation to the indigenous
population.[50] The Central government, however, did something
more than merely confining itself to the task of offering advice
to the Tashkent Soviet to rectify its past mistakes in the national
sphere. It deputed P. A. Kobozev, a Bolshevik stalwart who had
participated earlier in the revolutionary movement in Turkestan, to supervise in the Turkestan region the implementation
of all its directives and decrees and to organize the autonomy of
the region. The Central Committee and the Council of People's
Commissars of the RSFSR conferred wide powers on Kobozev to
enable him to make a success of his mission.[51]

On Kobozev's initiative, the Fifth Congress of the Soviets
of Turkestan assembled on 22 April 1918 to discuss the question of autonomy. In a message of greetings sent to the Congress
Lenin and Stalin stated:

> You can be assured, comrades, that the *Sovnarkom* will sup-
> port the autonomy of your region on a Soviet basis; we wel-
> come your initiative and are confident that you will cover the
> entire region with a set of soviets and will maintain intimate
> contact with the soviets already existing. We request you to
> send the Commission of the Constituent Congress of Soviets
> which you had undertaken to establish to Moscow for the
> purpose of determining the relations of the government of
> your region with the Council of People's Commissars.[52]

This Congress was attended by 263 delegates out of whom

---

48. Lenin and Stalin, *Stat'i i rechi o Srednei Azii i Uzbekistane* (Tashkent, 1940) 50-1.

49. *Ibid.*, 52.

50. Kh. Sh. Inoiatov, 'V. I. Lenin i stroitel'stvo natsional'noi gosudarstvennosti narodov Srednei Azii,' *Istoriia SSSR* (Moscow) 2 (1960) 73.

51. V. Ia. Nepomnin, *Istoricheskii opyt stroitel'stva sotsializma v Uzbekistane* (Tashkent, 1960) 83-4.

52. Lenin and Stalin, n.48, 53.

eightysix were Bolsheviks, seventy Left Socialist Revolutionaries, eightyseven non-party men, twenty Internationalists, Right Socialist Revolutionaries, etc. On 30 April 1918, the Congress adopted the 'Statute on the Turkestan Soviet Republic.' Pending the adoption, of a constitution, the statute defined the legal status and competence of the organs of the Turkestan Republic. The Turkestan Republic of the Russian Soviet Federation, as the new autonomous republic was called under this statute, was to consist of the entire Turkestan region within its geographical frontiers excluding Bukhara and Khiva. It was mentioned in the statute that the Turkestan Federated Republic is governed autonomously, recognizes and coordinates its work with the Central Government of the Russian Soviet Federation.'[53]

The statute designated the Congress of Soviets of Workers', Soldiers', Peasants' and Muslim-Dekkan Deputies as the highest legislative organ of the Turkestan Soviet Republic. When this body was not in session, the Central Executive Committee elected by the Congress was to function as the permanent legislative organ of the republic. The executive functions were entrusted to the Council of People's Commissars. At the lower rungs of administration the Soviets and their executive committees were to exercise the executive and legislative powers. The statute also envisaged the creation of a five-member commission for the purpose of resolving in collaboration with the Central Soviet government the problem of establishing a satisfactory and workable relationship between the Central and the regional governments.[54]

In conformity with the provisions of this statute, the Fifth Regional Congress of Soviets elected the first Central Executive Committee of Turkestan (*TsIK*) which consisted of thirtysix members with Kobozev as its chairman. Ten of these members were natives.[55] A sixteen-member *Sovnarkom* with all its earlier legislative powers duly shorn off was placed in charge of the executive functions of the republic.[56] The *Sovnarkom* consisted

53. *PVOSRT*, n.21, 206.
54. *Ibid.*, 206.
55. Safarov, n.6, 85 and Muraveiskii, n.2, 21.
56. Before the formation of the Central Executive Committee of the Turkestan Republic, the *Sovnarkom* of the Tashkent Soviet, in between

of the Commissariats of Justice, Food, Health, Nationality
Affairs, Military Affairs, Internal Affairs, Labour, Finance, Edu-
cation, Foreign Affairs, Industries, Communications, Posts and
Telegraph and the Administrative Matters of the *Sovnarkom*.[57]
The Commissariats of Justice, Internal Affairs, Nationality
Affairs and Health were headed by natives.[58]

Kobozev succeeded in winning certain other concessions to
the indigenous population. On his insistence, the Bolshevik
faction declared in the Fifth Congress of Soviets that the immediate tasks of the *Sovnarkom* and the Central Executive Committee of the Turkestan Republic was to draw a wide stratum of

the sessions of the Congress of Soviets, was in sole charge of both the
legislative and the executive functions.

57. The Left Socialist Revolutionaries held 50 per cent of the seats
in the Central Executive Committee. In the *Sovnarkom* the last eight
commissariats mentioned above were headed by them.

58. K. E. Zhitov, *Pobeda velikoi oktiabr'skoi sotsialisticheskoi revoliutsii
v Uzbekistane* (Tashkent, 1957) 201. The views of the local Bolsheviks and
the Left Socialist Revolutionaries on the issue of autonomy were such that
they countenanced hardly any interference by the Central government in
Turkestan affairs. Their insistence on creating within the Turkestan *Sovnarkom* the commissariats of military affairs, communications, post, telegraph
and foreign affairs on the pretext of the borderland position of the Turkestan
Republic did not meet with the approval of the Centre. A five-member
extraordinary Turkestan delegation which arrived in Moscow in June 1918
for discussing with the Central government the question of interrelations
between Moscow and Tashkent also took an intransigent attitude. The
delegation laid claim for a separate Turkestan citizenship, the right of the
Turkestan Central Executive Committee to nullify altogether or amend
the Centre's decrees, the right of the Turkestan Republic to establish
relations with neighbouring countries independently of the Centre, etc. In
view of the extraordinary nature of the demands put forward by the
Turkestan delegation, the talks ended in failure. Some time later the Sixth
Extraordinary Congress of Soviets of Turkestan meeting in October 1918
approved the first constitution of the Turkestan Republic. This constitution
left defence, foreign affairs, post and telegraph, and navy to the exclusive
jurisdiction of the Central government. But this constitution made it
obligatory for the Centre to carry on the administration in these spheres
not through its own commissariats but through the appropriate commissariats functioning within the Turkestan Council of People's Commissars.
In view of this the Central government refused to approve this constitution.
The dispute between the Centre and the Turkestan Republic on the
question of the competence of their commissariats was not resolved until
April 1921. See S. B. Krylov, 'Istoricheskii protsess razvitiia sovetskogo
federalizma,' *Sovetskoe pravo*, 5 (1924) 42-3; also see O. I. Chistiakov,
'Obrazovanie Rossiiskoi federatsii 1917-1918,' *Sovetskoe gosudarstvo i pravo*
10 (1957) 9-10; *MISGPUz*, n.47, 172.

the Muslim proletariat into participation in the constructive work of the region, in the adoption of correct measures in the sphere of education, health, finance, justice, agriculture, industry, labour, and in the work of creation of the revolutionary cadres among the indigenous population.'[59]

Notwithstanding Kobozev's persistent efforts, the prospects for making available the benefits of the autonomous government to the bulk of the indigenous population, did not appear to be bright. To find a large number of persons among the natives who, besides being proletarians, also possessed the requisite competence to run the national schools, organs of justice, administration, social and cultural institutions, etc., was indeed a difficult task. The few natives who possessed such competence did not hail from proletarian origins, and as such remained unacceptable to the government, which was still wedded to the slogan of 'self-determination of the toiling strata.' Though the newspaper *Pravda* wrote, 'amidst the loud applauses of the Muslim deputies the indestructible connection of Turkestan with the Russian Federation was ceremoniously announced,'[60] the Centre's intervention, as yet, did not yield any great benefits to the native population. That the attitude of a section of the immigrant Russian community towards the native population had not undergone any change became soon clear from an article which appeared in the newspaper *Nasha Gazeta* in July 1918. This article, appearing under the caption. 'On the

59. *Nasha Gazeta*, 90, 10 May 1918 as cited in Urazaev, n.18, 79. Soon after the Fifth Congress of Soviets some attempts were made to appease the native population. The Central Executive Committee decreed that the 'Turkish' language must be treated on a par with Russian as one of the state languages of the Turkestan Republic and that the organs of the government in their dealings with the native population must necessarily employ the Turkish language. Some time later, the Commissariat for Post and Telegraphs instructed all the post offices in the Turkestan Republic to accept telegrams written in the Turkish language. See *Turkestanskaia Pravda* (Tashkent) 15, 21 January 1923, and 7, 11 January 1923.

60. *Pravda* (Moscow) 94, 16 May 1918. The newspaper *Nasha Gazeta* wrote 'Having proclaimed the Turkestan region, an autonomous part of the great RSFSR, the Fifth Congress of Soviets handed over the fate of Turkestan into the hands of the people inhabiting it.' Cited by Kh. A. Aminov, 'Iz istorii bor'by za osushchestvlenie Leninskoi natsional'noi politiki v Turkestane (November 1917—June 1918),' *Trudy Uzbekskogo gosudarstvennogo universiteta im Alishera Navoi* (Samarkand, 1958) vypusk 83 (novaia seriia) 192.

Turkestan Autonomy' asserted, 'We (i.e. the Russians) cannot forget our status as conquerors and we must occupy a position in the republic which befits our importance. We continue to look upon the natives as only second-class citizens.... Our relation with the natives could never be the one that prevails between equals.'[61]

V. THE ESTABLISHMENT OF THE TURKOMNATS AND THE BEGINNING OF THE PROCESS OF DRAWING THE INDIGENOUS POPULATION CLOSER TO THE SOVIET ADMINISTRATION

An important outcome of the Fifth Congress of Soviets was the establishment of the People's Commissariat for Nationality Affairs (*Turkomnats*) within the Turkestan Republic. Though the abnormal conditions which then prevailed in Turkestan greatly handicapped its work, the *Turkomnats* to a considerable extent succeeded in drawing the representatives of the indigenous nationalities closer to the Soviet administration. Soon after its establishment the *Turkomnats* began to expand its activities. In accordance with a decree of the Central Executive Committee issued on 15 May 1918, the branches of the *Turkomnats* were established within various oblast' and uezd Soviets of the Turkestan Republic.[62]

The First Regional Congress of the Communist Party of Turkestan which met in June 1918, passed a resolution emphasizing the need for establishing the organs of the *Turkomnats* all over the republic. The resolution stated that these organs of the *Turkomnats* should be utilized for propagating the ideas of the Soviet régime among the indigenous population, for creating native cadres of propagandists and Red Army recruits, and for organizing the publication of communist literature in the local languages.[63]

In accordance with this decision, efforts were made to organize the so called 'Muslim Soviets' and to expand the activities of the organs of the *Turkomnats* within the oblast', uezd and

61. *Nasha Gazeta*, 142, 14 July 1918 as cited in Urazaev, n.18, 96-7.
62. L. M. Landa, 'Sozdanie narodnogo kommissariata po natsional'nym delam Turkestanskoi ASSR i ego deiatel'nost' v 1918-1919 godakh,' *Iz istorii sovetskogo Uzbekistana: sbornik statei* (Tashkent, 1956) 96.
63. *Nasha Gazeta*, 130, 29 July 1918. Cited in Safarov, n.6, 87.

volost soviets.[64] On 21 June 1918, the first issue of the Uzbek language newspaper *Istrakiun* made its appearance. At the oblast' and uezd levels the publication of several other newspapers and periodicals was also taken up.[65]

On 14 July 1918 the Turkestan Central Executive Committee recommended the adoption of the following measures for drawing the indigenous population nearer to the administration:

1. proclaiming the Uzbek and Kazakh languages as official languages of the Turkestan Republic besides Russian;
2. recognizing the equality of legal status of all citizens of the republic and ensuring adequate supply of food and other essential articles to all citizens irrespective of their national affiliations;
3. undertaking measures to draw the native workers and poor peasants within the orbit of the local soviets.[66]

By September 1918, besides the *Turkomnats* located in Tashkent, there functioned within the Turkestan Republic five oblast' and several uezd national commissariats. A collegium composed of the representatives of the various indigenous nationalities was created within the *Turkomnats*. Besides this, an organizational-agitational section, a cultural-educational section (which also included a press bureau) and a statistical section functioned within the *Turkomnats*. On 8 February 1919

64. Aminov, n.60, 196.
65. From December 1920 the newspaper *Istrakiun* was published under the name *Kizil Bairak* (The Red Banner) and was made the official news organ of the Central Committee of the Communist Party of the Turkestan Republic. Later it was renamed *Turkestan* and now it is being published under the title *Kizyl Uzbekistan*. Besides the *Istrakiun* issued from Tashkent, many other newspapers were also published from other cities of Turkestan. Notable among them were the *Mekhnatkashlar* of Samarkand, *Khalk Kolkhoni* of Namangan and *Khalk Gazetasi* of Kokand. From 1919 the newspaper *Erkinlik* was issued as the news organ of the Namangan branch of the *Turkomnats*. Between 1918-20, eleven newspapers were published in the Uzbek language. Besides them a number of papers were published in the Kazakh and Turkmen languages. The publication of books in the Uzbek language was begun with seven books in 1917. Subsequently their number rose to 33 in 1918, 91 in 1919 and 118 in 1920. See M. Vakhabov, *Formirovanie Uzbekskoi sotsialisticheskoi natsii* (Tashkent, 1961) 300-1.
66. The decree 'On equalizing the status of languages' was promulgated on 23 August 1918 but no serious effort was made to secure the realization of point 2 of these recommendations for a long time. See Muraveiski, n.2, 22.

a 'Statute of the Commissariat for Nationality Affairs of the Turkestan Republic' was published. This statute which was based on the instructions of the *Narkomnats* of the RSFSR, charged the *Turkomnats* with the following functions:

1. popularizing through the medium of the mother tongues of the indigenous nationalities the ideas and ideals of the Soviet régime among them;
2. implementing the decrees of the *Narkomnats* of the RSFSR;
3. implementing the decrees of the Turkestan Central Executive Committee, the *Sovnarkom* and the Congress of Soviets of the Turkestan Republic;
4. taking all measures for raising the cultural level and class consciousness of the nationalities inhabiting the territory of the Turkestan Republic;
5. organizing the fight against the counter-revolutionaries in all spheres; and
6. gathering statistical information on the number, composition and economic condition of the nationalities; the number of children of school-going and pre-school-going age, movements of population, increases and decreases of population, literacy, etc.[67]

Following the promulgation of this statute, in March 1919 separate national divisions of Uzbeks, Tadjiks, Turkmens, Kazakhs, Tatars, Ukrainians, native-Jews and Armenians were established within the *Turkomnats*. By this time the organs of the *Turkomnats* functioned within the uezd soviets of Tashkent, Hungry-steppe, Dzhizak, Katta-kurgan, Skobolev Andizhan, Kokand, Namangan, Khodzhent, Ura-Tube, Perovsk, Osh, Pishpek and twelve other uezd centres. By the end of 1919 the number of organs of the *Turkomnats* within the uezd soviets rose to twentyeight. Within the *Turkomnats* itself there functioned by this time ten national divisions and eight functional divisions.[68]

By February 1919 the number of natives within the Communist Party of Turkestan and the regional administration increased considerably. It was said that nearly half of the delegates who attended the Seventh Congress of Soviets, held in February 1919, represented the indigenous population.[69] During the same

67. Landa, n.62, 97.
68. *Ibid.*, 98.
69. Muraveiskii, n.2, 26.

month a 'Muslim National Section' was established under the chairmanship of Kobozev.[70] Soon afterwards several 'Muslim sections' were created within the party committees to facilitate agitational work among the natives. On 30 March 1919 the Second Regional Congress of the Communist Party of Turkestan decided to establish a Regional Bureau of the Muslim Organizations of the Russian Communist Party (also known as the Muslim Bureau or Musbureau). A statute published in May 1919 charged the newly created Muslim Bureau with the task of coordinating the activities of the various Muslim organizations of the Turkestan Republic and of drawing the soviet and party apparatuses closer to the indigenous population. The statute also envisaged the establishment of organs of the Muslim Bureau at the oblast, uezd and volost levels.[71] During the same month the First Regional Congress of the Muslim (Communist) Organizations of Turkestan met and reviewed the work of the Communist Party of Turkestan in the sphere of *nativizing* the party and soviet apparatuses. A resolution passed in this Congress criticized the recalcitrant attitude of the local Russian Communists and pointed out:

> We are forced to put up with a clearly indifferent attitude on the part of the representatives of the former privileged classes towards the indigenous working masses. This attitude could be noticed even among those who call themselves communists and who, behaving like 'bosses' treat the Muslims as their subjects. . . .[72]

Before the establishment of the Regional Muslim Bureau, the local organs of the *Turkomnats* were in charge of conducting the propaganda work among the indigenous population. They were also entrusted with the task of organizing the village cells and publishing communist literature in the various local languages. After the establishment of the Muslim Bureau all these functions were transferred to it and to its local organs. The Regional Muslim Bureau, towards the end of 1919, controlled a number of party units and also monopolized the propaganda work of the Soviet régime among the indigenous population. Headed by Turar Ryskulov, Tursun Khodzhaev, Mun-

---

70. Safarov, n.6, 96.
71. Vakhabov, n.65, 278-9.
72. Safarov, n.6, 97.

never Kary, Nezameddin Khodzhaev, Effendiev and other former Djadidist stalwarts, the Regional Muslim Bureau was able
to draw a large number of the indigenous people into the Communist Party of Turkestan and into the Regional administration.

The steadily growing strength and influence of the natives
(mostly former Djadidists) within the party and Soviet organs
of Turkestan began to cause a great deal of consternation to a
large number of local Russian Communists. In particular, a
group of so-called 'Old Communists' led by Tobolin and Kolesov (the former chairman of the *Sovnarkom*) openly expressed
its concern at the large-scale infiltration of erstwhile Djadidists
into communist organizations and sought to concentrate all key
positions in its own hands. Other Russian Communists like
Kazakov (chairman of the *TurkTsIK*), Uspenski and Solokin
began vehemently criticizing the activities of the Regional
Muslim Bureau and its organs. They argued that the existence
of the Regional Muslim Bureau, sooner or later, was bound
to transform the Communist Party of Turkestan into a nationalist organization and seriously undermine the communist influence in the Turkestan region. On the eve of the meeting of
the Third Regional Congress of the Communist Party of Turkestan (June 1919) a wide breach developed between the native
Communists led by Kobozev and the group of Russian Communists who were headed by Kazakov and Uspenski. These
Russian Communists did everything in their power to minimize
the growing influence of the natives. But when the Party Congress assembled the native Communists were able to muster
large-scale support and were able to successfully carry a number
of their resolutions in spite of the opposition of the Kazakov-
Uspenski group. Of particular significance was the passage of a
resolution which sought to define the rights and duties of the
'Muslim sections' which were functioning within the party committees. The resolution conferred upon them a status analogous
to the one enjoyed at the time by the party cells and brought
the 'Muslim sections' under the control of the local bureaus of
the 'Muslim Communists.[73] Even more significant was the election of Kobozev, Ryskulov, Effendiev, Nezameddin Khodzhaev

73. The full text of this resolution is cited in Manzhara, n.22, 132.

and Aliev to the Regional Committee of the Communist Party of Turkestan.[74] This 'parliamentary' victory of the native Communists, however, did not completely break the power of the Kazakov-Uspenski clique. It still held a majority of seats in the Regional Committee of the Party and Kazakov continued to remain the chairman of the Turkestan Central Executive Committee. Before long the rival groups were again involved in a bitter and long-drawn-out struggle.

The occasion for the renewal of the conflict was the receipt of a communication from the Central Committee of the Russian Communist Party on the question of ensuring a proportional representation of the natives in the regional administration. The Central Committee's directive stated:

> .... on the basis of the programme adopted by the Eighth Congress of the Russian Communist Party (B)[75] and in the interests of the workers'-peasants' government in the East, it is necessary (to ensure) *a wide proportional participation of the indigenous population of Turkestan in the state activities without the obligation of their belonging to the (Communist) Party,* it is enough if the candidates are workers of the Muslim organizations. Stop requisitioning the properties of the Muslims without the consent of the regional Muslim organizations, shun all kinds of frictions and creation of antagonisms. We hope... the Turkestan proletariat will undertake all measures to realize the objectives laid down by the Central government.[76]

A British Intelligence Officer, Colonel F. M. Bailey, who was in Tashkent at the time, stated that this communication caused great consternation in government circles because a proportional representation of the natives in the administration 'meant ninetyfive per cent and an end of the Bolshevik government' in Turkestan.[77] Kazakov, the Chairman of the Turke-

74. *Ibid.,* 134.

75. The Eighth Congress of the Russian Communist Party rejected the Bukharinist doctrine of 'self-determination for the toilers' and asserted that on the question of exercising the right of self-determination by any nation, the Russian Communist Party stood on the 'class-historical viewpoint.' See *Kommunisticheskaia partiia Sovetskogo Soiuza v rezoliutsiiakh i resheniiakh s'ezdov, konferentsii i plenumov, TsK, pt. I, 1898-1925* (Moscow, seventh edition, 1953) 417. (cited hereafter as *KPSS*)

76. *Leninskii sbornik* (Moscow) XXXV, 811. (emphasis added).

77. F. M. Bailey, *Mission to Tashkent* (London, 1946) 190-1.

stan Central Executive Committee, was quick to grasp the danger which the communication posed to the 'interests of the Russian workers' in the region and with the tacit approval of his supporters decided not to make its contents public. But these local Russian Communists found themselves in a highly embarrassing position when the Centre's emissary, Kobozev, not only made public the contents of this communication but also denounced the conduct of the Kazakov group. The hostile bickerings between the two rival groups which were so much in evidence in the Third Congress of the Communist Party, now once again flared up.

On 16 July 1919 a combined conference of the members of the Regional Muslim Bureau, the Regional Committee of the Party and several other communist organizations was summoned in the old part of Tashkent city to consider the Centre's communication. The speeches delivered in this conference by Munnever Kary, Nizameddin Khodzhaev, Mukhameddinov, Abduvakhit and other native communists fairly clearly indicated the amount of jubilation felt by them on the receipt of the Centre's directive. A resolution adopted by this conference demanded the immediate implementation of the directive and, in particular, suggested the reorganization of the Turkestan Central Executive Committee on the principle of proportional representation.[78]

The resolution passed by this conference was met with indignant remonstrance from the local Russian communist circles. A conference of Russian communist workers summoned on the initiative of the Kazakov-Uspenski group discussed this resolution threadbare for five days from 5 August. Many of them saw in it 'a mistrust of the intentions of the Russian proletariat' and attempts to squeeze out the Russian Communists from the local party and Soviet organizations. They turned their righteous indignation on Kobozev whom they accused of attempting to set the natives against the Russian workers. The situation, in fact, became so tense that Kobozev, fearing arrest, was forced to go into hiding. Following this conference Kazakov, in the name of the Turkestan Central Executive Committee, sent a cable informing the Central Committee of the Russian Com-

78. The resolution is cited in Manzhara, n.22, 137.

munist Party that the implementation of its directive 'might lead to an end of the Soviet regime in Turkestan and to a complete loss of our influence in the East.'[79] In another cable sent to Lenin, Kazakov demanded the immediate recall of Kobozev. He complained that Kobozev had flooded the party and Soviet organizations with non-class-conscious Muslim masses consisting mainly of former traders, interpreters etc., who lacked proletarian organizations and were generally characterized by 'the religious fanaticism of the native poor.'[80]

In the meantime the demand for the implementation of the principle of proportional representation began to mount. On 29 July the Samarkand city council demanded the adoption of the Centre's directive in full and without delay. On 2 August in an *in camera* session of the Tashkent City Committee (native part) the conduct of the Kazakov group was severely censured. A large number of conferences and meetings held all over the Turkestan region demanded that the Soviet regime of Turkestan should be based on the principle of proportional representation of the indigenous population. The party papers also took up the fight against 'chauvinistic attitude' of the local Russian Communists. A number of articles devoted to the elucidation of the tenets of the Soviet nationalities policy began to make their appearance in these newspapers. Significant was the appearance of an article in the *Istrakiun* under the caption 'Comrade Lenin on nation and on the national question.' This article reproduced Lenin's severe criticism of the Bukharinist doctrine of 'self-determination for toilers,' and also brought to light the decisions of the Eighth Congress of the Russian Communist Party on the national question.[81]

The native Communists led by Ryskulov, Tursun Khodzhaev, Nizameddin Khodzhaev and Effendiev sought to break their relations completely with the Kazakov group. Under the influence of these erstwhile Djadidist leaders, the Regional Muslim Bureau not only began to assert its independence from the Party's Regional Committee but also began to encroach upon the functions of the other organs of the party. In the following months such 'usurpations' increased to such an extent that the

79. The text of the cable is cited in *ibid.*, 134.
80. Vakhabov, n.65, 306-7.
81. *Ibid.*, 307-8.

Party's Regional Committee bitterly complained to the Central Committee of the Russian Communist Party that the Regional Muslim Bureau had virtually ignored it and often adopted measures which contradicted the policies of the Communist Party of Turkestan.[82]

The Eighth Congress of Soviets of Turkestan and the Fourth Regional Congress of the Turkestan Communist Party which met in September 1919 once again witnessed the grim drama of the two rival blocs trying to outmanoeuvre each other. In the Eighth Congress of Soviets, the Kazakov-Uspenski group in an attempt to undermine the interests of the natives, tabled and successfully carried a resolution which sought to abolish the People's Commissariat for Nationality Affairs. This resolution stated that the *Turkomnats* was 'an unnecessary, useless and harmful institution.'[83] But the Kazakov group found itself in a minority in the newly elected Turkestan Central Executive Committee which, for the first time, had native majority. Pressing their advantage, the native Communists tabled and successfully carried a resolution in the Congress of Soviets which had for its objective the dissolution of the Council of People's Commissars of the Turkestan Republic. This was their answer to the Kazakov group's attempt to abolish the *Turkomnats*. The functions of the *Sovnarkom* were transferred to three newly constituted councils within the Turkestan Central Executive Committee, viz:, the Council for Defence, the Council for Economic Affairs and the Council for Cultural and Educational Affairs.[84] The native Communists, however, failed to achieve similar successes in the Fourth Regional Congress of the Turkestan Communist Party. They had to be content with an equivocal resolution adopted in this Congress on the issue of proportional representation of the natives. The operative part of the resolution read:

> The principle of proportional representation in the Soviet organs of the Republic must be implemented in each individual case when it is officially demanded by the regional or local congresses of Soviets and under the general guidance

82. V. P. Nikolaeva, 'Turkkomissia kak polnomochnyi organ Ts.K. R.K.P. (B),' *Voprosy istorii KPSS* (Moscow) 2 (1958) 78-9.

83. Landa, n.62, 98.

84. Vakhabov, n.65, 309; also see Urazaev, n.18, 103.

of the regional and local committees of the Russian Communist Party and in accordance with the provisions of the Soviet constitution.[85]

The implications of this resolution were clear enough. While in principle the right of the indigenous population to participate in the governmental and party organs in proportion to their numerical strength was conceded, its implementation, however, was hedged with the proviso that in each individual case it required the concurrence of the regional and the local congresses of soviets and of the regional and local committees of the Russian Communist Party. The cardinal issue having been thus bypassed, the Party Congress did not grudge conceding certain relatively minor concessions such as 'the relaxation of the rigid class character of representation in the Regional Committee, in the Regional Muslim Bureau and in the local party organizations.'[86]

The Turkestan situation did not improve even when the control over the administration passed into the hands of the natives. Not only did the old bickerings between the rival blocs within the Turkestan Communist Party and the government continue but among the native Communists the pan-Turkic ideologues started gaining ascendancy. This group consisted mainly of the erstwhile Djadidist stalwarts like Ryskulov, Tursun Khodzhaev, Effendiev, Aliev and others. They had succeeded in transforming the Regional Muslim Bureau into a citadel of pan-Turkic ideology. The intermittent clashes of this group with the local Russian Communists created an explosive situation in Turkestan and paralyzed the work of the administration. Against such a background it is difficult to speculate what course the events would have taken if Turkestan continued to remain isolated for some more time from the Bolshevik Centre. However, fortunately for the peoples of Turkestan, the timely and effective intervention of the Centre prevented the situation from further deteriorating.

85. The full text of the resolution is cited in Muraveiskii, n.2, 27-8.
86. *Ibid.*, 28.

CHAPTER FOUR

The Turkestan Commission and the Consolidation of Soviet Rule in Turkestan, Khiva and Bukhara

1. THE APPOINTMENT OF THE TURKESTAN COMMISSION

TOWARDS the end of 1919 the Central Asian question had assumed considerable importance in the Centre. The Government of the RSFSR by that time had become fully aware of the great discrepancy which prevailed between the practices of the Russian Bolsheviks of Central Asia and its own precepts on the national question. This anomalous situation called for immediate rectification for more than one reason. As early as February 1919, the People's Commissar for Nationality Affairs, Stalin, had stated:

> Turkestan in its geographical position is a bridge connecting socialist Russia with the oppressed countries of the East, and in view of this the strengthening of the Soviet régime in Turkestan might have the greatest revolutionary significance for the entire East.[1]

But until September 1919 the Central government was prevented from effectively intervening in Central Asian affairs largely by its inability to break through the blockade imposed on the Central Asian region by the armed forces of Dutov. In the autumn of 1919, however, communications with Central Asia were once again restored following the defeat of Dutov's forces by the Red Army. The Central government seized this opportunity, and in October 1919, by a joint resolution of the

---

1. J. V. Stalin, 'Sovdepam i partiinym organizatsiiam Turkestana, *Zhizn' natsional'nostei* 7 (1919) reprinted in *Bolshevik Kazakhstana* (Alma-Ata) 9-10 (1935) 16. For Lenin's views on this issue see N. Narimanov, 'Lenin i vostok,' *Novyi vostok* 5 (1924) 11.

All-Russian Central Executive Committee and the Council of People's Commissars, created a high-power commission on Turkestan affairs and charged it with the task of completely reversing the policies pursued until then by the Government of the Turkestan Republic and bringing them in line with the policies of the Centre. To what extent this was to mean a departure from the earlier Bolshevik practices in Turkestan became at once clear from the wording of the resolution which brought the Commission into existence. The resolution asserted:

> The self-determination of the peoples of Turkestan and the abolition of all national inequality and all privileges of one national group over another constitute the foundation of all the policies of the Soviet Government of Russia and serve as a guiding principle in all the work of its organs, and it is only through such work that the mistrust of the native toiling masses of Turkestan for the workers and peasants of Russia, bred by many years of domination of Russian Tsarism, can be finally overcome.[2]

This was followed by the despatch of a personal letter from Lenin addressed to the 'Communist Comrades of Turkestan' in which he wrote:

> The establishment of correct relations with the peoples of Turkestan has now, for the Russian Socialist Federation of Soviet Republics, without exaggeration, a gigantic and world-wide historical significance. The relations of the Soviet workers'-peasants' republic to the people who have been weak and oppressed until now have a practical significance for all Asia, for the entire colonial world and for thousands of millions of people.[3]

In the same letter he exhorted the local Russian Communists to establish comradely relations with the peoples of Turkestan and to show in deeds 'the sincerity of our desire to root out all remnants of Great-Russian imperialism.'

The Turkestan Commission was composed of Sh. Z. Elieva (chairman), M. V. Frunze, V. V. Kuibyshev, F. I. Goloshchekin and Ia. E. Rudzutak.[4] It arrived in Turkestan in November

2. Text of this resolution is available in Lenin and Stalin, *Stat'i i rechi o Srednei Azii i Uzbekistane* (Tashkent, 1940) 91-2.

3. *Ibid.*, 94.

4. In the working of the Commission in Central Asia, M. V. Frunze and V. V. Kuibyshev soon emerged as outstanding figures and in May 1920, the latter was nominated the commission's chairman.

1919, and immediately began its work of 'rebuilding the Soviet organs on the model of the Centre.'[5] Before it stood a gigantic task. On the eve of its arrival, the situation in Turkestan had become almost catastrophic. The heavy demands of the civil war in the region had denuded the administrative machinery of all its efficient personnel. The control which the Soviet organs of power exercised on their local counterparts was only nominal. It had become extremely difficult to enforce laws and to collect taxes. Among the soldiers stationed in Tashkent, there was neither organization nor discipline.[6] The economic situation was worse. The total irrigated area in the Turkestan Republic had shrunk by fifty per cent between 1913 and 1920; in some oblasts like Transcaspia its shrinkage was to the tune of about seventy per cent. The cotton crop, which constituted the backbone of the region's economic life, had suffered immensely. In 1921 in Turkestan, Bukhara and Khiva, the cotton crop occupied less than ten per cent of the land which was under it in the prewar years. The industries had suffered a similar fate. Out of the 249 cotton-processing enterprises which were located on the territory of the Turkestan Republic, 229 had stopped working.[7] The Soviet and party organs had fallen into the hands of persons of shady background and shadier character. These people had nothing in common with the ideals of the new regime and had flocked under its banner only to use it in defending and strengthening their own position. Among them were to be found the former Tsarist officials, adventurers and *kulaks* who, in the name of class struggle, started oppressing and persecuting the native population of the Turkestan region. In the hands of such persons the Soviet regime had transformed itself, in many parts of Turkestan, into a weapon of national struggle.[8] Above all, the antagonism, hatred and distrust which characterized the re-

5. S. Muraveiskii, *Ocherki po istorii revoliustionnogo dvizheniia v Srednei Azii* (Tashkent, 1926) 29.

6. V. P. Nikolaeva, 'Turkkomissia kak polnomochnyi organ TsK RKP (B),' *Voprosy istorii KPSS* (Moscow) 2 (1958) 78.

7. Klych Momedovich Kuliev, *Bor'ba kommunisticheskoi partii za ukreplenie sovetskoi vlasti i osushchestvlenie natsional'noi politiki v Srednei Azii 1917-1925gg* (Ashkhabad, n.d.) 49; also see Iu. I. Iskhakov, *Razvitie khlopkovodstva v Uzbekistane* (Tashkent, 1960) 39-41.

8. Georgi Safarov, *Kolonial'naia revoliutsiia : opyt Turkestana* (Moscow, 1921) 133; also see A. I. Zevelev, *Iz istorii grazhdanskoi voiny v Uzbekistane* (Tashkent, 1959) 403.

lations between the Russian and the indigenous populations called for the immediate attention of the commission. Broido gave a graphic account of the Turkestan scene in the following words:

> Militant Great Russian chauvinism and the defensive nationalism of the enslaved colonial masses shot through with a mistrust of the Russians—that is the fundamental and characteristic feature of Turkestan reality.[9]

Thus, everywhere in Turkestan one came across the manifestations of either 'Great Russian chauvinism' or 'Muslim nationalism.' In particular, the Communist Party of Turkestan exhibited such 'deviations' in an acute form. M. V. Frunze, a member of the Turkestan Commission wrote:

1. The Communist Party of Turkestan never experienced unity. It was divided into two groups:
   (a) European Communists, mainly railway workers, who maintained the principle of pure dictatorship of the proletariat and attempted to apply this principle to life in spite of the fact that this actually meant the dictatorship of a small group of the local European population over the Muslim masses, and
   (b) a group of Muslim worker-communists who considered as unacceptable the position taken by the Europeans, and who emphasized instead the significance of the national problem.
2. The above disagreement took the form of an open or concealed struggle within the party; it brought about disintegration in the party, and made any constructive work impossible. On the one hand, Turkestan's peculiar situation (i.e. its isolation from Moscow) caused this struggle to take a most ugly form: petty intrigue, baiting, attempts to damage the position of another, and so forth....[10]

II. TURKESTAN COMMISSION AND LOCAL RUSSIAN COMMUNIST

At the time of the arrival of the Turkestan Commission in Tashkent the European wing of the party remained most belli-

---

9. *Zhizn' natsional'nostei* (Moscow) 23 (80) (18 July 1920). Cited in E. H. Carr, *The Bolshevik Revolution 1917-1923* (London, 1950) I, 334.
10. M. V. Frunze, *Sobranie sochinenii* (Moscow) I, 119-20. The document is available in Xenia Joukoff Eudin and Robert C. North, *Soviet Russia And The East 1920-1927: A Documentary Survey* (Stanford, 1957) 49.

gerent. It had sought on the one hand to prevent the participation of the indigenous population in the administration, and
on the other hand to minimize the scope for intervention by
the Central Soviet Government in Turkestan affairs. In fighting
this faction the Turkestan Commission encountered the hostility of the entire local Russian population. This was not un-
natural. All the immigrant Russians, whether they were the
peasant settlers of Semirechie, or the Tashkent railway workers,
or the miners of Kyzil-Kia, or the local Communists, saw in
the policies of the Commission a threat to their 'sovereign position' in the region.[11] In the face of this opposition, the
Turkestan Commission often was forced to depend upon the
Red Army units to enforce its decrees.

The Commission soon began the work of weeding out from
the party and Soviet organizations all persons who, in its opinion,
were responsible for bringing about the abnormal situation in
Turkestan. With the consent of the Central Committee of the
Russian Communist Party, the Commission ordered such
stalwarts of the local Communist movement as Kazakov,
Uspenski, Sorokin, Timliantsev and a host of others to leave
Turkestan immediately. At its instance, legal proceeedings were
instituted against a number of former Tsarist officials, gendarmes,
and speculators, who had managed to get into the local party
and Soviet organizations.[12] In accordance with the decision of
the Regional Committee and the Turkestan Commission of 21
November 1919, the party organization of the third railway
district was purged of all the recalcitrant members.

The Commission also paid attention to the question of weeding out such elements from the oblast party organizations. On
15 November 1919, at a combined conference of the Presidium
of the Turkestan Central Executive Committee, the Turkestan
Commission and the Party Regional Committee, the situation
prevailing in the Semirechie oblast was reviewed. Following this
a decree 'On the Soviet structure, party life and the economic
situation of the Semirechie oblast' was issued. This decree enjoined upon the Semirechie Oblast party organization to 'regulate
national antagonisms between the (Russian and native) populations by completely rooting out all colonists' impulses on the

11. Safarov, n. 8, 107.
12. Nikolaeva, n. 6, 81.

part of the Russian peasant settlers and by weakening the
economic power of the *peasant-kulaks*[13] Some time later, special
commissions were constituted and despatched to the Syr Daria
and Fergana oblasts to secure the realization of similar objectives.
These commissions in the process of re-registering the members
of the oblast party organizations, eliminated from them all
former Tsarist officials, speculators, traders etc. Out of the
number of persons who were exiled out of the Turkestan region
in 1919-20, there were 175 former police officials, 443 former
'whiteguards,' 340 bribe-takers, 92 who had indulged in extortion,
231 who had misused their official positions, 153 work-deserters
and 192 'chauvinists.'[14]

III. FIGHT AGAINST THE DJADIDISTS AND THE BASMACHIS

During this period the Commission was also engaged in fighting against what it termed 'the petty bourgeois nationalist
deviation' of some Muslim members of the party,[15] This faction
was represented by a group of nationalists who were led by
Ryskulov, Tursun Khodzhaev, Nezameddin Khodzhaev,
Munnever Kary, Effendiev and other erstwhile Djadidist
leaders.[16] The ideology of this group negated the aspirations of
the local national groups like the Turkmens, Uzbeks and
Kazakhs to develop their own languages, literature, culture, organs of administration etc., and instead, sought to unite all
national groups belonging to the Turkic race in a common
Turkic republic. Though the members of this group professed
outwardly to be Communists and swore allegiance to the party
ideals, they covertly did everything to minimize the spreading
of the influence of communism among the indigenous population. In the hands of such persons, the Regional Muslim Bureau
had become a citadel of the pan-Turkic ideology.

By November 1919, this group started propagating its views
openly. At its instance, the Regional Muslim Bureau, on 3 No-

13. Cited in E. Voskoboinikov and A. Zevelev, *Turkkomissiia VTsIK i
SNK RSFSR i Turkbiuro TsK RKP (B) v bor'be za ukreplenie Sovetskoi
vlasti v Turkestane* (Tashkent, 1951) 86.

14. *Zhizn' natsional'nostei*, 8 (14) (26 April 1922).

15. From Frunze's statement on the Turkestan situation, see Eudin
and North, n.10, 49.

16. See page 99.

vember 1919, passed a resolution seeking the abolition of the national divisions which functioned within the Turkestan People's Commissariat for Nationality Affairs and favouring the creation of a single 'Turkic' division in their place.[17] Confronted with such an open repudiation of the Soviet nationalities policy, the Turkestan Commission decided to eliminate the influence of the Ryskulov group on the working of local party and Soviet organs and to wind up the Regional Muslim Bureau. The Ryskulov group, for its part, began to plague the Commission by questioning, at every turn, its competence to undertake major reforms within the party and Soviet apparatuses and by seeking to secure its recall. This struggle continued throughout the first half of 1920.

In January 1920, against the opposition of the Ryskulov group, the Turkestan Commission adopted a special decree which stated that it was essential 'to recognize the need to carry out the administrative regrouping of Turkestan in conformity with the ethnographic and economic conditions of the region, and in particular, to demarcate the following groupings: Turkmen (Transcaspia), Uzbek-Tadjik (Samarkand, Fergana and a part of the Syr Daria oblast), and Kirgiz (i.e., the Kazakhs of a part of the Syr Daria oblast, the Amu Daria Division and the Semirechie oblast).'[18] The Ryskulov group stoutly contested the basic assumption underlying this proposal viz., that the Turkestan region was heterogeneous in its national composition and that the interests of the various nationalities demanded a re-

17. L. M. Landa, 'Sozdanie narodnogo komissariata po natsional'nym delam Turkestanskoi ASSR i ego deiatel'nosti v 1918-1919gg,' *Iz istorii sovetskogo Uzbekistana*: *sbornik statei* (Tashkent, 1956) 98. On the insistence of the Commission, the national divisions within the Commissariat for Nationality Affairs were reconstituted. Following the suspension of the activities of the commissariat from 10 December 1919, the national divisions were transferred to the Central Executive Committee. When the Commissariat for Nationality Affairs was reconstituted in September 1921, the national divisions were once again restored to their original place. *ibid.*, 98-9.

18. The approval of the Government of the RSFSR to this proposal was published in a decree of the All-Russian Central Executive Committee in August 1920. '*Izvestiia TurkTsIK*,' 27 August 1920, cited in M. Vakhabov, *Formirovanie Uzbekskoi sotsialisticheskoi natsii* (Tashkent, 1961) 325. It is interesting to note that this proposal for the administrative regrouping of the various oblasts already contained, in a rudimentary form, the outlines of the project on national-state delimitation of Central Asia of 1924.

grouping of its administrative divisions. Speaking before a combined conference of the Party Regional Committee, the Regional Muslim Bureau, the Committees of the Foreign Communists and the Turkestan Commission, held on 17 January 1920, Ryskulov asserted that 'Turkestan in its ethnographic and other conditions is a Turkic national republic.'[19] Shortly afterwards, speaking before the Third Regional Conference of the Muslim Bureau, Ryskulov stated:

> The Turkic nationalists must rectify a historical error, namely, that committed in relation to the peoples of Turkestan.... Turkic communists are fighting not only for the interests of the factory and railroad proletariat[20] but also consider it their duty to secure the cultural and economic interests of the peoples who live on the vast expanses of the thousand *verst-wide* deserts and in the kishlaks, by going into their midst.[21]

The resolution adopted in this conference outlined the scheme for the creation of a united Turkic republic. It stated:

> In the interests of the international unity of toilers and oppressed people, be it resolved that we shall oppose by means of communist agitation the strivings of the Turkic nationals to divide themselves into various national groups such as Tatar, Kirgiz, Bashkir, Uzbek etc., and (their desire) to establish small separate republics; instead, with a view to forge the solidarity of all Turkic people who so far have not been included with the RSFSR, it is proposed to unify them within a Turkic Soviet Republic, and wherever it is not possible to achieve this, it is proposed to unite different Turkic nationalities in accordance with their territorial proximity.[22]

If such words as 'the interests of the international unity of toilers and oppressed people' and 'communist agitation,' which were used to befuddle the Communists, are eliminated from this resolution, then there remain the following points:

1. to oppose the strivings of the Turkic peoples such as the Tatars, Kirgiz (Kazakhs), Bashkirs, Uzbeks etc., to form their own separate republics;
2. instead, to unite them in a single Turkic Soviet Republic;

19. Cited in Vakhabov, *ibid.*, 326-7.
20. The reference here is to the discriminatory practices of the local Russian Communists.
21. *Izvestiia*, 5 February 1920, cited in Safarov, n. 8, 109.
22. The text of this resolution is available in Muraveiskii, n. 5, 30.

3. within this united Turkic republic to include not only the
   Turkic peoples of the RSFSR but all Turks, even those living
   outside the frontiers of the RSFSR;
4. if it were not possible to unite the latter with the Turkic
   peoples of the RSFSR then to secure their unification in accordance with their territorial proximity.

If this was the long-term project of the Ryskulov group, its
immediate objectives were to secure a large measure of decen-
tralization in the civil and military administration, the renaming of the Turkestan Republic as 'the Turkic Republic' and
the Regional Communist Party of Turkestan as 'the Communist
Party of the Turkic Peoples.' The Third Regional Conference
of the Muslim Bureau also discussed these issues and passed a
resolution on the autonomy and the constitution of the
Turkestan Republic. In addition to the special rights and prerogatives claimed for the Turkestan Republic in the constitution
adopted at the Sixth Congress of Soviets in September 1919, the
Ryskulov group demanded the abolition of such supervisory
bodies like the Turkestan Commission, on the ground, that they
violated the autonomy of Turkestan.[23]

The claims put forward by the Ryskulov group only tended
to reinforce the determination of the Turkestan Commission to
secure the abolition of the Regional Muslim Bureau. On
15 January 1920 it adopted a decision which favoured the
creation of a monolithic structure within the Communist Party
of Turkestan and to abolish the Muslim Bureau and the Committees of the Foreign Communists.[24] The party unit of Tashkent city was the first to endorse this decision of the Commission.
The resolution adopted by the Tashkent party unit stated that
the existence of several party organizations, each formed on the
basis of the national affinities of its members, negated the
basic principles which governed the Bolshevik party organization
and tended to increase the nationalist sentiments among the
members of the party.[25] The Fifth Congress of the Communist
Party, meeting shortly afterwards, also endorsed these views
and adopted a resolution which stated:

23. Sh. Z. Urazaev, *Turkestanskaia ASSR i ee gosudarstvenno-pravovye
osobennosti* (Tashkent, 1958) 104; also see Nikolaeva, n. 6, 83.
24. Voskoboinikov and Zevelev, n. 13, 97.
25. *Izvestiia Kraikoma KPT i TurkTsIK* (Tashkent) 12, 18 January 1920.

Be it considered that it is abnormal to retain in Turkestan
equivalent and independent regional and uezd-city committees, such as: the Committees of the Party, the Muslim Bureau
and the Committees of the Foreign Communists; it is resolved
to unite all these independent national communist organizations in a single communist party headed by a single Regional
Committee which would be subordinated to the Central
Committee of the Russian Communist Party (Bolsheviks).[26]

The strategy of the Ryskulov group was not to oppose the
move for the abolition of the Muslim Bureau and the creation
of a unified Communist Party of Turkestan but to agitate for
the transformation of the Regional Party into the 'Communist
Party of the Turkic peoples.' Hence, soon after the decision was
taken to abolish the Muslim Bureau, the Ryskulov group tabled
a resolution in the Congress which stated: '... such a party
must be a party of the large native toiling mass of Turkic peoples.... The party must acquire the name "the Communist
Party of the Turkic peoples."'[27] Further, the Ryskulov group
also proposed the renaming of the Turkestan Republic as 'the
Turkic Republic.' In spite of the opposition of some delegates,
the resolution proposed by the Ryskulov group was adopted by
the Congress. Following this victory Ryskulov reasserted before
the party congress that it was wrong to divide the peoples of
Central Asia into separate national groups such as the Uzbeks,
Turkmens, Kazakhs etc., and that such divisions were artificial
and arbitrary. Further, it stated that few regions in Russia were
nationally as homogeneous as Turkestan and a great bulk of its
population belonged to the Turkic nationality.

The decision of the Fifth Party Congress to rename the party
'the Communist Party of Turkic Peoples' was in complete disagreement with the Bolshevik concept of a single and centralized
communist party for the entire Russian Republic (the All-
Russian Communist Party) with no independent regional communist parties whatever. Nor were the Communists prepared
to condone the manifestation of pan-Turkic or pan-Islamic
tendencies within their party organizations.[28] In view of this,
the thesis advanced by the Ryskulov group came in for a sharp
rebuttal at the hands of M. V. Frunze and V. V. Kuibyshev. In

26. *Izvestiia Kraikoma KPT i TurkTsIK*, 17, 25 January 1920.
27. Nikolaeva, n. 6, 83.
28. Eudin and North, n. 10, 28.

a conference of the Commission held on 23 February 1920, these two members asserted that the so called 'Turkic nation' never existed at any time and that it was only a figment of imagination of the Ryskulov group.[29] The Turkestan Commission rejected the demand for the creation of a Communist Party of the Turkic Peoples and also to rename the Turkestan Republic as the Turkic Republic. On 4 March, the Commission formally requested the Central Committee of the Russian Communist Party to give its verdict on the resolutions passed by the Third Regional Conference of the Muslim Bureau and the Fifth Congress of the Communist Party of Turkestan, and also on the draft worked out by itself on the question of interrelations between the RSFSR and the Turkestan Republic.[30] The Central Committee of the Russian Communist Party, after having reviewed all controversial issues of Turkestan, on 8 March 1920, communicated to the Turkestan Commission its authoritative opinion. The Central Committee of the Russian Communist Party rejected the Ryskulov group's demand for the creation of the Turkic Republic and the Communist Party of the Turkic Peoples. The Central Committee stated that there should exist in Turkestan a single Communist Party with a Central Committee at its head and that the party should be known as the Communist Party of Turkestan. Further, it stated that the Communist Party of Turkestan must be a part of the Russian Communist Party and that it should have a status of a provincial party organization.[31] Regarding the competence of the federal and the local organs of government, the Central Committee stated that all matters like defence, foreign affairs, railway, finance, post and telegraph must be left to the exclusive jurisdiction of federal organs and that all other matters be left within the competence of the Central Executive Committee of the Turkestan Republic. On 23 March 1920, the 'Statute on the autonomy of Turkestan,' which was approved by both the All-Russian Central Executive Committee and the Central Committee of the Russian Communist Party was published in the local papers. The statute stated that Turkestan was recognized as an Autonomous Repub-

29. Voskoboinikov and Zevelev, n. 13, 92-3; also see Zevelev, n. 8, 436.
30. Nikolaeva, n. 6, 84.
31. *Istortia Uzbekskoi SSR* (Tashkent, 1957) II, 112. (Cited hereafter as *IUzSSR*).

lic of the people inhabiting it, viz., Turkmens, Uzbeks and Kazakhs, with the oblast divisions corresponding to the existing national groupings, economic conditions and ethnic structure, and was to be known as the Turkestan Autonomous Republic of the Russian Soviet Federative Socialist Republic.[32]

The Ryskulov group, it was alleged, though it did not formally reject the verdict given by the Central Party organ, remained unrepentant. It was even alleged that the Ryskulov group tried to create a 'Muslim Army' and threatened to call upon all native workers to leave the Soviet and party organizations unless all its demands were met satisfactorily.[33] In May 1920, a delegation of this group headed by Ryskulov himself went to Moscow to convince the Central authorities of the justice of its demands. In Moscow the delegation was said to have claimed that it was authorized by the Turkestan Central Executive Committee and the Regional Committee of the Communist Party of Turkestan to carry on negotiations with the Government of the RSFSR and with the Third Communist International on all outstanding problems of the Turkestan region. This claim, however, was soon set at naught by two members of the Turkestan Commission, Elieva and Rudzutak, who also arrived in Moscow on the ostensible mission of discussing certain economic problems with the Central government, but in fact, to defend the policies pursued by the Commission in Turkestan and to minimize the damage the nationalists could do. They informed the Central Committee of the Russian Communist Party that the Ryskulov group represented neither the Central Executive Committee nor the Regional Committee of the Party of Turkestan.

The delegation submitted a representation signed by Ryskulov, Khodzhaev (*sic*) and Bek Imanov to the Central Committee of the Russian Communist Party. It contained a candid account of the Bolshevik misrule in Turkestan, and of the immense suffering inflicted on the native population (particularly on the

32. 'Izvestiia Kraikoma KPT i TurkTsIK', 65 (107), 24 March 1920.
33. Tursun Khodzhaev, a prominent former Djadidist and a member of the Ryskulov group, was reported to have confessed to all these things before an investigating commission in 1930. Further, he was supposed to have stated: 'I declare that if proper measures were not taken at that time, the strivings of the nationalists would have led to the establishment of a bourgeois state. If you had asked me in 1919, I would have told you that I desired it.' Cited in Voskoboinikov and Zevelev, n. 13, 94, 96.

nomads of Semirechie and Syr Daria oblasts) by the unchecked excesses of the Russian peasant settlers. Besides, the representation also elaborated the proposals for the creation of a Turkic Republic and a Communist Party of the Turkic Peoples, and reminded the Central Committee of the class solidarity and national homogeneity of the population of the Turkestan region. It declared that the Soviet and party organs in Turkestan had grown sufficiently strong to stand on their own legs without any assistance from the Turkestan Commission and that the continued existence of the latter in Tashkent compromised the autonomy of the Turkestan Republic.[34]

The Organization Bureau of the Central Committee, while considering the representation made by the delegation, elicited the views of Elieva and Rudzutak on the Turkestan situation. On 25 May 1920 the representation was taken up for consideration by the Politbureau of the Central Committee. Before giving its decision on the matter, the Politbureau constituted a commission to work out in detail the pattern of relationship that ought to exist between the RSFSR and the Turkestan Republic. The report prepared by this commission and the representation made by the Ryskulov group were considered also by Lenin. The basic demands made in the representation, viz., the demands for the creation of a Turkic Republic, and a Communist Party of the Turkic Peoples and the demand to wind up the Turkestan Commission were categorically rejected by Lenin. He, however, suggested that the Politbureau should work out ways and means for completely rooting out the lingering remnants of Russian colonialism in Turkestan, and for placing certain checks on the exercise of power by the Turkestan Commission. On 22 June the Politbureau considered Lenin's suggestions and decided to take the following measures:

1. to level down the land-holdings of the Russian peasant-émigrés in Turkestan to the size of the landholdings of the native *dekkans;*
2. to exile from Turkestan all Russian peasant-*kulaks;*
3. to give no authority to the Turkestan Commission to amend the laws which are in force without the consent of the Central Executive Committee, the Council of People's Commissars of the Turkestan ASSR and the Central government; and

34. *Ibid.,* 98-9.

4. to systematically take all measures to hand over power in Turkestan gradually but unflinchingly to the local Soviets of toilers under the control of reliable Communists.[35]

On 29 July 1920 these proposals, in a more elaborated form, were incorporated in a decree issued by the Central Committee of the Russian Communist Party under the title 'On the basic tasks of the Russian Communist Party in Turkestan.' The decree stated, among other things, that it was the immediate responsibility of the Russian Communist Party to restore to the Kazakh and Kirgiz nomadic population the lands seized from them by the Russian peasant-settlers during and after the rebellion of 1916, to provide land to the landless, to render ineffective and harmless the local Russian *kulaks,* to exile from Turkestan all former police and civil servants, speculators, and traders, to equalize the rights of the native and Russian urban population in the sphere of food distribution, to improve the food situation in the villages, to develop local industries etc.[36] Equally significant was the suggestion made by Lenin on 13 July 1920. He instructed the Turkestan Commission not only to undertake special measures to combat all manifestations of pan-Islamic and 'bourgeois nationalist' tendencies but also to commission the preparation of maps (ethnographic etc.) of Turkestan showing its subdivisions into Uzbek, Kirgiz (i.e., Kazakh) and Turkmen, and to elucidate in detail the conditions of fusion or division of those parts.[37] This proposal indicated the emerging trends of Soviet nationalities policy in Central Asia and, in fact, anticipated the scheme of national-territorial delimitation of 1924.

After the return of the Ryskulov group to Tashkent, its members were forced to accept their mistakes before a combined conference of the Turkestan Central Executive Committee, the party Regional Committee and the Turkestan Commission. Kuibyshev, who by then had become the chairman of the Turkestan Com-

---

35. Communicating this decision to V. V. Kuibyshev, Sh. Z. Elieva on 1 July 1920, wrote that 'in the opinion of the Politbureau and especially in the observations made by Lenin, the need to trust the Muslim masses to the maximum extent and the necessity of working in close cooperation with the active Muslim workers, were emphasized.' See Nikolaeva, n. 6, 85-6.

36. The full text of this document is available in K. Zhitov and V. Nepomnin, *Ot kolonial'nogo rabstva k sotsializmu* (Tashkent, 1939) 63-4.

37. *Leninskii sbornik* (Moscow) XXXIV, 326.

mission, stated in this conference that 'such members of the party, who do not share the views of the Centre on military affairs, on centralization, on the question of class-stratification among the indigenous population and on fighting against the local bourgeoisie, cannot enter into its guiding organs.'[38] Subsequently, all members of the Ryskulov group were excluded from the Presidium of the Central Executive Committee, which was newly constituted in a plenary session of the Central Executive Committee. Rakhimbaev, said to be a staunch Communist, was elected to replace Ryskulov as its chairman.[39] On 12 July 1920, following the receipt of the text of the decision of the Central Committee of the Russian Communist Party, the Turkestan Commission immediately began reorganizing the party apparatus. On 19 July a decree of the Commission secured the dissolution of the party Regional Committee. In its place a provisional fifteen-member Central Committee was constituted. Almost all the members of the Ryskulov group were excluded from this body also. The newly constituted Provisional Central Committee was composed mainly of 'reliable Communists' like N. Tiurakulov (chairman), Atabaev, I. Liubimov, Sultan Khodzhaev, T. Ustambaev, Khakimov, S. Kasym Khodzhaev, Babadzhanov, Rakhimbaev, Khodzhanov, Asfendiarov and four others.[40]

In a combined conference of the Tashkent party organizations held towards the beginning of August 1920, Frunze again denounced the activities of the Ryskulov group. He stated that the Turkestan Commission, by reorganizing the composition of the Central Executive Committee and the Central Committee of the party, was seeking to establish a single party line in Turkestan. 'Unity must be ensured' he insisted, 'and an undeviated implementation of a strict class viewpoint (must prevail) in the fight against the survivals of patriarchal-feudal relations among the Muslims and against the remnants of (Russian) colonialism.'[41] Subsequently, a number of nationalists including Ryskulov, were exiled from Turkestan region. Towards August 1920 the Commission, by excluding from the Communist Party of Turkestan

38. Cited in Voskoboinikov and Zevelev, n. 13, 102.
39. Safarov, n. 8, 121.
40. *IUzSSR*, n. 31, 113.
41. *Izvestiia Kraikoma KPT i TurTsIK*, 136, 19 August 1920.

all persons who had deviated towards either 'Great Russian chauvinism or pan-Turkic nationalism,' not only secured the unity in the party ranks but also ensured the normal working of the party on the model of the Russian Communist Party.[42] In September 1920, the Turkestan Commission also secured the approval of the 9th Congress of Soviets of Turkestan to a constitutional project it had worked out for the Turkestan ASSR. Chapter VI of this constitution which touched 'on the inter-relations between the Turkestan ASSR and the RSFSR,' was based upon the decision of the All-Russian Central Executive Committee 'on the Turkestan Republic.'[43] This constitution left to the exclusive jurisdiction of the federal organs, foreign affairs, foreign trade and defence. Further, it extended the scope of the decrees and directives of the Central government over the administration of post, telegraph and communications. The constitution placed the Turkestan Central Executive Committee under the obligation of seeking the previous consent of the Central People's Commissars for Post, Telegraph, Communications, Finance and Food before nominating the heads of the corresponding local commissariats. Similarly, the previous consent of the chairman of the All-Russian Council of National Economy became essential for nominating the head of the Central Council of National Economy of Turkestan ASSR.[44]

On 11 April 1922, the All-Russian Central Executive Committee gave the final legal affirmation to the constitution of the Turkestan ASSR. A decree issued by it stated that 'the Turkestan Soviet Socialist Republic composed of the oblasts: Syr Daria, Semirechie, Fergana, Samarkand, Transcaspia and the Amu Daria Division is declared an autonomous part of the RSFSR and is given the name—the Turkestan Soviet Socialist Republic.'[45] The decree stated that the Government of the Turkestan Republic should be organized on the basis of the constitution of the RSFSR. It envisaged no change in chapter VI of the constitu-

---

42. V. Ia. Nepomnin, *Istoricheskii opyt stroitel'stva sotsializma v Uzbekistane* (1917-1937) (Tashkent, 1960) 123; Nikolaeva, n. 6, 87.

43. See page 110.

44. Urazaev, n. 23, 112-3.

45. The full text of this decree is available in *Istoriia sovetskaia konstitutsiia (v dokumentakh) 1917-1957* (Moscow, 1957) 282-3. (Cited hereafter as *ISK*).

tion of the Turkestan Republic which dealt with the question of interrelations between the RSFSR and the Turkestan Republic.[46]

The resolution of the long-standing conflict between Turkestan and the RSFSR on the competence of their governmental organs within the frontiers of the Turkestan Republic marked the end of a phase of the work of the Turkestan Commission. Following this, in August 1920, most of its functions were entrusted to the newly-established Turkestan Bureau of the Central Committee of the Russian Communist Party (*Turkbureau of TsK of the RKP (b)*).[47]

Soon after its arrival in Tashkent in November 1919, the Turkestan Commission had also paid considerable attention to other issues like improving the conditions of living of the natives, curbing the activities of the Basmachis and extending the revolution to Khiva and Bukhara. In an attempt to win over the confidence of the indigenous population and to stop it from siding with the Basmachis, the Commission granted many concessions to the natives. On the one hand, the harsh practices of the Tashkent Soviet of indiscriminately requisitioning food articles from the semi-starved natives to feed the army and the privileged railway workers, the unauthorized confiscations of the properties of the local population, the arbitrary fixing of prices, etc., were discontinued.[48] On the other hand, a large number of natives were drawn into the orbit of governmental activities and placed in positions of responsibility. Besides, not only were the rights of the Russians and the native populations equalized in

46. Following the issue of this decree, a 'Provisional Commission of the All-Russian Central Executive Committee and the Council of People's Commissars of the RSFSR on Turkestan Affairs' was created (not to be confused with the Turkestan Commission) and it was charged with the task of strengthening the federal ties between Turkestan and the RSFSR by dealing directly with all issues falling within the exclusive jurisdiction of the Central government. This commission functioned in Turkestan until the proposal for effecting the economic unification of Turkestan, Bukhara and Khorezm was taken up. In August 1922, the Central Committee of the Russian Communist Party decided to wind up this commission. See S. B. Krylov, 'Istoricheskii protsess razvitia sovetskogo federalizma,' *Sovetskoe pravo* (Moscow) 5 (11) (1924) 43; also see Urazaev, n. 23, 116.

47. The Turkestan Bureau was composed of Sokol'nikov, Georgi Safarov Kaganovich and Peters. See Safarov, n. 8, 122.

48. G. Skalov, 'Sotsial'naia priroda basmachestva v Turkestane,' *Zhizn natsional'nostei*, 3-4 (1923) 56; also see I. Trainin, 'Postanovka natsional' nogo voprosa,' *Vlast'sovetov* (Moscow) 5 (1923) 30.

the sphere of distribution of food and of other essential articles, but the natives were even allowed to engage in small-scale trading and to have their own traditional schools and law courts. Even the *wakf* lands were restored to the clergy.[49] These reforms soon began to yield favourable results. Following the gradual improvement of their living conditions, the bulk of the natives overcame the resentment they had felt earlier against the Soviet regime. Even those who, in collaboration with the Basmachis, had taken up arms against it, began returning to normal living.[50]

These developments had a direct bearing on the change that began to take place within the Basmachi movement. With more and more people beginning to abandon its ranks in favour of settling down to peaceful living, the Basmachi movement in Turkestan began to lose the character of a popular political movement.[51] The Basmachi leaders found it difficult to retain under their control the war-weary and half-starved native population by employing slogans which, at one time, were so popular but had now become meaningless and without appeal.[52] The Turkestan Commission realized the growing weakness of the Basmachi movement and adopted energetic measures to secure the surrender of the recalcitrant Basmachi guerrillas. In January 1920, Monstrov with his 'peasant army' was compelled to surrender arms to the Soviets. In March, the same year, Madami Bek, who towards the end of 1919 had commanded nearly 7,000 men in Fergana, was also forced to surrender.[53] However, the attempt to organize the Basmachi guerrillas who had surrendered into a Soviet Basmachi force and set it against the real Basmachis, proved a fiasco. In September 1920, Madami Bek once again revolted and joined hands with his erstwhile kinsmen. This

49. Skalov, n. 48, 61.

50. *Turkestanskaia Pravda* (Tashkent) 12, 17 January 1923. To what extent this policy of appeasement succeeded becomes clear from a statement issued by the Council of the *Ulema*. Signed by some of the well-known *mullahs* like Kari Abullah, Mullah Ikram, Mullah Abdulrasul and others, the statement declared that the entire Orient including Central Asia owed a deep debt of gratitude to Lenin for liberating its peoples from the oppressive domination of the Europeans. See *Turkestanskaia Pravda*, 45 (322), 25 February 1924.

51. *Turkestanskaia Pravda*, 12, 17 January 1923.

52. Skalov, n. 48, 57.

53. Vasilevskii, 'Fazy basmacheskogo dvizheniia v Srednei Azii,' *Novyi Vostok* (Moscow) 29 (1930) 133.

episode and other events which took place in the course of the year 1920 in Khiva and Bukhara, gave a fresh lease of life to the Basmachi movement for a time.[54]

IV. EXTENSION OF REVOLUTION TO KHIVA AND BUKHARA

The Turkestan Commission's failure to secure the immediate disbandment of the Basmachi movement was more than compensated by the success which attended its policies in Khiva and Bukhara. These two native states where the anachronistic regimes of the Khan and the Amir still survived, remained untouched by the revolutionary currents which swept over the neighbouring Turkestan region. The Uzbek rulers of these two states, ever since the inception of their dynasties, had adopted a policy of most intransigent religious fanaticism and a dogged opposition to all modernizing trends. As a result, the medieval science and philosophy for which the two states were so justly famous had been replaced by a barren scholasticism which only succeeded in sterilizing all creative thinking and stultifying the growth of culture.[55] Even in the twentieth century, the Khan of Khiva and the Amir of Bukhara continued to administer their states in the same manner as their ancestors had done nearly three centuries ago. Faizulla Khodzhaev has left a vivid account of the Amir's rule in Bukhara. He wrote:

> No legislative organs besides the will of the Amir, no laws besides the religious laws of the *Shariat*, no guarantee or in-

54. After the downfall of his regime in Bukhara, Amir Said Alim Khan collaborated for a time with the Basmachis in the Eastern Bukhara and Hissar regions. More significant was the appearance of Enver Pasha in the midst of the Basmachis in spring 1922. Under his command the Basmachi movement regained its unity and posed a serious threat to the Bolshevik supremacy in Central Asia. Enver Pasha introduced modern methods of military training to his Basmachi recruits and gave them the rallying slogan 'Turkestan for the natives.' However, on 4 August 1922, Enver Pasha was killed in action and after his death, the Basmachi movement started disintegrating. By 1923 the Red Army managed to clear the whole of Fergana and considerable parts of Eastern Bukhara from Basmachi activity. Though several Basmachi bands continued to operate in some parts of Central Asia until 1928, by 1924 Basmachism ceased to constitute any great danger to the Soviet regime in the Central Asian region. *Ibid.*, 133-7.

55. V. V. Bartol'd, *Istoriia kul'turnoi zhizni Turkestana* (Leningrad, 1927) 79, 96-7, 107.

violability of the personal and property rights existed in Bukhara. At any moment any citizen of Bukhara could be thrown into prison and his property confiscated by the mere will of the Amir. The administration was carried out by the Amir's officials who were not answerable to the people. Under such conditions, corruption and arbitrariness blossomed in full swing. The people from whom the Amir's officials exacted such heavy taxes had no right to know where the money went. The administration of the entire country was carried on as though it was the household economy of the Amir.[56]

Conditions in Khiva were very similar. Besides, the Khanate suffered from acute political instability caused by the intermittent feuds between its Uzbek and Turkmen subjects.[57] The Khans of Khiva in the past had managed to remain in power partly by seeking the assistance of the Russian army stationed in the Amu Daria Division, and largely by successfully playing off the two major national groups one against the other. Administrative reform was long overdue in Khiva, and the newly organized Party of the Young Khivans made this issue the most important plank in its programme.[58] Towards the beginning of 1918 when the Russian armed forces were recalled from Khiva, the eruption of national feuds on a major scale became imminent. The Turkmens, united under Dzhunaid Khan, almost immediately marched on Khiva, killed its ruler and began systematically pillaging the Uzbek towns and villages. Dzhunaid Khan set up a puppet regime headed by the uncle of the de-

56. Faizulla Khodzhaev, 'O mlado-Bukhartsakh,' *Istorik Marksist* (Moscow) 1 (1926) 123-4.

57. O. Karklin, 'Pod znamenem sssr,' *Turkestanskaia Pravda*, 148 (425), 6 July 1924.

58. The Party of Young Khivans began to be organized soon after the 1905 Revolution in Russia. In its earlier stages of formation, like the Djadidist movements of Turkestan and Bukhara, the Young Khivan Party was confined to educational and cultural activities, and grew under the patronage of the Khivan ruler's two closest counsellors: Islam Khodzhaev and Hussain Bek. The Persian revolution of 1906 and particularly, the Turkish revolution of 1908, gave it a great stimulus. The Party of Young Khivans was modelled on and accepted the platform of the Young Turks Party. After 1917 it became active and successfully agitated for the establishment of the *Mejilis* (parliament), which after a short time was disbanded by the Khan with the help of Russian Cossack soldiers. See A. M. Samoilovich, 'Pervoe tainoe obshchestvo mlado-Bukhartsev,' *Vostok* (Leningrad) 1 (1922) 98; also see page 61.

ceased ruler and became the virtual dictator of the Khivan Khanate.[59]

With the accession of the Turkmens to the privileged position in the Khanate, the Party of Young Khivans abandoned the advocacy of the introduction of administrative reforms and emerged as a militant Uzbek nationalist party. For successfully challenging the hegemony of the Turkmens, the Young Khivan Party threw open its rank even to the obscurantist elements of the Khanate's Uzbek population. The Young Khivans also planned to utilize the ever-present internal dissensions among the Turkmens in order to bring about the downfall of Dzhunaid Khan's regime. As a result of such a manoeuvre, finally, two Turkmen leaders, Kosh Mohmedkhan and Guliam-Ali, who had quarrelled with Dzhunaid Khan, were won over to the side of the Party of Young Khivans. In return for their support, the dissident Turkmen leaders secured an assurance from the Young Khivan Party about the grant of autonomy to the Turkmen areas of Khiva, the regularization of the disputes between the Uzbeks and Turkmens by way of an equitable distribution of water, and the establishment of a representative government in Khiva.[60] After an agreement was reached between the Young Khivan Party and the dissident Turkmen leaders, an appeal was made to Tashkent for Soviet aid. In response to this appeal, on 25 December 1919 Red Army units consisting in all about 800 men started marching on Khiva. This coincided with the outbreak of a series of revolts against Dzhunaid's regime in Kunia-Urgench, Khodzheili, Tashauz and other towns of Khiva. In January 1920 Dzhunaid Khan was driven out to the Kara-kum desert, and in the following month he was decisively defeated.[61]

Following the deposition of Said Abdulla, the last Khan, in February 1920, a Provisional Revolutionary Government was constituted in Khiva. Soon after, the provisional government issued a manifesto in which it stated that 'the revolutionaries of Khiva have destroyed for ever the despotic administration of the Khan and his government and declare the funds and pro-

59. G. Skalov, 'Khivinskaia revoliutsiia 1920 goda,' *Novyi vostok*, 3 (1923) 248.

60. *Ibid.*, 249-51.

61. M. Abdullaev, *Obrazovanie Khorezmskoi sovetskoi narodnoi respubliki i osnovnye etapy ee razvitiia (1920-1924): Avtoreferat* (Tashkent, 1950) 9-10.

perties of the Khan, princes, *beks* and ministers as national property which shall be used for improving the life of the poor.'[62] The manifesto also spoke about the establishment of a people's government in Khiva. The Provisional Government of Khiva was not constituted on a strict class basis and it included the representatives of all those who had participated in the fight against Dzhunaid Khan. The provisional government was headed by the Young Khivan leader, Sultan Muratov.[63]

In April 1920, when preparations began to be made for summoning the First All-Khorezmian *Kuraltai* (congress), the nucleus of a communist party was established in Khiva under the protective guidance of the representatives of the RSFSR.[64] The ranks of the Communist Party of Khiva soon began to swell following the mass entry of the former Young Khivans into it after they had 'voluntarily' liquidated their party. On 4 April 1920 a Council of *Nazirs* (ministers) was constituted which was largely composed of the former Young Khivan and Turkmen tribal leaders.

The First All-Khorezmian *Kuraltai* of Soviets met in Khiva between 27-30 April, and proclaimed the formation of the

62. 'From the manifesto of the Khivan Revolutionary Committee on the confiscation of the property and lands of the Khan and *beks* and improving the life of toilers,' 14 February 1920, document No. 372, in *Turkmeniia vperiod inostrannoi voennoi interventsii i grazhdanskoi voiny (1918-1920 gg)*: *sbornik dokumentov* (Ashkhabad, 1957) 396-7.

63. Skalov, n. 59, 254-5.

64. Immediately after the establishment of the Provisional Government in Khiva, the Government of the RSFSR nominated G. B. Skalov as its representative in Khiva. Some time later, a new Extraordinary Commission composed of the representatives of the Tashkent group of Young Khivans and a number of Bukharan Communists was created under the chairmanship of G. I. Broido. The Commission was charged with the task of establishing the Communist Party of Khorezm and a revolutionary government in Khiva. Alimdzhan Akchurin, a Tatar by origin, played an important role in the establishment of the communist party in Khorezm, and in May 1920, he was elected the head of its Central Committee. The Turkestan Commission took particular care to point out to its representatives in Khiva of the need to avoid the mistakes which were committed by the earlier Bolsheviks in Turkestan. On 17 May 1920 it wrote to them that 'in all our work in Khiva it is necessary to take the greatest amount of care and to see that it does not take the form of attempts to impose European culture by force.... All aspects of local life: customs, ethnic peculiarities, and even the religious beliefs of the people must be borne in mind.' See K. Mukhammedberdyev, *Kommunisticheskaia partiia v bor'be za pobedu narodnoi sovetskoi revoliutsii v Khorezme* (Ashkhabad, 1959) 151, 153, 155.

Khorezmian Soviet People's Republic. The *Kuraltai* approved
the constitution of the new Republic which was drafted by the
provisional government. It also constituted a seven-member
Council of People's *Nazirs* headed by the former Young Khivan
leader, Palvan Niaz Iusupov.[65] In June 1920, a delegation of the
Government of Khorezem was sent to Moscow, where it signed
with the Government of the RSFSR a mutual alliance treaty. By
this treaty the RSFSR recognized the full independence of the
Khorezmian Soviet People's Republic (Article 1) and abrogated
all previous treaties concluded between Tsarist Russia and the
Khanate of Khiva which had placed certain limitations on the
sovereignty of Khiva (Article 2). Besides, the Russian Republic
transferred the title of all movable and immovable properties
which belonged to it by virtue of its being the successor state
to the Tsarist Russian empire and also renounced all claims to
concessions which were formerly granted by the Khan of Khiva
to Russian citizens, industrial or commercial enterprises (Article 3). Both the parties to this treaty agreed not to allow their
territories to be made use of by any other governments, organizations, groups or persons having hostile motives or seeking to
carry out either direct or indirect warfare against either one
of them or against any other Soviet republic (Article 16). The
treaty also envisaged the establishment of a common plan, common direction and training of forces for defence purposes, and
also bound the two parties to conclude simultaneously a military-
political alliance treaty (Article 17). The Russian Republic
offered to supply to Khorezm instructors, literature, teachers,
printing presses (Article 18) and also a subsidy of 500,000,000
rubles (Article 19). The Khorezm Republic, for its part, agreed
not to grant any mining, transport, land or industrial concessions
to any other states except to Soviet states (Article 20).[66]

The events which took place in Khiva in the first half of 1920
were bound to have their repercussions on Bukhara. There the
resistance to the despotic rule of the Amir came mainly from
the Party of Young Bukharans.[67] This party was a political off-

65. 'Khorezmskaia sovetskaia narodnaia respublika,' *Zhizn' natsional'-
nostei* 1 (1923) 183. (Cited hereafter as KhNSR).
66. For the text of the treaty see *ISK*, n.45, 237-40.
67. The Party of Young Bukharans, in all essentials, was a party of
the petty bourgeoisie and urban middle class intellectuals. Neither among
the native *dekkhans* and landless agricultural workers who constituted the

shoot of the former Djadidist movement of Bukhara, and in the
early stages of its development, like the Djadidist movements of
all other Muslim regions of Russia, had interested itself mainly
in cultural revival activities and in attempts at modernizing the
educational system. By 1917, however, it had transformed itself
into a political party, and started agitating for the establishment
of a responsible government in Bukhara. Though by then it had
built up a network of party organizations throughout the main
cities of Bukhara and possessed a group of capable and talented
political workers, the Party of Young Bukharans lacked organizational unity. A section of the party led by Sadriddin Aini
and his group sought to restrict its activities only to the cultural
sphere. Another section, particularly its old members like Abdul
Vakhit Burkhanov, Mukhtidin Rafaat, Musa Seidzhanov and
Akhmedzhan Maksum opposed the adoption of any radical or
revolutionary policies by the party. Yet another section led by
the more militant young men like Fitrat, Usman Khodzhaev
and Faizulla Khodzhaev advocated the organization of an armed
attack on the Amir's government for achieving the objectives
of the party.[68] These differences which characterized the thinking of the various segments of the Young Bukharan Party tended
to increase with the deepening of the political crisis in Bukhara.
Following the proclamation on 17 March 1917 of a manifesto
on reforms by the Amir and his subsequent attempt to disband
the Young Bukharan Party by force, these differences increased
and in fact, led to an open breach between the moderates and

bulk of the population of Bukhara nor among the economically powerful
and socially influential landlords, *beks* and the clergy did the Party of
Young Bukharans have any following. Agrarian unrest was rife in
Bukhara because nearly eightyfive per cent of the land was concentrated
in the hands of the Amir and a small group of land owners but the
Young Bukharans were not radical enough to propose large-scale agrarian
reforms and thereby gain the support of the discontented peasantry. See
D. Soloveichik, 'Revoliutsionnaia Bukhara,' *Novyi vostok*, 2 (1922) 273;
also see Khodzhaev, n. 56, 125-8.

68. Khodzhaev, n. 56, 129, 134-5. It is interesting to note that there
was a strong undercurrent of pan-Islamic, pan-Turkic and anti-Russian
bias in the thinking of several Young Bukharans. Some of them took
cudgels against the Amir's despotic and feudal regime and against the
obscurantism of the Bukharan clergy because they thought that these two
elements were responsible for subjecting the Muslim culture and civilization of Central Asia to the domination of the Europeans. In Turkestan
too there were many Djadidists who thought similarly.

the radicals. From then onwards, radical rather than moderate programmes became popular in Young Bukharan circles and control over the party passed into the hands of its more militant members.[69]

After the events of March 1917, the Young Bukharans were no longer able to carry on their political agitation openly in Bukhara. Therefore many of them moved into Kagan, the headquarter of the former Russian Resident in Bukhara where Russia enjoyed extra-territorial rights, and from there began to organize the party activities. On 6 December 1917 the Young Bukharan Party sent a delegation consisting of Faizulla Khodzhaev and Preobrazhenskii to Tashkent to solicit Soviet aid for organizing an armed attack against the Amir's regime in Bukhara.[70] The armed attack which Kolesov launched on the Amirate in response to the appeal made by the Young Bukharan Party not only failed but provoked Amir Said Alim Khan to resort to severe reprisals against the Young Bukharan Party. As a result, nearly 1,500 members and sympathizers of the Young Bukharan Party were killed and the party was left badly maimed. Following this, the surviving members of the party abandoned Bukhara altogether and took up residence in Tashkent and Samarkand.

During this period yet another rift developed among the Young Bukharan émigrés in Turkestan. They split into 'the Young Bukharan Revolutionaries' and 'the Young Bukharan Communists.'[71] The latter organized their party on the initiative of Mukhtar Saidzhanov, Iakub Zade, Azimdzhan Khusainov, Aminov and Akchurin. The Young Bukharan Revolutionaries established their 'Central Turkestan Bureau' in Tashkent and published in its name the programme of their faction which was drafted by Fitrat.[72]

69. Faizulla Khodzhaev, *K istorii revoliutsii v Bukhare* (Tashkent, 1926) 32.

70. Even at this stage, the Party of Young Bukharans were against deposing the Amir from his throne. Instead, they sought to retain him as a sort of constitutional head of the Bukharan state with all real authority vested in the government which they hoped to form. *Ibid.*, 46.

71. Dervish, 'Bukharskaia sovetskaia narodnaia respublika', *Zhizn' natsional'nostei*, 1 (1937) 197.

72. Curiously enough, this programme in comparison with the earlier programme of the party was not revolutionary at all. It sought to retain the Amir as the head of the Bukharan state and repeated the earlier

Relations between the Young Bukharan Revolutionaries and the Young Bukharan Communists were invariably strained and the attempts made by the Turkestan communists to bring about a reconciliation between them did not meet with any great success. The Turkestan Commission sought to reconcile the two factions with a view to speed up the revolution in Bukhara. But the communist faction of the Young Bukharans openly accused the Party of the Young Bukharan Revolutionaries as a 'clerical-national, pan-Islamic and anti-Soviet organization with leanings towards Afghanistan.'[73] But towards August 1920, the Young Bukharan Revolutionaries themselves began to veer more and more towards communism although they still opposed the immediate merger of their group with the Bukharan Communist Party. The Turkestan Bureau of the Young Bukharan Revolutionaries proposed a merger of the two factions soon after a successful revolution in Bukhara.[74] But the Bukharan Communists did not give up their demand for the immediate disbandment of the Party of the Young Bukharan Revolutionaries and the inclusion of its members within the Young Bukharan Communist Party. To resolve the deadlock between the two factions

Djadidist demands for regularizing and modernizing the administration and raising the cultural level of the Bukharan people. It did not even seek to abolish the *wakf* lands but declared that it was a valuable institution and proposed reform only regarding the method of utilizing the funds accruing from the *wakf* lands. Minor reforms were suggested in the method of managing the state's finances and in the realm of provincial administration. A suggestion was made in this programme to invite specialists and experts from among the Muslims of Russia, Azerbaidzhan and Turkey. A brief resume of this programme is available in Khodzhaev, n. 69, 35-9.

73. *IUzSSR*, n. 31, 74. The Turkestan Commission sought to utilize the Party of Young Bukharan Revolutionaries only for the sake of fighting the Amir. It did not desire that the Bukharan Communists should collaborate with it after the Amir was overthrown. On 30 June 1920 the Commission issued a circular which stated that 'only Communists and their sympathizers must be associated in establishing the central and provincial organs of government in Bukhara and all coalitions (with others) must be avoided.' *Ibid.*, 175.

74. The Turkestan Bureau of the Young Bukharan Revolutionaries was aware that though the leaders of the party were increasingly leaning towards communism, its rank and file as well as the bulk of the sympathizers of the party were opposed to communism. In order not to alienate these people from the party, the Turkestan Bureau of the Young Bukharan Revolutionaries opposed the immediate merger with the Communist Party of Bukhara. See Khodzhaev, n. 69, 72-3.

of the Young Bukharans, the Turkestan Bureau of the Russian Communist Party suggested that both of them should collaborate to bring about the speediest downfall of the Amir's regime in Bukhara on the basis of a working formula. Though this formula suggested by the Turkestan Bureau was more on the lines of the proposal earlier put forward by the Young Bukharan Revolutionaries, the Bukharan Communists were forced to accept it.

In the meantime, discontent against the Amir's rule in Bukhara was on the increase. The general unrest in Bukhara was further augmented by the propaganda of the Young Bukharan Revolutionaries and the Bukharan Communists. The peasants in several parts of Bukhara refused to pay taxes and attempts to collect them forcibly often resulted in the massacre of the Amir's officials. Discontent was also rife in the army, and there were many instances of the Amir's soldiers deserting and joining hands with Young Bukharan rebels. Against the background of such an explosive situation, the Bukharan Communists in the latter half of August 1920 held their fourth congress in Chardzhui. Incited by the Bukharan Communists, the warlike Turkmen population of Chardzhui rose in rebellion against the Amir's rule on 25 August. The Chardzhui rebellion signalled the eruption of similar revolts in other parts of Bukhara and following this, the Young Bukharan Revolutionaries sent a formal appeal to the RSFSR and the Red Army for help.[75]

General M. V. Frunze, who commanded the local Red Army units, anticipated the events in Bukhara well in advance. On 12 August 1920 he issued a directive to his troops to take up positions near Chardzhui, Kagan, Katta-kurgan, Kushka, Takhta-Bazar and alerted the Amu Daria flotilla on the ground that 'in the nearest future, an open rebellion of the Bukharan people against the Amir's government is awaited' and instructed his troops to be in combat readiness.[76] His directive of 25 August 1920 declared that 'the peoples of Bukhara who have been oppressed for centuries by the Amir, the greedy officials and the wealthy strata, have revolted against their enslavers and have hoisted the banner of freedom.' In order to render 'fraternal revolutionary aid to the peoples of Bukhara,' Frunze ordered

75. *Ibid.*, 75-6.
76. 'Direktiva voiskam Turkestanskogo fronta,' no. 3504, 12 August 1920 in M. V. Frunze, *Izbrannye proizvedeniia* (Moscow, 1957) I, 335-9.

his troops to march into Bukhara on the morning of 29 August 1920.[77] Soon after the outbreak of hostilities, one town after another began falling into the hands of the Red Army and its Young Bukharan collaborators. But the battle for the city of Bukhara was keen and bloody and the Red Army suffered heavy losses.[78] Finally, however, on 2 September 1920, the city of Bukhara was taken, and in a telegram sent to Lenin, Frunze declared, 'the fortress of old Bukhara was taken today by the Red Bukharan and our forces. The last pillar of Bukharan obscurantism.... has fallen. The Red banner of world revolution is flying triumphantly over the Registan.'[79]

Shortly before the fall of Bukhara the Amir fled from his capital, and his government collapsed. Following this a Revolutionary Committee and a Council of People's *Nazirs* were constituted. Abdusaidov was nominated the head of the Revolutionary Committee and Faizulla Khodzhaev.became the Chairman of the Council of People's *Nazirs*. In both the organs of the new government, the Young Bukharan Revolutionaries held a predominant position.[80] On 11 September 1920 the Party of Young Bukharan Revolutionaries dissolved itself and its members joined the Bukharan Communist Party *en masse*. As a result, the membership of the latter rose to 14,000.[81]

Following the success of the revolution in Bukhara, the Government of the RSFSR nominated V. V. Kuibyshev, who was until then the chairman of the Turkestan Commission, as its plenipotentiary in Bukhara. Kuibyshev was nominated also the representative of the Central Committee of the Russian Communist Party and of the Third Communist International in Bukhara and he was charged by them to help the Bukharan Communist Party in consolidating the gains of the revolution in Bukhara. In discharging these dual functions, Kuibyshev in effect, played

77. 'Direktiva voiskam Turkestanskogo fronta,' no. 3667, 25 August 1920. *Ibid.*, 339-41.

78. In a telegram despatched to V. V. Kuibyshev, General Frunze stated that the Red Army lost more than five hundred soldiers in the battle for Bukhara and he attributed it to 'unwise commanding and the absence of proper management.' See 'Telegrama v shtab Turkfronta Tov. Kuibyshevu, *ibid.*, 343.

79. 'Telegrama v revvoensovet respubliki glavkomu, Tov. Leninu, redaktsiiam *Izvestiia* i *Pravda*,' no. 00274/psh, 2 September 1920, see *ibid.*, 344.

80. See Khodzhaev, n. 69, 76.

81. See *IUzSSR*, n. 31, 187.

a contradictory role. On the one hand, as the representative of the RSFSR, he assured the new Bukharan government that his state respected the complete independence of Bukhara and on the other hand, as the representative of the Russian Communist Party and the Communist International, he exhorted the party and Government of Bukhara to hasten Bukhara's socialist transformation.[82]

Bukhara was proclaimed a People's Soviet Republic in October 1920 by the First All-Bukharan *Kuraltai* of People's Representatives, which began its session on 6 October 1920 in the Summer Palace of the Amir. The *Kuraltai* designated itself as the supreme legislative organ of the republic, and when it was not in session its functions were delegated to the Revolutionary Committee. The Council of People's *Nazirs* was nominated as the highest executive organ of the republic. Before winding up its session, the *Kuraltai* approved the decision of the Revolutionary Committee to despatch a high-power delegation to Moscow for the purpose of concluding a treaty of friendship and mutual aid with the RSFSR.[83] On 4 March 1921 this delegation concluded a 'Treaty of Union' with the RSFSR on more or less the same lines as the one earlier concluded between Khorezm and the RSFSR.[84]

V. CONSOLIDATION OF SOVIET REGIME IN CENTRAL ASIA

The establishment of the soviet form of government in Bukhara and Khorezm in 1920, the merging of the Young Bukharan and the Young Khivan parties within the communist parties of these republics and the conclusion of mutual alliance and military-political agreements with them by the RSFSR marked the beginning of the extension of Soviet influence on these two

82. A. A. Gordienko, *Sozdanie narodno-sovetskogo gosudarstva i prava i ikh revoliutsionno-preobrazuiushchaia rol'v Khorezme i Bukhare* (Tashkent, 1959), 41-2, 53.

83. Before this delegation left for Moscow, Kuibyshev on 3 November 1920 concluded on behalf of the RSFSR a 'Military-political Agreement' and 'a Provisional Agreement on the Former Russian Settlements in Bukhara' with the Revolutionary Committee. *Izvestiia TurkTsIK*, 1 December 1920, cited in *IUzSSR*, n. 31, 183-4.

84. For the text of the treaty between Bukhara and the RSFSR see *ISK*, n. 45, 271-4.

extremely backward regions. However, in view of the fact that these two republics came within the orbit of Soviet influence relatively late, and also because of the semi-feudal conditions which prevailed in them; their immediate socalist transformation was difficult to achieve. Though they were firmly set on the path of socialism yet, in 1920, Bukhara and Khorezm represented two 'bourgeois democratic' republics within the constellation of Soviet socialist republics which surrounded the RSFSR. A glance at the constitutions of these two republics clearly indicates their non-socialist character.[85]

The constitutions of Bukhara and Khorezm contained a whole series of deflections from the socialist principles which were enshrined in the constitutions of the RSFSR and other Soviet republics. They made no reference whatsoever either to the 'Rights of the Toiling and Oppressed Peoples' or to the dictatorship of the proletariat which were embodied in all Soviet constitutions of the time. On the contrary, they conferred rights on all the peoples inhabiting their territories irrespective of their class affiliations.[86] Perhaps the most striking departure from Soviet constitutional practice was made by Bukhara in declaring in Article 26 of its constitution that 'no published laws of the republic may contradict the foundations of Islam.'[87] The recognition accorded by the constitutions of Bukhara and Khorezm to the institution of private property and to the law of inheritance was no less significant. Further, the constitution of Bukhara bestowed upon its citizens freedom of conscience (Article 7), speech, press and assembly, and the inviolability of person (Article 8) and of home (Article 9). Article 10 of this constitution sought to defend the citizens of Bukhara against arbitrary action by the government. Article 58 conferred on all citizens of Bukhara of both sexes who had

---

85. The constitution of Bukhara was adopted by the second All-Bukharan Congress of Soviets of People's Deputies in September, 1921 and he constitution of Khorezm was approved by the first All-Khorezmian Kuraltai held in April 1920. The constitution of Bukhara is partly reprinted in ISK, *ibid.*, 369-71.

86. Article six of the constitution of Bukhara.

87. K. Arkhipov, 'Bukharaskaia narodnaia respublika: obzor konstitutsii', *Sovetskoe pravo*, 1 (1923) 136-7; also see Dervish, n. 71, 197-8; *KhSNR*, n. 65, 193-4.

attained the age of eighteen the right to vote for their deputies.[88]
Though the constitution of Bukhara envisaged the establishment
of the same pattern of government in Bukhara as existed at that
time in the RSFSR and other Soviet republics, and more or less
the same method of election of the deputies to the all-Bukharan
Congress of Soviets, yet, unlike the Soviet practices elsewhere,
it conferred far greater powers on the Congress of Soviets of
Bukhara and the Bukharan Central Executive Committee. The
Council of People's *Nazirs,* on the other hand, was reduced to
an organ of secondary importance.[89]

The relations which subsisted between the RSFSR and the two
Central Asian people's republics between 1920-24 also displayed
certain other interesting features. Though the 'full independence' of these two republics was recognized by the RSFSR in the
initial treaties it concluded with them, its later practices, however, tended to compromise the sovereignty of Bukhara and
Khorezm. The military-political agreements concluded by the
RSFSR with these two republics enabled the former to secure control over the armed forces and the military organizations located
in Bukhara and Khorezm. The right of independent action of
the two Central Asian republics in the economic sphere was also
considerably curtailed by two other agreements concluded between the RSFSR and Bukhara on 4 March 1921 and between
the RSFSR and Khorezm on 13 September 1920. These agreements,
which sought to regulate the economic and financial policies
among their signatories, placed Bukhara and Khorezm under
the obligation to seek the previous consent of the RSFSR before
granting trade concessions to any other foreign states and to
carry on trade with the RSFSR on a commodity-exchange basis.[90]
In addition, the RSFSR formed a single customs union with

88. The following article, however, deprived the big landlords, capitalists
and all the former state officials of their right to vote. Similar provisions
existed in almost all the Soviet constitutions of the time. See Arkhipov,
ibid., 135.

89. *Ibid.,* 135-6. It is also interesting to note that the constitution of
Bukhara did not entirely do away with the traditional administrative
institutions. For instance, it retained the institution of the *aksakal* at the
lowest rung of the administration, however, it rendered the office of the
aksakal an elective post. *Ibid.,* 137.

90. I. I. Kryl'tsov, 'Gosudarstvennoe razmezhevanie Sredne-Aziatskikh
respublik', (publichno-pravovye predposylki i posledstviia razmezhevaniia),
Vestnik iustitsii Uzbekistana (Tashkent) 1 (1925), 18-21.

Bukhara and Khorezm by securing the abolition of all internal customs barriers among the three republics. On 20 May 1921 the RSFSR concluded with Khorezm an agreement 'on the administration of post, telegraph, telephone and radio,' and on 21 September 1921 it concluded another agreement 'on the distribution of the ships of the Amu Daria flotilla' with Bukhara and Khorezm. The latter agreement was replaced on 30 April 1923 by a fresh treaty which placed the management of the Amu Daria flotilla in the hands of the Commissariat of Naval Communications of the RSFSR.[91] The culmination of the process of orientating Bukhara and Khorezm towards the other Soviet republics, and especially towards the Turkestan ASSR, occurred in 1923 when the Central Asiatic Economic Council was established.

The question of securing the economic unification of Turkestan, Bukhara and Khorezm was put forward by the Central Committee of the Russian Communist Party. On its instruction, the Turkestan Bureau as early as 9 March 1922 had examined the feasibility of this proposal. In a conference held on that date the Turkestan Bureau recognized the homogeneity of interests of the three Central Asian republics in the spheres of agriculture, finance, irrigation, transport, internal and external trade.[92] On 23 January 1923, the Central Asian Bureau of the Central Committee of the Russian Communist Party[93] decided to summon a conference of the representatives of the governments of Turkestan, Bukhara and Khorezm republics to secure the implementation of the directive of the Central Committee on the question of bringing about the economic unification of these republics. On 5 March 1923, this conference met in Tashkent and decided to set up the Central Asian Economic Council.

on the contrary

91. *Ibid.*, 21.

92. A. I. Ishanov, 'Bukharskaia narodnaia sovetskaia respublika', *Uchenye zapiski Tashkentskogo iuridicheskogo instituta* (Tashkent, 1955) I, 49.

93. On 2 February 1922 the Politbureau of the Central Committee of the Russian Communist Party took a decision in favour of merging the communist parties of Bukhara and Khorezm with the Russian Communist Party. In order to coordinate and supervise the work of the communist parties of Turkestan, Bukhara and Khorezm, the Central Committee of the Russian Communist Party on 18 May 1922 reorganized the Turkestan Bureau into the 'Central Asian Bureau of the Central Committee of the Russian Communist Party.' Following this, the Turkestan Commission was abolished. See A. A. Gordienko, *Sozdanie sovetskoi natsional'noi gosudarstvennosti v Srednei Azii* (Moscow, 1959) 125; also see *IUzSSR*, n. 31, 211.

The conference elected its presidium, consisting of nine members.[94] The legal position and the functions of the Central Asian Economic Council were precisely defined in a statute issued after the Second Economic Conference of these republics in April 1924.[95]

The statute designated the Central Asian Economic Council as a permanent executive organ entrusted with the task of regulating, supervising and coordinating, on the basis of a single unified plan, the policies of the Central Asian republics on all economic issues such as industrial, commercial, financial, agricultural, etc., which had significance for the entire Central Asian region or the USSR.[96] The Central Asian Economic Council was to be periodically elected by the conference of the representatives of the governments of the Central Asian republics and the USSR. Its directives were made binding on all the economic coun-

94. Of the nine members of the Presidium of the Central Asian Economic Council, one belonged to the RSFSR, four to the Turkestan ASSR, two to Bukhara and two to Khòrezm. See G. Skalov, 'Ekonomicheskoe ob'edinenie Sredne aziatskikh respublik kak faktor natsional'noi politiki,' *Zhizn'natsional'nostei,* 5 (1923) 42.

95. Following the establishment of the Central Asian Economic Council, separate economic councils were established within each of the three local republics and they were charged with the function of coordinating the work of the commissariats of finance, agriculture and trade as well as of the transport, fuel and statistical divisions. See Gordienko, n. 82, 138.

96. The proposal to effect the union of the then existing Soviet republics in a Union of Soviet Socialist Republics was taken up in the XI Congress of the Russian Communist Party held in March 1922. Subsequently, the Central Committee of the Russian Communist Party created a commission under the chairmanship of Stalin to work out concrete proposals for establishing such a union. In September 1922, this commission put forward a proposal known as 'autonomization' which envisaged the entrance of the Soviet Republics of Ukraine, Byelorussia and the republics of the Transcaucasian Federation (Georgia, Armenia and Azerbaidzhan) into the RSFSR as its autonomous parts. This proposal, however, was strongly criticized by Lenin in a letter addressed to the members of the Politbureau on 27 September 1922. Lenin proposed instead, the formation of a new Union of Soviet Socialist Republics on the basis of equality and voluntary entry of all its members including the RSFSR. On the basis of this suggestion made by Lenin, the commission of the Central Committee worked out a scheme which was subsequently approved by the plenary session of the Central Committee of the Russian Communist Party. Finally, the First All-Union Congress of Soviets adopted the historic decision on the formation of the Union of Soviet Socialist Republics on 30 December 1922. While the Turkestan ASSR as an autonomous unit of the RSFSR became a part of the USSR, Bukhara and Khorezm remained outside it. Speaking before the Tenth All-Russian Congress of Soviets on

cils located within the Turkestan ASSR, the republics of Bukhara and Khorezm.[97]

The establishment of the Central Asian Economic Council, though it facilitated the speedier economic reconstruction of Central Asia tended, to a considerable extent, to restrict the freedom of action of the governments of the Central Asian republics in the economic sphere. It was not always easy to precisely determine which of the many problems that beset each of these republics had a significance only to the republic concerned or to Central Asia as a whole. In practice, however, the Central Asian Economic Council tended to extend the sphere of its activities by concerning itself with many problems which really had no significance of wider dimensions.[98] The reduction of freedom of action of the governments of the Central Asian republics which resulted from such a practice was strongly resented by many. In particular, the former Young Bukharan and Young Khivan leaders who headed the governments in Bukhara and Khorezm, and whose conversion to the communist ideology was by no means complete, strongly resented what they termed 'the attempts to destroy the individuality of Bukhara and Khorezm' and the undermining of their sovereignty. In a vain bid to stop the establishment of the Central Asian Economic Council, the Bukharan Communists argued that Bukhara constituted a distinct economic unit by itself and as such, there was no need to tag it on to the other two Central Asian republics.[99] But this objection, like their earlier objection to the merger of the Bukharan Communist Party with the Russian Communist Party,

26 December 1922, Stalin stated that Bukhara and Khorezm were not admitted into the USSR 'for the sole and exclusive reason that these republics are not socialist.' For the relevant documents on the formation of the USSR see *ISK*, n.45, 389-403; also see J. V. Stalin, *Marxism and the National and the Colonial Question* (London, n.d.) 124.

97. Gordienko, n. 82, 139.

98. The Central Asian Economic Council suggested to the governments of Bukhara and Khorezm to undertake a series of reforms in land, tax structure, system of agricultural credits, private trading etc., in order to hasten the transition to a socialist economy. In particular, it concerned itself with resolving the national frictions which plagued both Bukhara and Khorezm. It suggested to these governments to eradicate the economic inequality which prevailed among the Uzbek, Turkmen and Kazakh populations, which, in the Council's opinion, was the main cause for the national frictions. See Ishanov, n. 92, 50; Skalov, n. 94, 42-5.

99. Ishanov, n. 92, 49.

was overruled. The reluctance of the Communists of Bukhara and Khorezm to fall in line with the policies framed by the Central Asian Bureau led to their expulsion from the communist parties of their states. On the plea that many merchants and speculators, by infiltrating into the communist parties of Bukhara and Khorezm were trying to hinder the sovietization of these two republics, the Central Asian Bureau began an extensive purge campaign. In Bukhara the purge campaign commenced in 1922 when the membership of its communist party touched the record figure of 16,000 persons. By the end of that year, nearly 15,000 Bukharan Communists lost their membership cards.[100] In Khorezm, it was alleged that nearly fifty per cent of the members of the communist party hailed from among traders and speculators. The purges were started there in 1923 and when completed, only a few hundred of the several thousand members of the communist party remained within its ranks.[101]

In the meantime, the policies of the governments of Bukhara and Khorezm also came in for severe criticism at the hands of the People's Commissar for Nationality Affairs, Stalin. In the Fourth Conference of the Central Committee with the Responsible Workers of the National Republics and Regions held on 10 June 1923, Stalin vehemently criticized the composition of the Bukharan Council of *Nazirs* and the manner in which the funds of the State Bank of Bukhara and the cattle seized from the Amir were allocated.[102] He declared that the policies pursued

100. A considerable number of the Bukharan Communists who were former Young Bukharan revolutionaries voluntarily left the party after it became clear to them that the so-called independence of Bukhara was a mere fiction. Several of them went over to the side of Enver Pasha who, by then, had placed himself at the head of the Basmachi movement. Prominent among them was Usman Khodzhaev, a noted Young Bukharan revolutionary who had been at first the *Nazir* for Finance and then the Chairman of the Bukharan Central Executive Committee. In Khorezm, the first government headed by the Young Khivan leader, Palvan Niaz Iusupov, was averse to implementing socialist reforms. In March 1921, a Soviet-inspired insurrection brought about the downfall of the Iusupov government. The government subsequently installed in Khorezm was more responsive to the demands of the Central Asian Bureau. See Khodzhaev, n. 69, 15; N. Chekalin, 'Sobytiia v Khorezmskoi respublike,' *Voennaia mysl* (Moscow) 1 (1921) 228-9; Abdullaev, n. 61, 11-2.

101. Rudolf Schlesinger, *The Nationalities Problem and the Soviet Administration* (London, 1956) 71-2.

102. Stalin stated that in Bukhara, which was exclusively a peasant country, there was not even a single peasant in the Bukharan Council of

by the Government of Bukhara were neither socialist nor popular, and unless they were radically revised immediately, the Republic of Bukhara could not be admitted into the USSR. The same applied to Khorezm as well.

The refusal to admit Bukhara and Khorezm into the USSR and Stalin's criticism of the policies of their governments, soon led to the introduction of large-scale reforms in these republics. In October 1923, only four months after the Moscow Conference of the Responsible Workers, the Fourth All-Khorezmian *Kuraltai* of Soviets met in Khiva and decreed the immediate rectification of all anomalies and inadequacies which hindered the complete transformation of Khorezm into a socialist republic. Before the end of its session, the *Kuraltai* formally renamed Khorezm 'the Khorezmian Soviet Socialist Republic.'[103]

Bukhara was proclaimed a socialist republic considerably later, although the orientation of its policies in that direction began towards the end of the 1923 itself. On 19 September 1924, the Fifth All-Bukharan *Kuraltai* of Soviets formally reorganized Bukhara into a Soviet socialist republic. The resolution of the *Kuraltai* which proposed this reorganization also spoke about the establishment of the 'dictatorship of the proletariat (of the toiling and exploited mass of workers and poor peasants) in Bukhara.'[104]

Nazirs, and that the latter was dominated by traders, intellectuals and *mullahs*. The nature of the composition of the ministry largely determined also the nature of the policies of the Bukharan government. Stalin alleged that 75 per cent of the credits advanced by the State Bank of Bukhara was to private traders (about 7 million gold rubles) and only two per cent (less than a quarter million gold rubles) to the peasant cooperatives. Besides, out of the 2,000 head of cattle confiscated from the Amir, only 200 head of cattle were given to the peasants and the remainder had gone into the hands of well-to-do people. See V. G. Granberg, 'Obrazovanie Tadzhikskoi avtonomnoi sovetskoi sotsialisticheskoi respubliki,' *Trudy iuridicheskogo fakul'teta Tadzhikskii gosudarstvennyi universitet* (Stalinabad, 1955) 26; also see G. Rizaev, *Sel'skoe khoziaistvo Uzbekistana za 40 let* (Tashkent, 1957) 46; Schlesinger, n.-101, 73.

103. *Turkestanskaia Pravda*, 60 (337) 14 March 1924.

104. The full text of this resolution is available in *ISK*, n. 45, 484-5. On 17 October 1924 a Bukharan government delegation headed by the Chairman of the Bukharan Central Executive Committee, Parsa Khodzhaev, arrived in Moscow and reported to M. Kalinin, the Chairman of the VTsIK on the work of the Fifth All-Bukharan *Kuraltai* on transforming Bukhara into a Socialist Republic. See *Turkestanskaia Pravda*, 234 (511) 20 October 1924.

By 1924, all the internal and external dangers which threatened the safety and stability of the Soviet regimes in Turkestan, Bukhara and Khorezm had been removed, and the adoption of socialist policies by these republics was fully ensured. In the process of achieving this, both the Government of the RSFSR and the Central Committee of the Russian Communist Party had established and strengthened multiple links with the Central Asian republics. Though centralization had become the dominant trend in all policies pursued in the Central Asian republics, care was taken, nevertheless, to ensure that those policies in the region were implemented by the natives themselves. Besides, the establishment of the Central Asian Bureau and the Central Asian Economic Council as guiding and supervisory organs further ensured that the policies laid down in Moscow were fully and faithfully implemented in Central Asia.

After the Tenth Congress of the Russian Communist Party held in March 1921, the speediest eradication of the economic, political and cultural backwardness of the peoples of Central Asia, the removal of the national frictions among them, and assisting the Central Asian republics to catch up with the more advanced central regions of Russia, became the main goals of the Soviet nationalities policy.[105] In order to achieve these objectives, the Russian Communist Party was charged by the Tenth Party Congress to undertake the following measures:

1. the development and consolidation of the Soviet state system in forms consistent with the national character of these peoples;
2. the organization of their own courts, administrative bodies, economic organs and government organs functioning in the native language and recruited from among the local people acquainted with the customs and psychology of the local poulation, and

105. Stalin in his 'Report on the immediate tasks of the party in connection with the national question' which was approved by the x Party Congress, stated that 'although under the Soviet regime in Russia and in the republics associated with Russia we no longer have ruling nationalities or subject nationalities, mother country or colonies, exploited or exploiters, nevertheless the national problem still exists in Russia. The crux of the national problem in the RSFSR lies in the obligation to put an end to that backwardness (economic, political and cultural) of the nationalities which we have inherited from the past and to afford the backward peoples the opportunity of catching up with central Russia politically, culturally and economically.' See Stalin, n. 96, 103.

3. the development of a press, schools, theatres, clubs and cultural and educational institutions generally, functioning in the native language.[106]

In an article written in *Pravda* on 8 May 1921, the People's Commissar for Nationality Affairs, Stalin, declared that national equality, although in itself an important political acquisition, ran the risk of remaining merely an empty phrase if adequate resources and opportunities for exercising it did not exist. He pointed out that many backward nationalities of Russia, including those which inhabited the Central Asian region, in view of their cultural and economic backwardness were unable to make adequate use of the rights granted to them. 'We cannot remain content ourselves with national equality,' wrote Stalin, 'and that national equality must be extended by means of measures for securing the real equality of nationalities.'[107] The Twelfth Congress of the Russian Communist Party also recognized that 'the equality of legal status of nations in itself does not solve the whole national problem.' The resolution on the national question approved by this congress stated that the backward nationalities of Russia, including those of Central Asia, would be unable to achieve a higher level of development and catch up with the more advanced nationalities unless they received real and prolonged assistance from outside.[108] In his report to the Congress on 'national factors in party and state,' Stalin stated:

> We have proclaimed equality of legal status and are practising it; but equality of legal status... is still a long way from true equality. Formally all the backward nationalities and all the tribes enjoyed all the rights enjoyed by the other, more advanced nationalities of our federation. But the trouble is that some nationalities... have never passed through the stage of industrial development, or even entered that stage, are frightfully backward culturally and are entirely unable to

---

106. *Kommunisticheskaia partiia sovetskogo soiuza v rezoliutsiiakh i resheniiakh s'ezdov, konferentsii i plenumov Tsk* (Moscow, 1953) I, 559. (Cited hereafter as *KPSS*).

107. Stalin, n. 96, 115. In order to achieve this objective, Stalin recommended that the Party should undertake (1) the study of the economic conditions, social life and culture of the backward nations and peoples; (2) the development of their culture; (3) their political education; (4) their gradual and painless incorporation into the higher forms of economic life and (5) the organization of economic cooperation between the toilers of the backward and advanced nationalities. *Ibid.*, 115-6.

108. *KPSS*, n. 106, 713-4.

take advantage of the rights granted to them by the revolution. This is a question of greater importance than the question of schools.... The schools will not get you far. The
schools are developing, so are the languages; but actual inequality is the basis of all discord and friction... the Russian
proletariat must take all necessary measures to establish centres of industry in the border regions (which) were formerly
looked upon as sources of raw materials. Certain attempts
have already been made in this direction. Bukhara has taken
one factory, and might have taken four. Turkestan is taking
one large factory. Thus the conditions now exist enabling
these republics, which are backward economically to establish
with the aid of the Russian proletariat their own centres of
industry.... [109]

The Twelfth Party Congress endorsed Stalin's view that the
immediate eradiction of national inequality to a considerable
extent was rendered difficult by certain other factors. These consisted, on the one hand, of 'the arrogant, negligent and soullessly
bureaucratic attitude on the part of the Russian officials towards
the needs and the requirements of the national republics' and
on the other, of the existence of national squabbles and wrang-
lings in regions which were inhabited by more than one nationality. In Turkestan, Bukhara and Khorezm, it was alleged that
Uzbek nationalism had turned 'into aggressive nationalism, into
outright chauvinism... directed against... the Turkmens and
Kirgiz (Kazakhs).'[110] The Congress condemned both these deviations as 'harmful and dangerous to the cause of communism'
and called upon the members of the party to combat them.[111]
The Congress also suggested the adoption by the Party of a
number of practical measures for drawing the indigenous populations of the borderland regions into the process of building
up the party and Soviets, for raising the cultural level and economic standards of these peoples, and for creating centres of
industry in the borderland areas, etc.

On the basis of these suggestions, the Central Committee of
the Russian Communist Party worked out a number of concrete
proposals for implementation in the borderland regions like

109. 'Natsional'nye momenty v partinnom i gosudarstvennom stroitel'-
stve' (Doklad I. Stalina na zasedanii XII s'ezda R.K.P. (B), 23 Aprelia
1923 g), see *Zhizn' natsional'nostei*, 3-4 (1923) 16.

110. *KPSS*, n. 106, 715.

111. *Ibid.*, 718.

Central Asia. Responsible party and government officials from Turkestan, Bukhara, Khorezm and other borderland regions were summoned to Moscow in June 1923, for reviewing the progress made in the economic and cultural spheres after the Tenth Party Congress and for implementing the recommendations of the Twelfth Party Congress. After acquainting himself with the report made by the delegates from Turkestan, Stalin declared:

> ... we have to admit that the present position in Turkestan is the most unfavourable and alarming one. The picture is one of cultural backwardness, a devastatingly low percentage of literacy, isolation of the state apparatus from the language and life of the peoples of Turkestan, a devastatingly slow rate of development... Turkestan as it is now is the weakest point of the Soviet regime. The task is to transform Turkestan into a model Republic, into the outpost of revolution in the East.... We have to solve this task, cost what it may, without sparing our strength or shirking sacrifices.[112]

In order to overcome the cultural and economic backwardness of the borderland regions, the Central Committee called upon the Communists of those regions to implement the following measures immediately. In the cultural sphere they were asked, (a) 'to organize (non-party) clubs and other educational institutions for popular enlightenment in the local language;' (b) 'to extend the network of educational establishments of all grades in the local languages;' (c) 'to draw in the more or less loyal national teachers;' (d) 'to establish a network of societies spreading literacy in the local languages;' and (e) 'to organize the publishing business.' In the economic sphere they were asked, (a) 'to regulate and, where required, to stop migration;' (b) 'to provide the local working population with land out of the state land fund;' (c) 'to grant the local population agricultural credit on easy terms;' (d) 'to intensify irrigation work;' (e) 'to move factories and plants to republics which are rich in raw materials;' (f) 'to set up trade and technical schools;' (g) 'to arrange courses on agriculture' and finally, (h) 'to assist in every way the cooperative movement and, in particular, the producers' cooperatives (in order to attract handicraftsmen).'[113]

Though greater emphasis began to be laid on the rapid in-

---

112. See Schlesinger, n. 101, 70-1.
113. *Ibid.*, 66.

dustrialization of the Central Asian region, the immediate task
of the governments of Turkestan, Bukhara and Khorezm, consisted in rehabilitating agriculture. This meant also the recom-
missioning such industries which were primarily concerned with
the processing of agricultural products and raising the cattle
stock. Ever since its inception, the Central Asian Economic
Council concerned itself with the task of improving the irrigation facilities in Turkestan, Bukhara and Khorezm.[114] Thanks
to the intensive work done in this field and to the generous
allocation of funds from the Central government, the total irrigated area within the Turkestan Republic, between 1922-24,
rose from 1,289,000 to 1,887,000 hectares. In Khorezm, in addition
to repairing the canals which had been damaged, the construction of a fresh irrigation canal system was also taken up. In
Bukhara, where no serious damage was done to the irrigation
system, the rehabilitation work proved relatively easier.[115]

The extension of irrigational facilities gave considerable
stimulus to the raising of agricultural production. By 1924, it
was claimed that within the Turkestan Republic almost two-
thirds of the land that was under cultivation in the prewar
period was once again brought back under the plough. In particular, there was a significant increase in the area of land under
the cotton crop. Between 1922-24 the land under cotton rose
from 63,428 to 311,443 *desiatins*. This meant that within Turkestan, nearly 71.4 per cent of the cotton production of the pre-
war years was restored.[116] In Bukhara, it was claimed that cotton
production was fully restored to its prewar level by 1923 itself.[117]
The success attained in the rehabilitation work in the agricultural sector was attributed mainly to the establishment and development of the agricultural cooperatives and to the aid provided
by the Centre.[118]

114. *Turkestanskaia Pravda*, 34 (325) 15 February 1923.
115. S. A. Radzhabov, 'Natsional'no-gosudarstvennoe razmezhevanie
Srednei Azii,' *Uchenye zapiski Tashkentskogo iuridicheskogo instituta*
(Tashkent, 1955) I, 63-5.
116. *Narodnoe khoziaistvo Srednei Azii* (Tashkent) 10-12 (1927) 22 and
5 (1924) 17. In 1923 a five-year plan was adopted for rehabilitating the
cotton production in the Turkestan Republic. The plan envisaged the
complete rehabilitation of cotton production by the end of 1927. See
Iskhakov, n. 7, 43.
117. *IUzSSR*, n. 31, 216.
118. By 1924, it was claimed that the agricultural cooperatives had

Production in the industrial sector also made modest progress following the re-commissioning of many factories which had gone out of production, the enlargement of their productive capacities and the transfer of a number of industries from central Russia to Turkestan, Bukhara and Khorezm. The Turkestan Republic was supplied with a textile mill, a paper mill and a celluloid manufacturing industry; Khorezm received a paper mill, a glass factory and a hydroelectric station. Bukhara was provided with a textile mill, a leather tanning factory, a paper mill and a soap manufacturing industry. Intensive work was undertaken in all the republics to raise the production of the cotton-processing and the cotton-ginning enterprises to prewar level.[119] The moderate progress made in the industrial sector led Stalin to state before the Twelfth Party Congress that the industrial base had been laid in Central Asia to facilitate the region's subsequent industrial development.[120]

The implementation of the recommendations of the Tenth and Twelfth Party Congresses relating to the improvement of the cultural and educational standards of the peoples of Central Asia and the creation and development of judicial, economic and administrative organs functioning in the native languages, however, did not prove easy. It was easy enough for the Central party and government organs, often lacking an intimate knowledge of the chaotic situation which prevailed in Central Asia, to be indignant at the region's 'devastatingly low percentage of literacy, the isolation of the state apparatus from the language and life of the people and a devastatingly slow rate of development,' and to flood the local organs with a spate of directives exhorting them to speed up their work. But the rectification of the anomalous situation which prevailed in Central Asia posed almost insurmountable hurdles. The extremely low percentage of literacy, the absence of trained native officials, the national and linguistic heterogeneity of the people, the presence of national and tribal feuds and frictions, the tendency on the part of the dominant nationalities to ignore, and often to deli-

brought within their fold 213,000 peasant cultivators. In 1923 nearly 92 per cent of cotton cultivators within Turkestan were supplied with state credits through the instrumentality of the agricultural cooperatives. See Radzhabov, n. 115, 63.

119. *IUzSSR*, n. 31, 211, 216 and Radzhabov, n. 115, 64.
120. See page 138 above.

berately undermine the interests of the weaker national and ethnic groups, accounted for the extremely slow rate of development in the education and cultural spheres.[121]

The preponderance of illiteracy had a direct bearing on the slow rate of progress made in *nativizing* the state apparatus and in training native officials to man the party and state organs. In 1924, Vareikis, the Secretary of the Central Committee of the Communist Party of Turkestan, stated that although considerable progress was made in *nativizing* the administrative apparatus at the oblast, uezd and volost levels, yet, at the centre nearly 70 per cent of the government posts were still held by persons of European origin.[122] The statistical data relating to the year 1924 also reveals that 90 per cent of the posts in 28 different 'institutions having a Central Asian significance' were held by persons of European origin. Out of the 99 'responsible workers' allocated to the Uzbek Soviet Socialist Republic when it was formed, 55 were persons of European origin and only 43 were Uzbeks.[123] The number of trained personnel among the Turkmens, Tadjiks, Kirgiz, Kazakhs, and Kara-Kalpaks was far lower than among the Uzbeks.

Progress in cultural and educational spheres was retarded by certain other factors besides illiteracy. To some extent it was impeded by the lack of a sound knowledge of the national and

121. The 1897 census revealed that the general level of culture which prevailed in Central Asia was far lower than even the semi-wild Yakut region. When the next census was taken in 1920 (excluding Fergana oblast) it was found that literacy in Turkestan ranged between 4 to 9 per cent. A higher percentage of literacy was recorded in the Syr Daria and the Semirechie oblasts where there was a sizable Russian immigrant population. A comparison of the results of the 1897 and 1920 census reports reveals that literacy among the indigenous populations of Central Asia, during the intervening period of twentythree years went up by only one per cent. The degree of illiteracy among the Kazakhs of Semirechie was 97 per cent and in Syr Daria oblast 97.5 per cent. Illiteracy ranged between 98 to 99 per cent among the Kurama of the Angren river valley and was almost 99 per cent among the inhabitants of Samarkand and Transcaspian oblasts. According to the estimates of Magidovich, literacy in the Fergana oblast in the early twenties of this century ranged between 1.5 per cent among the Uzbeks, Tadjiks and Kipchaks to 4.5 per cent among the Kirgiz. According to the 1920 census a relatively higher percentage of literacy was recorded among the Kirgiz population of the Semirechie oblast also. See *Turkestanskaia Pravda* 24 (35), 3 February 1923 and 25 (36), 4 February 1923.

122. *Turkestanskaia Pravda*, 100 (377), 8 May 1924.

123. *Vlast' Sovetov*, 48, 29 November 1925.

ethnic divisions, linguistic affinities and differences, customs and ways of living of the peoples of Central Asia. Thus, for instance, in 1918, the Turkestan Central Executive Committee had decreed that the 'Turkish language' was to be treated on par with Russian as one of the state languages of the Turkestan Republic.[124] Subsequently however, it was found that the notion of linguistic homogeneity of Central Asian peoples held by the earlier Bolsheviks, had no basis in fact and that they had mistaken the language of the Uzbeks for the so-called 'Turkish language.' This discovery led to the complete reversal of earlier policy and to an attempt to provide a fair deal to other languages whose claims had been overlooked.[125] In doing so, the Bolsheviks further learnt to their consternation that the languages of Central Asia not only differed from one another considerably but also existed at different stages of historical development. This demanded the formulation of linguistic and educational policies which took note of all their diverse features and ensured their unhindered growth. Besides, there was the need to ensure that the administrative apparatus and judicial and economic organs also functioned in the languages which were comprehensible to all the national and ethnic groups which inhabited Central Asia. All these immensely complicated the work of the governments and led to the establishment of cumbersome administrative mechanisms.

The orientation of the policies of the Turkestan Republic in this direction started taking place with the establishment of the People's Commissariat for Nationality Affairs in 1918. During the period of its existence, the *Turkomnats* had within its composition separate national divisions of Uzbeks, Tadjiks, Turkmens, Kirgiz, Tatars, Ukrainians, Native Jews and Armenians.[126] On 31 March 1921, a separate Kazakh National Division was created within the Turkestan Central Executive Committee

124. *Turkestanskaia Pravda,* 15, 21 January 1923.

125. Many minor national groups such as the Kirgiz, Kara-Kalpaks etc., possessed only oral traditions and had no literary languages of their own. Many orientalists, linguists and ethnographers were commissioned to make detailed studies of such backward national groups and to suggest ways and means of improving their languages, culture and ways of living. See M. Dzhunusov, *K voprosu o formirovanii Kirgizskoi sotsialisticheskoi natsii* (Frunze, 1952) 122-3.

126. See page 92.

and it was charged with the task of shaping the policies of the Turkestan Government in a manner conducive to the maximization of the wellbeing of the Kazakh-inhabited areas of the republic.[127] After the abolition of the Commissariat for Nationality Affairs on 14 June 1922, the national divisions which functioned within it were once again transferred to the Central Executive Committee where they enjoyed a status similar to the Kazakh National Division. These national divisions did much to improve the living conditions, culture and languages of the people they represented. They presented before the Central Executive Committee the needs and requirements of the nationalities concerned and exhorted it to adopt the necessary measures.

On the basis of a special decree adopted by the Turkestan Commission in January 1920,[128] the All-Russian Central Executive Committee, in August 1920, directed the Turkestan Central Executive Committee to

> set to work on the redivision of the administrative districts of Turkestan in conformity with their national compositions so that real freedom of cultural and economic development of the toiling masses of the indigenous peoples of Turkestan is ensured and any possibility of national inequality is removed.[129]

In accordance with this directive, the Turkestan Central Executive Committee, by a decree issued in April 1921, reorganized the Transcaspian oblast into the 'Turkmen oblast.'[130] In April 1922, the Central Executive Committee secured the establishment of a separate Kirgiz oblast by amalgamating several Kirgiz-majority areas of Semirechie, Syr Daria and Fergana oblasts.[131]

---

127. *Sbornik dekretov, rasporiazhenii i postanovlenii Tsentral'nogo Ispol'nitel'nogo Komiteta sovetov Turkestanskoi respubliki*, 9 sessii (Tashkent, 1921) 166, 172-3.

128. See page 106.

129. Cited in M. F. Mukhamed'iarov, 'K istorii provedeniia natsional'nogosudarstvennogo razmezhevaniia Srednei Azii v 1924,' *Sovetskoe vostokovedenie* (Moscow) 1 (1965) 46.

130. The suggestion to reorganize the Transcaspian oblast was mooted in the Second Transcaspian Oblast Congress of Soviets. It was stated that the reorganization of the oblast, to a considerable extent, stimulated the growth of national consciousness among the Turkmens. See V. Karpych, 'K istorii vozniknoveniia Turkmenskoi SSR,' *Turkmenovedenie*, 10-1 (1928) 41.

131. I. Khodorov, 'Natsional'noe razmezhevanie Srednei Azii,' *Novyi*

Political, economic and cultural inequalities were more pronounced among the national groups which inhabited Khorezm
and Bukhara. In addition, the Soviet governments of these two
republics inherited from the former regimes of the Khan and
the Amir a legacy of national feuds and frictions. Soon after the
inauguration of popular regimes in these republics, equality
before law of all citizens irrespective of their national affiliations
was proclaimed. But in Khorezm and Bukhara the formal proclamation of equality before law did not go very far in remedy-
ing the basic 'inequality in the distribution of land and water'
which was at the bottom of all national frictions.[132] The intransigence of Uzbek nationalists who were securely entrenched
in the government and party organs of Khorezm and Bukhara
nullified the initial attempts which were made to ameliorate the
conditions of the Turkmens, Kazakhs, Kara-Kalpaks and
Tadjiks.[133]

In Khorezm, it was only after the fall of the Young Khivans'
government in March 1921 that the second All-Khorezmian
Kuraltai addressed itself to the task of introducing certain reforms which sought to ease national tensions and to restore
peace among the warring national groups. The *Kuraltai* created
a separate Turkmen National Division within the Central Executive Committee. Composed of seven Turkmen members of the
Central Executive Committee, the Turkmen National Division
was charged with the task of making a special study of the economic, social and cultural needs and requirements of the Turkmen areas and of suggesting concrete proposals for their improve-

vostok 8-9 (1925) 66. In the economic conference of the Turkestan
Republic held in 1923, the creation of the Kirgiz oblast was criticized on
the ground that it was economically inexpedient. See *Otchet 2-oi ekonomicheskoi konferentsii Turkestanskoi respubliki* (Tashkent, 1923) 85.

132. *Turkestanskaia Pravda*, 148 (425), 6 July 1924.

133. In Khorezm, its first popular government headed by Palvan Niaz
Iusupov not only repudiated the promises it had made to the Turkmens
of granting autonomy to the Turkmen regions and improving the economic conditions of the Turkmens by securing an equitable distribution of
land and water, but even resorted to force to quell the unrest among the
non-Uzbek populations. Several Red Army units composed exclusively of
Uzbeks were always stationed in the Turkmen areas to thwart any
attempts at rebellion. See *KhNSR*, n. 66, 187 and I. I. Kryl'tsov, 'Pravovoe oformlenie natsional'nykh respublik Srednei Azii: Turkmenistan,
Vestnik iustitsii Uzbekistana, 6-8 (1926) 12-13.

ment.[134] The Kazakh-Kara-Kalpak National Division was established by the Third All-Khorezmian *Kuraltai* for safeguarding the interests of the Kazakh and the Kara-Kalpak populations of the republic and to help in promoting their wellbeing.[135]

In addition to these measures taken to promote the development of the weaker national groups of Khorezm, the reorganization of the administrative units in conformity with the distribution of national groups was also taken up. On the basis of the recommendations of the Fourth All-Khorezmian *Kuraltai,* the entire territory of the Khorezmian Republic was divided into three national oblasts and one national area. A Kazakh-Kara-Kalpak oblast was established by amalgamating the *shuros* of Kungrad, Kunia-Urgench, Khodzheili and Chumanai. The Novo-Urgench oblast was formed by amalgamating in it the Uzbek *shuros* of Besh-Aryk, Gurlen, Dargan-Ata, Kipchak, Kiiat-Kungrad, Kiiat, Mangyt, Novyi Urgench, Pitniak, Sadyvar, Shabad, Khazarasp, Klanki and Khtai. The Turkmen oblast of Tashauz was constituted by combining in it the *shuros* of Ambar-Manak, Il'ialy, Klych-Bai, Kak-chaga, Porsu, Tashauz and Takhta-Bazar. A separate Khiva Area composed mainly of the Uzbek majority areas of Ak-derbent, Astana, Gazavat, Gudzha, Kirman, Khiva and Iangi-Aryk, was also formed.[136] These reforms not only stabilized the Soviet regime in Khorezm but also helped in removing national frictions which had plagued the political life of Khorezm for centuries.[137]

A separate Turkmen National Division was established within the Central Executive Committee of Bukhara. Towards the end of 1923, the Government of Bukhara decided also to constitute a separate Turkmen oblast by incorporating in it all the

134. *KhNSR*, n. 65, 187-8.
135. *Ibid.,* 192; also see *Turkestanskaia Pravda,* 171 (448) 6 August 1924.
136. It has, however, to be noted that only the Kunia-Urgench oblast and the Khiva Area were nationally homogeneous. The Uzbeks constituted in them 97 and 96 per cent respectively. The Kazakh-Kara-Kalpak oblast had 32.5 per cent Uzbeks, 34.8 per cent Kazakhs, 8.3 per cent Kara-Kalpaks and 23.5 per cent Turkmens. The national composition of the Tashauz oblast was 54 per cent Uzbeks, 0.2 per cent Kazakhs and 45.8 per cent Turkmens. See *Materialy po raionirovaniiu Srednei Azii: territoriia i naseleniia Bukhary i Khorezma* (Khorezm) (Tashkent, 1926) II, pt. 2, 34, 90.
137. *Turkestanskaia Pravda,* 12, 17 January 1923.

Turkmen majority *vilaiets* of Bukhara and making Chardzhui its administrative centre.[138] The eastern *vilaiets* of Garm, Diushambe, Kuliab and Sary-Asi were amalgamated in a semi-autonomous oblast of Eastern Bukhara. The administration of this predominantly Tadjik-inhabited region was entrusted to the Central Executive Committee of Eastern Bukhara formed on 28 May 1924.[139] The proposal to establish a Kazakh national division, however, did not find the approval of the Bukharan government.[140]

In addition to the creation of national divisions and the formation of national oblasts within each of the Central Asian republics, attempts were also made to provide adequate representation to all nationalities within the administrative organs. At all levels of administration—from the local organs of authority up to the Central Executive Committee and the Council of People's Commissars—a number of posts was reserved for the representatives of all nationalities.[141] The introduction of such reforms not only led to the gradual improvement of the political, economic and cultural conditions of the more backward nationalities of Central Asia, but also stimulated the growth of national consciousness among them.

The proposal to establish the Kazakh Autonomous Soviet

138. The All-Bukharan Turkmen *Kuraltai*, meeting on 19 September 1923, enthusiastically greeted the decision to form a separate Turkmen oblast. The *Kuraltai* declared that the establishment of a separate Turkmen oblast would greatly facilitate the speedier solution of all the administrative, economic and educational problems of the Turkmen population of Bukhara. See *Turkestanskaia Pravda*, 200, 23 September 1923.

139. *Materialy po raionirovaniiu Srednei Azii: territoriia i naseleniia Bukhary i Khorezma* (Bukhara) (Tashkent, 1926) I, pt. 1, 68.

140. An article which appeared in an August issue of the *Turkestanskaia Pravda* (vide 178, 29 August 1923) alleged that the Government of Bukhara had completely neglected the Kazakh-inhabited areas of Bukhara. It claimed that the Kazakhs constituted nearly one-sixth of the population of Bukhara (i.e. 500,000 persons) and were in a compact majority in the former *bekdoms* of Nur-Ata, Karshi, Boisu and Kuliab. It pleaded for the establishment of a separate Kazakh national division in Bukhara and urged the Bukharan government to enlist the services of Kazakhs of the Turkestan and Kazakh republics to work among the backward Kazakh areas of Bukhara. It is to be noted, however, that the strength of the Kazakh population of Bukhara was highly exaggerated in this article. The materials on the regionalization of Bukhara placed the Kazakh population in Bukhara at only 24,268 persons. See n. 139, 165.

141. Mukhamed'iarov, n. 129, 46.

Socialist Republic brought to the forefront the question of integrating in it the Kazakh-inhabited areas of the Turkestan Republic. The Kazakhs of the Steppe region and also those living within the Turkestan Republic had long expressed a desire that the Kazakh Autonomous Republic should include all the Kazakh population of the Ural region, the Kazakh steppe, western Siberia and Turkestan.[142] The Government of the RSFSR viewed with sympathy the desire of the Kazakh population to be united under a single administration. This found expression in the decree of the All-Russian Central Executive Committee and the *Sovnarkom* 'On the formation of the Autonomous Kirgiz (Kazakh) Socialist Soviet Republic' issued on 26 August 1920. While Section D of Clause I of this decree envisaged the inclusion of the Mangyshlak uezd and two other volosts of the Krasnovodsk uezd of the Transcaspian oblast within the Kazakh ASSR, Clause 2 envisaged the incorporation of the other Kazakh-inhabited areas of the Turkestan Republic within the Kazakh ASSR on the basis of the freely expressed wishes of the population of those areas.[143] Clause 11 of this decree stated that in order to facilitate the formulation and implementation of uniform policies in all the Kazakh areas including those which were within the Turkestan administration, a plenipotentiary of the Kazakh Revolutionary Committee should be included within the Presidium of the Turkestan Central Executive Committee. This Kazakh plenipotentiary was made responsible to the Kazakh Revolutionary Committee and was charged with the task of supervising the implementation of its directives.[144]

After protracted negotiations between the Kazakh Revolutionary Committee and the Turkestan Central Executive Committee, the latter agreed to transfer to the Kazakh ASSR the Mangyshlak

142. As early as October 1918 the Kazakh population of the Mangyshlak uezd of the Transcaspian oblast expressed itself in favour of integrating the Mangyshlak uezd with the Kazakh Republic. See S. N. Pokrovski, ed., *Obrazovanie Kazakhskoi ASSR: sbornik dokumentov i materialov* (Alma-Ata, 1957) document 55, 93-4.

143. Document 167, *ibid.*, 251-2. A note appended to this decree stated that in the event of a controversy arising between the Kazakh Revolutionary Committee and the Turkestan Central Executive Committee on the question of transferring the Syr Daria and Semirechie oblasts to the Kazakh ASSR, the matter would be taken up by the Central institutions of the RSFSR for finding an appropriate solution.

144. *Ibid.*, 255.

uezd and two Kazakh majority volosts of the Krasnovodsk uezd
of the Transcaspian oblast.[145] Towards the end of 1920 the
Secretary of the All-Russian Central Executive Committee demarcated the frontier between the Kazakh and the Turkestan
Republics in the Adaev uezd of the Transcaspian oblast.[146] The
Turkestan Government, however, demurred on the question of
transferring to the Kazakh ASSR the Syr Daria and Semirechie
oblasts.[147]

Following its failure to secure the concurrence of the Turkestan Central Executive Committee to the question of ceding to
the Kazakh Republic the Syr Daria and the Semirechie oblasts,
the Government of the Kazakh Republic, towards the beginning
of 1922, appealed to the *Narkomnats* to resolve this issue. On 21
March 1922 the *Narkomnats* decided to take up this issue at the
Eleventh Congress of the Russian Communist Party and also to
summon a conference of the Turkestan and Kazakh delegates
attending this Congress, to thrash out an agreement on securing
to the Kazakh ASSR the Syr Daria and the Semirechie oblasts.
This conference which met on 4 April 1922, also failed to reach
an agreement on this issue. It only resolved to ask the Central
Committee of the Turkestan Communist Party and the Oblast
Committee of the Russian Communist Party of Kazakhstan to
elicit the views of their party members on the question of transferring the two oblasts to the Kazakh ASSR.[148]

The proposal to cede the Syr Daria and Semirechie oblasts to
the Kazakh Republic did not find a favourable response in the
party and governmental circles of the Turkestan Republic until
1924. Georgi Safarov, a member of the Turkestan Bureau of
the Central Committee of the Russian Communist Party, linked
up the question of transferring the Syr Daria and the Semirechie

145. *Statisticheskii spravochnik Turkmenskoi oblasti 1920-1924* (Poltoratsk, 1924) 5-6.
146. *Sovetskaia politika za 10 let po natsional'nomu voprosu v* RSFSR
(Moscow, 1928) 79; also see *Turkestanskaia Pravda*, 88 (363) 17 April
1924.
147. According to the statistical data available for 1915, the Kazakhs
constituted almost three-fourths of the total population of the Semirechie
oblast. In absolute figures, out of the oblast's total population of
1,223,000 persons the Kazakhs constituted 883,000 persons. See *Turkestanskaia Pravda*, 28 (39) 8 February 1923.
148. A. Nusupbekov, *Ob'edinenie Kazakhskikh zemel' v Kazakhskoi
sovetskoi sotsialisticheskoi respublike* (Alma-Ata, 1953) 57.

oblasts to the Kazakh Republic with the basic question of resolving the future course of development of the Turkestan ASSR. He wrote:

> Before Turkestan there are two possible ways of development: one consists in effecting a political and economic reorganization on the basis of the national principle (i.e., creation of separate Uzbek, Kirgiz (Kazakh) and Turkmen republics) and another, in its further development in the form of a single political unit with a broad measure of self-determination to the different national oblasts. The final decision on the question of incorporating the Syr Daria and Semirechie oblasts within Kazakhstan is directly dependent on the question as to which of these two paths of development the Turkestan Republic takes.[149]

Towards the beginning of 1924 the first of the two alternatives suggested by Safarov was accepted by the Turkestan Communist Party as the most satisfactory and expedient course for the Turkestan Republic to follow. With this, the question of transferring the Syr Daria and the Semirechie oblasts to the Kazakh ASSR merged itself within the larger question of redrawing the frontiers of the Turkestan Republic on the nationality principle. The Central Asiatic Bureau of the Central Committee of the Russian Communist Party began eliciting the views and opinions of the communists of Bukhara and Khorezm on the possibility of bringing within the orbit of the proposed national-territorial delimitation even Bukhara and Khorezm. The following chapter is devoted to a detailed study of this momentous territorial reorganization of the Central Asian republics.

149 *Zhizn' natsional'nostei,* 10 (1922) 4.

CHAPTER FIVE

National-Territorial Delimitation of Central Asia

THE national territorial delimination of Central Asia which brought into existence several national republics in place of the former multinational political entities of Turkestan, Bukhara and Khorezm, has given rise to an acute controversy between Soviet and non-Soviet scholars. Soviet scholars generally see in this reform a 'second revolution' and a consummation of the Soviet nationalities policy in Central Asia.[1] They claim that only as a result of the creation of nationally homogeneous republics, peaceful and harmonious relations have been established among the different national groups of Central Asia in place of the intermittent clan-tribal feuds and national frictions which plagued their lives in the the past. The non-Soviet critics of the reform, however, see quite different things in it. Mustafa Chokaev alleged that the plan of 'the division of Turkestan into tribal states' was invented by the Bolsheviks at Moscow to counter the attempt made by the 'Mussalman Communists' to secure the unification of all the Turkic tribes around the nucleus of Soviet Turkestan.[2] Prince Labanoff-Rostovsky, a Russian emigré scholar, has expressed the view that the national delimitation plan 'was less concerned with solving the ethnographical puzzle than with the political aspect arising from the problem' and that it was merely the Bolsheviks' reply to the Basmachi uprising.[3] Yet others

1. *Turkestanskaia Pravda,* 141 (481) 27 June 1924.
2. Mustafa Chokaev, 'Turkestan And the Soviet Regime,' *Journal of the Royal Central Asian Society* (London) xviii (1931) 414. Like his Djadidist associates Mustafa Chokaev subscribed to the view that Turkestan was 'nationally and linguistically homogeneous since a predominant part of its population belonged to the Turkic nationality.'
3. Lobanoff-Rostovsky, 'The Muslim Republics in Central Asia', *Journal of the Royal Institute of International Affairs* (London) 7 (1928) 249-50.

see in this reform a manifestation of the principle of 'divide and rule' and hold Stalin as its chief architect.[4]

Though the timing of the reform might have been prompted by other considerations, there can be no denying that the principle underlying the plan of reform stemmed directly from the Soviet nationalities policy itself. It is interesting to note in this connection that as early as 1913 the Central Committee of the Russian Social Democratic Workers' Party (RSDRP) in its Poronin Conference included a provision in the party's programme on the national question which ensured the national minorities and ethnic groups which did not choose to opt for secession from Russia:

> a wide measure of regional autonomy and full democratic local self-government; *the demarcation of the boundaries of the regional autonomies and self-governing units by the local populations themselves in conformity with their economic, ethnic distinctions and national composition etc.*[5]

This provision was restated again in full by the Seventh Conference of the RSDRP held in April 1917, and it also found expression in a number of public pronouncements made by the Government of the RSFSR after 1917.[6] The People's Commissariat for Nationality Affairs gave concrete shape to this provision when it established separate national state formations for the Byelorussians, Georgians, Armenians, Azerbaidzhanis, Tatars, Bashkirs, Chuvash, Kalmyks and others. In Central Asia, however, the implementation of this provision was delayed on account of the extremely fluid political situation which prevailed there until the close of 1923.[7] It was only when the Bolsheviks successfully overcame the Basmachi resistance and extended their influence and control over Bukhara and Khorezm were they free to give their attention to other issues.

4. *The Central Asian Review* (London) 8 (1960) 342-3.

5. *Kommunisticheskaia partiia Sovetskogo Soiuza v rezoliutsiiakh i resheniiakh s'ezdov, konferentsii i plenumov TsK, pt. I, 1898-1925* (Moscow, 7th edition, 1953) 346. (emphasis added).

6. See *Politika Sovetskoi vlasti po natsional'nym delam za tri goda 1917-1920* (Moscow, 1920) 5-8; also see S. L. Ronin, 'Stalinskoe uchenie o natsii i o mnogonatsional'nom sovetskom gosudarstve,' *Sovetskoe gosudarstvo i pravo* (Moscow) 2 (1950) 5-6.

7. In a communication sent on 5 June 1920 to the Presidium of the All-Russian Executive Committee and to the Central Committee of the Russian Communist Party, the Turkestan Commission had stated that the

The Bolsheviks, as early as 1920, had decided to break up the multinational state structure of the Turkestan ASSR and to re-draw its administrative boundaries in conformity with its ethnographic divisions. This decision was clearly reflected in the decree promulgated by the Turkestan Commission in January 1920 and in the instructions given by Lenin to the Turkestan Commission on 13 July 1920.[8]

While the Turkestan Commission continued with the preparatory work for a full scale territorial reorganization of the Turkestan ASSR, the governments of Turkestan, Bukhara and Khorezm republics, between 1920-24 sought to meet half-way the demands of the various national groups for autonomous existence. The creation of national divisions, the establishment of national autonomous oblasts, the development of the languages, literatures, press, etc., of the indigenous nationalities, were bound to stimulate their national consciousness and accentuate their demands for the establishment of separate national state formations. How quickly and to what extent, these demands did in fact develop became evident from the somewhat stormy debate which took place in the Thirteenth Congress of Soviets of the Turkestan Republic. The Congress received a 'Declaration of the Thirty Fergana Delegates' which contained a demand for the autonomous separation of Fergana from Turkestan and its direct inclusion in the RSFSR.[9] The Kirgiz and

political situation which then prevailed in Turkestan dictated the necessity of retaining for some more time an undivided Turkestan Republic and that its immediate division into a number of national units was bound to plunge all work into chaos and help the nationalist elements. See A. Nusupbekov, *Ob'edinenie Kazakhskikh zemel' v Kazakhskoi sovetskoi sotsialisticheskoi respublike* (Alma-Ata, 1953) 55.

8. See pages 111 and 113 of this book.

9. The Fergana oblast was inhabited by three distinct nationalities: Uzbeks, Tadjiks and Kirgiz. Each of them constituted a compact majority in different uezds and volosts and culturally and economically were closely connected with their kinsmen in the adjoining areas. In view of this, in a combined conference of the Central Asiatic Bureau of the *Tsk RKP* (B) and the Executive Bureau of the *TsK* of the Communist Party of Turkestan held on 13 January 1924, it was stated that 'to take up the question of carving out Fergana into an autonomous oblast in the given circumstances and in the form suggested by the Comrades of Fergana is incorrect, since the division of national territories into oblasts must proceed on the lines suggested by the decisions of the VIII, X and XII Congresses of the Party.' Cited in Kh. T. Tursunov, *O natsional'no—gosudarstvennom razmezhevanii Srednei Azii* (Tashkent, 1957) 13.

the Kazakh delegates also put forward similar demands. The
Turkmens led by Aitakov, Atabaev, and Sakat Muratov began
pleading for the establishment of a separate Turkmen national
republic.[10] Such demands on the part of the representatives of
the local nationalities provided a popular setting to the proposed
reform.

I. NEED FOR NATIONAL DELIMITATION

The necessity for undertaking such an extensive territorial
reorganization of Central Asia arose from the desire to remedy
the complex national tangle which considerably hindered the
development of a socialist order within the region. The bewildering heterogeneity of national composition, the linguistic,
economic and cultural affinities and differences of the peoples of
Central Asia have been discussed in the earlier part of this
book.[11] In spite of the utter complexity of the national problem
in Central Asia, no serious effort was ever made in the pre-
revolutionary period to find out a remedy for it. On the contrary,
the demarcation of the political and administrative frontiers of
the Turkestan region on the basis of only the military, strategic
and political exigencies of the time of the Russian conquest had
increased the complexity of the national problem.[12] Not only
did the old political and administrative frontiers drawn in a
haphazard manner completely ignoring the existing ethnographical divisions, but they also cut across areas of homogeneous population and set at naught their natural affinities and common eco-

---

10. V. Karpych, 'K istorii vozniknoveniia Turkmenskoi SSR', *Turkmenovedenie* (Ashkhabad) 10-11 (1928) 45.

11. See chapter I.

12. In 1873, when the question of demarcating the frontier between
Turkestan and Bukhara arose, the Governor-General of Turkestan simply
ordered that the frontier be fixed at 9 versts to the south of the route
through which the Russian armies were then marching in connection with
the Khivan expedition. The sole objective of this order was to ensure the
Russian possession of a considerable number of wells. The frontier thus
demarcated cut across the territory inhabited mainly by Uzbeks and
Kazakhs into two parts one going to Bukhara and another to Turkestan.
The same criterion was followed in demarcating the frontier between
Turkestan and Bukhara in the Zerafshan basin and the western frontier
of the Khanate of Khiva. The demarcation of frontiers among the three
states only on the basis of political and strategic considerations further
complicated the already complex ethnographic map of the Central Asian
region. See *Turkestanskaia Pravda* (Tashkent) 191 (408), 29 August 1924.

nomic interests. In addition to this, the practice of the former regimes of Turkestan, Bukhara and Khiva of setting one national
group against another and kindling inter-tribal feuds created
great tensions and rendered the peaceful coexistence of several
national groups within the framework of a single state formation
extremely difficult.[13]

The revolution in Central Asia did not change the political
and administrative frontiers which had come into existence as
a result of the historical events of the past and of the policies
of the Tsarist government. Within each territorial unit different national groups continued to be herded together, and the
problem of reorganizing the boundaries of the Central Asian
republics on a more satisfactory basis still remained.[14] An idea
of the complexity of the national composition of the populations of Turkestan, Bukhara and Khorezm could be had from
the following tables.

Table 1

NATIONAL COMPOSITION OF THE POPULATION OF THE
TURKESTAN REPUBLIC[15]

National groups	*Number*	*Percentage of total population*
1. Uzbeks	2,347,491	41.4
2. Kazakhs	1,097,677	19.4
3. Kirgiz	607,551	10.7
4. Tadjiks	437,656	7.7
5. Turkmens	266,672	4.7
6. Kara-Kalpaks	77,825	1.4
7. Kurama	49,697	1.1
8. Taranchi	44,989	0.8
9. Kipchaks	42,449	0.7
10. Jews	15,465	0.3
11. Russians	540,674	9.5
12. Persians	35,296	0.6
13. Tatars	21,826	0.4
14. Armenians	19,886	0.3
15. Dungans	10,971	0.2
16. Others	48,329	0.8
Total	5,664,454	100.0

13. *Vlast' sovetov* (Moscow) 1 (1925) 15.
14. M. Nemchenko, 'Natsional'noe razmezhevanie Srednei Azii', *Mezhdunarodnaia zhizn'* (Moscow) 4-5 (1924) 91.
15. *Statisticheskii ezhegodnik 1917-1923 gg* (Tashkent, 1924) I, pt. 3,
45-8. The figures given in this table are based upon the 1920 census and

Table II

NATIONAL COMPOSITION OF THE POPULATION OF BUKHARA [16]

National groups	Number	Percentage of total population
1. Uzbeks	777,768	50.7
2. Kazakhs	24,268	1.6
3. Kirgiz	8,215	0.5
4. Tadjiks	475,589	31.6
5. Turkmens	164,993	10.3
6. Kara-Kalpaks	2,095	0.1
7. Arabs	47,179	3.1
8. Bukharan Jews	6,842	0.4
9. Others	24,066	1.7
Total	1,531,015	100.0

Table III

NATIONAL COMPOSITION OF THE POPULATION OF KHOREZM [17]

National groups	Number	Percentage of total population
1. Uzbeks	364,404	79.0
2. Kazakhs	19,638	4.3
3. Turkmens	67,431	14.6
4. Kara-Kalpaks	4,262	0.9
5. Russians	830	0.2
6. Persians	1,504	0.3
7. Arabs	1,248	0.3
8. Tatars	1,190	0.3
9. Others	398	0.1
Total	460,905	100.0

they considerably differ from the figures given by the Commission on the Economic Unification of the Central Asian Republics. According to the estimates of this Commission the total population of the Turkestan Republic was placed at 5,299,162 persons. See *Sredne Aziatskii ekonomicheskii raion* (Tashkent, 1922) 21. The oblast-uezd-wise distribution of the national groups of the Turkestan Republic is shown in Appendix B.

16. *Materialy po raionirovaniiu Srednei Azii: territoriia i naselenie Bukhary i Khorezma* (Bukhara), (Tashkent, 1926) I, pt. 1, 165-6. (Cited hereafter as *MRSA(B)*). The Commission on the Economic Unification of the Central Asian Republics placed the total population of Bukhara at 2,029,512 persons. The *vilaiet-wise* distribution of the national groups of Bukhara is shown in Appendix C.

17. *Materialy po raionirovaniiu Srednei Azii: territoria i naselenie*

NATIONAL COMPOSITION OF THE CENTRAL ASIAN REPUBLICS BEFORE DELIMITATION

LEGEND

UZBEKS

TURKMENS.

TADJIKS.

KIRGIZ.

KARA-KALPAK

KAZAKHS.

From these tables and from the ethnographical map of the Central Asian region shown on page 158 it becomes clear that national frontiers of Central Asia overlapped and cut across the region's political and administrative frontiers. In other words, the existing political and administrative frontiers had no relation to the pattern of settlement of the national groups in the Central Asian region. The Uzbeks, Kazakhs, Turkmens and Kara-Kalpaks inhabited all the three Central Asian republics, and the Tadjiks and the Kirgiz inhabited both the Turkestan and the Bukharan republics.

The Uzbeks within the Turkestan Republic inhabited mainly the Fergana and Samarkand oblasts. A considerable portion of them also lived in the Tashkent, Mirzachul, Turkestan and Chimkent uezds of the Syr Daria oblast.[18] The Uzbeks constituted a compact national group in the Baisun, Bukhara, Guzar, Karshi, Kermen, Nur-Ata, Shakhrisiabz, Shirabad and Sary-Assi *vilaiets* of the Republic of Bukhara.[19] Within Khorezm the Uzbeks lived mainly in the Novo-Urgench oblast and in the Khiva area.[20]

The Kazakh population of the Turkestan Republic was concentrated mainly in the Syr Daria and Semirechie oblasts. They constituted a compact majority in Alma-Ata, Dzharkent, Lepsinsk, Taldy-Kurgan uezds of the Semirechie oblast and in Ak-Mechet, Aulie-Ata and Kazalinsk uezds of the Syr Daria oblast. There was also considerable Kazakh population in Turkestan, Chimkent, Mirzachul and Tashkent uezds.[21] In Bukhara the Kazakhs lived in and around the Urt-kul, Dzhilikul and Kurgan-Tube area.[22] In Khorezm, the Kazakhs were concentrated mainly in the Amu Daria delta and constituted as much as 47 per cent of the population of Kungrad district and 47.9 per cent of the

Bukhary i Khorezma (Khorezm) (Tashkent, 1926) II, pt. 2, 90. (Cited hereafter as *MRSA(K)*). According to the estimates of the Commission on the Economic Unification of the Central Asian Republics, the population of Khorezm was placed at 640,844 persons. The oblast-wise distribution of the national groups of Khorezm is shown in Appendix D.

18. *Materialy po raionirovaniiu Turkestana: proekt administrativno-khoziaistvennogo deleniia TSSR* (Tashkent, 1924) 125-6, 129, 132, 135. (Cited hereafter as *MRT*.)

19. *MRSA(B)*, n. 16, 83, 92, 95, 99-100, 103, 124.

20. *MRSA(K)*, n. 17, 37, 91, 96, 98-101, 102.

21. *MRT*, n. 18, 108-109, 114-5, 118, 120.

22. *MRSA(B)*, n. 16, 83-6.

population of Khodzheili district.[23]

The Kirgiz inhabited mainly the territory of the Turkestan Republic. They lived in a compact mass in the Karakol (formerly Przhevalsk), Pishpek (now Frunze), and Naryn uezds of the Syr Daria oblast, in the Osh uezd, Dzhalal-Abad volost and the north-eastern part of the Pamir region of the Fergana oblast.[24]

The Tadjiks within Turkestan republic lived mainly in the Samarkand and Fergana oblasts. Within the former, they inhabited Samarkand city and the hilly areas situated in the southern and southeastern parts of the Samarkand, Pendzhikent, Ura-Tube and Khodzhent. In the Fergana oblast, the Tadjiks were to be found in Isfara, in the southeastern parts of the Pamir region and in Kanibadam.[25] The bulk of the Tadjik population was concentrated in the hilly region situated in the eastern part of the Republic of Bukhara, the so-called Eastern Bukharan region.[26]

The Turkmens inhabited mainly the former Transcaspian oblast of the Turkestan Republic, the Chardzhui oblast of Bukhara and the Turkmen and Tashauz oblasts of the Khorezm Republic.[27]

The bulk of the Kara-Kalpak population was divided between the Turkestan and Khorezm republics. Within the former, they constituted a relative majority of the population of the Amu Daria district. A small portion of the Kara-Kalpak population lived also in the Kokand and Andizhan uezds of the Fergana oblast.[28] In Khorezm the Kara-Kalpaks lived mainly in the northern Kazakh-Kara-Kalpak oblast.

More significant was the fact that, barring the Uzbeks, no other major national group of Central Asia constituted a compact majority in any of the three republics. In Turkestan, Bukhara and Khorezm, all of them were swamped by the numerical predominance of other national groups. How serious this situation really was is shown in Table IV.

23. *MRSA(K)*, n. 17, 107.
24. *MRT*, n. 18, 112, 115, 132, 135, 137.
25. Nemchenko, n. 14, 85.
26. *MRSA(B)*, n. 16, 68, 125-8.
27. *MRT*, n. 18, 122-3; *MRSA(B)*, n. 16, 71, 77-82; *MRSA(K)*, n. 17, 43-4, 49, 102-103.
28. *MRT*, n. 18, 120, 132, 135.

Table IV

REPUBLICWISE DISTRIBUTION OF THE MAJOR NATIONAL GROUPS OF CENTRAL ASIA AND THE PROPORTION OF EACH NATIONAL GROUP TO THE TOTAL POPULATION OF EACH REPUBLIC(29)

Name of the major national groups	TURKESTAN		BUKHARA		KHOREZM	
	Percentage of each nationality in relation to its total strength in Central Asia	Percentage of each nationality in relation to the population of the republic	Percentage of each nationality in relation to its total strength in Central Asia	Percentage of each nationality in relation to the population of the republic	Percentage of each nationality in relation to its total strength in Central Asia	Percentage of each nationality in relation to the population of the republic
Uzbeks	66.5	41.4	22.2	50.1	11.3	61.1
Turkmens	43.2	4.7	27.0	10.6	29.8	28.8
Tadjiks	47.7	7.7	52.3	31.0	—	—
Kirgiz	98.6	10.8	1.4	0.5	—	—
Kara-Kalpaks	68.1	1.4	2.0	0.1	29.9	5.4
Kazakhs	95.9	19.3	2.1	1.5	2.0	3.5

29. The table is reproduced from Ilias Alkin, 'Natsional'no-gosudarstvennoe razmezhevanie Srednei Azii i VII s'ezd sovetov SSSR,' Revoliutsionnyi vostok (Moscow) 6 (1934) 115.

It becomes clear from this table that on the eve of the national delimitation of Central Asia, 66.5 per cent of the total Uzbek population of Central Asia lived in Turkestan, 22.2 per cent in Bukhara and 11.3 per cent in Khorezm and constituted respectively 41.4 per cent, 50.1 per cent and 61.1 per cent of the total population of these republics. Similarly, 43.2 per cent of the total Turkmen population of Central Asia lived in the Turkestan Republic, 27.0 per cent in Bukhara and 29.8 per cent in Khorezm. However, in relation to the total populations of these republics the Turkmens constituted only 4.7 per cent in Turkestan, 10.6 per cent in Bukhara and 28.8 per cent in Khorezm. The Tadjik population of Central Asia was divided between the Turkestan and Bukharan republics in the order of 47.7 per cent and 52.3 per cent respectively, but in relation to the total populations of these two republics, the Tadjiks constituted only 7.7 per cent and 31 per cent respectively. Almost the entire Kirgiz population of Central Asia (98.6 per cent) lived in the Turkestan Republic where, however, it was reduced to the status of an insignificant minority (10.8 per cent). Similar was the condition of the Kara-Kalpak and the Kazakh populations.

Such a heterogeneous composition of the population of the Central Asian republics raised a number of problems. For one thing, the various national groups which inhabited Turkestan, Bukhara and Khorezm did not exist on the same level of political, economic social and cultural development, and they also differed from one another in language, ways of life, customs and traditions. In view of this, the Soviet authorities experienced great difficulties in adopting uniform economic, judicial and educational policies for all their subjects and in promoting their welfare in equal measure. Within Turkestan, the smaller and more backward nationalities did not comprehend the laws, decrees and directives which were issued either in Russian or in the languages of the other dominant nationalities. Besides, the Kazakhs, Kirgiz and Turkmens who were just emerging from their time-honoured nomadic way of life to sedentary living possessed economic, social and cultural distinctions which sharply differentiated them from the sedentary Uzbeks and Tadjiks who were engaged in cotton cultivation, gardening and handicrafts, and also possessed thriving urban commercial centres and rich cultural and literary traditions.[30] Thus, the pursuit of a uniform economic policy for the different national groups within Turkestan was extremely difficult. In the sphere of cooperatives, for instance, the form, method, and structure of organization had to be different for the sedentary agricultural people from what was required for the nomadic cattle breeders.[31]

The Governments of Bukhara and Khorezm also experienced similar difficulties. Sultan Kary, the Chairman of the Central Executive Committee of Khorezm, complained that it was almost impossible to apply the same set of laws to both the Uzbeks and Turkmens of Khorezm. The government of Khorezm was confronted with yet another problem. The Turkmens, as a rule, paid their taxes to their clan leaders which seldom reached the treasury and the burden of taxes fell almost exclusively on the Uzbek population. When the government started incurring expenditure on welfare measures for Turkmens, it encountered opposition from the Uzbeks.[32]

In formulating a standardized educational policy for all their subjects, the governments of Turkestan, Bukhara and Khorezm experienced similar difficulties. Linguistic diversity and uneven levels of cultural development of the national groups demanded individual attention to the cultural and educational needs of each nationality.[33] More disturbing was the presence of national and inter-tribal frictions which often led to outbreaks of violence and rendered the preservation of law and order and the pro-

---

30. *Turkestanskaia Pravda*, 182 (459) 19 August 1924; also see S. P. Tolstov, 'Velikaia pobeda Leninsko-Stalinskoi natsional'noi politiki (k dvadtsttriletiiu natsional'nogo razmezhevaniia Srednei Azii),' *Sovetskaia Etnografiia* (Moscow) 1 (1950) 9.

31. *Ibid.*

32. *Turkestanskaia Pravda*, 186 (463), 24 August 1924.

33. E. M., 'Razmezhevanie Srednei Azii,' *Vlast sovetov*, 1 (1925) 15. National distinctions which are manifest in the ways of life, religious influences and the uneven levels of cultural development of the various national groups' wrote Kozhudov, the Deputy Commissar for Education of the Turkestan Republic, 'cause great hindrances for formulating a uniform educational policy by the People's Commissariat of Education. The establishment of separate republics will provide full opportunity to the commissariats of education of these republics to carry on their work in accordance with the distinctions of life of the peoples of those republics.' See *Turkestanskaia Pravda*, 187 (464), 25 August 1924.

motion of normal economic development difficult. In spite of
the best efforts made by the Soviet authorities, national feuds
and frictions continued to linger on in Turkestan, Bukhara and
Khorezm.[34] For instance, in the middle of July 1923, about 2,000
Kazakh nomads raided the Turkmen areas of the Turkestan Republic and occupied the wells of Guimat, Goekdere, Chagyl
and Kemal. The Turkmens, who at first retreated into Persia,
later reappeared and drove the Kazakhs out. In autumn and
winter the raids on each other's settlements continued. A commission appointed by the Government of Turkestan, after investigating the causes which led to these raids, found that the
clan leaders of the two groups had taken advantage of the deep-
seated national prejudices of their followers and incited them
into such raids.[35] In fact, one of the factors which proved decisive
in inducing the Soviet authorities to break up the multi-national
state structures of Turkestan, Bukhara and Khorezm was their
belief that the establishment of nationally homogeneous state
formations in Central Asia was bound to undermine the influence

34. Inter-national frictions and antagonisms within the Central Asian
republics grew mostly out of the political and economic inequalities which
existed among the different nationalities. The Uzbeks constituted the
dominant nationality in all the three republics, and not only possessed the
bulk of the fertile lands, and trade and industrial monopoly, but also
exercised effective control over the organs of administration. Uzbek
motives were always suspect in the eyes of other national groups who, in
the past, were subjected to the oppressive rule of Uzbek khans and amirs
and exploited by the Uzbek landlords, and merchants. National friction
and antagonisms began to grow partly as a result of the survival of
memories of such experiences in the consciousness of the non-Uzbek
national groups, and mostly out of the disregard shown by the Uzbek
nationalists for the needs and interests of the minor nationalities. See
Karpych, n. 10, 43-4. Speaking before the second session of the All-Union
Central Executive Committee on 24 October 1924, the Turkmen delegate
Atabaev, alleged that the first Revolutionary Government of Khorezm
headed by the 'Uzbek bourgeoisie' had practised a sort of 'massacre of
St. Bartholomew' on the Turkmen population. He stated that more than
one thousand Turkmens were done to death in a single night. The
Turkmens retaliated by pillaging Uzbek villages and massacring Uzbek
peasant families. In doing this they were reported to have more than ful-
filled the quota set: 'ten Uzbeks for every one Turkmen.' See 'Zasedan
vtoroi sessii TsIK SSSR 24 Oktiabria 1924 g,' *Narodnoe khoziaistvo
Srednei Azii* (Tashkent) 4 (1924) 204. (Cited hereafter as *ZVS TsI
SSSR*).

35. *Turkestanskaia Pravda*, 211, 6 October 1923; also see *Zhiz
matsional'nostei* (Moscow) 10 (1924) 8.

of the clan-tribal leaders among their peoples and help class stratification. In reply to their critics, who saw an apparent contradiction in this belief, the Bolsheviks argued that once the almost 'elemental longing' of the nationalities to possess their own state formations was satisfied, the people were bound to see clearly that none other than their own clan-tribal leaders stood in the way of their economic wellbeing.[36] It became almost a hardened conviction among the local Communists that the then existing political and administrative frontiers inevitably bred national frictions and antagonisms.[37] Faizullah Khodzhaev, the Chairman of the Council of *Nazirs* of the Republic of Bukhara, declared that it was extremely difficult to promote the development of all national groups in an equal measure unless the multinational structure of the Central Asian republics was scrapped and nationally-homogeneous political units were created.[38] Other eminent local communist leaders also argued that the establishment of separate states for each of the nationalities was the only possible means to overcome the existing national frictions and antagonisms and to promote their economic and cultural development. They added that, when every nationality possessed its own state and was able to manage its

---

36. *Turkestanskaia Pravda*, 102 (379), 12 May 1924; 185 (462), 22 August 1924.

37. *Turkestanskaia Pravda*, 99 (376), 7 May 1924. A thesis on national delimitation issued on 15 July 1924 by the Central Asiatic Bureau declared that 'national antagonisms which were strengthened in the past are now firmly entrenched in the economic conditions which prevail among the peoples of Central Asia and hamper the work of emancipating them not only from the Russian colonialists but also from the local exploiting classes, they (i.e., national antagonisms) relegate to the background class contradictions and accentuate nationalism among the different nationalities; the weaker and backward nationalities instead of being assisted and aided by the more dominant nationalities only continue to be exploited by them.' The thesis went on to say that only by establishing separate state formations for each of these nationalities could the existing national antagonisms be overcome and favourable conditions be created for promoting the economic and cultural development of all nationalities. See *Turkestanskaia Pravda* 165 (442), 30 July 1924.

38. *Ibid.* Speaking later before the second session of the All-Union Central Executive Committee, Faizulla Khodzhaev stated that the 'peoples of Central Asia would gain less in the struggle with their own handicaps than they could gain with the unification along national and economic lines.' See *ZVS TsIK SSSR*, n. 34, 198.

own affairs unhindered by others, there existed the objective pre-requisites for the promotion of its welfare.[39]

11. PRELIMINARY DISCUSSION OF THE DELIMITATION SCHEME

Among the Communist Party organizations of Central Asia the Bukharan Communist Party took the lead in bringing up the national delimitation project for discussion. On 25 February 1924 a plenary session of the Central Committee of the Bukharan Communist Party after debating this issue adopted a resolution which stated that conditions within the Central Asian republics were ripe for the division of their territory into a number of republics on the nationality principle.[40] The Executive Bureau of the Central Committee of the Communist Party of Bukhara followed this up by adopting a resolution on 10 March which favoured the establishment of the Uzbek and Turkmen Union Republics and a Tadjik Autonomous Oblast.[41] On 10 April the Central Committee of the Communist Party of Bukhara created a five-member commission and charged it with the task of working out the details of the proposals put forward by the Central Committee of the Bukharan Communist Party. The commission was also asked to prepare a report on national delimitation for the perusal of the Central Asiatic Bureau. The members of the commission were instructed to work in close co-operation with the Uzbek workers of Turkestan and Khorezm.

A representative of the Central Asiatic Bureau on 3 March 1924 initiated the discussion on the national delimitation project at a conference of the Executive Bureau of the Central Committee of the Communist Party of Khorezm. As later disclosed by Sultan Kary, the Chairman of the Khorezm Central Executive Committee, the conference failed to arrive at any clearcut decision in view of the divergent opinions held by the members of the Party on the national delimitation issue. Although a large section of them favoured the secession of the Turkmen areas of

39. *Turkestanskaia Pravda*, 179 (456), 15 August 1924; 182 (459), 19 August 1924; 183 (460), 20 August 1924; 184 (461), 21 August 1924; and 186 (463), 24 August 1924.
40. A. A. Gordienko, *Sozdanie sovetskoi natsional'noi gosudarstvennosti v Srednei Azii* (Moscow, 1959) 156.
41. Kh. T. Tursunov, *Obrazovanie Uzbekskoi sovetskoi sotsialisticheskoi respubliki* (Tashkent, 1957) 117.

Khorezm, they steadfastly opposed the proposal to incorporate
the Uzbek areas of the republic in Uzbekistan.[42] It was true that
towards the middle of March, a conference of 'responsible Party
workers' of Khiva, adopted a resolution which favoured the
delimitation of Khorezm on the nationality principle. But for
a long time, neither the Party Central Committee nor the
Khorezm Central Executive Committee committed themselves to
the national delimitation project.[43]

In Turkestan the preliminary discussions on national delimitation were begun in March 1924. On 10 March a joint session
of the Central Committee of the Turkestan Communist Party
and the Presidium of the Turkestan Central Executive Committee discussed the national delimitation question. Though at
the end of the conference a resolution was adopted favouring
the delimitation of the Turkestan Republic, the discussions in
this conference were characterized by acute differences of
opinion. Rakhimbaev, a prominent Uzbek communist, opposed
the proposal to merge the Kazakh-inhabited regions of Turkestan with the Kazakh ASSR on the ground that it was likely to
greatly enlarge the territory of the Kazakh Republic![44] Khodzhanov, the delegate from the Kazakh areas of Turkestan, and
Paskutsii, who was later to become a member of the Turkmen
National Bureau, rejected the national delimitation scheme
in toto. Paskutsii stressed the need, not of dividing the central
Asian region into a number of national republics, but of merging
the existing republics of Central Asia in one large Soviet
republic. The views expressed by Khodzhanov and many other
delegates almost resembled the views once expressed by the
'Moslem Communists' led by Ryskulov. On 23-24 March a
plenary session of the Central Committee of the Turkestan Communist Party once again reviewed the national delimitation
question. A resolution adopted in this session recognized that the
time was appropriate to take up the question of delimitation of
Turkestan into autonomous republics.[45] The Central Committee
of the Turkestan Communist Party favoured the division of
Turkestan into three national republics of Uzbeks, Kazakhs and

42. *Turkestanskaia Pravda*, 186 (463), 24 August 1924.
43. Tursunov, n. 41, 125.
44. *Ibid.*, 118.
45. *Ibid.*, 124.

Turkmens, and also proposed the establishment of autonomous oblasts for the Tadjiks and the Kirgiz.[46] It, however, opposed the idea of merging the Kazakh-inhabited areas of Turkestan with the Kazakh Republic and proposed instead the establishment of a separate Kazhkh Republic out of those areas.

After these preliminary discussions on the national delimitation question were completed by the Communist Party organizations of Turkestan, Bukhara and Khorezm in the first quarter of 1924, the question was taken up for review by the Politbureau of the Central Committee of the Russian Communist Party on 5 April 1924. In view of the absence of relevant materials on the national delimitation project, the Politbureau decided to defer its decision on the question until the end of May 1924, and in the meantime, it instructed the Central Asiatic Bureau to prepare a detailed report on delimitation project and forward it and other relevant materials (political and ethnographic maps, etc.) to the Central Committee of the Russian Communist Party.[47]

The Central Asiatic Bureau soon began the work of compiling a systematic and comprehensive report on the proposed reform. To accomplish this work, the Central Asiatic Bureau created a special Commission on National Delimitation and also Uzebek, and Turkmen National Commissions.[48] The National Commissions were asked to work out the details of the national delimitation scheme concerning their respective state formations and to submit their reports to the National Delimitation Commission not later than 9 May 1924.

In the meantime the national delimitation project came up for discussion at the Eighth Congress of the Communist Party of Turkestan which was held toward the beginning of May 1924. Ia. E. Rudzutak, a former member of the Turkestan Commission, was deputed by the Central Committee of the Russian Communist Party to attend this Congress and acquaint himself

---

46. *Ibid.*, 125.

47. Kh. T. Tursunov, 'Natsional'noe razmezhevanie Srednei Azii i obrazovanie Uzbekskoi SSR,' *Voprosy istorii* (Moscow) 10 (1954) 45.

48. The represestatives of the Kirgiz were included in the Kazakh National Commission and the Tadjik representatives in the Uzbek National Commission. These two Commissions were instructed to make their proposals also on the state formations of the Kirgiz and the Tadjiks. See Tursunov, n. 41, 126.

with the views of the members of the Communist Party of Turkestan on the delimitation question. Vareikis, the Secretary of the Central Committee of the Turkestan Communist Party, in the course of his report to the Congress, dealt at length on the delimitation question. Vareikis asserted that national delimitation was a 'progressive step forward' in the implementation of the Soviet nationalities policy in Central Asia, and that it was bound to weld together the mosaic of clans and tribes which were ethnically and culturally related to one another and consolidate them in a single socialist nation.[49] Further, he stated that national delimitation, by making it possible for the Uzbeks, Kazakhs, Turkmens and Tadjiks of Turkestan to unite with their kinsmen living in Bukhara and Khorezm, would enhance the prospects for their economic and cultural development.[50] Segizbaev, a Tadjik delegate, declared before the Party Congress that if the proposed reform were to be dropped for any reason, then, national frictions were bound to continue to hamper the work of socialist construction.[51] Rudzutak in his address to the Congress sounded a note of warning. He stated that the public discussion of the national delimitation question was bound to accentuate nationalist feelings among the peoples of Central Asia and give rise to a movement of 'brain waves' on many issues. He declared that it was the task of the responsible Party workers to see that these 'brain waves' were channelled into the 'healthy Communist path'.[52]

Shortly after the Eighth Congress of the Communist Party of Turkestan concluded its session, the National Commissions sub-

49. *Turkestanskaia Pravda*, 100 (377), 8 May 1924. Speaking before the Combined Conference of Party Workers of Tashkent on 20 August 1924, Vareikis further elaborated this view by analysing the effects of national delimitation on the Turkmens. He stated that among the Turkmens the process of consolidation of their nation was not yet complete and its completion was considerably hindered by clan-tribal enmities. The formation of the Turkmen national state, in Vareikis' opinion, was bound to accelerate the process of consolidation and development of the Turkmen nation. See *Turkestanskaia Pravda*, 185 (462), 22 August 1924.

50. *Turkestanskaia Pravda*, 100 (377), 8 May 1924.

51. *Ibid*. In its editorial the newspaper *Turkestanskaia Pravda* wrote that national delimitation 'is bound to put a final end to the internal friction which now impedes economic and political work and it would lead the peoples of Central Asia along the road of national consolidation and economic rehabilitation.' See *ibid*., 102 (379), 12 May 1924.

52. *Turkestanskaia Pravda*, 181 (458), 18 August 1924.

mitted their proposals to the National Delimitation Commission. None of these Commissions, however, had succeeded in deciding upon the criteria for determining the frontiers of the future state formations. This difficulty arose mainly from the fact that ethnic boundaries in Central Asia were not always clearcut and in many places were mostly indeterminable. In resolving this thorny problem the question arose as to what prinicples should serve as bases for resolving the controversies on the frontiers. There were two opposing principles before them—the national-political principle and the economic principle. The national-political principle demanded the resolution of all controversies on the basis of the study of the national composition of the peoples of a given area and of the need to maintain unity of territory. This principle took as its basis the predominance of any given nationality which lived in a compact mass and excluded the possibility of creation of any national corridors or islands which was bound to destroy the principle of territorial unity. The economic principle demanded the fixation of frontiers only after studying the economic links and orientation of a given territory to its adjoining areas, the presence in it of means of communication, irrigation systems, etc.[53] On 10 May 1924 the Natonal Delimitation Commission examined this question. It recommended that the national-political principle be taken as the basis for drawing the frontiers in most cases, since its application in a majority of cases was easier and also because it stemmed directly from the Bolshevik programme on the national question.[54] The Commission also attached great importance to the economic principle since after a detailed study of the different regions, it was found that its claims to recognition could not be overlooked. The decision to preserve certain economic, technological and scientific organizations as the common properties of the future state formations indicated the recognition accorded to the economic principle.[55]

The Uzbek National Commission recommended the formation

53. I. Khodorov, 'Natsional'noe razmezhevanie Srednei Azii,' *Novyi vostok* (Moscow) 8-9 (1925) 68; also see Zelenski, 'Natsional'noe-gosudarstvennoe razmezhevanie Srednei Azii,' *Turkestanskaia Pravda*, 201 (479) 11 September 1924.

54. V. Ia. Nepomnin, *Ocherki sotsialisticheskogo stroitel'stva v Uzbekistane* (1917-1937 gg) (Tashkent, 1957) 112.

55. Khodorov, n. 53, 68.

of the Uzbek republic by merging in it the regions of Turkestan, Bukhara and Khorezm republics which were inhabited predominantly by the Uzbek population.[56] These regions were the Fergana oblast without its Kirgiz majority areas; the Samarkand oblast without five nomadic volosts of the Dzhizak uezd; Tashkent city; the Tashkent and Mirzachul uezds of the Syr-Daria oblast; the territory of the Republic of Bukhara excluding the region situated on the left bank of the river Amu Daria (part of Chardzhui and Kerki *vilaiets*), and the territory of the Khorezm Republic without its Turkmen and Kazakh areas. The Uzbek National Commission also proposed the formation of a separate Tadjik Autonomous Oblast (within the Uzbek Republic) by amalgamating the Pamir and Matcha areas of the Samarkand oblast and Garm, Darvaz and Kuliab regions of the Republic of Bukhara.[57]

A large section of the members of the Kazakh National Commission favoured the incorporation of the Kazakh-inhabited areas of the Turkestan Republic within the Kazakh ASSR and the retention of the Kazakh Republic within the Central Asiatic Federation for the creation of which they made a strong case.[58] The Turkmen National Commission recommended the formation of a separate Turkmen Republic by merging in it the Turkmen-inhabited areas of Turkestan, Bukhara and Khorezm.

The recommendations of the National Commissions on the formation of the future state formations of Central Asia were scrutinized by the National Delimitation Commission on 10 May 1924. The Commission favoured the establishment of the Uzbek and Turkmen republics and the Tadjik and Kirgiz autonomous oblasts. The Commission, however, rejected the recommendations of the Kazakh National Commission to merge the Kazakh-inhabited areas of Turkestan with the Kazakh ASSR and to establish a Central Asiatic Federation.[59]

56. The fact that the Uzbeks of Khorezm, at this stage, still refused to join the proposed Uzbek Republic, it would appear, had no influence on the members of the Uzbek National Commission in making this recommendation.

57. Text of the recommendation of the Uzbek National Commission 'On the formation of the independent Uzbek Republic' is available in Nepomnin, n. 54, 112.

58. Nusupbekov, n. 7, 63.

59. Neither at this stage nor later did the Soviet authorities give any convincing reasons for refusing to establish the Central Asiatic Federation.

The recommendations of the National Delimitation Commission, together with the decisions of the Communist Party organizations of Turkestan, Bukhara and Khorezm, were embodied in the report forwarded by the Central Asiatic Bureau to the Central Committee of the Russian Communist Party. On 2 and 12 June 1924 the Politbureau of the Central Committee of the Russian Communist Party scrutinized this report. On 12 June the Politbureau adopted a decree 'On national delimitation of the republics of Central Asia (Turkestan, Bukhara and Khorezm)'. In this decree it was stated that

1. The proposals of the Central Committees and *Sovnarkoms* of Bukhara and Turkestan be accepted in the following manner:
   (a) to carve out the Turkmen parts of Turkestan, Bukhara and Khorezm and establish an independent Turkmen Republic;[60]
   (b) to carve out from Bukhara and Turkestan their Uzbek areas and establish an independent Uzbek Republic;
   (c) to retain the Khorezm Republic in its present form after separating from it the Turkmen areas;
2. to merge the Kirgiz (i.e., the Kazakh) areas of Turkestan with the KASSR;
3. to create an Autonomous Kara-Kirgiz (i.e., Kirgiz) Oblast and to include it within the RSFSR;
4. to carve out within the Uzbek Republic a separate Autonomous Oblast of the Tadjiks;
5. to conclude a treaty between the USSR and the independent Turkmen and Uzbek Republics on their entrance into the Union in the forthcoming Congress of Soviets of the USSR.[61]

It is evident from this decree that the Politibureau made significant changes in the recommendations made by the National Delimitation Commission and the Communist Party organizations of Turkestan and Bukhara on the national delimitation scheme. Firstly, being aware of the treaty obligation of the RSFSR

In the subsequent months when the national delimitation question was taken up for public discussion the demand for the establishment of such a federation grew more and more.

60. A note appended to this clause stated that 'the question of the form and time of carving out the Turkmen (areas) from the Khorezm Republic is to be taken up for consideration by a commission, the establishment of which is envisaged by clause 11 of the present decree.'

61. For the text of this decree see Nepomnin, n. 54, 113.

to continue to recognize the independence of Khorezm and of the opposition of the Communists of Khorezm to the delimitation scheme, the Politbureau decided in favour of retaining the Khorezm Republic as a separate entity. Secondly, the Politbureau rejected the National Delimitation Commission's suggestion to form a separate state formation from the Kazakh-inhabited areas of Turkestan and decreed instead the immediate merger of those areas with the Kazakh Republic. Thirdly, the Politbureau decided in favour of including the Kirgiz Autonomous Oblast within the RSFSR.[62]

Equally significant was the decision of the Politbureau to retain the Central Asiatic Bureau as the coordinating and guiding organ over the Communist Party organizations of the state formations of Central Asia. The jurisdiction of the Central Asiatic Bureau was extended over the Communist parties of Uzbekistan, Turkmenistan, Khorezm and the oblast Party organizations of Tadjikistan and Kirgizia. The Politbureau also favoured the reconstitution of the Central Asiatic Economic Council in accordance with the changes which were envisaged by the delimitation scheme. The Central Asiatic Economic Council was charged with the task of coordinating the economic activities of the new republics and autonomous oblasts.[63]

The Central Committee of the Russian Communist Party gave elaborate instructions to the Central Asiatic Bureau on the manner in which the national delimitation project was to be steered to its completion and specifically asked the latter to complete the work of delimitation by the end of the budget year (i.e., October 1924).[64] The Central Asiatic Bureau was asked to constitute a Territorial Commission consisting of representatives of the various nationalities of Central Asia and to charge this Commission with the task of delineating the frontiers of the new republics and autonomous oblasts.[65] The Central Committee also favoured the launching of an intensive

---

62. The National Delimitation Commission had not stated clearly whether the Kirgiz Autonomous Oblast was to be included within any other state formation or was to exist in its own right as an independent entity.

63. See Gordienko, n. 40, 164.

64. *Kommunisticheskie partii Turkestana, Bukhary i Khorezma v period natsional'no-gosudarstvennogo razmezhevaniia v Srednei Azii* (Tashkent, 1959) 47-8. (Cited hereafter as *KPTBKh.*)

65. *Ibid.*, 47.

propaganda campaign to enlighten the peoples of Central Asia
on the significance of the new reform and to secure their
support.[66]

The Central Asiatic Bureau on 26 June 1924 resolved to proceed with the work of national delimitation on the lines suggested by the Central Committee of the Russian Communist Party.
Accordingly, it established a Central Territorial Commission and
charged it with the task of working out a concrete plan of delimitation. In its work the Territorial Commission was asked to
take the assistance of the newly-established Statistical and Economic Commissions.[67] Besides, the Uzbek, Turkmen, Kazakh,
Kirgiz and Tadjik National Bureaux were organized to work out
the political, economic and administrative measures which were
required for the establishment of the new republics and autonomous oblasts.[68] At the same time, the Central Asiatic Bureau
also decided to launch an intensive propaganda campaign among
the masses to explain to them the significance and objectives of
the delimitation project. In order that this campaign might be
conducted in conformity with the aims and objectives of the
proposed reform, the Central Asiatic Bureau on 15 July 1924
issued a 'thesis on national-territorial delimitation of Central
Asia for reporters.' In this thesis the Central Asiatic Bureau
instructed the reporters and propagandists to explain to the
people the factors which induced the Soviet authorities to embark upon so radical a reform as the national delimitation of
Central Asia and the objectives it sought to achieve.[69]

Beginning from August 1924 the national delimitation project was taken up for renewed discussion by innumerable organizations associated with the Communist parties of Turkestan and

66. *Turkestanskaia Pravda*, 162 (439), 27 July 1924.
67. These Commissions were charged with the task of processing and
studying the available materials and also of conducting an area-wise study
of the different regions in order to determine their national-linguistic
structures, economic set-up etc. The Territorial Commission was asked to
base its recommendations on an objective evaluation of the data made
available by the Statistical and Economic Commissions. See E. Shteinberg,
Ocherki istorii Turkmenii (Leningrad, 1934) 110; also see K. N. Nurbekov,
'Obrazovanie Kirgizskoi suverennoi sovetskoi sotsialisticheskoi respubliki,'
Sovetskoe gosudarstvo i pravo (Moscow) 9 (1958) 44.
68. See Gordienko, n. 40, 165-6.
69. For the full text of the thesis see *Turkestanskaia Pravda*, 165 (442),
30 July 1924.

Bukhara. Besides the oblast, uezd and volost organs of these parties, the party cells, trade unions, the unions of 'Koshchi,'[70] collective farms, industrial and commercial establishments, educational institutions, etc., discussed the delimitation scheme and adpoted resolutions favouring it.[71] A plenary session of the Tashkent (old part) District Committee meeting on 11 August stated that the thesis issued by the Central Asiatic Bureau provided the correct approach to the problem of national delimitation.[72] A resolution adpoted by the members of the Central Asiatic State University stated that the timing of the reform was well set and the formation of nationally homogeneous states was bound to put an end to the existing national antagonisms and frictions among the peoples of Central Asia.[73] A resolution adopted by a conference of Uigur workers, while welcoming the delimitation scheme, reminded Party organizations of the need to keep in view the interests of such national minorities as the Uigurs, Kashgaris, Taranchis, Dungans etc.[74] A conference of the non-Party workers and soldiers of the Red Army on 30 August, after having heard a report on the delimitation project by Karklin, the Vice-Chairman of the Central Asiatic Bureau, stated in a resolution that 'the delimitation of the Central Asian republics on the national-territorial principle is a matter of great importance and will provide wide opportunities for class stratification and class war.'[75] A conference attended by Party members, trade unionists, Komsomol members, workers and soldiers of the Red Army held in Merv greeted the proposal to establish a separate Turkmen republic and stated that such a

70. Peasant organizations which included landless and small peasants, agricultural workers, tenant farmers, share croppers and village *kustars*. The union of *Koshchi* was a mixture of rural trade unions and cooperatives and was predominantly political in its character. See Alexander G. Park, *Bolshevism in Turkestan 1917-1927* (New York, 1957) 146.

71. Texts of these resolutions are available in the following numbers of *Turkestanskaia Pravda*, 179 (456), 15 August 1924; 181 (458), 18 August; 182 (459), 19 August; 183 (460), 20 August; 184 (461), 21 August; 186 (463); 24 August; 187 (464), 25 August; 188 (465), 26 August; 189 (466), 27 August; 190 (467), 28 August; 192 (469), 31 August; 194 (471), 2 September; 200 (477), 9 September; 233 (510), 19 September; and 240 (517), 27 October.

72. *Turkestanskaia Pravda*, 179 (456), 15 August 1924.

73. *Turkestanskaia Pravda*, 190 (467), 28 August 1924.

74. *Turkestanskaia Pravda*, 192 (469), 31 August 1924.

75. *Turkestanskaia Pravda*, 194 (471), 2 September 1924.

step was bound to create favourable conditions for drawing the bulk of the Turkmen population into the constructive actvities of the state, for raising their cultural level and for the most efficient exploitation of the natural resources of the region.[76] A conference of peasants and members of the Union of *Koshchi* held in Samarkand stated that the delimitation project fully satisfied the behests of Vladimir Ilych Lenin on the national question.[77] The Regional Conference of Trade Union Organizations of the Turkestan Republic, meeting in Tashkent in September, hailed the national delimitation project as a prudent device which not only facilitated the overcoming of national frictions but also helped the promotion of the economic and cultural development of the various nationalities of Central Asia.[78] Speaking before the conference of the Party workers of Tashkent, Vareikis, Secretary of the Central Committee of the Turkestan Communist Party, asserted that 'a time will come when national delimitation will be viewed as a second revolution which has fundamentally altered the inter-relations among the toilers of Central Asia.'[79] A resolution adopted at this conference emphasized the need for conducting the work of national delimitation in the spirit of genuine internationalism and solidarity of interests of the peoples of the Central Asian region.[80]

On 14 September 1924 a plenary session of the Central Committee of the Turkestan Communist Party examined the views expressed by the members of the Party on national delimitation. It noted with some consternation that while the leaders of the Party and its rank and file had expressed their views on the national delimitation question, the vast peasant masses had remained, more or less, indifferent to it. In order to win over the support of the peasantry to the proposed reform, the Secretary of the Central Committee of the Turkestan Communist Party addressed a circular-letter to 'all oblast committees, uezd committees, cell bureaux and to all members and candidates of the Party' urging them to mobilize all their resources to launch an

76. *Turkestanskaia Pravda*, 187 (464), 25 August 1924.
77. *Turkestanskaia Pravda*, 200 (477), 9 September 1924.
78. *Turkestanskaia Pravda*, 209 (486), 19 September 1924.
79. *Turkestanskaia Pravda*, 185 (462), 22 August 1924.
80. *Ibid.*

intensive campaign among non-Party workers and peasants and influence their opinions in favour of the delimitation project.[81]

In the days that followed the campaign seeking to popularize the national delimitation scheme among the peasant masses grew in depth and dimension. As instructed by the Central Committee of the Turkestan Communist Party, legions of propagandists and agitators penetrated the remotest corners of the region and canvassed support for the new reform.[82]

During the period of public discussion of the national delimitation project the local newspapers invited the public to express its opinions in their columns. A large number of persons hailing from different walks of life and pursuing diverse occupations discussed all aspects of the delimitation issue in a thoroughgoing manner. However, not everything went as planned by Communist leadership. Notwithstanding the constant reminders from above that the discussion and agitation on national delimitation must be carried on in a spirit of genuine internationalism, frequent nationalistic manifestations were in evidence everywhere. On 11 September 1924 N. Zelenski, the Secretary of the Central Committee of the Russian Communist Party (who later became the head of the Central Asiatic Bureau), complained that several members of tht Party 'were losing the common perspective on the national question and instead of upholding the Party line, had started approaching many issues from the narrow nationalistic angle.'[83] He further alleged that many Party newspapers, judged by their writings and the type of articles they had published, also appeared to have lost perspective.[84] This was, in fact, only natural. The tremendous propaganda on national delimitation which was carried out for the best part of the year 1924 could not but accentuate the national consciousness of the various national groups. Zelenski himself admitted that there was an increase in the national consciousness.

81. *Turkestanskaia Pravda*, 205 (482), 15 September 1924.
82. In Bukhara also the propagandists of the reform carried out an intensive campaign. After the adoption of a thesis on national delimitation by the Central Committee of the Bukharan Communist Party in July 1924, the question was discussed at innumerable conferences and meetings of party and non-party men. By the middle of August the campaign reached its apogee. See *Turkestanskaia Pravda*, 188 (405), 26 August 1924.
83. *Turkestanskaia Pravda*, 201 (479), 11 September 1924.
84. *Ibid.*

of not only the dominant national groups, but even among the smaller and weaker nationalities such as the Kara-Kalpaks, the Kazakh population of Bukhara, the Kashgaris, Taranchis, Dungans, etc.[85] Once the public interest and enthusiasm on the question of establishing national republics were roused, it became difficult to keep the discussion within the narrow limits set by the Communist leadership.[86] The 'movement of brain waves' on many issues of national delimitation to which Rudzutak had made a reference in the Eighth Congress of the Communist Party of Turkestan, was now in evidence everywhere. Many started alleging that in reorganizing the state frontiers of the Central Asian region the Bolsheviks were parcelling out the ancient territories of the East. The Bukharan clergy pleaded for the retention of Bukhara as an independent Muslim state. The Kazakh nationalists put forward a grandiose scheme for the establishment of a 'Greater Kazakhstan' with its territorry stretching from the Bukharan steppe and Siberia to the Volga. The Uzbek and Kirgiz nationalists came out with their plans for the establishment of a 'Great Uzbek State' and 'Great Kirgizia.' All of them saw in the national delimitation scheme an excellent opportunity to enlarge the size of the territories of their republics at the cost of their neighbours. Thus, for instance, the Khorezmians, who until then had shown only a lukewarm interest in the national delimitation project, suddenly put forward a proposal to constitute a federated republic of Khorezm composed of the Uzbek regions of Khorezm, Turkestan and Kara-Kalpakia. Yet other sections of the public voiced their demands for the establishment of 'separate autonomies,' 'union of free tribes,' 'independent cities,' etc.[87] Rudzutak, it may be recalled, had

85. *Ibid.*

86. An example of the attempt made by the Turkestan Communist Party to counter the growth of national exclusiveness among the peoples of Central Asia while discussing the national delimitation project could be seen in a thesis it issued during this period. The thesis declared that 'the toiling masses of Central Asia should firmly get to learn that the creation of separate independent Soviet republics does not place before them exclusively nationalistic tasks and aims... on the contrary, proletarian internationalism lies at the bottom of all the future work of the national republics. All those who think otherwise—either consciously or otherwise—are the enemies of the workers'-peasants' government.' Cited in Tursunov, n. 47, 45.

87. S. Radzhapov, 'Etapy razvitiia sovetskogo gosudarstvennogo stroia

enjoined upon the 'responsible Party workers' to channel such 'movement of brain waves' into the 'healthy Communist path.' But it soon became evident that many prominent local Communists were more interested in throwing the weight of their influence for securing the realization of the territorial and financial demands put forward by the national groups to which they belonged rather than in upholding the Party line on national delimitation. It was found that the Party propagandists who were sent around to explain to the public the essence of the new reforms had themselves begun an agitation for demarcating the frontier of a given territory in a particular manner and on the advisability of including this volost or that village within this or that republic.[88] Such 'deviations towards nationalism' began to assume an acute form especially among the Uzbek and Kazakh Party workers when the question of deciding the future of the Mirzachul' and Tashkent uezds of the Syr-Daria oblast and of the city of Tashkent was taken up.[89] The Kazakh Party workers led by Khodzhanov and Asfandiiarov launched a vigorous campaign to seek a revision of the decision of the Politbureau which had assigned Tashkent City to the future Uzbek Republic. They also demanded that the Mirzachul' and Tashkent uezds in an unmutilated form be transferred to the Kazakh ASSR. The Uzbek nationalists in turn claimed not only that the two uezds including the city of Tashkent be merged with Uzbekistan but that some of the cities of the Syr-Daria oblast which had considerable Uzbek populations be organized into autonomous cities.[90] These

v Srednei Azii,' *Sovetskoe gosudarstvo i pravo,* 11 (1948) 66; by the same author 'Natsional'no-gosudarstvennoe razmazhevanie Srednei Azii,' *Uchenye zapiski Tashkentskogo iuridicheskogo instituta* (Tashkent, 1955) I, 74; Nusupbekov, n. 7, 67.

88. Such detractions from the Party line on the national delimitation issue led the editor of *Ak Zhol,* Tokhtybaev, to state that 'in discussing the national delimitation scheme great attention must be paid to the voice of the Russian proletariat, because unlike the local national groups which are likely to express only their narrow nationalist interests, the Russian proletariat, not itself being a party to any local controversies, is bound to take a broader and more objective view.' See *Turkestanskaia Pravda,* 184 (461), 21 August 1924.

89. Zelenski revealed on 10 September 1924 that no less than three national groups, the Uzbeks, the Kazakhs and the Kirgiz had advanced their claims over the city of Tashkent. See *Turkestanskaia Pravda,* 201 (479), 11 September 1924.

90. The Uzbeks constituted 44.6 per cent of the population of Aulie-Ata, 70.6 per cent of the population of Turkestan and 74.1 per cent of

controversies assumed such an acrimonious character that it
looked as though national exclusiveness rather than proletarian
internationalism had won the day.[91]

III. ATTITUDE OF THE KHOREZM COMMUNISTS TO THE DELIMITATION QUESTION

The Communists of Khorezm, perhaps, caused the greatest
embarrassment to the Bolshevik leadership on the national
delimitation question. It was noted earlier in this chapter
that the initial discussions on national delimitation held at the
conference of the Executive Bureau of the Central Committee
of the Communist Party of Khorezm in March 1924 had not led
to any clearcut decision. Subsequently, however, the Communist
Party and Government of Khorezm came out openly against
the delimitation scheme. Towards the beginning of May, the
Secretary of the Central Committee of the Khorezm Communist
Party and a few members of the government submitted a report
to the Central Asiatic Bureau in which they stated their desire

---

the population of Chimkent. However, the rural areas which surrounded
these cities had a predominantly Kazakh population. See *Otchët Syr-
Dar'inskogo oblastnogo ekonomicheskogo soveshchaniia za 1921-1922:
khoziaistvennyi god* (Tashkent, 1923) 20. (Cited hereafter as *OSDOES*).
91. Both the Kazakhs and the Uzbeks contended that they alone constituted a majority of the population of the Tashkent uezd and that the
Kurama, an ethnic group formed by the fusion of the Kazakh and the
Uzbek tribes (Kurama in Uzbek means 'sewn together' or 'mongrel') which
constituted 14.1 per cent of the population of the uezd was more intimately related to them alone. A similar dispute arose between the Kazakh
and Uzbek representatives on the Territorial Commission on the future
status of the Kara-Kalpaks of the Amu-Daria region. Both of them
demanded that the region be included in their own republics. The 1926
census showed that there were 169,748 Uzbeks as against only 1,972
Kazakhs within the city of Tashkent. It also showed that in the former
Tashkent district of the Syr-Daria oblast there were 328,359 Uzbeks as
against 86,874 Kazakhs. Further, it was found that the Kurama, over
whom both the Kazakhs and the Uzbeks disputed, ethnically and culturally were more intimately connected with the latter. As such, the
Tashkent uezd minus ten of its thirtyone volosts, the Mirzachul' uezd
minus two of its eight volosts and the city of Tashkent were assigned to
the Uzbek Republic. However, the claims of the Uzbek nationalists to
organize certain cities with predominantly Uzbek populations such as
Turkestan, Aulie-Ata, Chimkent etc., into 'autonomous cities' were rejected on the ground that such a device was bound to destroy the economic
and territorial unity of the Kazakh Republic. See *S.E.* n. 15, 3; *Vsesoiuznaia perepis' naseleniia 1926 g* (Moscow, 1928) XV, Section 1, 36; Nusupbekov, n. 7, 70-5; Gordienko, n. 40, 168.

to retain the Republic of Khorezm in its existing form. On 2 July 1924 the Central Committee of the Communist Party of Khorezm fully endorsed this view in a telegram it sent to the Central Asiatic Bureau.[92] In view of this negative stand taken by the Soviet and Party organizations of Khorezm on the delimitation question, the Politbureau was forced to agree to leave the bulk of the territory of the Khorezm Republic outside the scope of the delimitation plan.

A resolution adopted by the Executive Bureau of the Central Committee of the Communist Party of Khorezm on 9 July gave an impression that the Communist Party of Khorezm was about to reverse the negative stand it had taken earlier on the delimitation issue. The resolution stated that the delimitation of the territory of Khorezm was the only correct method for resolving the national question.[93] That this resolution was adopted under outside pressure and that, as yet, there was no change of attitude of the Khorezm Communist Party to the delimitation issue became clear from the fact that the Executive Bureau did not propose to follow up the adoption of this resolution by any concrete action. On the contrary, on 16 July 1924 the Central Committee of the Communist Party of Khorezm openly chided some of its members who sought to rally popular support for the delimitation plan and threatened to expel them from the Party.[94]

Confronted with such an open defiance of the 'Party line' by the Central Committee of the Communist Party of Khorezm, the Central Asiatic Bureau decided to act. Its Vice-Chairman, Karklin, was rushed to Khorezm in the latter half of July 1924. A statement issued to the press by Karklin after his return to Tashkent towards the beginning of August did not disclose the real purport of his visit to Khorezm and the statement gave an impression that the tour was merely a routine one.[95] However, quite significant was Karklin's observation that an extensive tour of the Turkmen, Kazakh-Kara-Kalpak and Uzbek areas of Khorezm had convinced him that the peoples of those areas were very keen to secede from Khorezm in order to unite with their kinsmen who were about to come into possession of their

92. Gordienko, n. 40, 161.
93. *Ibid.*, 161.
94. *Ibid.*, 169.
95. *Turkestanskaia Pravda*, 171 (448), 6 August 1924.

own national republics. Karklin also stated that only by opting
for national delimitation could Khorezm eradicate national
frictions among its heterogeneous population.[96] The fact that
Karklin's visit to Khorezm coincided with the adoption by the
Central Committee of the Communist Party of Khorezm a resolution 'welcoming the decision of the Politbureau of the Central
Committee of the Russian Communist Party on national delimitation' could not have been a mere chance occurrence.[97] That
it was not so became clear from a statement issued to the press
by Sultan Kary, the Chairman of the Central Executive Committee of Khorezm, a few days later. In this statement Sultan
Kary stated:

> ... the great economic significance of the delimitation of
> Khorezm did not strike us until Comrade Karklin, two weeks
> before, made a fresh report. Only then we (i.e., the Uzbek
> Communists) understood that we do not have a better way
> out than to incorporate ourselves with Uzbekistan.[98]

It is beyond dispute that Karklin succeeded in his mission of
bringing the recalcitrant Uzbek Communists of Khorezm into line
with the Communist parties of Turkestan and Bukhara on the
national delimitation question by telling them that a truncated
Khorezm bereft of its Turkmen and Kara-Kalpak regions was
not economically viable and perhaps also by hinting that the
Central subsidies which were required to keep Khorezm in
existence as a separate entity might not be forthcoming. Confronted with such a threat of economic impoverishment, the

---

96. Equally significant was Karklin's observation that the pace of economic development of Khorezm was extremely slow and that sizable
subsidies from the Centre were needed to bolster up its economy. In
other words, what Karklin meant was that Khorezm was not an economically viable unit and that it was quite a problem to bridge its revenue
deficits. See *ibid;* also see *Turkestanskaia Pravda*, 258 (535), 19 November 1924.

97. The resolution adopted by the Executive Bureau of the Central
Committee of the Communist Party of Khorezm on 26 July requested the
Central Asiatic Bureau to prevail upon the Central Committee of the
Russian Communist Party to carry out the necessary amendments in the
decree of the Politbureau relating to Khorezm. The resolution further
stated that the Central Committee of the Khorezm Communist Party considered it expedient to merge the Uzbek areas of Khorezm with the Uzbek
Republic, and that the Kara-Kalpaks were free to unite with the republic
of their choice. See Gordienko, n. 40, 169 and Tursunov, n. 41, 146.

98. *Turkestanskaia Pravda*, 186 (463), 24 August 1924.

Uzbeks of Khorezm had no other alternative but to agree to merge with the Uzbek Republic.

On 5 August 1924 the Central Asiatic Bureau formally considered the 'request' of the Central Committee of the Communist Party of Khorezm to approve the decision of its Executive Bureau (of 26 July 1924) on merging the Uzbek areas of the Republic with Uzbekistan. The Central Asiatic Bureau, after giving its own approval to this proposal, asked the Central Committee of the Russian Communist Party 'to fulfil the request of the Khorezm Communist Party on amending points (b) and (c) of the decree of the Politbureau of 12 June in relation to the Khorezm ssr'[99] The Central Committee of the Russian Communist Party subsequently carried out the appropriate amendments which completed the process of bringing Khorezm in line with Turkestan and Bukhara on the national delimitation question.

IV. COMMUNIST ATTITUDE TO PROPOSAL TO ESTABLISH THE CENTRAL ASIATIC FEDERATION AND RETENTION OF KAZAKH ASSR WITHIN THE CENTRAL ASIATIC ECONOMIC COUNCIL

In the course of working out the details of the national delimitation plan by the various national commissions, and in the subsequent public discussion of that plan, a large number of Communists both in Turkestan and in the Kazakh republics favoured the retention of the intimate economic links which had evolved in the past between the Syr-Daria and Semirechie oblasts which were about to be transferred to the Kazakh ASSR and the remaining parts of the Central Asian region. While a large section of them desired to retain the Kazakh Republic as a constituent member of the Central Asiatic Federation, others taking their stand on the 'thesis on national delimitation' issued by the Central Asiatic Bureau on 15 July 1924, preferred to retain the Kazakh Republic within the orbit of the Central Asiatic Economic Council.[100] When the delimitation plan

99. Gordienko, n. 40, 169-70.
100. The architect of the Central Asiatic Federation scheme was said to be Khodzhanov, a prominent Kazakh Communist leader. He was supported by Faizulla Khodzhaev, Asfandiiarov, Atabaev, Iu. Abdurakhmanov

was taken up for discussion, a large section of the people showed a keen interest for 'retaining the Kazakh Republic within the Central Asiatic political and economic union.' And numerous resolutions which favoured such a union began pouring into the Central Asiatic Bureau and the Central Committee of the Communist Party of Turkestan. Within Tashkent City alone more than fifty Party cells were reported to have come out in support of this union.[101] Some of the prominent local Communist leaders, being not yet sure of the attitude of the Central Asiatic Bureau to this question, spoke in equivocal terms. But such equivocal statements deceived no one since it was generally known that these leaders were the advocates of the Central Asiatic Federation. Abdurakhmanov, Secretary of the Turkestan Central Executive Committee, declared in August that

> the formation of independent republic and autonomous oblasts is a step forward to the establishment of a single state of toilers of Central Asia. Through national delimitation to international unification of the toiling masses of Central Asia, to the creation of a Central Asiatic Federation—such is the slogan of our Party.[102]

Eskaraev, the Chairman of the Syr-Daria Oblast Executive Committee, complained that 'voices are already heard among us on isolating the Kazakh Republic, and I hope that merely because the Kazakh Republic has an extensive territory, the Party will not exclude it from the future economic unification of Central Asia.'[103] Speaking before the Central Committee of the Communist Party of Turkestan in August 1924, Vareikis stated that

> the idea of Central Asiatic Federation has become extremely popular among the members of the Party. The prospects for the creation of such a federation are bright. Therefore, it would be a great mistake to categorically speak against the possibility of establishing the Central Asiatic Federation.[104]

However, this optimism about the establishment of the

and many other noted native Communist leaders. See Radzhapov, 'Natsional'no- gosudarstvennoe razmezhevanie Srednei Azii,' n. 87, 45.

101. *Turkestanskaia Pravda*, 184 (461), 21 August 1924 and 181 (458), 18 August 1924.

102. *Turkestanskaia Pravda*, 186 (463), 24 August 1924.

103. *Turkestanskaia Pravda*, 181 (458), 18 August 1924.

104. *Turkestanskaia Pravda*, 185 (462), 22 August 1924.

Central Asiatic Federation was soon to fade. On 14 September 1924 Vareikis announced at a plenary session of the Central Committee of the Turkestan Communist Party that 'the idea of forming a federation, though it has a large number of adherents among the Party members, has been considered as premature by the higher organs of the Party.'[105] No other reason was publicly given either then or in the years that followed by any Soviet authorities or scholars for not establishing the Central Asiatic Federation.

The proposal to retain the Kazakh Republic within the Central Asiatic Economic Council also met with a similar fate. The Vice-Chairman of the Central Asiatic Bureau stated that the thesis of the Central Asiatic Bureau had never envisaged the retention of the Kazakh ASSR within the Central Asiatic Economic Council[106] and that it was either misunderstood or misconstrued by the members of the Party. In Karklin's opinion, neither the Central Asiatic Bureau nor the Central Asiatic Economic Council was in a position to discharge its coordinating and supervisory functions efficiently if its jurisdiction was extended over such large and remote regions which were included within the frontiers of the Kazakh Republic.[107] He stated further that 'such a work of co-ordination is impracticable at the present moment in view of our extremely weak and bad means of communication.'[108] A few days later, Zelenski, Secretary of the Central Committee of the Russian Communist Party, asserted that, barring a few Party organizations of Tashkent City, the bulk of the Communist Party organizations of Turkestan were opposed to having any relations with the Kazakh ASSR. Zelenski stated that such an attitude was justified in view of the fact that the Kazakhs were oriented more towards Omsk and Orenburg than towards Tashkent.[109] Though Zelenski conceded that the Syr-Daria and Semirechie oblasts had close economic ties with the other parts of the Central Asian region, he argued that this

105. *Turkestanskaia Pravda*, 205 (482), 15 September 1924.
106. In fact, it was true that the thesis had not envisaged the extension of the jurisdiction either of the Central Asiatic Economic Council or of the Central Asiatic Bureau over the Kazakh Republic. See the text of the thesis in *Turkestanskaia Pravda*, 165 (442), 30 July 1924.
107. *Turkestanskaia Pravda*, 181 (458), 18 August 1924.
108. *Ibid.*
109. *Turkestanskaia Pravda*, 199 (476), 8 September 1924.

alone was not sufficient to justify the inclusion of the Kazakh
Republic within the orbit of the economic unification of Central
Asia.[110] He repeated the argument earlier advanced by Karklin
that 'to guide the economic activities of the distant areas of
Kazakhstan which bordered on Siberia and the Trans-Ural region
from Tashkent or Turkestan with the existing means of communication is an extremely difficult task.'[111] The fact that the proposal to effect the economic intergration of the Kazakh regions
with Central Asia has never been taken up since then, in spite
of the fact that during these years the means of communication
have improved greatly, indicates that there were other considerations to force the Kazakh Republic into political and economic
isolation from its southern neighbours.[112]

V. WORK OF TERRITORIAL COMMISSION AND ITS RECOMMENDATIONS

While the Party organs were preoccupied in resolving the political controversies which had arisen in the course of the public
discussions on the delimitation scheme, the Central Territorial
Commission and the National Bureaux proceeded with the work
of giving a concrete shape to the delimitation plan.[113]   They

110. Zelenski stated that the economic importance of the Syr-Daria and
Semirechie oblasts to the Turkestan region was unduly exaggerated. Their
contributions either in foodstuffs or in cattle products to the economy of
the Turkestan Republic, in his opinion, were insignificant. It is interesting
to note that a senior member of the Turkestan Government thought otherwise on this issue. Sergazibaev, the Vice-Chairman of the *Sovnarkom* of
the Turkestan Republic, stated that these two oblasts constituted the
main source of cattle wealth of the Turkestan Republic. In the years
immediately preceding their transfer to the Kazakh Republic, the Syr-
Daria and Semirechie oblasts contributed to the Turkestan Republic 67.3
per cent of its leather, 69.5 per cent of its furs, and 46.5 per cent of its
wool. See *Turkestanskaia Pravda*, 190 (467), 28 August 1924.
    111. *Turkestanskaia Pravda*, 201 (479), 11 September 1924.
    112. Within the Central Asian region itself the new republics and
autonomous oblasts had no other choice before them except to join the
Central Asiatic Economic Council. When Zelenski learnt that some people were not favourably disposed towards this proposal, he denounced
their attitude as 'a manifestation of out-right local chauvinism.' See
Turkestanskaia Pravda, 199 (476), 8 September 1924.
    113. The information available on the work of the Territorial Commis-
sion is next to nothing. Its report was never published and the newspapers of this period also fail to throw much light on its work. Though
many Soviet writers have published books and articles on the National

sought to determine the size of the territory and population of
each state formation and to fix its frontiers on the basis of a
study of the national composition and economic set-up of the
different regions and to work out projects for the establishment
of the political, administrative and economic institutions of the
future national republics and autonomous oblasts. The fact that
by that time the republics of Turkestan, Bukhara and Khorezm
had already organized several national oblasts whose contours,
to a large extent, anticipated the future frontiers of the national
republics and autonomous oblasts rendered the work of the
Territorial Commission and National Bureaux relatively easier.
But their work was also beset with great difficulties on account of
the scanty, imprecise and contradictory character of the data on
which they had to rely. While the Government of the Turkestan
Republic was able to provide the territorial Commission and
the National Bureaux with some valuable materials,[114] the governments of Bukhara and Khorezm had practically nothing to
offer them. Since no census of population was conducted in
Bukhara and Khorezm before 1926, the Territorial Commission
and the National Bureaux were forced to draw heavily upon the
highly controversial estimates of the Commissions on Regionalization and the Central Asiatic Economic Council.[115] In addition
to this, the practice which still persisted among some sections
of the peoples of the Central Asian region of calling themselves
by their clan-tribal names made it more difficult to determine
correctly the national composition of several areas.[116] To over-

Delimitation of the Central Asian Region, none of them has tried to give
any additional information on the Commission's work. Similarly, there is
paucity of material on the work of the various National Bureaux. Steinberg and Karpych have provided some useful details on the working of
the Turkmen National Bureau, and the newspaper, *Turkestanskaia Pravda,*
also occasionally reported on its working. The members of the Turkmen
National Bureau were Aitakov, Atabaev, Sakat Muradov, Paskutsii, B.
Nazarov and Artyk Rakhmanov.

114. These consisted mainly of the 1917 and 1920 census reports, two
volumes of official statistical compilations on the economy and population
of the Republic, and the reports of the Commission on Regionalization
and Administrative-economic Divisions. The 1917 census was wholly out
of date and the 1920 census was incomplete. The latter did not cover
Fergana—the most populous oblast' of the Turkestan Republic.

115. How radically these estimates differ from one another was seen in
the earlier part of this chapter. See pages 155-6.

116. The 1920 census reports revealed that among the Uzbeks of

come these difficulties the Territorial Commission often deputed groups of expert investigators to conduct systematic studies of those areas on which either there was no information at all or the available information was faulty, and to place their findings before the members of the Commission.

By the beginning of September 1924, the Territorial Commission completed the task assigned to it. The details of its recommendations on merging the different regions of Turkestan, Bukhara and Khorezm in the new republics and autonomous oblasts are given below.

1. *The Uzbek Republic.* The Commission recommended the inclusion of the following areas of Turkestan and Bukhara in the Uzbek Republic:[117]

> (1) the Dzhizak uezd excluding its six volosts inhabited by the Kazakhs, the Samarkand uezd excluding its three volosts inhabited by Tadjiks, the Katta-Kurgan and Khodzhent uezds of the Samarkand oblast;
>
> (2) the Tashkent uezd excluding its ten Kazakh volosts and a part of the Mirzachul' uezd of the Syr-Daria oblast;
>
> (3) the Kokand uezd excluding its two volosts inhabited by the Kirgiz population, the Andizhan uezd excluding its ten Kirgiz volosts, the Namangan uezd excluding its ten Kirgiz volosts, the Fergana uezd minus four volosts, and the two volosts of Bulak-Bashi and Maniak of the Osh uezd of the Fergana oblast;
>
> (4) Bukhara, Kermin, Nur-Ata, Karshi, Shakhrisiabz, Guzar, Baisun, Sary-Assi (excluding the Karatag *tuman*) and Shirabad (excluding the Kelifa *tuman*) *vilaiets* of the Republic of Bukhara. [118]

2. *The Tadjik Autonomous Oblast.* According to the recommendations of the Territorial Commission the following areas

Turkestan there were many who still regarded themselves as Sarts and others who called themselves by their clan-tribal names such as Bargin, Dzhalair, Mitan, Naiman etc. The findings of the Commission on the Regionalization of Bukhara and Khorezm indicated that such practices were in vogue on a much larger scale in those republics. See *Perepis' naseleniia v Turkestanskoi respublike* (Tashkent, 1924) V, 35-6; *MRSA(K)*, n. 17, 96.

117. The Territorial Commission did not recommend the inclusion of the Uzbek regions of Khorezm in the Uzbek Republic since the decision of the Central Committee of the Russian Communist Party on this issue was not yet made available.

118. *Turkestanskaia Pravda,* 201 (479), 11 September 1924.

were proposed to be included within the Tadjik Autonomous Oblast :

(1) the Kurgan-Tube *vilaiet;*
(2) the Kuliab *vilaiet;*
(3) the Diushambe *vilaiet;*
(4) a part of the Syr-Daria *vilaiet* (the Regar area and Karatag);
(5) The Garm *vilaiet;*
(6) the upper Zarafshan region situated in the eastern part of the Samarkand oblast;
(7) the Western Pamir region including Roshnan, Sugnan, Ishkashim and Liangar;
(8) the Sarasui area (the Oroshor volost);
(9) a part of the territory of the Wakhan volost located to the east of the frontier of the Bukharan Republic and extending up to the lake Zor-kul. [119]

3. *The Turkmen Republic.* The Commission recommended the incorporation of the following areas of Turkestan, Bukhara and Khorezm in the Turkmen Republic:

(1) the entire Turkmen oblast (the former Transcaspian oblast) of the Turkestan Republic;
(2) the whole of Kerki and Chardzhui *vilaiets* and the Kelifa *tuman* of the Republic of Bukhara;
(3) Tashauz, Ilialy, Porsu, Kunia-Urgench regions; the entire area situated between the Turkmen areas of Khorezm and the frontier of the Kazakh Republic, the southern and north-western portions of Khodzheili, western Kipchak, Mangyt, Ambar-Manak, northern Khozavat, Sadavar, Tuiu-Muian and Dargan-Ata areas of the Republic of Khorezm.[120]

4. *The Kirgiz Autonomous Oblast.* The following areas of the Turkestan Republic were proposed to the included within the Kirgiz Autonomous oblast:

(1) the Karakol uezd;
(2) a part of the Pishpek uezd (the Naryn region) including the Pishpek city and its seven Kirgiz volosts;[121]

119. *Ibid.*
120. *Ibid.*
121. Only three volosts of the Pishpek uezd were left outside the composition of the Kirgiz Autonomous Oblast. They were Giorgievsk, Zachuisk and Karakun.

(3) a part of the Aulie-Ata uezd consisting of fourteen Kirgiz-inhabited volosts;[122]
(4) the ten Kirgiz volosts of the Andizhan uezd;[123]
(5) the ten Kirgiz volosts of the Namangan uezd;[124]
(6) the four Kirgiz volosts of the Fergana uezd;[125]
(7) the two Kirgiz volosts of the Kokand uezd;[126]
(8) the Osh uezd excluding its two volosts inhabited by the Uzbeks;[127]
(9) the eastern portion of the Pamir region.

5. *The Kazakh inhabited regions of the Turkestan Republic transferred to the Kazakh ASSR* :

(1) the Ak-Mechet uezd, twenty-four Kazakh volosts of the Aulie-Ata uezd including the Aulie-Ata town, the Kaza-linsk uezd, a part of the Mirzachul' uezd, a part of the Tashkent uezd (its ten Kazakh-inhabited volosts), the Turkestan uezd and the Chimkent uezd of the Syr-Daria oblast;
(2) the Alma-Ata, Dzharkent and Lepsinsk uezds, three Kazakh inhabited volosts of the Pishpek uezd and the Taldy-Kurgan uezd of the Semirechie oblast;
(3) six Kazakh-inhabited volosts of the Dzhizak uezd of the Samarkand oblast.[128]

VI. THE KARA-KALPAK
AUTONOMOUS OBLAST

The proposal to establish the Kara-Kalpak Autonomous Oblast was entirely new. During the initial discussions on the national delimitation scheme neither the Kara-Kalpaks them-

122. These volosts were Kurkurez, Karakol, Bau-Terek, Kenkol, Tolko-novosk, Ur-Machal, Dzhalilev, Kara-Balti, Uch-Kurgan, Dmitrievsk, Niko-laipolsk, Orlovsk, Aleksandrovsk and Grodekov. See *Pravda Vostoka* (Tashkent) 1 (540), 25 November 1924.
123. Karakul'-Sary-Sui, Kenkol-Karadyr, Kugart, Maili-Sai, Chenkent, Aimsk, Bazar-Kurgan, Massi, Naukent, and Dzhalal-Abad (including the Dzhalal-Abad town). See *ibid*.
124. Arym, Kyzyl-Dzhar, Kurk-Ugul, Sarnisk, Susamyr, Chatkal, Kutluk-Seid, Bagysh, Baiston and Mastur. *Ibid*.
125. Iaukesh-Boston, Ichkilik, Naiman and Aravan volosts.
126. Lialiaik and Naigut-Kipchak volosts.
127. The volosts of the Osh uezd which were merged with Kirgizia were Ak-Dzhar, Allai, Gul'chin, Karatash, Kipchagai, Iassyn, Akburin, Kurbash, Turuk-Naukat, Kashgar-Kishlak, Uzden and Osh (including Osh town).
128. These volosts were Kyzyl-Kum, Ata-Kurgan, Fistali-Tau, Kok-Tube, Kurgan-Tube and Char-Darya. See Nusupbekov, n. 7, 70-4.

selves nor others had mooted this question. However, as the popular enthusiasm for the establishment of the national republics and autonomous oblasts began to grow, several representatives of the Kara-Kalpaks began to press for the establishment of their own national state formation. In August 1924, Doshnazarov, the Chairman of the Party Collegium of the Kara-Kalpak Oblast Committee of the Amu-Daria Oblast issued a statement to the press stating that the Central Asiatic Bureau at last had agreed to form the Kara-Kalpak Autonomous Oblast.[129] Doshnazarov felt that in view of the close cultural ties which existed between the Kara-Kalpaks and the Kazakhs, the Kara-Kalpak Autonomous Oblast should be included within the composition of the Kazakh ASSR. A general conference of the Kara-Kalpak Party workers which met in September also demanded that the Kara-Kalpak Autonomous Oblast be included within the Kazakh ASSR.[130]

The Central Asiatic Bureau having decided to establish the Kara-Kalpak Autonomous Oblast referred this question for detailed study to the Territorial Commission. On 6 September 1924, the latter adopted a resolution which recognized the feasibility of the proposal to establish the Kara-Kalpak Autonomous Oblast. The decision of the Territorial Commission was formally approved by the Central Asiatic Bureau and later by the Central Committee of the Russian Communist Party.[131] The Kara-Kalpak Autonomous Oblast was proposed to be formed by merging the Kara-Kalpak-inhabited regions of the Amu-Daria oblast of the Turkestan Republic and the Kazakh-Kara-Kalpak oblast of the Khorezm Republic.[132]

The bulk of the recommendations of the Territorial Commission was accepted by the different national groups without dispute. However, some minor controversies did arise over the future of certain regions. The Kazakhs did not agree to the inclusion of the three volosts of the Tashkent uezd within the

---

129. *Turkestanskaia Pravda*, 192 (469), 31 August 1924.
130. *Turkestanskaia Pravda*, 219 (496), 2 October 1924.
131. Tursunov, n. 41, 137.
132. The Kara-Kalpaks constituted only a relative majority of the population of the Amu-Daria oblast' (39.1 per cent). Within the Kungrad and Khodzheili regions which constituted the Kazakh-Kara-Kalpak oblast' of the Khorezm Republic, the Kara-Kalpaks constituted only 15.1 per cent and 7.3 per cent respectively of their populations. See *MRT*, n. 14, 120 and *MRSA(K)*, n. 17, 107.

Uzbek Republic on the ground that their population was predominantly Kazakh in composition. They also objected to the inclusion of the Kazakh-inhabited regions of the former Bukharan Republic within the Uzbek Republic.[133] The Shurakhan uezd became a bone of contention between the Uzbeks and the Kara-Kalpaks, and the Uzbeks and the Kirgiz were ranged against one another over the future of certain parts of the Osh uezd. At a later stage the Tadjiks began an agitation for the inclusion of the Khodzhent uezd within their state formation.[134] However, these controversies were insignificant in view of the fact that the disputed areas in all did not exceed more than one per cent of the territory of the Central Asian region and comprised only 2.1 per cent of its population.[135] All the unresolved disputes over territories and frontiers were placed before the Central Committee of the Russian Communist Party which in turn created a special commission under the chairmanship of V. V. Kuibyshev to resolve them.[136]

133. Speaking before the All-Russian Central Executive Committee on 14 October 1924, the Kazakh delegate, Saifulin, expressed dissatisfaction over the inclusion of the Kazakh-inhabited regions of Bukhara and the Mirzachul' uezd within the Uzbek Republic. He demanded the establishment of a separate autonomous oblast within the Uzbek Republic consisting of the Kazakh regions of the former Bukharan Republic and the immediate transfer of the Mirzachul' uezd to the Kazakh ASSR. The Chairman of the All-Russian Central Executive Committee informed the delegate that while some of the controversies over the fixation of boundaries of the various republics of Central Asia were being looked into by its Presidium, the *VTsIK* did not have the competence any more to decree the establishment of an autonomous oblast for the Kazakhs within the Uzbek Republic. Saifulin was asked to take up this question with the Central Executive Committee of the Uzbek Republic. See *Vserossiiskii tsentral'nyi ispolnitel'nyi komitet XI sozyva : vtoraia sessiia : stenograficheskii otchët* (Moscow, 1924) 317-24. (Cited hereafter as *VTIK* (s.o.)).

134. The 1926 census indicated that the Tadjiks constituted a majority of the population of the Khodzhent uezd. In view of this the Khodzhent uezd was constituted into a Tadjik national district and later was transferred to the Tadjik Republic. See Mumin Khodzhaev, 'Sed'maia soiuznaia,' *Sovetskaia Aziia* (Moscow) 3-4 (1930) 247.

135. See *Turkestanskaia Pravda*, 201 (479), 11 September 1924.

136. This Commission recommended that, excluding the Irdzhar and Slaviansk volosts, all other volosts of the Mirzachul' uezd be merged with the Uzbek Republic. Irdzhar and Slaviansk volosts were given to the Kazakh ASSR. The Commission also favoured the inclusion of the six disputed volosts of the Tashkent uezd and the Chinaz area within the Uzbek SSR. It allocated the Shurakhan uezd to the Kara-Kalpak Autonomous Oblast. See *Turkestanskaia Pravda*, 258 (530), 13 November 1924.

In September 1924 the national delimitation plan was reviewed and approved by the Central Committees of the Communist Parties of Turkestan, Bukhara and Khorezm. On 15 September an Extraordinary Session of the Central Executive Committee of the Turkestan Republic assembled to give its legal affirmation to the proposal of delimiting the territory of the Turkestan Republic on the national principle. On the following day it adopted a decree which conferred upon the Uzbeks, Turkmens, Kazakhs, Tadjiks and Kirgiz the right to opt out of the composition of the Republic and establish their own national state formations.[137] The *Kuraltais* of Soviets of Bukhara and Khorezm, meeting respectively on 20 and 29 September 1924, also conferred similar rights on the major national groups which inhabited those republics.[138] Armed thus with the legal sanction of the legislative organs of their republics on the national delimitation plan, delegates from Turkestan, Bukhara and Khorezm proceeded to Moscow to secure the approval of the Central legislative organs to these decisions. The All-Russian Central Executive Committee on 14 October 1924 took up for consideration the national delimitation project and acquainted itself with the decision taken on this question by the Turkestan Central Executive Committee. After making certain relatively minor modifications in the delmitation project,[139] the All-Russian Central Executive Committee decided to permit the Turkestan Republic to secede from the RSFSR and to delimit its territory on the nationality principle.[140] On 27 October the Central Executive Committee of the USSR after having heard the reports of Faizullah Khodzhaev and Atabaev on the national delimitation of the Central Asian republics, decreed the dissolution of the multi-national state structures of Turkestan, Bukhara and Khorezm and the establishment in their place of the Uzbek and Turkmen Soviet Socialist Republics, the Tadjik Autonomous

137. *Stenograficheskii otchët 3-ti chrezvychainoi sessii TurkTsIK 15-16 Sentiabria 1924 g* (Tashkent, 1924) 32-3.

138. *Turkestanskaia Pravda*, 214 (491), 25 September 1924; and 248 (525), 5 November 1924.

139. The Tadjik Autonomous Oblast was elevated to the status of an Autonomous Republic; the Kara-Kalpak Autonomous Oblast was included within the Kazakh ASSR and the Kirgiz Autonomous Oblast was included within the RSFSR.

140. *VTIK* (s.o.), n. 133, 300-21.

Republic, and the Kirgiz and Kara-Kalpak Autonomous Oblasts. The decree also effected the immediate merger of the Kazakh-inhabited areas of the Turkestan Republic with the Kazakh ASSR.[141]

Following the approval of the delimitation project by the Central Executive Committee of the USSR, the formation of the new republics and autonomous oblasts of Central Asia was formally proclaimed on 27 October 1924. On 18 November 1924 the Central Executive Committees of Bukhara and Turkestan passed decrees on the dissolution of the governments of those republics. On 22 November the Central Executive Committee of Khorezm also passed a similar decree.[142] Several provisional revolutionary committees were created to look after the administration of the new republics and autonomous oblasts until the Constituent Congresses of Soviets of the new state formations created the permanent organs of government. The Turkmen Revolutionary Committee was composed of twentyfive members and was headed by Aitakov. Faizulla Khodzhaev was elected the Chairman of a sixteen-member Uzbek Revolutionary Committee. The Kirigiz Revolutionary Committee consisted of fourteen members and was headed by Aitorbek.[143] The Tadjik Revolutionary Committee had as its chairman Nusratulla Maksum and was composed of fourteen members.[144] These revolutionary committees at once began the work of organizing the administrative apparatuses of the new republics and autonomous oblasts. They created within themselves several departments or divisions on education, justice, agriculture, administration, workers-peasants inspectorate, economic affairs, internal trade, finance, etc. The revolutionary committees also gave their attention to the creation of a uniform pattern of administrative divisions, introduction of a unified system of laws, establishment of judicial organs at the different levels of administration, eradication of illiteracy, organization of oblast, uezd and volost Congresses of Soviets, and preparations for

141. *ZVS TsIK SSSR*, n. 34, 196, 208.

142. *Turkestanskaia Pravda*, 260 (537), 21 November 1924; G. Nepesov, 'Vozniknovenie Turkmenskoi sovetskoi sotsialisticheskoi respubliki, *Voprosy istorii*, 2 (1950) 11.

143. *Vlast' sovetov*, 1 (1925) 16.

144. *Pravda Vostoka*, 4 (543), 28 November 1924.

summoning of the Constituent Congresses of their republics or autonomous oblasts.[145]

Following the abolition of the Party organizations of the former Central Asian republics, Provisional Party Organizational Bureaux of the Uzbek and Turkmen SSRs, the Tadjik Autonomous Republic and the Kirgiz and Kara-Kalpak Autonomous Oblasts were established.[146] These Organizational Bureaux were charged with the task of undertaking all necessary measures for the establishment of the Communist parties of the new republics and autonomous oblasts and with making preparations for the summoning of the Party Congresses.

While the preparatory work for the establishment of the permanent party and governmental organs of the new state formations was under way, several commissions such as the Central Asiatic Liquidation Commission,[147] the Territorial, Economic and National Commissions worked upon the question of implementing the delimitation project. The Territorial Commission and the Central Asiatic Liquidation Commission estimated that the territory and population of the Central Asian region which came within the orbit of the delimitation plan consisted of 1,745,400 square kilometres and 8,131,062 persons.[148] They allocated the territory and population of the Central Asian region among the new republics and autonomous oblasts as shown in the following table.

145. *Vlast' sovetov*, 4 (1925) 14.

146. Tursunov, n. 41, 174-5.

147. Shortly before winding up its work the Presidium of the Central Asiatic Economic Council established the Central Asiatic Liquidation Commission composed of the representatives of the USSR and the new state formations of Central Asia. This Commission was charged with the task of co-ordinating the work of the liquidation committees of Turkestan, Bukhara and Khorezm on the distribution of the assets and liabilities of the defunct states among the new republics and autonomous oblasts. The Liquidation Commission also supervised the work of winding up the administrative apparatuses of Turkestan, Bukhara and Khorezm. In accordance with the decree of its Presidium, the Central Asiatic Economic Council wound up its activities from 26 November 1924 and handed over all its functions, assets and liabilities to the Council of Labour and Defence. See *Pravda Vostoka*, 3 (542), 27 November 1924.

148. The total population of the Turkestan Republic was placed at 5,254,584 persons and that of Bukhara and Khorezm at 2,236,437 persons and 640,044 persons respectively.

Table V[149]

Names of Republics/ Autonomous Oblasts	Allocation of territory (in sq. kms.)	Allocation of population	
		In absolute figures	In percentages
1. The Uzbek SSR	167,500	3,963,285	48.7
2. The Tadjik ASSR	145,800	739,503	9.1
3. The Turkmen SSR	443,500	855,114	10.5
4. The Kirgiz A.O.	190,700	714,648	8.8
5. The Kara-Kalpak A.O.	112,000	219,106	2.7
6. Regions transferred to the Kazakh ASSR	685,900	1,468,724	18.1
7. Disputed regions	—	170,684	2.1
Total	1,745,400	8,131,064	100

The population of the former Turkestan Republic (5,254,584 persons) was allocated among the new republics and autonomous oblasts in the following order: 2,323,764 or 44.2 per cent to the Uzbek SSR, 1,35,665 or 2.6 per cent to the Tadjik ASSR, 350,000 or 6.7 per cent to the Turkmen SSR, 714,648 or 13.6 per cent to the Kirgiz A.O., 91,098 or 1.7 per cent to the Kara-Kalpak A.O., 1,468,724 or 28.0 per cent to the Kazakh ASSR. The disputed regions of the Tashkent and Mirzachul' uezds had a population of 170,684 persons (2.1 per cent) which was subsequently allocated between the Uzbek and Kazakh republics.[150] The distribution of the population of the former Bukharan Republic (2,236,437 persons) among the new state formations was as follows: 1,319,498 or 59 per cent to the Uzbek SSR; 603,338 or 27 per cent to the Tadjik ASSR; and 313,101 or 14 per cent to the Turkmen SSR. The population of the Khorezm Republic (640,044 persons) was distributed in the following order: 320,023 or 50 per cent to the Uzbek SSR; 192,013 or 30 per cent to the Turkmen SSR and 128,008 or 20 per cent to the Kara-Kalpak Autonomous Oblast.[151]

149. This table is based on the following sources: S. K. Kondrashov, 'Sredne-Aziatskoe razmezhevanie,' Planovoe Khoziaistvo (Moscow) 4 (1925) 255-8; Ilias Alkin,· n. 29, 124; Khodorov, n. 53, 70; Sh. F. Mukhamed'iarov, 'K istorii natsional'no-gosudarstvennogo razmezhevaniia Srednei Azii,' Sovetskoe vostokovedenie (Moscow) 1 (1955) 55; Biulleten' tsentral'nogo statisticheskogo upravleniia Uzbekistana (Tashkent, 1925) I, 13; G. Cherdantsev, Sredne-Aziatskie respubliki (Moscow, 1928) 9 and Nusupbekov, n. 7, 74.

150. See footnote 136 of this chapter.

151. Gordienko, n. 40, 185.

VI. THE ECONOMIC DELIMITATION

The national delimitation scheme envisaged not only the reorganization of state frontiers but also the distribution of the economic wealth of the Central Asian region among its new state formations. This work, usually referred to as economic delimitation, commenced soon after the delimitation plan was approved in the Centre and continued until the beginning of 1926. In September 1924 the governments of Turkestan, Bukhara and Khorezm were asked to provide detailed information on the value of their industrial and commercial establishments, area of land sown to different crops, head of cattle available in each republic, etc. These governments in turn instructed the commercial and industrial establishments which came under their jurisdiction to compile lists of their assets and liabilities and balance sheets of their trade and industrial turnovers. The data thus made available served as the basis for estimating the value of the properties coming within the scope of economic delimitation. The data was at first scrutinized by the Liquidation Commission of each republic and later by the Central Asiatic Liquidation Commission.

Before setting about the actual work of distributing the various kinds of properties among the new republics and autonomous oblasts, the Central Asiatic Liquidation Commission had to decide upon the principle or principles governing the economic delimitation. In the distribution of a large number of properties the Commission took as the basis the size of the population of the new republics and autonomous oblasts. It divided the assets of organizations dealing with fodder stocks on the basis of the head of cattle possessed by each state formation. The immovable properties were allocated to the state on whose territory they were located. The funds of agricultural credit banks were divided on the basis of the volume of land under different crops and the size of their production. The properties of the silk and bee-keeping industries were divided on the basis of the size of the production of those industries within the new state formations.[152] The manner in which the assets of

---

152. I. I. Kryl'tsov, 'O printsipakh ekonomicheskogo razmezhevaniia Sredne-Aziatskikh respublik,' *Narodnoe khoziaistvo Srednei Azii*, 8-9 (1926) 135, 139.

some important organizations were distributed among the new state formations is shown below.

The value of the state properties of the former Turkestan Republic was placed at 46.5 million rubles and of Bukhara and Khorezm at 26.4 million rubles and 2.4 million rubles respectively. The share of these properties allocated to the different republics and autonomous oblasts was in the following order: 45.8 million rubles or 60.8 per cent to the Uzbek SSR; 7 million rubles or 9.3 per cent to the Tadjik ASSR; 10.4 million rubles or 13.8 per cent to the Turkmen SSR; 3.6 million rubles or 4.7 per cent to the Kirgiz Autonomous Oblast; 6.2 million rubles or 8.2 per cent to the Kazakh ASSR; and 0.8 million rubles or 1.0 per cent to the Kara-Kalpak Autonomous Oblast.[153]

The total livestock of the Central Asian region was estimated at 13,629,000 head of cattle. Of this the three former republics of Turkestan, Bukhara and Khorezm possessed each respectively 10,321,000, 2,571,000 and 737,000 head of cattle. The number of head of cattle allocated to the different republics and autonomous oblasts was in the following order: 2,589,063 or 19 per cent to the Uzbek SSR; 962,054 or 7.1 per cent to the Tadjik ASSR; 1,701,100 or 12.5 per cent to the Turkmen SSR; 5,845,370 or 42.9 per cent to the Kazakh ASSR; 1,881,658 or 13.8 per cent to the Kirgiz Autonomous Oblast and 380,745 or 2.8 per cent to the Kara-Kalpak Autonomous Oblast.[154]

Closely connected with the distribution of livestock was the question of allocation of summer pastures. In this connection a dispute arose between the representatives of the Kazakh ASSR and the Kirgiz Autonomous Oblast regarding the utilization of the summer pastures located in the Susamyr, Karkara, Kok-Airak and Chon-Kiben areas. Through the good offices of the Central Asiatic Liquidation Commission the Kazakh ASSR and the Kirgiz Autonomous Oblast were persuaded to conclude an agreement between themselves on the common utilization of these summer pastures.[155]

The funds of the Central Asiatic Commercial Bank and the Central Asiatic Agricultural Credit Bank which totalled

153. Khodorov, n. 53, 77; Kondrashov, n. 149, 258.
154. Kryl'tsov, n. 152, 136; Kondrashov, n. 149, 256.
155. Kryl'tsov, n. 152, 136.

5,161,000 rubles were distributed in the following manner: 2,876,000 rubles to the Uzbek SSR; 1,428,000 rubles to the Tadjik ASSR; 777,000 rubles to the Turkmen SSR; 20,000 rubles to the Kirgiz Autonomous Oblast; 42,000 rubles to the Kazakh ASSR; 13,000 rubles to the Kara-Kalpak Autonomous Oblast and 5,000 rubles to the disputed areas.[156]

The distribution of land under different cultures among the new republics and autonomous oblasts is shown in table VI.

Table VI[157]

Names of republics/ aut. oblasts	In desiatins	Percentage of total acreage in Central Asia	Percentage of cultivated area within the republic
I. *The Uzbek SSR*			
a. cotton	236,359	67.3	16.96
b. cereals	1,005,738	40.7	72.18
c. lucerne	102,087	50.4	7.32
e. orchards & vineyards	47,219	62.4	3.39
II. *The Tadjik ASSR*			
a. cotton	—	—	—
b. cereals	628,165	25.5	97.75
c. lucerne	6,049	3.0	0.94
d. tobacco	30	1.1	0.00
e. orchards & vineyards	8,399	11.1	1.31
III. *The Turkmen SSR*			
a. cotton	47,590	13.6	21.31
b. cereals	145,625	5.9	65.21
c. lucerne	19,903	9.8	8.91
d. tobacco	22	0.8	0.01
e. orchards & vineyards	10,192	13.5	4.56
IV. *The Kazakh ASSR*			
a. cotton	21,204	6.1	4.48
b. cereals	405,689	16.4	85.70
c. lucerne	40,810	20.2	8.62
d. tobacco	314	11.7	0.05
e. orchards & vineyards	5,387	7.1	1.14

156. *Ibid.*, 142.
157. This table is based on the figures given by Kondroshov, n. 149, 257.

V. *The Kirgiz AO*

a. cotton	13,268	3.8	5.38
b. cereals	212,526	8.6	86.21
c. lucerne	19,120	9.5	7.76
d. tobacco	191	7.1	0.08
e. orchards & vineyards	1,416	1.9	0.57

VI. *The Kara-Kalpak AO*

a. cotton	1,622	0.9	4.66
b. cereals	28,304	1.2	81.33
c. lucerne	4,774	2.4	13.72
d. tobacco	15	0.6	0.04
e. orchards & vineyards	88	0.1	0.25

VII. *Disputed Areas*

a. cotton	28,858	8.3	34.52
b. cereals	42,101	1.7	50.36
c. lucerne	9,621	4.7	11.51
d. tobacco	71	2.6	0.08
e. orchards & vineyards	2,950	3.9	3.53

The total area of land under the various crops was estimated to be 3,097,743 *desiatins*. Its division among the new republics and autonomous oblasts was in the following order: 1,393,444 *desiatins* to the Uzbek SSR; 642,643 *desiatins* to the Tadjik ASSR; 223,332 *desiatins* to the Turkmen SSR; 473,404 *desiatins* to the Kazakh ASSR; 246,516 *desiatins* to the Kirgiz Autonomous Oblast and 34,803 *desiatins* to the Kara-Kalpak Autonomous Oblast.

The gross income from the agricultural sector in Central Asia for 1923-24 was estimated at 454,738,000 rubles. This sum was distributed among the new state formations in the following order:

Uzbek SSR	316,915,000	rubles	69.7 per cent
Tadjik ASSR	20,406,000	"	4.5 "
Turkmen SSR	28,220,000	"	6.2 "
Kirgiz AO	30,525,000	"	6.7 "
Kazakh ASSR	49,587,000	"	10.9 "
Kara-Kalpak AO	9,085,000	"	2.0 "

The income from the industrial sector was meagre and did not constitute more than 15.1 per cent of the national income of the Central Asian region in 1924. Among the industries of the Central Asian region the cotton-processing enterprises were of great significance, and they were located mainly in the cotton growing areas. Since a major portion of the cotton growing areas fell to the share of the Uzbek Republic, a majority of the cotton processing enterprises (110 out of 132 enterprises) were allocated to the Uzbek SSR.[158]

In 1924 there existed three cotton joint-stock companies in the Central Asian region, one each in Turkestan, Bukhara and Khorezm. The total share capital of these companies was estimated at 68,394,000 rubles. In the course of delimitation these joint-stock companies were abolished and their share capital was distributed among the new republics and autonomous oblasts in the following order: 7,342,000 rubles to the Uzbek SSR; 1,328,000 rubles to the Turkmen SSR; 557,000 rubles to the Kazakh ASSR; 411,000 rubles to the Kirgiz AO and 57,927,000 to the USSR.[159]

The division of assets of the fodder-stock organization of the Turkestan Republic was done on the basis of the head of cattle possessed by each of the new state formations. The value of the raw material stocks held by this organization on 1 July 1924 was estimated at 436,310,059 rubles. The allocation of this sum among the new republics and the autonomous oblasts was as follows: 2,183,295 rubles to the Kazakh ASSR; 871,311 rubles to the Kirgiz Autonomous Oblast; 1,032,745 rubles to the Uzbek SSR and the Tadjik ASSR and 275,747 rubles to the Turkmen SSR.[160]

The fuel industries of the Central Asian region were allocated to the states on whose territory they existed at the time of delimitation. The coal mines of Shurab and the oil fields of Santo and the oil plants located at Kokand, Namangan, Fergana, Andizhan, Tashkent, Katta-Kurgan and Samarkand were allocated to the Uzbek SSR. The oil and ozocerite fields of the Cheleken area and the plants located in Krasnovodsk, Merv and Poltoratsk were given to the Turkmen SSR. The coal mines of Kizyl-kia and Kok-Iangak and the oil plant of Dzhalal-Abad city were allocated to the Kirgiz Autonomous Oblast. The saksaul stores of the northern Syr-Daria region, the Lenger coal mines and the oil plants

158. Khodorov, n. 53, 74.
159. Kondroshov, n. 149, 259.
160. *Pravda Vostoka*, 3 (542), 27 November 1924.

of Chimkent and Aulie-Ata were handed over to the Kazakh
ASSR.[161]

The Kazakh ASSR was allocated the textile industry located in
Alma-Ata and the Uzbek Republic was given the hydro-electric
station situated on the Boz-su.[162] The Central Asiatic Liquidation Commission decided not to allocate certain educational,
scientific and technical institutions to any state formations but
to retain them for the common utilization of all the republics
and autonomous oblasts. These comprised chiefly the Central
Asiatic State University, the Central Asiatic Communist University, the Central Asiatic Chemical and Bacteriological Labora-
tories, etc.[163] Similarly, the technical institutions of forestry,
medicine and engineering located in the city of Tashkent were
left to the common utilization of all the republics and autonomous oblasts until such time the new state formations were able
to establish their own technical institutes.[164]

The implementation of the national delimitation project,
for all practical purposes, was completed by the end of 1924,
even though the work of allocating the funds and properties of
the former republics of Turkestan, Bukhara and Khorezm among
the new state formations continued up to the beginning of 1926.
As a result of this reform, each of the major national groups of
the Central Asian region came to possess not only its own
separate state formation, but also the means to develop its economy, language and culture. An attempt is made in the following chapter to evaluate the significance of the establishment of
national state formations to each of these nationalities and to
analyse the historical process by which the Tadjiks, Kirgiz and
Kara-Kalpaks attained their present status within the Soviet
Union.

161. *Pravda Vostoka*, 15 (554), 11 December 1924; 19 (557), 16
December 1924.
162. *Pravda Vostoka*, 1 (540), 25 November 1924; 6 (545), 1 December
1924.
163. *Pravda Vostoka*, 6 (545), 1 December 1924.
164. *Pravda Vostoka*, 4 (543), 28 November 1924.

CHAPTER SIX

The New National State Formations of Central Asia

A T T H E T I M E of the implementation of the national delimitation project, the Central Asian region possessed an area of 1,745,000 square kilometres and an estimated population of 8,131,064 persons. In accordance with the decree of the Politbureau of the Central Committee of the Russian Communist Party of 12 June 1924, in the course of implementing the delimitation scheme 685,900 square kilometres of territory having a population of 1,468,724 persons was ceded to the Kazakh ASSR. As a result, the Central Asian region lost more than one-fourth of its territory and 18.1 per cent of its population.[1] The area transferred to the Kazakh ASSR comprised parts of the Syr-Daria, Semirechie and Samarkand oblasts of the former Turkestan ASSR. The remaining areas of Central Asia were divided among the Uzbek and Turkmen SSRS, the Tadjik ASSR, and the Kirgiz and Kara-Kalpak Autonomous Oblasts. In the following pages,

Following the distribution of the economic resources of the Central Asian region among its new state formations, the Kazakh ASSR was given 5,845,370 head of cattle (which represented 42.9 per cent of the entire cattle stock of Central Asia), 49,587,000 rubles which constituted 10.9 per cent of income from agriculture, 2,183,295 rubles worth of assets of the fodder-stock organization of the Turkestan Republic, and 6.2 million rubles worth of state properties. In the territory transferred to the Kazakh ASSR there was 473,404 *desiatins* of cultivable area; 21,204 *desiatins* (4.48 per cent) of this area was under cotton, 405,689 *desiatins* (85.70 per cent) under cereals, 40,810 *desiatins* (8.62 per cent) under lucerne, 314 *desiatins* (0.05 per cent) under tobacco and 5,387 *desiatins* (1.14 per cent) under orchards. Before delimitation, the regions transferred to the Kazakh ASSR supplied large quantities of food stuffs and cattle products to the Turkestan ASSR, and at the time of delimitation, it was feared that the transfer of these areas to the Kazakh ASSR might bring about a crisis in the food situation in the Central Asian region. The proposal to retain the Kazakh ASSR within the Central Asiatic Economic Council was put forward by many, mainly to overcome this difficulty. See pp. 183-6, 197-202.

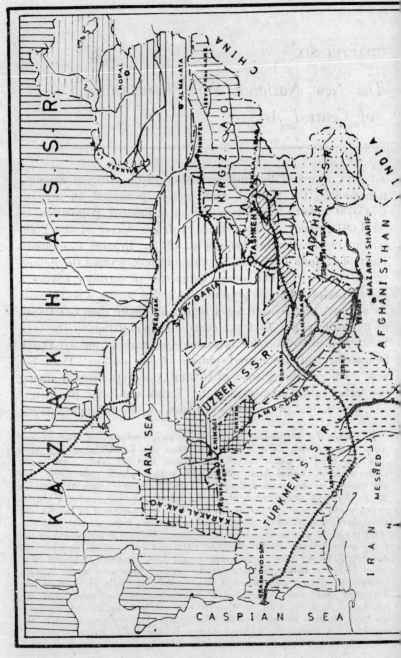

an attempt is made to provide details on the size of territory, population and economic resources which accrued to these new state formations as well as to analyse the national composition of their population structures, their constitutional and administrative set-ups, etc.

I. THE UZBEK SOVIET SOCIALIST REPUBLIC

The Uzbek Soviet Socialist Republic occupied a territory of 167,500 square kilometres with a population of 4,447,555 persons. The following areas which previously constituted parts of the republics of Turkestan, Bukhara and Khorezm, and which were inhabited predominantly by the Uzbek population, were merged within the Uzbek Republic.

(1) forty-one volosts of the Dzhizak, Katta-Kurgan and Khodzhent uezds of the Samarkand oblast, twenty-four volosts of the Tashkent and Mirzachul uezds of the Syr-Daria oblast, seventy volosts of the Andizhan, Kokand, Namangan and Fergana uezds and seven village communities (Shakhimardan, Vuadil, etc.) of the Fergana oblast;[2]

(2) the Zerafshan area (consisting of the Bukhara, Kermin and Nur-ata *vilaiets*), the Kashka-Daria region (consisting of Bek-Budi, Guzar, Shakhrisiabz *vilaiets*), a part of the Surkhan-Daria region (including the whole of the Baisun *vilaiet* and two *tumans* of the Shirabad *vilaiet*) and the western border areas of the Eastern Bukharan oblast (The Sary-Assi and Iurchi *tumans* of the Sary-Assi *vilaiet*);[3]

(3) the south-eastern part of the territory of the Khorezm Republic which was subsequently organized into the Gurlen, Novo-Urgench and Khiva uezds.[4]

The frontiers of the Uzbek SSR bordered in the north with the Kazakh ASSR, in the east with the Kirgiz Autonomous Oblast and the Tadjik ASSR, in the south with Afghanistan and in the west with the Turkmen SSR.

2. Kh. T. Tursunov, *Obrazovanie Uzbekskoi sovetskoi sotsialisticheskoi respubliki* (Tashkent, 1957) 157.

3. *Materialy po raionirovaniiu Srednei Azii: territoriia i naselenie Bukhary i Khorezma* (Tashkent, 1926) I, pt. 1 (Bukhara) 69 (cited hereafter as *MRSA(B)*).

4. *Materialy po raionirovaniiu Srednei Azii: territoriia i naselenie Bukhary i Khorezma* (Tashkent, 1926) II, pt. 2 (Khorezm) 37 (cited hereafter as *MRSA(K)*).

Among the various nationalities of the Central Asian region, the Uzbeks emerged as the richest as a result of national delimitation. The territory which was included within the Uzbek Republic represented one of the most fertile, economically advanced and densely populated areas of the Central Asian region. Not only did the bulk of the irrigated areas of the Central Asian region come into the possession of the Uzbek SSR (it acquired nearly 80 per cent of the lands which were irrigated in the pre-war years) but the presence on its territory of the Amu-Daria, the Syr-Daria and the Zerafshan rivers ensured wide opportunities for further extension of the facilities of irrigation and the development of hydro-electric power. Besides, the Uzbek SSR also possessed the Hungry Steppe Irrigation Canal System, the second biggest irrigation system of Central Asia, which provided water to as much as 60,000 *desiatins* of land.[5] Of the total of 3,097,743 *desiatins* of cultivated land of the Central Asian region, 1,393,444 *desiatins*, i.e. nearly half of the entire sown area of Central Asia fell to the share of the Uzbek Republic. Within the Uzbek SSR nearly one-sixth of this land, located in the fertile Fergana valley, Samarkand, Tashkent, Bukhara and Khorezm regions, was under the cotton crop and it represented 85.2 per cent of the entire cotton growing areas of the Central Asian region.[6] More significant was the fact that out of the gross income of 454,738,000 rubles which accrued to the Central Asian region from its agricultural sector, as much as 316,915,000 rubles (i.e. 69.7 per cent) was allocated to the share of the Uzbek SSR.[7] In livestock also the Uzbek SSR was well placed. Nineteen per cent of the total livestock of Central Asia (2,589,063 head of cattle) fell to the share of the Uzbek SSR.[8] At the time of its formation small peasant holdings with an average of 2.1 *desiatins* of land and 5.2 head of cattle characterized the predominantly agricultural economy of the Uzbek

---

5. *Pravda Vostoka* (Tashkent) 1 (540), 25 November 1924.

6. In 1923-24 out of the 14.2 million poods of raw cotton grown in the Central Asian region, the territories merged within the Uzbek SSR accounted for as much as ten million poods. See *Istoriia Uzbekskoi SSR* (Tashkent, 1957) II, 236 (cited hereafter *IUzSSR*).

7. See p. 200.

8. See pp. 198-9.

Republic.[9]   Besides cotton, the Uzbek Republic also produced considerable quantities of rice and cereals.   In 1923-24 the Uzbek areas accounted for 73,584,000 poods of cereals.[10]

In the allocation of the properties of the former republics of Turkestan, Bukhara and Khorezm among the new state formations, the scale was heavily tilted in favour of the Uzbek SSR. It secured 45.8 million rubles worth of properties (i.e. 60.8 per cent) out of a total of 75.3 million rubles worth of properties of the former Central Asian republics.[11]   In the industrial sector also the Uzbek SSR was most favourably placed.   It secured 110 out of the 132 cotton-processing industries which existed in Central Asia.[12]   Besides, most of the fuel industries, wine manufacturing enterprises, silk-reeling factories, flour-mills and soap-making plants came under the control of the Uzbek SSR.[13] No less significant was the fact that the Uzbek Republic secured 49.8 per cent of the railway network of the Central Asian region.[14]

In the sphere of educational facilities again the Uzbek SSR was better placed than the other republics of the Central Asian region.   To its share came 981 primary and middle schools with an estimated student population of 75,000 persons, 23 *technicums*, 8 professional-industrial schools, 8 industrial schools, etc.[15]   More important was the location of the Central Asiatic

9. *Turkestanskaia Pravda*, 201 (479), 2 September 1924.

10. *Pravda Vostoka*, 1 (540), 25 November 1924.

11. See p. 198; also see *Pervyi vseuzbekskii, s'ezd sovetov*: *stenografi-cheskii otchët* (Tashkent, 1925) 25 (cited hereafter as *PVSS*).

12. In 1924-25, the cotton-processing industries of the Uzbek SSR earned 70.1 million rubles, which was 65.6 per cent of the income that accrued to the Republic from its industrial enterprises. See Tursunov, n. 2, 164.

13. *Turkestanskaia Pravda* (Tashkent) 196 (473), 4 September 1924. In 1924-25 there were 185 industrial establishments on the territory of the Uzbek SSR which employed 8,700 workers. The gross income which accrued from these industries was estimated to be 106.9 million rubles. See Tursunov, n. 2, 163.

14. *Pravda Vostoka*, 1 (540), 25 November 1924.

15. Within the former Turkestan Republic, the Uzbek areas were relatively better provided with educational facilities than the non-Uzbek regions. After delimitation most of the educational institutions which existed in the Uzbek areas came under the control of the Uzbek SSR. See *Turkestanskaia Pravda*, 260 (537), 21 November 1924.

State University and the Communist University of Tashkent. In 1925 the Central Asiatic State University had a student population of 3,331. The Uzbek SSR was also better equipped than the other republics in respect of libraries, clubs, hospitals, ambulances, etc.

The territory of the Uzbek SSR was not only the most densely populated region of Central Asia, but the one in which the process of urbanization had made most headway. According to the 1926 census, the Republic's urban population was placed at 1,062,288, which represented 23.8 per cent of its total population.[16] Almost all the major cities of Central Asia such as Tashkent, Samarkand, Bukhara, Khiva, Kokand, Margelan, Andizhan and Namangan came under the Uzbek SSR.

The population composition of the Uzbek SSR was more homogeneous than that of the Kirgiz and Kara-Kalpak Autonomous oblasts and of the Kazakh ASSR. The Uzbeks constituted as much as 74.7 per cent of its total population. An approximate picture of the national composition of the Republic's population structure oblast-wise emerges from the following table:[17]

Table VII

Oblasts	Uzbeks	Tadjiks	Turkmens	Kirgiz	Kazakhs	Russians	Others
Zerafshan	75	10.4	2.6	—	0.5	1.2	10.3
Kashka-Daria	83.8	9.4	1.4	—	0.3	—	5.1
Samarkand	74.3	14.6	—	—	0.3	4.3	6.5
Surkhan-Daria	62.3	32.3	—	—	—	0.5	4.9
Tashkent	57.7	1.8	—	0.2	15.5	19.0	5.8
Fergana	72.2	12.9	—	5.7	0.6	1.8	6.8
Khorezm	97.7	—	—	—	0.6	0.4	1.3
Kenimekh Area	16.9	—	—	—	77.7	—	5.4
Total	72.2	10.8	0.4	2.5	3.2	4.3	6.6

Note: The figures are in percentages.

Soon after its formation, the Revolutionary Committee of the Uzbek SSR issued a proclamation in which it assured the non-

16. *Vsesoiuznaia perepis' naseleniia 1926 g* (Moscow, 1928) XV, 8-9.
17. These figures are taken from *Vsia Sredniaia Aziia: spravochnaia kniga na 1926 khoziaistvennyi god* (Tashkent, 1926) 385. Though the figures given in this table are not absolutely precise, a fairly clear picture of the distribution of the national groups among the several oblasts of the Uzbek SSR emerges from it.

Uzbek population of the Republic that their interests would be fully safeguarded. It was stated in this proclamation that

The nationalities policy of the Soviet Government ensures the complete equality of all nations. The Revolutionary Committee of the Uzbek ssr declares that henceforth there is no place on the territory of the Uzbek ssr for national antagonisms. All national minorities included within the Uzbek ssr are guaranteed all necessary facilities for their cultural and economic development (and the right to employ) their mother tongues in administration, law courts and educational institutions.[18]

The Revolutionary Committee created a special Commission on National Minorities and charged it with the task of working out schemes for effectively safeguarding the interests of the national minorities inhabiting the territory of the Uzbek ssr.[19] On the recommendation of this Commission the Revolutionary Committee sought to establish an administrative system which, besides rendering the authority of the government more effective, also accommodated the interests of the national minorities. The predominantly Kazakh-inhabited Kenimekh region of the former Republic of Bukhara was organized into a national area (*raion*) and its administration became the direct responsibility of the Central Executive Committee of the Uzbek ssr.[20] Similarly, the Khodzhent region in which the majority of the population were Tadjiks was organized into a national district. Besides these two major national units, a large number of smaller national administrative divisions such as national volosts, and sel'sovets (village soviets) were also established. There came into existence twelve national volosts and as many as 306 national sel'sovets. Of these national sel'sovets, 107 were possessed by the Tadjiks, 51 by Kazakhs, 31 by Kuruma, 24 by Russians, 3 by Uigurs, 10 by Kipchaks, 18 by Kara-Kalpaks, 13 by Turkmens, 12 by Arabs and 4 by Persians.[21] Within each one of these national divisions the people who inhabit-

18. The text of the proclamation is available in *Pravda Vostoka,* 10, 5 December 1924.
19. *Vlast' sovetov* (Moscow) 11 (1925) 17.
20. *Vsia Sredniaia Aziia,* n. 17, 383-4.
21. G. Cherdantsev, *Sredne-Aziatskie respubliki* (Moscow, 1928) 69-70; also see *PVSS,* n. 11, 31.

ed it was given facilities to run its administration and to organize their cultural and educational institutions through the medium of their mother tongue. A decree of the Revolutionary Committee 'On the *nativization* of the state and administrative apparatuses of the Uzbek SSR', while making the use of the Uzbek language compulsory at all levels of administration, also decreed that in areas where a majority of the population employed a non-Uzbek language, their administrative work should be conducted in both the language of the majority population and in the Uzbek language.[22]

The former republics of Turkestan, Bukhara and Khorezm, in ceding parts of their territories to the new state formations, also had bequeathed to them the administrative and legal systems which existed on those territories. Soon after their establishment, the Revolutionary Committees of the new republics and autonomous oblasts were confronted with the task of creating a uniform pattern of administration and unified norms of legislation. The Uzbek SSR, for instance, inherited no less than three distinct types of administrative divisions. In the areas which came to it from the former Turkestan Republic, the administrative units conformed to a four-tier pattern: oblasts, uezds, volosts and sel'sovets. The territory of the former Republic of Bukhara was divided administratively into *vilaiets, tumans, kents* and *amindoms*. The territory ceded by the former Khorezm Republic to the Uzbek SSR had its own distinct type of administrative divisions: oblasts, uezds, *shuros* and *aksakaldoms*. On 29 January 1925 the Revolutionary Committee of the Uzbek SSR decided in favour of adopting the pattern of administrative divisions which existed in the former Turkestan Republic. Subsequently, the entire territory of the Uzbek SSR was divided into 7 oblasts, 23 uezds, 239 volosts and 1,152 sel'sovets. The newly-organized oblasts were Tashkent, Fergana, Samarkand, Zerafshan, Kashka-Daria, Surkhan-Daria and Khorezm.[23] Soon after

22. *Vlast' sovetov*, 8 (1925) 14.
23. In the following year the Central Executive Committee of the Uzbek SSR embarked upon a fresh administrative reorganization. In accordance with its decision, the territory of the Uzbek SSR was divided into districts (*okrugs*), areas (*raion*) and sel'sovets. In place of the seven oblasts which existed until then ten districts were organized and the number of sel'sovets was increased from 1,152 to 1,730. The new districts

this administrative reorganization, a decision was taken to make the city of Samarkand the capital of the Uzbek Republic. On 3 April 1925 the Government of the Uzbek SSR shifted from Tashkent to Samarkand.[24]

The delimitation of Central Asia also led to fundamental changes in the Communist Party organizations of the region. Following the abolition of the communist parties of Turkestan, Bukhara and Khorezm, there came into existence the communist parties of Uzbekistan and Turkmenistan and the oblast party organizations of Tadjikistan, Kirgizia and Kara-Kalpakia. At the time of its formation, the Uzbek Communist Party had a total membership of 16,371 persons of which 6,883 (42.2 per cent) were Uzbeks, 6,666 (40.7 per cent) were Russians and 946 (6.8 per cent) were Tadjiks.[25] A Provisional Organizational Bureau managed the affairs of the Uzbek Communist Party until February 1925, when the first congress of the Communist Party of the Uzbek SSR was held. The Party Congress proclaimed the Uzbek Communist Party an integral part of the All-Russian Communist Party (Bolsheviks), and elected its permanent organs. The newly elected Central Committee of the Uzbek Communist Party replaced the Povisional Organizational Bureau.[26]

Soon afterwards, the First Constituent Congress of Soviets of the Uzbek SSR assembled in Bukhara on 13 February 1925. The Congress was attended by 588 delegates among whom were 404 Uzbeks, 66 Tadjiks, 65 Russians, 5 Kirgiz and 48 from other national minorities of the Uzbek SSR.[27] The Congress adopted a 'Declaration on the Formation of the Uzbek Soviet Socialist Republic' and then addressed itself to the task of establishing the permanent legislative and executive organs of the Republic. It elected a Central Executive Committee consisting of 160 members and 44 candidate members with Iuldash Akhunbabaev,

were Andizhan, Zerafshan, Kashka-Daria, Samarkand, Surkhan-Daria, Tashkent, Fergana, Khodzhent, Khorezm and Bukhara. See Tursunov, n. 2, 168-70.

24. *Pravda Vostoka*, 75 (675), 5 April 1925.

25. Tursunov, n. 2, 174-5.

26. A. Agzamkhodzhaev and Sh. Z. Urazaev, *Razvitie sovetskoi gosudarstvennosti v Uzbekistane* (Moscow, 1960) 66.

27. *PVSS*, n. 11, 100-3.

a veteran Uzbek communist of humble peasant origin, as its chairman. The Congress also unanimously elected Faizulla Khodzhaev as the chairman of the new Council of People's Commissars of the Uzbek Republic. A separate resolution adopted by the Congress approved the proposed entry of the Uzbek SSR into the Soviet Union. The resolution stated, 'the toiling mass of Uzbek people declare... their unswerving decision on the voluntary entrance (of Uzbekistan) into the USSR as an equal member on the basis of the declaration of the First Congress of the USSR guaranteeing the security and freedom of national development of peoples.'[28]

A conference of the Central Executive Committee of the Uzbek SSR held between 12-15 April 1925 once again discussed the question of integration of Uzbekistan into the USSR. The conference favoured the sending of a delegation of the Uzbek SSR to participate in the Third All-Union Congress of Soviets. In particular, the Central Executive Committee urged Iuldash Akhunbabaev and Faizulla Khodzhaev to lead this delegation and to convey to the Congress of Soviets of the USSR 'the desire of the people and government of the Uzbek SSR' for the inclusion of the Uzbek Republic within the USSR.[29] In accordance with this decision of the Central Executive Committee, a sixty-member delegation from the Uzbek SSR was sent to Moscow towards the beginning of May 1925. After a formal request was made by the Uzbek delegation, the Third Congress of Soviets of the USSR on 13 May took a decision to admit the Uzbek Republic into the Soviet Union. The Congress favoured the conclusion of a treaty between the USSR and the Uzbek Republic on the admission of the latter into the Soviet Union, and it charged its Presidium with carrying out all the necessary amendments to the constitution of the USSR to facilitate the admission of the new member and with submitting those amendments to the Congress for approval. A resolution passed by the Congress on this question stated, 'the entrance of the said republics[30] into the USSR is a new demonstration of the fact that the USSR

28. *Ibid.*, 106.
29. *Vlast' sovetov*, 23-24 (1925) 28.
30. The Turkmen Republic was also admitted as a constituent member of the USSR along with the Uzbek Republic.

is really a voluntary union of equal peoples and a reliable bulwark of the formerly oppressed people.'[31]

II. THE TURKMEN SOVIET SOCIALIST REPUBLIC

The Turkmen Soviet Socialist Republic, which was formed on the basis of the recommendations of the Territorial Commission, acquired an area of 443,500 square kilometres and a population of 855,114 persons. It was constituted from the Turkmen majority areas of the former republics of Turkestan, Bukhara and Khorezm. These areas were

(1) the Turkmen oblast (the Transcaspian oblast) of the former Turkestan ASSR, consisting of Poltoratsk, Tedzhen, Krasnovodsk and Merv uezds;

(2) The Kerki and Chardzhui *vilaiets* and the Kelifa *tuman* of the former Bukharan SSR;[32]

(3) Dargan-Ata, Il'ialy, Kunia-Urgench, Porsu, Tashauz and the Takhta-Bazar areas of the former Khorezm SSR.[33]

Situated in the westernmost part of the Central Asian region, the new Turkmen SSR bordered in the south on Persia and Afghanistan, in the east on the Uzbek SSR and the Kara-Kalpak Autonomous Oblast, in the north on the Kazakh ASSR and in the west on the eastern shore of the Caspian sea.

The territory which came into the possession of the Turkmen SSR sharply differed in many ways from the territory included within the Uzbek Republic. Compared with the latter, which consisted mostly of fertile river valleys and oasis regions, the Turkmen territory was less fertile, economically more backward, and more sparsely populated. More than 80 per cent of its territory was covered with the sands of the Kara-kum and other deserts, and the remaining parts also were not so well supplied with water resources. Only the southern portion of the Republic and a narrow strip of land situated on the left bank of the river Amu-Daria had adequate water resources. The presence of rivers such as the Murgab, the Tedzhen and the Atrek, and the

31. *S'ezdy Sovetov SSR v postanovleniiakh i rezoliutsiiakh* (Moscow, 1939) 78; also see *Pravda Vostoka*, 105 (705), 17 May 1925.

32. *MRSA(B)*, n. 3, 71.

33. Four out of the seven *shuros* of the Tashauz oblast, two *shuros* of the Kunia-Urgench oblast and one *shuro* of the Kazakh-Kara-Kalpak oblast were incorporated in the Turkmen SSR. See *MRSA(K)*, n. 4, 35.

small rivulets which flowed down from the Kopet-Dag mountains, rendered the southern part of the Turkmen SSR an important region from the standpoint of agriculture. Besides, this region also possessed the largest irrigation canal system of the Central Asian region. The Bairam-Ali irrigation canal system, as it was called, provided water to 285,000 *desiatins* of land, and in the pre-war years it had irrigated as much as 326,000 *desiatins*.[34]

Though in size the territory of the Turkmen SSR was considerably larger than that of the Uzbek Republic, its cultivable land was less than one-sixth of the latter's sown area. In all, the area under cultivation within the Turkmen SSR did not exceed 223,332 *desiatins*. About 12.5 per cent of the total livestock of Central Asia, a share amounting to 1,701,100 head of cattle, was allocated to the Turkmen SSR. Its value was estimated to be about 20 million rubles.[35] An average of about 2.5 *desiatins* of land and 12.7 head of cattle was owned by each individual peasant holding within the Turkmen SSR. These figures were slightly higher than those for the Uzbek SSR at this time. The reason for this was that the Turkmen SSR was more sparsely populated than the Uzbek SSR, and also possessed considerably larger territory.[36] In the economy of the Turkmen SSR both agriculture and stock-raising played an equally important role. About 52 per cent of its income was derived from agriculture and 48 per cent from stock-raising. However, the income which accrued from both agriculture and stock-raising did not exceed more than 33 million rubles.[37] Of the total sown area of the Turkmen SSR, 47,590 *desiatins* (21.3 per cent) was under cotton, 19,903 *desiatins* (8.91 per cent) under lucerne, 145,625 *desiatins* (65.21 per cent) under cereals, 22 *desiatins* (0.05 per cent) under tobacco, and 10,192 *desiatins* (4.56 per cent) consisted of orchards and vineyards.[38] Turk-

34. G. Karpov, 'Turkmeniia i Turkmeny,' *Turkmenovedenie* (Ashkhabad) 10-11 (1929) 37.

35. *Turkestanskaia Pravda*, 199 (476), 8 September 1924; also see 198-9.

36. *Turkestanskaia Pravda*, 196 (473), 4 September 1924.

37. *Ibid*. See also 200-1.

38. S. K. Kondrashov, 'Sredne-Aziatskoe razmezhevanie,' *Planovoe khoziaistvo* (Moscow) 4 (1925) 257.

menistan's chief articles of export consisted of dry fruits, cotton, carpets, karakul wool, oil, etc. The Republic possessed great potentialities for the development of water transport, and it had acquired 1,364 *versts* of railway network.

The population composition of the Turkmen SSR was largely homogeneous. The Turkmens constituted 70.2 per cent of the total population of the Republic. Among the other national groups which inhabited the Turkmen SSR, there were 104,900 (11.7 per cent) Uzbeks, 6,000 (0.7 per cent) Kazakhs, 1,000 (0.01 per cent) Kirgiz, 74,000 (8.2 per cent) Russians and 82,900 (9.1 per cent) persons belonging to other minor national groups.[39] An approximate picture of the district-wise distribution of the various national groups of the Turkmen SSR emerges from the following table.[40]

Table VIII

Name of district	Turkmens	Uzbeks	Kazakhs	Russians	Others
Poltoratsk	64.4	—	1.5	17.2	16.9
Merv	84.1	0.6	0.4	6.3	8.6
Chardzhui	66.8	25.9	—	4.3	3.0
Kerki	83.4	15.4	—	0.4	0.8
Tashauz	86.2	13.9	—	—	—
Total	77.9	9.8	0.4	5.8	6.1

Note: The figures are in percentages.

The Turkmen Republic, like the Uzbek SSR, inherited diverse types of administrative divisions and legal norms. At the time of its formation there were within the Turkmen Republic two oblasts, three *vilaiets,* 4 uezds, 10 *tumans,* 7 *shuros,* 36 *kents,* 272 *aksakaldoms,* 20 volosts and 267 *aulsovets.* By a decree of the Revolutionary Committee of the Turkmen SSR of 24 January 1925, all the old administrative units of the Republic were abolished and new administrative divisions were established. The whole territory of the Turkmen SSR was divided into 5 dis-

39. *Vsesoiuznaia perepis' naseleniia 17 dekabria 1926 goda*: *kratkie svodki: narodnost' i rodnoi iazyk naseleniia SSR* (Moscow, 1928) III, 3, 16-17 (cited hereafter as *VPN*(K.S.)); G. Karpov, 'Natsional'nye menshinstva TSSR: kratkie svedeniia o chislennom sostave i istoricheskom proshlom,' *Turkmenovedenie,* 3-4 (1931) 65.
40. These figures widely differ from the 1926 census figures for the Turkmen SSR. The value of this table consists in that it gives an approximate picture of the district-wise distribution of the national groups which inhabited the Turkmen SSR.

tricts, 26 areas (*raions*), 7 volosts, 272 *aksakaldoms* and 307 aulsovets.[41]

On 15 December 1924 the Revolutionary Committee of the Turkmen SSR promulgated an ordinance by which the jurisdiction of the laws of the USSR was extended over the entire territory of the Turkmen Republic. The task of rationalizing the conflicting laws of the former Turkestan, Bukhara and Khorezm republics which were still in force in different parts of the Turkmen SSR was entrusted to a special commission.[42] The reorganization of the judicial apparatus of the Republic was also undertaken and towards the end of 1924 the High Court of the Turkmen SSR was established.[43]

The question of creating the permanent organs of the Turkmen Communist Party and of the government of the Turkmen SSR was taken up by the First Congress of the Communist Party of Turkmenistan and the First Constituent Congress of Soviets which simultaneously began their sessions on 14 February 1925. The Turkmen Party Congress elected a new Central Committee to replace the Provisional Organizational Bureau as the guiding organ of the Communist Party of Turkmenistan, and decreed that the newly established Turkmen Communist Party should function as an integral part of the All-Russian Communist Party (Bolsheviks). On 20 February, the Congress of Soviets of the Turkmen SSR adopted a 'Declaration on the Formation of the Turkmen Soviet Socialist Republic'. It was stated in this declaration that the Turkmen SSR was formed 'on the territory which for a long time had been inhabited by the Turkmen people' and these areas consisted of the districts of Poltoratsk, Merv, Kerki, Leninsk (Chardzhui) and Tashauz.[44] Point eleven of

41. A Gordienko, 'Obrazovanie i razvitie Turkmenskoi SSR,' *Uchenye zapiski iuridicheskogo fakul'teta SAGU* (Tashkent, 1956) II, 130; also see *Turkmenskaia SSR: administrativno-territorial'noe delenie na I Aprelia 1940 goda* (Ashkhabad, 1940).

42. I. I. Kryl'tsov, 'Pravovoe oformlenie natsional'nykh respublik Srednei Azii: Turkmenistan,' *Vestnik iustitsii Uzbekistana* (Tashkent) 6-8 (1926) 15.

43. Gordienko, n. 41, 131.

44. See *Khronologicheskoe sobranie zakonov Turkmenskoi SSR, ukazov prezidiuma verkhovnogo soveta, postanovlenii i rasporiazhenii pravitel'stva Turkmenskoi SSR (1925-1944)* (Ashkhabad, 1960) I, 7-8 (cited hereafter as KSZTSSR).

this declaration recognized the equality of rights of all citizens (including women) irrespective of their racial and national affiliations, and assured full freedom of development to all national minorities inhabiting the territory of the Turkmen ssr. One of the rights of the national minorities recognized in this declaration was the right to employ the mother-tongues of the minority groups in local organs of administration, educational and cultural institutions and law courts.[45] The Congress of Soviets of Peasants', Workers' and Red Army Deputies' of the Turkmen ssr was designated as the supreme organ of power of the Republic, and in the period between its sessions, the Central Executive Committee was designated as the highest repository of all powers within the Turkmen ssr. The Congress charged the newly established Central Executive Committee to constitute a Council of People's Commissars and to prepare the draft constitution of the Republic. The Central Executive Committee was asked to submit this constitution to the Second Congress of Soviets of the Turkmen ssr for its approval.[46]

The First Congress of the Communist Party of Turkmenistan as well as the First Constituent Congress of Soviets adopted resolutions which indicated the desire of the Turkmen people 'for the voluntary entrance of the Turkmen ssr as an equal member into the ussr.' In accordance with these resolutions, the Central Executive Committee of the Turkmen ssr in one of its conferences decided in favour of sending a delegation of the Turkmen ssr to participate in the Third Congress of Soviets of the ussr and to request the latter to accept the Turkmen ssr as a member of the Soviet Union. On 13 May 1925 the Third Congress of Soviets of the ussr resolved to admit both the Turkmen and the Uzbek ssrs into the Soviet Union.

III. THE TADJIK AUTONOMOUS SOVIET SOCIALIST REPUBLIC

The newly formed Tadjik Autonomous Soviet Socialist Republic occupied an area of 145,000 square kilometres and possessed a population of 827,000 persons. The following areas which were

45. *Ibid.*, 8-9.
46. Gordienko, n. 41, 135.

inhabited predominantly by Tadjiks were incorporated within the
Tadjik ASSR:

(1) the entire Pamir region[47] of the former Fergana oblast,
the upper Zerafshan area situated between the river
Matcha and the Iskander-kul lake, and the northern
slopes of the Turkestan range situated between the rivers
Ak-su and Gul'draut;[48]

(2) the Eastern Bukharan region of the former Republic of
Bukhara consisting of the *vilaiets* of Garm, Hissar, Kuliab,
Kurgantube, Diushambe and a part of the Sary-Assi *vilaiet*
(the Regar and the Kara-tag areas).[49]

.The southen and eastern frontiers of the Tadjik ASSR coincide
with the international frontiers of the USSR with Afghanistan
and China respectively. In the south-east, the territory of the
Tadjik Republic is separated from India by a four-hundred-
kilometres-wide strip of territory, the so-called Afghan corridor.
To the north of the Tadjik ASSR lay the territory of the Kirgiz
Autonomous Oblast and to its west, the territory of the Uzbek
SSR.[50]

Consisting mostly of either hilly regions or high mountain
ranges, the territory of the Tadjik ASSR represented one of the
most backward and neglected parts of the Central Asian region.
Though the river Piandzh (the upper course of the river Amu-
Daria) and its tributaries—Gunt, Vortang, Kizil-su, Vaksh and
Kafirnigan—flowed through it, most of the territory of the
Republic was unsuited for cultivation because of its mountainous character. It had no urban centres, and the process of
industrialization had left it wholly untouched. More than 95 per
cent of its population was dependent on agriculture, and in
parts of its territory primitive barter economy prevailed. The
bulk of the population of the Tadjik Republic was concentrated
in its western part. This region, which was watered by the

47. The Territorial Commission had divided the Pamir region between
the Tadjik ASSR and the Kirgiz Autonomous Oblast, but this decision was
reversed by the VTsIK and the entire Pamir region was allocated to the
Tadjik ASSR. See *Turkestanskaia Pravda*, 255 (532), 16 November 1924.

48. *Biulleten' tsentral'nogo statisticheskogo upravleniia Uzbekistana*
(Tashkent, 1925) I, 5-6.

49. *MRSA(B)*, n. 3, 69; *Pravda Vostoka*, 1 (540), 25 November 1924.

50. Mumin Khodzhaev, 'Sed'maia soiuznaia,' *Sovetskaia Aziia* (Moscow)
3-4 (1930) 247.

rivers Kizil-su, Vaksh, Ak-su and Kafirnigan, represented the most fertile part of the Tadjik ASSR.

When the economic resources of the former republics of Turkestan, Bukhara and Khorezm were distributed among the new state formations of Central Asia, the Tadjik ASSR was allocated seven million rubles' worth of state properties, 962,504 head of cattle and 1,428,000 rubles from the funds of the Central Asiatic Agricultural Credit Bank. Its share included 642,643 *desiatins* of cultivated land of the Central Asian region which yielded a gross income of 20,406,000 rubles. Nearly 97.75 per cent of this area (628,165 *desiatins*) grew cereals. About 6,049 *desiatins* of land grew lucerne and another 8,399 *desiatins* were occupied by orchards.[51] A considerable number of people, especially in southern Tadjikistan, were engaged in stock-raising.

The Tadjiks constituted the bulk of the population of the Republic. Out of the Republic's total population of 827,200 persons, the Tadjiks constituted as much as 74.6 per cent (617,100 persons). The remaining part of its population consisted of 175,000 (21.2 per cent) Uzbeks, 4,100 (0.5 per cent) Turkmens, 11,400 (1.4 per cent) Kirgiz, 1,600 (0.2 per cent) Kazakhs, 5,600 (0.7 per cent) Russians and 11,900 (1.4 per cent) persons belonging to other national groups.[52]

In reorganizing the administrative units of the Tadjik ASSR, the Revolutionary Committee of the Republic decided to adopt the *vilaiet* system of administrative divisions which had previously existed in the Republic of Bukhara. The entire territory of the Republic was divided into eight vilaiets. The newly established *vilaiets* were Garm, Gorno-Badakhshan, Diushambe, Kuliab, Kurgan-tube, Pendzhikent, Sary-Assi and Ura-tube.[53] The Pamir region was at first organized into the Gorno-Badakhshan *vilaiet* and later into the Gorno-Badakhshan Autonomous Oblast.[54]

51. See pp. 198-9.

52. VPN (K. S.), n. 39, 3; also see A. V. Pankov, 'Polozhenie, granitsy, sostav i administrativnoe delenie Tadzhikistana,' *Tadzhikistan* (Tashkent, 1925) 1-8.

53. *BTsSUUz*, n. 48, 10-11.

54. *Vsia Sredniaia Aziia*, n. 17, 542. In its national composition the Pamir region was divided sharply into two parts: the Tadjik-inhabited south-western part and the Kirgiz-inhabited north-eastern part. The Tadjiks constituted 87.7 per cent and the Kirgiz 12.2 per cent of the total

In a proclamation addressed to 'All Toilers of Tadjikistan', the Provisional Revolutionary Committee on 7 December 1924 officially proclaimed the formation of the Tadjik Autonomous Soviet Socialist Republic. On 12 March 1925, people all over Tadjikistan celebrated the formation of their national republic. Even though from November 1924 the Provisional Revolutionary Committee began to make preparations for the meeting of the First Constituent Congress of Soviets of the Tadjik ASSR, this body did not meet until the end of 1926. On 1 December 1926 the Constituent Congress of Soviets of Tadjikistan adopted with great ceremony a declaration on the formation of the Tadjik Autonomous Soviet Socialist Republic. After scrutinizing the report of the Provisional Revolutionary Committee on its work since November 1924, the Congress took up the question of establishing the permanent governmental organs of the Republic. The Provisional Revolutionary Committees, both central and local, were abolished, and authority was vested in the newly-elected soviet organs. All the legislative functions of the Republic were entrusted to the newly-created Central Executive Committee of the Tadjik ASSR.[55] A Council of People's Commissars was established to take charge of the Executive functions. The Congress also adopted a resolution on the inclusion of the Tadjik ASSR within the Soviet Union as an autonomous part of the Uzbek SSR. This resolution stated, '...the First All-Tadjik Constituent Congress of Soviets on behalf of the *dekkans* of Tadjikistan declares...its unswerving decision on the voluntary entrance (of the Tadjik ASSR) into the USSR through the Uzbek SSR in the capacity of an autonomous Republic.'[56]

population of the region. In its socio-economic and linguistic set-up the Pamir region differed from the rest of the Tadjik areas. Its average density of population was only 0.3 persons per square kilometre and an area of nearly 50,000 square *versts* was inhabited by only 16,400 persons. See *Materialy po raionirovaniiu Turkestana*: *proekt administrativno-khoziaistvennogo deleniia TSSR* (Tashkent, 1924) II, 137; N. D. Degtiarenko, 'Sozdanie i razvitie Tadzhikskoi sovetskoi sotsialisticheskoi gosudarstvennosti,' *Uchenye zapiski Tashkentskogo iuridicheskogo instituta* (Tashkent, 1955) I, 226.

55. S. A. Radzhabov, 'Natsional'no-gosudarstvennoe razmezhevanie Srednei Azii,' *Uchenye zapiski Tashkentskogo iuridicheskogo instituta* (Tashkent, 1955) I, 77.

56. Cited in Tursunov, n. 2, 213. A decree issued by the Central Executive Committee of the Uzbek SSR on 22 July 1925 stated that the

IV. THE KIRGIZ AUTONOMOUS OBLAST

The Kirgiz Autonomous Oblast[57] was formed by merging those parts of the former Turkestan ASSR which were inhabited predominantly by the Kirgiz population. This territory consisted of the Karakol and Naryn uezds and a part of the Pishpek uezd of the former Semirechie oblast; fourteen Kirgiz-majority volosts of the Aulie-Ata uezd of the former Syr-Daria oblast; thirty-eight volosts of the Andizhan, Namangan, Fergana, Kokand and Osh uezds of the former Fergana oblast.[58]

Situated in the north-eastern corner of Central Asia, the Kirgiz Autonomous Oblast occupied an area of 190,700 square kilometres and possessed a population of 993,000 persons. The territory of Kirgizia is surrounded on almost all the four sides by mountain ranges which act as its natural frontiers with the adjoining states. In the south-east its frontier with China passes along the Kok-shaal-Tau range and the Tien-shan ranges. In the south the Zaalai and Turkestan ranges constitute Kirgizia's natural frontier with the Tadjik Republic. Again, the mountain ranges located in the north and north-eastern part of Kirgizia separate its territory from the territory of the Kazakh Republic. In the west, for about 300 kilometres its frontier with Uzbekistan runs along the plains adjoining the Alatau mountains and through the Chu river valley. In the south-west where the territories of Kirgizia and Tadjikistan meet in the Fergana valley, the frontier between these two state formations has been demarcated along the foot-hills and piedmont plains.[59]

Tadjik ASSR was an autonomous part of the Uzbek SSR. On the basis of the declaration on the formation of the Uzbek SSR adopted by the First Congress of the Uzbek SSR, this decree sought to determine the competence of the legislative, executive and judicial organs of the Uzbek SSR over the territory of the Tadjik ASSR. See I. Ananov, 'K preobrazovaniiu Sredne-Aziatskikh respublik,' *Sovetskoe pravo* (Moscow) 4 (1925) 136.

57. At the time of its formation, Kirgizia was known as the Kara-Kirgiz Autonomous Oblast. The epithet 'Kara', which means 'black', was subsequently dropped in accordance with a decree of the *VTsIK* issued on 25 May 1925. See *Sovetskaia politika za 10 let po natsional'nomu voprosu v RSFSR* (Moscow, 1928) 86.

58. For details about these territories see p. 190 (footnotes).

59. S. N. Riazantsev and V. F. Pavlenko, *Kirgizskaia SSR* (Moscow, 1960) 3. The frontiers of the Kirgiz Autonomous Oblast with the Uzbek SSR, the Tadjik and Kazakh ASSRs underwent some minor changes consequent upon the transfer of some areas from the Kirgiz AO to the neigh-

The territory of Kirgizia abounds not only in mountains but also in valleys, rivers and lakes. Its biggest rivers are the Naryn, Chu and Kara-Daria. In the eastern part of the territory of Kirgizia is situated the Issyk-kul lake—the second biggest lake in the Soviet Union and one of the largest lakes in the world. The rivers flowing through the Kirgiz territory have considerable importance for irrigation, and the rich pasture lands located in the foothill regions, their adjoining plains and the river valleys are well suited for agriculture. The territory of Kirgizia also has considerable forest wealth and mineral resources. Chief among them are coal, lead, zinc, tin, quick-silver, antimony, marble, gold, salt and oil deposits. At the time of its formation nearly half of the territory of the Kirgiz Auto-nomous Oblast consisted of mountain pastures which ensured an adequate supply of fodder to its livestock. To the share of the Kirgiz Autonomous Oblast had come 13.8 per cent of the total cattle wealth of Central Asia which amounted to 1,881,658 head of cattle. Nearly 64.1 per cent of the income of Kirgizia was derived from its livestock.[60]

At the time of its formation, the Kirgiz Autonomous Oblast's total cultivated area amounted to 246,516 *desiatins*. According to the data available an income of 30,525,000 rubles accrued to the Kirgiz Autonomous Oblast from agriculture in 1923-24.[61] In 1924, within Kirgizia 13,268 *desiatins* (5.38 per cent) of land was under the cotton crop, 212,526 *desiatins* (86.21 per cent) under cereals, 19,120 *desiatins* (7.76 per cent) under lucerne,

bouring republics and *vice versa*. Between 1927 and 1929 the Kirgiz AO ceded the Grodekov and Besh-agach villages of the Talass canton to the Kazakh ASSR. In turn the Kazakh ASSR transferred to the Kirgiz AO the Kamyshansk village of the Dzhetysuisk *gubernia*. The Uzbek SSR ceded to Kirgizia the village of Uch-Kurgan which had a population of 6,116 persons. The frontier between the Kazakh ASSR and Kirgizia in the Karakol canton underwent some change consequent upon the inclusion in the latter of the Dzhaulan area. Again, in accordance with a decree passed by the *TsIK* of the USSR on 4 May 1927, several villages from the *Uzbek* SSR were transferred to the Kirgiz AO. By a decree of the *TsIK* of the USSR passed on 8 June 1927, the Sulliukta coal-mine was transferred from the Uzbek SSR to the Kirgiz AO. See *Otchet o rabote pravitel'stva Kirgizs-koi ASSR za 2 goda: Mart 1927—Aprel 1929* (Frunze, 1929) 2-3 (cited hereafter as *ORPKASSR*).

60. *Pravda Vostoka*, 1 (540), 25 November 1924.

61. See pp. 198-9.

191 *desiatins* (0.08 per cent) under tobacco and 1,416 *desiatins* under orchards and vineyards.[62] About 35.9 per cent of the income of the Kirgiz Autonomous Oblast was derived from agriculture.[63]

In its population composition the Kirgiz Autonomous Oblast was less homogeneous than some of the other new state formations of Central Asia.[64] The Kirgiz constituted 66.6 per cent (661,200 persons) of Kirgizia's total population of 993,000 persons. Among its non-Kirgiz population there were 103,800 (11.1 per cent) Uzbeks, 1,800 (0.2 per cent) Kazakhs, 116,400 (11.7 per cent) Russians and 103,800 (10.4 per cent) persons belonging to other national groups. Though inexact, the following table provides an approximate picture of the districtwise distribution of the nationalities of the Kirgiz Autonomous Oblast.[65]

Table X

Districts	Kirgiz	Uzbeks	Kazakhs	Russians	Others
Pishpek	44.8	4.2	4.6	41.4	5.0
Karakol-Naryn	71.8	2.3	1.8	21.3	2.8
Dzhalal-abad	71.7	21.5	—	4.2	2.6
Osh	60.0	35.6	—	2.2	2.2
Total	61.2	17.5	1.6	16.6	3.1

Note: The figures are in percentages.

Soon after the formation of the Kirgiz Autonomous Oblast, the Provisional Revolutionary Committee began to organize a number of national cantons, volosts and sel'sovets in order to provide the national minorities all facilities for their development. On the territory inhabited by the people of European origin (Great Russians, Ukrainians and Germans) the Revolutionary Committee created one national canton, eleven national volosts and seventy-one national sel'sovets. The Uzbek-inhabited areas of the Kirgiz AO were organized into one national volost and nineteen national sel'sovets. Besides these, there came into existence 2 Tatar national sel'sovets, 1 Dungan national sel'sovet, and 21 national sel'sovets of mixed Euro-

62. See pp. 199-200.
63. *Pravda Vostoka*, 1 (540), 25 November 1924.
64. See *VPN (K.S.)*, n. 39, 16-17.
65. *Vsia Sredniaia Azii*, n. 17, 651.

pean population.[66] The national minorities were given facilities
to manage the administration of their own national units and
to run their educational and cultural institutions through the
medium of their mother-tongue.

The bulk of the population of the Kirgiz AO lived in the rural
areas, and its urban population did not exceed 11.6 per cent
of its total population. Kirgizia's average density of population
was only 5.07 persons per square kilometre. It ranged from
40.2 persons per square kilometre in the Pishpek region to only
1.92 persons per square kilometre in the Naryn area.[67] Administratively the entire territory of the Kirgiz AO was divided into
four districts: Karakol-Naryn, Pishpek, Dzhalal-Abad and Osh.
Pishpek city, which at the time had a population of only 13,000
persons, became the capital of the Kirgiz AO. Later on Pishpek
was renamed Frunze.[68]

The Constituent Congress of the Kirgiz Autonomous Oblast
met in Pishpek between 27-30 March 1925. In place of the Provisional Revolutionary Committee which until then was in
charge of the administration of Kirgizia, the Congress constituted an elected Executive Committee. A resolution adopted by
this Congress demanded that Kirgizia should be given a higher
constitutional position than a mere autonomous oblast and to
realize this it instructed the newly-constituted Executive Committee to open negotiations with the All-Russian Central Executive Committee.[69] In a plenary session of the Executive
Committee of the Kirgiz AO held on 31 March 1925 a Presidium
was constituted. On 5 April 1925 by a decree of the Presidium
of the Executive Committee of the Kirgiz AO the organs of state
administration were established. These consisted of the Departments of Land, Finance, Labour, Health, Education, Justice,
Nationalities, Social Security, Internal Trade and Planning.

On 6 December 1925 the Executive Committee of the Kirgiz

66. *Kratkii obzor sovetskogo stroitel'stva i narodnogo khoziaistva
Kirgizii: materialy k dokladu Ispolkoma KAO 3-tei sessii VTsIK RSFSR
XI sozyva* (Frunze, 1926) 2-3; also see Cherdantsev, n. 21, 70.
67. ORPKASSR, n. 59, 3.
68. *Pravda Vostoka*, 1 (540), 25 November 1924.
69. K. N. Nurbekov, 'Obrazovanie Kirgizskoi suverennoi sovetskoi
sotsialisticheskoi respubliki,' *Sovetskoe gosudarstvo i pravo* (Moscow) 9
(1958) 45.

AO formally requested the *VTsIK* of the RSFSR to confer on Kirgizia the status of an autonomous republic. Subsequently, two delegates from the Kirgiz AO, Urazaev and Fat'ianov, pleaded before the third session of the *VTsIK* (of the XII Congress) for the enhancement of the constitutional status of the Kirgiz AO.[70] The All-Russian Central Executive Committee, after acquainting itself with the report of the Executive Committee of the Kirgiz AO, resolved to confer upon Kirgizia the status of an autonomous republic, and soon issued a decree on this question. This decree was confirmed by the thirteenth congress of Soviets of the RSFSR on 15 April 1927.[71]

After the reorganization of Kirgizia into an autonomous republic, a central executive committee consisting of 150 members was established by the first Constituent Congress of the Kirgiz ASSR in March 1927. In a plenary session of the Central Executive Committee of the Kirgiz ASSR held on 12 March 1927, a presidium was constituted. The Presidium was composed of two chairmen, two vice-chairmen and seventeen members. The executive organs of the Republic—the Council of People's Commissars, consisting of 39 members—was also constituted. Pending the adoption of the constitution of the Kirgiz ASSR, the functions of its governmental organs were regulated by a provisional decree issued by the Presidium of the Central Executive Committee of the Kirgiz ASSR on 22 March 1927 and by 'the Statute on the state organization of the Kirgiz ASSR' issued by the *Sovnarkom* of the RSFSR on 4 February 1927.[72]

70. *Vlast' sovetov*, 48 (1925) 5.
71. A resolution approved by the Thirteenth Congress of Soviets of the RSFSR which confirmed this decree stated, 'on the basis of the sovereign rights of the peoples proclaimed by the October Revolution, in conformity with the aspirations of the workers and peasants of Kirgizstan and also in view of the general economic and political importance of Kirgizstan and the unity of its national territory, the Thirteenth All-Russian Congress of Soviets confirms the decision of the Third Session of the All-Russian Central Executive Committee of the XII Congress, on the reorganization of the Kirgiz Autonomous Oblast into an autonomous republic of the RSFSR, and grants permission for the election of its Central Executive Committee in the First All-Kirgiz Congress of Soviets and for beginning the organization of the government of the republic.' See *Sovetskaia politika za 10 let po natsional'nomu voprosu*, n. 57, 90.
72. Nurbekov, n. 69, 47; A. Zorin, '10 let sovetskoi Kirgizii,' *Revoliutsionnyi vostok* (Moscow) 6 (1934) 161-3.

V. THE KARA-KALPAK AUTONOMOUS OBLAST

The newly-established Kara-Kalpak Autonomous Oblast occupied an area of 112,000 square kilometres and possessed a population of 363,470 persons. The Kara-Kalpak AO was constituted by amalgamating the Khodzheili and Kungrad regions of the former Khorezm Republic with the Chimbai and Surakhan uezds of the former Amu-Daria oblast.[73]

Most of the territory of the Kara-Kalpak AO located near the Aral Sea is covered by the sands of the Kizyl-kum desert. The territories situated on the right bank of the Amu-Daria and on the right portion of its delta are relatively more fertile. These areas possess much alluvial soil and are irrigated by the waters of the Amu-Daria.[74] At the time of its formation the Kara-Kalpak Autonomous Oblast possessed 34,803 *desiatins* of cultivable land and 380,745 head of cattle. Among the various crops grown on its territory, cotton occupied 1,622 *desiatins* (4.66 per cent), cereals 28,304 *desiatins* (81.33 per cent), lucerne 4,774 *desiatins* (13.72 per cent) and orchards 88 *desiatins* (0.25 per cent). According to the data available for 1923-24, a sum of 9,085,000 rubles accrued to Kara-Kalpakia from agriculture.[75]

Unlike the other state formations of Central Asia which were largely homogeneous in their national composition, Kara-Kalpakia was and continues to remain heterogeneous in its national composition. According to the 1926 census its territory was inhabited by 38.1 per cent Kara-Kalpaks, 28.5 per cent Kazakhs, 27.6 per cent Uzbeks, 1.6 per cent Russians and 3.2 per cent Turkmens.[76] Though at the time of the establishment of the Kara-Kalpak AO the Kara-Kalpaks constituted a relative

73. According to the recommendations of the Territorial Commission, the Surakhan uezd had been allotted to the Uzbek SSR, but by a decree issued on September 1924, the Central Executive Committee of the USSR transferred the Surakhan uezd including Turtkul town to the Kara-Kalpak AO. See Ia. M. Dosumov, *Ocherki istorii Kara-kalpakskoi ASSR 1917-1927* (Tashkent, 1960) 252, 254.

74. The Amu-Daria is the only river which flows through the Kara-Kalpak region and the areas irrigated by its water are the most densely populated part of the Kara-Kalpak AO. See *Uzbekistan: ekonomiko-geograficheskaia kharakteristika* (Tashkent, 1950) 287-90.

75. See pp. 198-200.

76. Ilias Alkin, 'Natsional'no-gosudarstvennoe razmezhevanie Srednei Azii i VII s'ezd sovetov SSSR,' *Revoliutsionnyi vostok*, 6 (1934) 125.

majority of its population, in subsequent years, largely as a result of assimilation by the culturally more advanced Uzbeks, the size of the Kara-Kalpak population began to fall sharply. According to the 1939 census the Kara-Kalpaks constituted a little less than 27 per cent of the population of Kara-Kalpakia. The downward trend discernible in the growth of the Kara-Kalpak population and the absence of strong cultural traditions and national consciousness among them have imparted an artificial character to the Kara-Kalpak nation.[77]

Administratively the entire territory of the Kara-Kalpak AO was divided into four districts and twenty-five volosts. From the territory which came into its possession from the former Khorezm Republic, the Khodzheili and Kungrad districts were constituted. The Khodzheili district was divided into six volosts and the Kungrad district into four volosts. That part of the territory of the former Amu-Daria oblast which was merged with the Kara-Kalpak AO was divided into the Turtkul and Chimbai districts The Turtkul district was divided into seven volosts and the Chimbai district into nine volosts.[78] Chimbai town became the capital of the Kara-Kalpak AO.

The First Constituent Congress of Soviets of the Kara-Kalpak Autonomous Oblast met in Turtkul between 15-19 February 1925. The Congress adopted a formal 'Declaration on the Formation of the Kara-Kalpak Autonomous Oblast' and created an Oblast Executive Committee to take charge of the administration of the territories of Kara-Kalpakia. The Congress also formed a 40-member delegation to attend the Fifth All-Kazakh Congress of Soviets and instructed it to express before the latter the desire of the Kara-Kalpak people and government for the inclusion of the Kara-Kalpakia AO as a federative part of the Kazakh ASSR. The Fifth All-Kazakh Congress of Soviets which met in Kyzyl-Orda between 15-19 April 1925, in accordance with the wishes of the Kara-Kalpaks, decreed the inclusion of Kara-Kalpakia as an autonomous part of the Kazakh ASSR.[79]

77. Alexandre Bennigsen and Chantal Quelquejay, *The Evolution of the Muslim Nationalities of the USSR and their Linguistic Problems* (London, 1961) 32-3 (trans. from French by Geoffrey Wheeler).

78. Dusumov, n. 73, 254.

79. *Ibid.,* 253.

VI. SIGNIFICANCE OF THE NATIONAL DELIMITATION

The political map of the Central Asian region underwent a radical change as a result of the implementation of the national delimitation scheme. In place of the former republics of Turkestan, Bukhara and Khorezm, which under different names had existed on the political map of Central Asia since the days of the Russian conquest of the region, there now came into existence as many as five separate state formations. Of these the Uzbek and Turkmen republics were immediately elevated to the rank of Union Republics which entitled them to the right of direct entrance into the Soviet Union and to a constitutional position which at that time was enjoyed within the USSR by the Russian Federative Soviet Socialist Republic, the Ukrainian SSR the Byelorussian SSR and the Transcaucasion Federation. Of the three remaining political formations, Tadjikistan was given the status of an Autonomous Republic within the Uzbek SSR and Kirgizia and Kara-Kalpakia were organized as Autonomous Oblasts, the former within the RSFSR and the latter within the Kazakh ASSR. The fact that the republics in which Tadjikistan, Kirgizia and Kara-Kalpakia were included were members of the Soviet Union also made these three state formations of Central Asia members of the USSR though in an indirect way.

The main significance of the national delimitation of Central Asia lay in the fact that it enabled the unification within the framework of nationally homogeneous republics of the different segments of the Uzbek, Turkmen, Tadjik, Kirgiz, Kara-Kalpak and Kazakh populations which previously were scattered over the territories of the republics of Turkestan, Bukhara and Khorezm.[80] Thus, if formerly 66.5 per cent of the total Uzbek

80. In an address delivered on 18 May, 1925, to the students of the University of the Peoples of the East, Stalin emphasized this aspect of the reform. He stated, 'in the pre-revolutionary era, both these countries (i.e. Uzbekistan and Turkmenistan) were torn into fragments, into various khanates and states, and were a convenient field for the exploiting machinations of the "powers that be." The time has now come when these scattered fragments can be *re-united* into independent states, so that the toiling masses of Uzbekistan and Turkmenistan can be united and welded with the organs of government. The delimitation of the frontiers in Turkestan is primarily the *reunion* of the scattered parts of these countries

population of Central Asia lived within the Turkestan ASSR, 22.2 per cent within the Republic of Bukhara and 11.3 per cent within the Khorezm Republic, within the newly-established Uzbek Republic as much as 82.6 per cent of the entire Uzbek population of Central Asia was unified. The attempt made to unify territorially the scattered segments of the Turkmen population met with greater success. If formerly 43.2 per cent of the Turkmen population of Central Asia lived within the Turkestan Republic, 27.0 per cent within Bukhara and 29.8 per cent within Khorezm, within the newly-established Turkmen SSR as much as 94.2 per cent of the entire Turkmen population of Central Asia was brought together. The reform proved equally beneficial to the Tadjiks, Kirghiz, Kara-Kalpaks and the Kazakhs. Within the Tadjik ASSR 75.2 per cent of the entire Tadjik population of the Central Asian region was unified; 86.7 per cent of the entire Kirgiz population of the Central Asian region was brought within the framework of the Kirgiz Autonomous Oblast and 79.3 per cent of the entire Kara-Kalpaks of Central Asia now lived within the Kara-Kalpak AO.[81] The merger of the Kazakh-inhabited regions of the former Turkestan Republic within the Kazakh ASSR led to the increase of the Kazakh population of the latter from 46.6 per cent to 61.3 per cent.[82] As a result of national delimitation, the population of the new republics and autonomous oblasts acquired a greater degree of homogeneity than had existed in the former republics of Turkestan, Bukhara and Khorezm. Though none of them approximated to the ideal of a uni-national state, within each one of them its dominant nationality constituted a compact majority of its total population.[83] Thus, within the Uzbek SSR the Uzbeks constituted 74.7 per cent of the total population, and the Turkmens constituted 70.2 per cent of the population of the Turk-

into independent states.' See I. V. Stalin, *Sochineniia* (Moscow, 1948) VII, 136-7.

81. Sh. F. Mukhamed'iarov, 'K istorii natsional'no-gosudarstvennogo razmezhevaniia Srednei Azii v 1924 g,' *Sovetskoe vostokovedenie* (Moscow) 1 (1955) 55; Ilias Alkin, n. 76, 115.

82. A. Nusupbekov, *Ob'edinenie Kazakhskikh zemel' v Kazakhskoi sovetskoi sotsialisticheskoi respublike* (Alma-Ata, 1953) 80.

83. This statement requires qualification in relation to the Kara-Kalpaks who constituted only a relative majority of the total population of the Kara-Kalpak Autonomous Oblast.

men SSR. Wihin the Tadjik ASSR the Tadjiks constituted as much
as 74.7 per cent of the total population. The Kirgiz constituted
66.4 per cent of the total population of Kirgizia.[84]

The significance of the national delimitation of Central Asia
was not merely political. It had considerable significance for
the economic, cultural and national consolidation of the major
nationalities of the region. In the economic sphere, the delimitation of Central Asia resulted in the territorial bifurcation of
the areas practising a nomadic cattlebreeding economy from the
areas of sedentary agricultural economy. The areas merged
within the Kazakh and the Kirgiz Republics, which were Central Asia's traditional centres of cattlebereding economy, sharply
differed from the regions of sedentary agricultural economy
which, after the delimitation of 1924, were situated mainly in
the Uzbek and Tadjik Republics. The Turkmen and the Kara-
Kalpak regions, in whose economy both agriculture and stock-
raising played an equally important part, also differed from both
the typically cattlebreeding areas of Kazakhstan and Kirgizia
and the typically agricultural regions of Uzbekistan and Tadjikistan. The inclusion of such distinct economic regions within the
framework of separate state formations enabled the governments
of the newly-created republics and autonomous oblasts to attempt a systematic study of the economic potential and to undertake a planned development of their resources.

In the educational and cultural sphere the establishment of
nationally homogeneous state formations enhanced prospects
for systematically combating illiteracy and raising the cultural
level of the people. Before 1924, whatever educational and
cultural institutions there were in Central Asia, existed as a rule
in the more advanced Uzbek regions, and the peripheral non-
Uzbek areas were utterly neglected. With the establishment
of their own national state formations, the Turkmens, Tadjiks,
Kirgiz and Kara-Kalpaks acquired the necessary means to catch
up not only with the culturally more advanced regions of Central Asia but also with European Russia.[85] Equally significant

84. VPN (K.S.), n. 39, 3, 16-17.
85. Between 1924-27 the number of schools within the Uzbek SSR
increased by four times and within the Turkmen SSR, the number of students increased from 12,000 to 23,000 persons. Within Kirgizia at the

was the stimulus the languages of the nationalities of Central Asia received following the establishment of the new state formations. Their large-scale use in administration, in cultural and educational institutions, and in the publication of newspapers, books and periodicals, provided ample scope for the development of these languages and for the growth of national literatures.[86]

In the national sphere the immediate outcome of the establishment of the new state formations was the disappearance of national antagonisms, feuds and frictions which had plagued the Central Asian region for such a long time. The territorial separation of the different national groups from one another, and the removal of the economic causes which in the past had roused national passions and frictions, led to the establishment of peaceful and harmonious relations among the different national groups.

Equally significant was the fact that following the establishment of nationally-homogeneous state formations, the Uzbeks, Tadjiks, Turkmens and Kirgiz acquired the objective prerequisites not only for preserving their national identity but also for consolidating their nations by way of assimilating their kindred ethnic groups, tribes and clans. Under the former multi-national state structures of Turkestan, Bukhara and Khorezm, the economically weak and culturally backward national groups had faced the danger of losing their national identity and being assimilated and absorbed by the more dominant national groups. The weaker national groups were freed from this threat of national extinction following the changed political, economic and social conditions which came to prevail in Central Asia after 1924.

Another important outcome of the delimitation of Central Asia was that it rendered possible the rapid socialist transforma-

time of its formation there were only 70 schools and 16 doctors. By 1927 Kirgizia had 480 schools and 100 doctors. Within Tadjikistan by 1927 there were 154 schools which within the following two years doubled in number. See S. Dimanshtein, 'Desiat' let natsional'noi politiki partii i sovvlasti,' *Novyi vostok* (Moscow) 19 (1927) XII-XIII; V. N. Shumilin, 'Puti razvitiia narodnogo khoziaistva Tadzhikistana,' *Novyi vostok*, 29 (1930) 125.

86. A. Potseluevskii, 'Razvitie Turkmenskogo iazyka,' *Turkmenovedenie*, 10-11 (1929) 71.

tion of the region. From the standpoint of Bolshevik leadership, in fact, this was the main significance of the reorganization of the national frontiers of Central Asia. It is important to note in this connection that the Bolsheviks, unlike others to whom the establishment of nationally homogeneous state formations appeared as an end in itself, emphasized from the beginning that one of the important factors which induced them to undertake the reform of 1924 was the increased prospects it held for building socialism. In view of past experiences this line of reasoning appeared quite justified. In the former republics of Turkestan, Bukhara and Khorezm, the Bolsheviks found that the presence of inter-tribal frictions and antagonisms, and the preoccupation of the people with national rather than with socialist slogans had greatly hindered their objectives of promoting class stratification and building socialism. With the creation of the new national republics and autonomous oblasts, the Bolsheviks believed that national passions would abate and the objective conditions would be created for the establishment of a socialist order. This belief was forcefully expressed by M. I. Kalinin before the First Congress of the Communist Party of Uzbekistan in the following words:

> He who thinks of state, including an autonomous state, as an end in itself, commits a grievous error and he ceases to be a communist. In our Soviet Union all state formations and the USSR itself are only means for (achieving) the victory of communism. Therefore, in resolving the national question the communist should never let from his view this most fundamental aim.[87]

In view of these facts it is not surprising that the national delimitation of Central Asia appeared to many Communists as a 'second revolution' which fundamentally altered the relations which subsisted among Central Asia's various national groups. This also explains the passion with which they defend the reform of 1924 against its critics. A speech delivered by Faizulla Khodzhaev before the Second Congress of Soviets of Uzbekistan contains the most eloquent defence of the national delimitation of Central Asia. Drawing the attention of the critics to some of

---

87. *I s'ezd Kommunisticheskoi partii (Bolshevikov) Uzbekistana*: stenograficheskii otchët (Tashkent, 1925) 24.

the beneficial aspects of the reform, Faizulla Khodzhaev in this speech stated:

> If you desire to see what we have achieved as a result of na-
> tional-state delimitation, look upon the territory of the present
> Uzbek Republic, see how the relations between the various
> nationalities are established, see how the wide strata of
> workers and peasants have been associated with the entire
> administration in this Republic; see and tell us who rules this
> country. Look at the number of schools which the Soviet
> Government has established and also the work it is carrying
> out in the educational sphere; look at the mutual relations
> which have evolved between the Soviet republics and the
> Soviet Union into which Uzbekistan, on its own free volition,
> has entered as an equal member; look at the complete na-
> tional peace which now prevails, the growth of our industries,
> agriculture and trade which have already attained the pre-
> war level (of development). See all these and be convinced
> about all that national delimitation has given to Central Asia.[88]

Notwithstanding this panegyric on the national delimitation of Central Asia, it would be wrong to presume that the reform satisfied all sections of the people or that its results were wholly beneficial. In fact, its negative results were also of some significance inasmuch as the disappointment and bitterness it gave rise to among certain sections of the people were as pro-found as the jubilation it roused in its advocates and supporters. The partition of Central Asia into numerous national republics seriously undermined the old sense of unity that had evolved in

88. Cited in B. Kul'besherov, 'Sovetskoe stroitel'stvo v Srednei Azii i ego zadacha k 10-letiiu Oktiabr'skoi revoliutsii,' *Novyi vostok*, 19 (1927) XXXII. It is interesting to note in this connection that later on when confronted with the upsurge of nationalist sentiments among the Uzbeks and other nationalities of Central Asia, the Bolsheviks tried to play down the significance of national delimitation. Speaking before a conference of the Uzbek Communist Party workers in 1929, Zelenski, the Chairman of the Central Asiatic Bureau, declared, 'a view is prevalent among the responsible Party members that the economic development of Uzbekistan is the result of national delimitation. This is wrong. The economic develop-ment of Uzbekistan is due to the creation of the Uzbek *Soviet* Republic, is the result of the establishment of the dictatorship of the proletariat, is a result of the October Revolution. The creation of a national republic is not the cause of its economic development, but it is only due to the inclusion of Uzbekistan within the USSR and is the result of the help rendered by the Union to the backward economy of Uzbekistan.' See *Pravda Vostoka*, 51 (1847), 4 March 1929.

the region on the basis of certain racial, religious and cultural affinities. There were still many people to whom the ideals of the common Islamic civilization and culture of Central Asia held greater emotional and spiritual appeal than the ideals of parochial nationalism. Of course, it was true that this sense of unity was not strong enough to stem the tide of the centrifugal forces which were ushered into the body politic by the growing economic, national and linguistic differentiations. But the traditionalists were not prepared to support on this account what they termed as 'parcellization of their ancient territory' into 'artificial tribal republics'. Nor did the neo-radical section of the population represented by the erstwhile Djadidist intellectuals feel happy over the partition of Central Asia. These people, who under the inspirational glow of Gaspirali's *'Tardjuman'* had started inculcating among the peoples of Central Asia the ideal of a common 'Turkic' nation, culture and language, found that their entire life's work was being swept away in one sweep by the reform of 1924. The resulting bitterness manifested itself in angry denunciations, and they charged the Bolsheviks with the sinister design of dividing for political reasons the Central Asian region, which according to them, was 'nationally and culturally homogeneous.' Whatever might have been the motives of the Bolsheviks, it remains true that the reform which they undertook in 1924 had the effect of driving the last nail into the coffin of the idea of the 'Turkic nation' which was professed for a long time by the Djadidists in Central Asia.

The delimitation of Central Asia also marked the beginning of the process of drawing the peoples of the region away from the political and cultural influences of the adjoining countries of the Middle East and particularly from Turkey. This process was to culminate in the changes introduced in the scripts of the languages of Central Asia first from the Arabic to the Latin script and later from the Latin to the Cyrillic script. These changes were also accompanied by attempts made to orient the new republics of Central Asia towards European Russia.

Thus, viewed from whatever angle, the delimitation of Central Asia appears to be one of the most significant events in the recent history of the region. Not only did it radically alter the political map of Central Asia but it also rendered ineffective the old racial, religious and cultural bonds which had historically evolved in the region. Over the ruins of the old order it set the stage for the emergence of the new 'socialist nations' of Central Asia and paved the way for the momentous socialist experiment. In fact, it marked that great dividing line which separates two distinct periods in the history of recent times of the Central Asian region.

VII. ELEVATION OF TADJIKISTAN,
      KARA-KALPAKIA AND KIRGIZIA TO
      HIGHER FORM OF STATEHOOD

Barring the reorganization of the Kirgiz Autonomous Oblast into an Autonomous Republic in 1926,[89] the political set-up which emerged in Central Asia as a consequence of national delimitation, did not undergo any major changes until 1929. But beginning from 1929 the political set-up of some state formations began to undergo significant changes following the introduction of a number of reforms. In 1929 the Tadjik ASSR was separated from the Uzbek SSR and raised to the status of a union republic and was included directly within the USSR. In 1932 the Kara-Kalpak Autonomous Oblast was detached from the Kazakh ASSR, elevated to the status of an autonomous republic and was included within the RSFSR. Four years later, it was once again separated from the RSFSR and included within the Uzbek SSR. In 1936, following the adoption of a new constitution of the USSR, the Kirgiz ASSR was separated from the RSFSR, raised to the status of a union republic and was included directly within the USSR. The economic and political causes which led to these changes are worth examining.

While the other republics and autonomous oblasts of Central Asia were able to switch over to constructive activities soon after their establishment, the Tadjik Republic was preoccupied for a long time with the task of mopping up the remnants of the Basmachi guerrillas. Normal conditions came to prevail within Tadjikistan only from 1926 onwards. However, within the short span of only three years the Republic made considerable headway in rehabilitating its shattered economy. By

89. See pp. 224-5.

1929 the sown area within Tadjikistan had already reached the pre-war level and the area under the cotton crop, during this period, was nearly twice as much of the area which was under this crop in 1914. In the territory included within the Tadjik Republic, the cotton crop in 1914 had occupied about 35,000 hectares. By 1928-29 Tadjikistan had 61,000 hectares under the cotton crop. This rise was particularly impressive in view of the fact in 1925-26 the area under cotton had shrunk to 9,000 hectares.[90]

Tadjikistan, which had practically no industrial establishments at the time of its formation, by 1928-29 had established a number of cotton-processing and cotton-ginning enterprises. The establishment of the Termez-Diushambe railway line helped in linking the territory of Tadjikistan with other parts of the Soviet Union with modern means of communication. In the educational sphere also Tadjikistan made considerable progress. In 1927-28 there were 154 schools and 3 pedogogical *technicums* on the territory of the Tadjik ASSR. In 1929 the number of schools increased to more than three hundred.[91]

The resources of the Tadjik Republic were wholly inadequate to meet the requirements of the ambitious development programme which was launched in 1926. Its 1925-26 budget placed the total revenue of the Republic at 511,000 rubles and its expenditure at 5,139,000 rubles. About 90 per cent of the overall deficit for the year 1925-26 was covered by subsidies provided by the Government of the USSR. In 1929 the total revenue of Tadjikistan had risen to 3,844,000 rubles and its expenditure to 14,340,000 rubles. In that year Tadjikistan received a subsidy of 10,420,000 rubles from the Centre.[92]

By 1929 the Communists of Tadjikistan had begun to express their misgivings on the constitutional arrangement made in 1925 by virtue of which the Tadjik ASSR became an autonomous part of the Uzbek SSR. By then the feeling was widespread among the Tadjik Communists that their Republic was not get-

90. *Pravda Vostoka*, 174 (1970), 30 July 1929.

91. M. Irkaev and others, *Ocherk istorii Sovetskogo Tadzhikistana* 1917-1957 g (Stalinabad, 1957) 160-7.

92. *Pravda Vostoka*, 59 (1855), 15 March 1929; see also N. D. Degtiarenko, *Razvitie sovetskoi gosudarstvennosti v Tadzhikistane* (Moscow, 1960) 109.

ting a fair deal at the hands of the Government of the Uzbek SSR. In July 1929, Khodzhibaev, the Chairman of the Council of People's Commissars of the Tadjik ASSR, complained that

> the preoccupation of the Uzbek organs with their own problems has inevitably resulted in setting aside a number of needs of Tadjikistan. The Uzbek Government, for very obvious reasons, cannot give sufficient attention to our problems.[93]

That such complaints were not altogether without foundation becomes clear from the statement made by Tadzhiev, a member of the Central Committee of the Communist Party of Uzbekistan. Tadzhiev stated:

> In my opinion, the basic evil is that Uzbek nationalism in certain spheres is indistinguishable from a predatory movement, especially in relation to other nationalities. The Central Committee of the Party has done nothing to check such ugly manifestations and our directives in many places are not always implemented.[94]

The strains and stresses which characterized the relations between the two republics came to a head when the Third Congress of Soviets of the Uzbek SSR rejected a draft constitution of the Tadjik ASSR which was sent for its approval by the Second Congress of Soviets of the Tadjik ASSR. Following this the Tadjiks began to plead for the secession of the Tadjik Republic from the Uzbek SSR and also intensified their campaign for the incorporation of the Khodzhent uezd within their Republic. A number of conferences of Soviet and Party organizations including the Diushambe City Soviet passed resolutions favouring the reorganization of the Tadjik ASSR into a union republic and its direct inclusion within the Soviet Union.[95]

On 12 June 1929, the Presidium of the Central Executive Committee of the USSR, in response to the demand put forward by the Communists of Tadjikistan, adopted a decree on the secession of the Tadjik ASSR from the Uzbek Republic and on the reorganization of Tadjikistan into a union republic.[96] Fol-

93. *Pravda Vostoka*, 174 (1970), 30 July 1929.
94. *Pravda Vostoka*, 59 (1855), 15 March 1929.
95. *Pravda Vostoka*, 174 (1970), 30 July 1929.
96. This decree adopted by the Presidium of the Central Executive Committee of the USSR stated, 'Consideration having been taken of the

lowing this the Presidium of the Central Executive Committee of the USSR appointed a special commission to resolve all problems which arose in connection with the reorganization of the Tadjik ASSR into a union republic. All issues connected with the secession of the Tadjik ASSR from the Uzbek Republic and its elevation to the status of a union republic were discussed in a plenary session of the Central Executive Committee of the Tadjik ASSR on 10 September 1929, and later by the Third Extraordinary Congress of Soviets of Tadjikistan on 15 October 1929. On 16 October the Extraordinary Congress adopted a 'Declaration on the Formation of the Tadjik Soviet Socialist Republic'. This declaration also sanctioned the inclusion of the Tadjik SSR within the Soviet Union.[97]

On 6 November 1929 an Extraordinary Session of the Central Executive Committee of the Uzbek SSR gave its consent to the separation of the Tadjik ASSR from the Uzbek SSR. Following this the question was placed on the agenda of the Central Executive Committee of the USSR.[98] On 5 December 1929 the Central Executive Committee of the USSR gave its approval to the inclusion of the Tadjik Soviet Socialist Republic as the seventh member of the Soviet Union.[99] This decision was formally confirmed in March 1931 by the Sixth Congress of Soviets of the USSR.[100]

In 1932 certain changes were introduced in the political set-up of the Kara-Kalpak Autonomous Oblast. A decree of the All-Russian Central Executive Committee promulgated in March

fact that the Tadjik ASSR in its economic, national and geographical features is wholly different from the Uzbek SSR and in order to promote the successful economic and cultural development of Tadjikistan, it is time to take up the question of separating the Tadjik Republic from the composition of the Uzbek SSR and of its inclusion within the Union of Soviet Socialist Republics as an independent Republic.' Cited in Irkaev and others, n. 91, 183.

97. *Ibid.*, 184; also see D. L. Zlatopol'skii, *Obrazovanie i razvitie SSSR kak soiuznogo gosudarstva* (Moscow, 1954) 153.

98. *Pravda Vostoka*, 261 (2057), 10 November 1929. Following the separation of the Tadjik Republic from the Uzbek SSR, the Central Executive Committee of the Uzbek Republic issued a decree on the transfer of the Khodzhent uezd to the Tadjik SSR.

99. For the text of this decision see *Izvestiia TsIK Soiuza SSR i VTsIK*, 289, 9 December 1929.

100. See S. Radzhabov, *Tadzhikskaia SSR — suverennoe sovetskoe gosudarstvo* (Stalinabad, 1957) 201; Ikraev and others, n. 91, 185.

that year elevated the Kara-Kalpak Autonomous Oblast to the status of an autonomous republic. Following this Kara-Kalpakia was separated from the Kazakh ASSR and included within the RSFSR.[101]

The causes which brought about this change in the political set-up of Kara-Kalpakia are not clear. In the case of the Tadjik Republic there were certain definite economic and political causes, which, to a large extent, rendered its reorganization in 1929 justifiable. But in the case of Kara-Kalpakia no such causes existed at the time. There is no reason to believe that the Government of the Kazakh ASSR pursued in relation to the Kara-Kalpak Autonomous Oblast policies which adversely affected the latter. Nor is it clear that the Kara-Kalpaks themselves at this time agitated for the separation of Kara-Kalpakia from the Kazakh ASSR in the manner the Tadjiks had done in 1929 for the secession of the Tadjik ASSR from the Uzbek SSR.

If it is difficult to discover the political causes which led to these changes, it is also not easy to unravel the economic motivations underlying them. In 1932 Kara-Kalpakia had not any outstanding economic achievements to its credit, on the basis of which it could have put forth a claim for the advancement of its political status. On the contrary, there is reason to believe that the Kara-Kalpak Autonomous Oblast had failed to realize its targets of economic development. A directive sent to the Communist Party of Kara-Kalpakia by the Central Asiatic Bureau in 1932 called attention to this question.[102] In this directive the Central Asiatic Bureau alleged that both the Communist Party and Government of Kara-Kalpakia had failed in their tasks of providing a socialist basis to the economy of the Kara-Kalpak Autonomous Oblast and in fully utilizing the resources for promoting its economic development. Further, in the sphere of *nativizing* the state and party apparatuses similar inadequacies were discovered. The Central Asiatic Bureau chided both the Government and the Communist Party of the Kara-Kalpak Autonomous Oblast for continuing to employ the

---

101. K. Vikulin, 'Kara-kalpakskaia avtonomnaia SSR,' *Sovetskoe stroitel'-stvo* (Moscow) 5 (1932) 101.
102. *Pravda Vostoka*, 118 (2876), 24 May 1932.

Russian language in their work.[103] If these allegations had any substance in them, then it is difficult to see how the Kara-Kalpak Autonomous Oblast qualified for the higher form of statehood which was conferred upon it in 1932.

In 1936, following the constitutional reforms introduced in the USSR, the Kara-Kalpak ASSR was separated from the RSFSR and included within the Uzbek Soviet Socialist Republic.[104] The fact that during these years the Uzbek population of the Kara-Kalpak ASSR registered a sharp rise might have been a decisive factor which led to the inclusion of Kara-Kalpakia within the Uzbek Republic.[105]

In 1936 when the Kirgiz ASSR was elevated to the status of a union republic, conditions within Kirgizia in the economic, social and cultural spheres had undergone significant changes. Within a decade of the establishment of the separate Kirgiz Autonomous Oblast, the Kirgiz emerged as an authentic socialist nation. The clan-tribal differences, the patriarchal mode of life and the dialectal variations which, for a long time, impeded the growth and consolidation of the nationhood of the Kirgiz, had by then started disappearing. The economic and cultural developments which rendered the consolidation of the Kirgiz nation possible within such a short span of time are worth examining.

During the period of the First and Second Five Year Plans, the nature of the economy of Kirgizia underwent a radical change. If at the time of its formation the Kirgiz Autonomous Oblast had an essentially nomadic cattlebreeding economy, at the end of the Second Plan period a sizable portion of its income began to be realized from agriculture and industry. In the agricultural sector individual peasant holdings had become largely things of the past. The process of collectivization which began in 1928 had by 1934 amalgamated 68.5 per cent

103. *Ibid.*
104. *Bol'shaia sovetskaia entsiklopediia* (2nd edn.) XX, 117.
105. In 1926 the Uzbeks constituted 27.6 per cent of the total population of the Kara-Kalpak Autonomous Oblast. In 1939 their number increased to more than 50 per cent of its total population. During these years the Kara-Kalpak population fell from 38.1 per cent to less than 27 per cent of the total population of Kara-Kalpakia. See Bennigsen and Quelquejay, n. 77, 33.

of the peasant holdings into large collective farms. About 127,524 small peasant holdings were merged into 1,762 large collective farms.[106] In addition to this, large tracts of virgin land were brought under agriculture. If at the time of its formation Kirgizia had only 269,328 hectares of cultivated land, by 1935 its sown area exceeded a million hectares. In 1933 the collective farms yielded a gross income of about 68.4 million rubles, out of which about 46 million rubles were realized from agriculture alone.[107] The growth of agriculture made a deep impact on Kirgizia's traditional nomadic way of life. By 1933 about 45,000 nomads and semi-nomads were settled on land.

During the First Five Year Plan the basis of industrialization was laid. Subsequently, a number of coal-mining, textile, leather, food-processing, oil-drilling and light metal industries began to be established. By 1933, there were about 1,500 small industrial enterprises, two thermal power and one hydro-electric stations in the Kirgiz ASSR. During the First Plan Period the capital investment in industrialization amounted to about 65 million rubles.[108]

A factor of some significance which helped the national consolidation of the Kirgiz was the growth and expansion of modern means of communication. A network of state highways which came into existence in the early thirties not only made the remoter parts of the Republic accessible but also put an end to their traditional isolation. Equally significant was the establishment of the railways. A beginning was made in this sphere by the construction of the Dzhalal-Abad-Kok Iangak, Karasu-Osh, Frunze-Kang and Kang-Tokmak railway lines. By 1936, the Kirgiz Republic possessed more than 3,000 automobiles.[109]

Progress in the educational and cultural spheres went hand in hand with economic development. At the time of its forma-

106. Nurbekov, n. 69, 48-9.

107. *Istoriia Kirgizii* (Frunze, 1957) 153.

108. *Ibid.*, 153-4. Between 1932-37 the industrial output of Kirgizia increased by 171 per cent, the number of workers by 61.3 per cent, labour productivity by 108 per cent and annual average of wage increase by 114 per cent. See *Formirovanie i razvitie Kirgizskoi sotsialisticheskoi natsii* (Frunze, 1957) 151.

109. *Ibid.*, 153.

tion only 2 per cent of the population of the Kirgiz Republic
were able to read and write. Within ten years after its establishment nearly 50 per cent of the population of the Kirgiz
Republic became literate. By 1934 nearly 82 per cent of children of school-going age were provided with educational facilities, and between 1924-34 the number of schools increased from
463 to 1,580.[110] Besides these schools, about one hundred pro-
fessional-technical schools were also established by 1934. Education in most of these institutions was imparted through the
medium of the Kirgiz language. With the rise in literacy the
number of libraries, clubs, theatres, 'Red Chaikanas', newspapers, journals, and books also started growing. The publication of the first Kirgiz newspaper, *Erkin-Too* was begun as
early as 1924. Another newspaper, *Leninchil Zhash* and the
journal *Kommunist* began their publication in 1926. Between
1921-29 two Russian language newspapers, *Krasnoe utro* and
Batratskaia Pravda were published.[111]

The changes which took place in Kirgizia between 1924-36
reflected to some extent the profound transformation which had
taken place during these years in the USSR itself. Rapid industrialization and collectivization of agriculture wrought far-
reaching changes in the structure of Soviet society. The USSR
was no longer the backward agrarian country it had been in
1924 when its first constitution was adopted.[112] The new constitutional project published on 12 June 1936 drew attention to
these facts and to the numerous problems which were brought
into existence by the rapidly expanding economy of the USSR.
It stated that in view of such changes a need had arisen for

> giving more precise definition to the social and economic basis
> of the Constitution by bringing the Constitution into confor-
> mity with the present relation of class forces in the USSR (the
> creation of a new socialist industry, the demolition of the
> *kulak* class, the victory of the collective farm system, the
> consolidation of socialist property as the basis of Soviet
> society, and so on.[113]

110. *Ibid.*, 196-7.
111. *Ibid.*, 196.
112. I. Tsamerian, *Sovetskoe mnogonatsional'noe gosudarsto, ego osobennosti i puti razvitiia* (Moscow, 1958) 132-47.
113. J. Stalin, *Problems of Leninism* (Moscow, 1947) 540.

In his comments on the 'Amendments and Addenda to the Draft Constitution', Stalin laid down three specific conditions which were to govern the elevation of an autonomous republic to the status of a union republic. These were

(1) the republic concerned must be a border republic, not surrounded on all sides by the territory of the USSR;
(2) the nationality which gives its name to a given Soviet Republic must constitute a more or less compact majority within that republic; and
(3) the republic should have a population of not less than a million.[114]

At the time of promulgating the new constitution of the USSR all those Soviet autonomous republics which fulfilled these conditions were elevated to the status of union republics. Since the Kirgiz ASSR also fulfilled these conditions, it was separated from the composition of the RSFSR, raised to the status of a union republic and included directly in the USSR.

The process of building the national state formations in the Central Asian region which was begun in the early twenties of the present century was thus brought to completion in 1936. At the end of this period the inequality of political status which prevailed among the state formations of the Uzbeks, Turkmens, Tadjiks and Kirgiz had disappeared. The Tadjik and the Kirgiz Republics had attained a political status equal not only to their more advanced Central Asian neighbours but also to the other constituent member republics of the USSR. Among the eleven republics which constituted the USSR in 1936 as many as four were republics of the Central Asian region.[115] Though subsequently the membership of the USSR increased, the political set-up established within the Central Asian region in 1936 has remained unaltered.

114. *Ibid.*, 562-3.
115. See Article 13 of the Soviet Constitution in *Istoriia sovetskoi konstitutsii* 1917-1956 (Moscow, 1957) 711.

CHAPTER SEVEN

Conclusions

ON THE EVE of the Russian conquest, the peoples of Central Asia exhibited two interesting but mutually conflicting historical tendencies. The first was centripetal as reflected in the cultural and religious affinities which bound them together and the geographical contiguity of the region which they inhabited. The second was the bewildering ethnic, linguistic and social differences which held them apart and strengthened the centrifugal tendency. The disintegrating forces which were inherent in the latter tendency were kept in check for a long time by the pervasive influence of Islam, the essentially feudal character of the political and economic set-up and by Central Asia's proverbial isolation from the more advanced countries of Asia and Europe. After the Russian conquest, not only did Central Asia's age-old isolation become a thing of the past, but, the impact of the advanced Russian culture and civilization wrought significant changes in its political, economic and social life. These changes began to take place in spite of the passive character of the Russian official policies pursued in relation to Central Asia.

By the beginning of the twentieth century two divergent trends had begun to manifest themselves in Central Asia's political life. A relatively small group of newly-awakened native intelligentsia, desirous of checking the russification of language and culture of the local population, began propagating the ideals of the Djadidist movement. The Central Asian Djadidists, who first came into prominence as reformers of the native social and educational system were under the strong influence of the pan-Turkic ideology. In their political activities the Djadidists of Central Asia were drawn into the fold of the All-Russian Muslim movement which, under the leadership of the

Volga Tatars, strived for the establishment of a single 'Turkic state', 'a Turkic language' and 'a Turkic culture'.

The introduction of the capitalist mode of economy, on the other hand, steadily began to weaken the hold of the traditional bonds of unity among the peoples of Central Asia. Consequently, they started emphasizing on the primacy of the claims and objectives of their own nationalism over those of the pan-Turkic movement. As in other regions of Russia, local nationalism in Central Asia began to clash with the ideals propagated by the Djadidists. The latter by persistently denying the existence of the local nationalist movements got alienated from the masses and ceased to wield any influence over them. The tragedy of the Djadidist movement in Russia (including Central Asia) was that it remained, until the end, essentially a movement of a handful of intellectuals who failed to comprehend the tempo and impact of national and linguistic differentiations which had taken place among Russia's Muslim population in the first quarter of the twentieth century. On the contrary, they sought to superimpose on them an ideology which had lost its emotional appeal. The extent to which the pan-Turkic ideal had lost its hold on the bulk of the Muslim population of Russia was forcefully demonstrated by the near-pandemonium which broke out in the First All-Russian Muslim Congress held in May 1917 when a Tatar-backed resolution sought to frustrate the move to introduce territorial autonomy in various Muslim regions of Russia. The Congress witnessed as never before the upsurge of nationalist sentiments and aspirations among the different Muslim nationalities of Russia, and those who still championed the cause of the pan-Turkic ideal were stigmatized as agents of the Tatars. Though the Djadidists continued to champion the cause of the pan-Turkic movement even after this Congress, it was clear that the battle had already been lost nearly six months before the Bolsheviks emerged victorious in Russia. The Bolsheviks, by their policy of stimulating the aspirations of the smaller national groups to possess their own territorial autonomy, accelerated the ultimate disappearance of the pan-Turkic ideology from Russia.

The application of the Soviet nationalities policy in Central

Asia was rendered difficult by the chaotic situation which came to prevail there after the collapse of the authority of the Imperial régime and by the early misrule of the local Russian Bolsheviks. The spirit of Great Russian chauvinism which indeed characterized the policies of the Tashkent Soviet and the manner in which it handled the ill-fated Autonomous Government of Turkestan and the Turkmen National Committee, dealt a grievous blow to the Bolshevik prestige in Central Asia and rendered difficult the reconciliation of the local population to the Soviet régime. Notwithstanding the repeated attempts made by the Centre's emissary, Kobozev, to check the reckless policies of the local Russian Bolsheviks and to draw the natives into the fold of the Party and the government, the nationalities policy of the Soviet régime remained consigned to cold storage until the arrival of the Turkestan Commission in November 1919.

It was, largely, through the instrumentality of the Turkestan Commission and the Turkestan Bureau of the Central Committee of the Russian Communist Party (later reorganized into the Central Asiatic Bureau) that the nationalities policy of the Soviet régime began to be implemented in Central Asia. Being organs of the Central Party Organization and composed almost exclusively of Russians who were deputed from the Centre, these agencies were as much concerned with the objective of re-establishing the Centre's control over the region as with the task of broadening the basis of the local Soviet régime by bringing into its fold a large number of natives. Within a year after its arrival in Tashkent, the Turkestan Commission not only normalized the political situation within the Turkestan ASSR, but also succeeded in extending the Bolshevik control and influence over Khiva and Bukhara—the two former vassal states which had managed to retain a large degree of internal autonomy until 1920. Until 1922, the Bolsheviks were content to accept the outward professions of loyalty to the communist ideals exhibited by their Young Bukharan and Young Khivan collaborators. But from 1922 onwards, the process of sovietizing Bukhara and Khorezm was started in a thoroughgoing manner which resulted in the reduction of the so-called independence of these states to a mere fiction. The purge campaigns conducted at the instance of the Central Asiatic Bureau within the communist parties of Bukhara and Khorezm in 1922 and 1923 led to the expulsion of all those erstwhile Djadidists who still cherished the ambition of retaining Bukhara and Khorezm as independent states and succeeded in bringing the policies of these two republics in line with Bolshevik principles. By 1924, though the governments of Turkestan, Bukhara and Khorezm were headed by the natives themselves, the Central Asian region was brought definitely within the Soviet orbit.

Not until the Bolsheviks were convinced that the Soviet régimes in Turkestan, Bukhara and Khorezm had grown sufficiently strong, did they embark upon the task of reorganizing the national frontiers within the Central Asian region. It is true that the Bolsheviks were moving with the current of history in assisting the major national groups of Central Asia to establish their own separate national state formations. The process of evolution and consolidation of nationhood of such people as the Uzbeks, Turkmens, Tadjiks and Kirgiz had set in a long time before. In forming the new national republics within the Central Asian region, the Bolsheviks recognized the legitimate nationalist aspirations of these people. But in doing so they also tried to safeguard the local Soviet régimes from the danger of any manifestation of the pan-Turkic nationalism in future. How much the Bolsheviks were really concerned in combating this danger becomes clear from their reluctance to establish the Central Asiatic Federation as proposed by many local Communists in 1924 and from their policy of isolating the Kazakh Republic from its southern neighbours.

While evaluating the Soviet nationalities policy in Central Asia between 1917-1936, one cannot fail to notice two broad trends which, notwithstanding their outward divergent appearance, worked in a complementary manner. The first was the application of a policy of thoroughgoing centralization which subordinated the regional interests to the interests of the Union. The other was the encouragement and promotion of national and linguistic distinctions of the peoples of Central Asia within the overall socialist set-up. These two trends although they appeared to work at cross purposes, in fact, helped to realize a common objective, viz. the consolidation of the Soviet régime in Central Asia.

The policy of centralization, to some extent, inevitably resulted in the russification of the methods and procedures of local party and governmental organs and in the promotion of non-regional (i.e., non-national) and all-Union loyalties among the peoples of Central Asia. The formulation of the objectives of economic and educational policies on an all-Union scale, the presence within the party and governmental organs of the Central Asian republics of a sufficiently large number of Russians, and the monolithic structure of the Communist Party of the Soviet Union, all these naturally facilitated, and to some extent made inevitable, the application of a policy of centralization. By the end of 1934, when the Central Committee of the All-Union Communist Party and the Council of People's Commissars of the USSR decided to wind up the Central Asiatic Bureau and the Central Asiatic Economic Council, the policy of centralization had already borne substantial results in strengthening multiple ties between the Centre and the republics of Central Asia. As such the retention of these twin agents of centralization had become no longer necessary.

No less impressive were the results achieved in establishing Soviet institutions in forms consistent with the national and linguistic distinctions of the peoples of Central Asia. While the establishment of the national republics of Central Asia enabled the Uzbeks, Turkmens, Tadjiks, Kirgiz and Kara-Kalpaks to consolidate their nationhood and to overcome the national and tribal feuds and frictions which had plagued their lives in the past, the economic policies, which were subsequently pursued in relation to Central Asia, conferred upon these local nationalities a substantial degree of material prosperity. After the Tenth Congress of the Russian Communist Party, a greater emphasis was laid on rendering all assistance to the Central Asian region to overcome its economic backwardness and to catch up with the economically more advanced parts of the Soviet Union. The process of formation and consolidation of the national territorial autonomous units of the peoples of Central Asia reached its culmination in 1936. But the economic objective of the Soviet nationalities policy viz., the elimination of the economic disparity between the Central Asian region and other well developed regions of Russia, had not been realized till then. The attainment of this objective became the primary concern of subsequent Soviet policies.

An Outline of the Soviet Nationalities Policy[1]

The Background

Within the sprawling boundaries of the Russian Empire which encompassed one-sixth of the total land surface of the world, there lived a bewilderingly large number of races and ethnic groups diverse in language, religion, culture and customs. The first all-Russian census taken in 1897 estimated that nearly 104 distinct nationalities inhabited the territory of the Tsarist Empire.[2] A more systematic census of a later period revealed even greater diversity of the population composition of Russia.[3]

Official policy, grounded as it was on the triple principles of orthodoxy, autocracy and nationality (the Great Russian nationality of course), rarely took into account the national, linguistic, religious and cultural diversity of the population.[4] For all practical purposes, the imperial government assumed that Russia was a uni-national state and accorded the position of privilege in all walks of life only to the Great Russian nationality. The pursuance of such a policy in the multi-national Russian Empire resulted, as could be expected, in great suffering for all non-Great Russian nationalities, including the two nationalities belonging to the Slavic group, the Ukrainians (also known as the Little Russians) and the Byelorussians. But, in the end, it became clear that the policy of the 'hammer and anvil' which was attended by such dismal failure in the other multi-national empires of the time like Germany, Austria-Hungary and Ottoman Turkey, could hardly produce better results in Russia. Its only outcome was the

---

1. This outline formed part of an article published in the April issue (1963) of the *International Studies* (New Delhi). Here it is reproduced with the permission of the editor of the journal.

2. Avrahm Yarmolinsky, *The Jews and Other Minor Nationalities under the Soviets* (New York, 1928) 141.

3. The 1926 census which covered much less territory than the 1897 census revealed that there were as many as 175 ethnic groups speaking 149 languages. See Frank Lorimer, *The Population of the Soviet Union : History & Prospects* (Geneva, 1946) 50-65.

4. An Imperial manifesto issued on 3 June 1907 rather bluntly told the non-Great Russian nationalities of the empire that "the Russian Duma created in order to strengthen the Russian state, should be Russian also in spirit. Other peoples who are included in our empire should have representatives in the State Duma to state their needs, but they cannot be and shall not be represented in such number as to enable them to decide purely Russian questions." Cited in W. R. Batsell, *Soviet Rule in Russia* (New York, 1929) 99.

growth of incipient nationalist movements all over the Empire and the emergence of the national question as an outstanding issue in Russian political life.(5)

In spite of the growing importance of the national question, few political parties except the Russian Social Democratic Workers Party (RSDRP) gave serious consideration to it. The dominant position held by the nationalistically-minded Great Russians in the other political parties and their utter unwillingness to abdicate the number of privileges they enjoyed by belonging to the ruling nationality, came in the way of these parties developing popular nationalities policies. Even the liberal Cadets and the Mensheviks fared no better, and their nationality planks were built on the dubious scheme of cultural national autonomy.

The RSDRP, however, endeavoured to break away completely from the pernicious influence of Great Russian nationalism.(6) Its growing awareness of the importance of the national question was indicated by the manifesto it issued in its founding Congress in 1898. Its national programme was based upon the decision of International Socialist Congresses which had advocated the right of nations to self-determination. A more explicit assertion of this right was embodied in Point 9 of the programme which the RSDRP adopted at its second Congress in 1903. This point recognized 'the right of self-determination for all nations entering the composition of the (Russian) state.'(7)

The adoption by the RSDRP of the right of nations to self-determination, however, did not indicate unanimity of opinion on this issue in the Social Democratic circles. The Polish Social Democrats and the Jewish Bund bitterly opposed its inclusion. The Polish delegation to the 1903 Congress of the Party sought to amend Point 9 in such a way as to ensure only the establishment of 'institutions guaranteeing full freedom of cultural development to all nations incorporated in the (Russian) state.'(8) The

---

5. See Hans Kohn, *Nationalism in the Soviet Union* (London, 1933).

6. Later Stalin was to describe Great Russian nationalism as "the rankest kind of nationalism, which strives to obliterate all that is not Russian, to gather all the threads of administration into the hands of Russians and to crush everything that is not Russian." See his *Marxism and the National And Colonial Question: A collection of Articles and Speeches* (London, n.d.) 154.

7. Point 3 of this programme demanded "wide local self-government, regional self-government for those localities which are differentiated by their specific habits, customs and population." Point 7 recognized "complete equality of rights for all citizens irrespective of sex, religion, race or nationality." Point 8 recognized "the right of the population to receive education in their native languages, the right of every citizen to speak at meetings in his native language, the introduction of the native language on a par with the official state language in all local, public and state institutions." See *Kommunisticheskaia partiia Sovetskogo Soiuza v rezoliutsiiakh i resheniiakh s'ezdov, konferentsii i plenumov Tsk, 1898-1925* (7th edition, Moscow, 1953) I, 40. (Cited hereafter as *KPSS*).

8. V. I. Lenin, *Sochineniia* (2nd edition, Moscow, 1935) XVII, 466.

Jewish Bund, more or less, was also inclined in favour of such an amend-
ment, but for different reasons.(9) The Party Congress, while rejecting
all attempts of the Polish and Jewish delegations to restrict the right of
nations only to the cultural sphere, not only asserted the right to free self-
determination but also insisted that this right must always be construed
as a political right, i.e., the right to political separation from the Russian
state.(10) In the preceding year, Plekhanov, while defending the draft programme of the Party, had insisted that the right of self-determination,
while not obligatory to the bourgeois democrats, was obligatory for Social
Democrats. Further he had declared, 'if we were to forget or hesitate to
advance it, for fear of offending the national prejudice of the present
generation of Great Russians, the call . . . "workers of all countries unite"!
on our lips would become a shameful lie.'(11)

The controversy on the right of nations to self-determination in the

---

9. The Bundists' opposition to the adoption of the right of nations to
self-determination by the RSDRP was understandable. The Jews in Russia
nowhere constituted a compact majority and were scattered all over the
empire in little pockets or islands amidst non-Jewish peoples. Living thus
without a compact territorial basis they were unable to take advantage of
the right to self-determination recognized by the RSDRP. In view of this,
the Russian Jewish leaders, while rejecting the nationalities plank of the
RSDRP as unsuitable, advocated the adoption of the so-called cultural
national autonomy. The latter was an ingenious scheme propounded by
two Austrian Social Democrats, Karl Renner (more familiarly known as
Springer) and Otto Bauer. This scheme, devised mainly to solve the
national tangle of the Dual Monarchy, while granting each national group
the right to organize its national councils on a non-territorial, personal
basis for promoting its educational and cultural development, left the
political, economic and administrative matters of the empire outside its
jurisdiction. In accordance with this scheme, the Austrian Social Democratic
Party in 1897 became a federation of six autonomous national parties—
German, Czech, Polish, Ruthenian, Italian and Yugoslav. In 1899, in the
Brünn Congress, the Austrian Social Democratic Party resolved to reorganize
Austria as a "federation of nationalities." The Russian Jews found in this
scheme an ideal solution for their peculiar problem and enthusiastically
began to advocate its adoption in Russia. Besides, they demanded that the
RSDRP should recognize the Bund as the sole representative organization
of Russian Jews. See Edward Hallet Carr, *The Bolshevik Revolution
1917-1923* (London, 1950) I, 418-9.

10. In view of this clear interpretation of the right of self-determination
given by the Party itself, the opinion of Mr. Richard Pipes that the only
interpretation not held by those who voted this statement into the
Party's programme was that it implied the right to secession and the
formation of independent states, seems to be hardly in consonance with
facts. The minutes of the 1903 Congress on this issue clearly indicate that
the Party meant only one thing, the right to political separation and
formation of independent state. See Lenin, n. 7, 467; Richard Pipes, *The
Formation of the Soviet Union* (Cambridge, Mass., 1954) 43.

11. G. V. Plekhanov, *Sochineniia* (Moscow, 1926) XII, 238.

Social Democratic circles did not end there. The Polish Social Democrats and the Bundists who had unsuccessfully tried to prevent the adoption of Point 9 in the 1903 Congress, began an energetic campaign against it openly. They charged that Point 9 was 'vague', 'sweeping', 'a mere platitude', 'a fashionable term', etc.(12) They were joined by Russian Social Democrats of more leftist persuasions who were inclined to believe that nations were obsolete and self-determination was mere nonsense. The Polish Social Democrat, Rosa Luxemburg, charged that the recognition accorded by RSDRP to the right of nations to self-determination was tantamount to supporting the bourgeois nationalism of the oppressed nations.(13) How much Lenin was concerned by such criticisms becomes clear from a letter he wrote to Maxim Gorky in February 1913:

> Regarding nationalism, I share your opinion that we should concern ourselves more with it. We have a fine Georgian here (the reference here is to Stalin) who is writing a big article for the *Prosveshchenie*, for which he has collected all Austrian, and other data.... Here and in the Caucasus, the Social Democrats have worked among the Georgians, Armenians, Tatars, Russians, jointly in a *single* Social Democratic organization for more than ten years. That is... the proletarian solution of the national question.... No, we shall never have such dirty business as in Austria. We shall never tolerate it...(14)

In an article entitled 'On Cultural National Autonomy,' Lenin roundly condemned the Austrian thesis.(15) A more elaborate refutation of it was

---

12. Liebman of the Bund, attacking the RSDRP's stand on national self-determination, was to write later "when Russian Social Democrats in its programme, fifteen years ago, advanced the point about the right of every nationality to "self-determination," everyone asked himself: what does this fashionable term really mean? No answer was given to this. This word was left enveloped in fog. In fact it was difficult at that time to dissipate the fog. The time had not yet come when this point could be made concrete—they used to say at that time—let it remain enveloped in fog for the time being and life itself will indicate what content is to be put into this point." See Lenin, n. 7, 469.

13. *Ibid.*, 442.

14. Cited in Demetrio Boersner, *The Bolsheviks and the National and Colonial Question 1917-1928* (Geneva, 1957) 36.

15. Lenin, n. 7, 92-5, 188. Also see vol. XII, 67. An authoritative party pronouncement on cultural national autonomy became available after the Poronin Conference of the Central Committee of the Party in 1913. The resolution on the national question adopted at the Seventh Party Congress held in April 1917 declared that "the proletariat firmly denounces the so-called cultural national autonomy i.e., taking the schools out of the state jurisdiction and transferring them to the national 'councils' or the like. The workers living in the same locality and even working in the same enterprises, when following this cultural national autonomy, will be artificially divided and apportioned to one or another 'national culture;' in other words, it will promote the relation of the working masses with the bourgeois culture of separate nations, while the aim of the Social Demo-

contained in Stalin's work, *Marxism and the National Question,* published
during this time. This work, which established Stalin's reputation as a
Marxist theoretician of note on the national question, expressed concern
at the growing tide of nationalism all over Russia. In his opinion this was
bound to affect adversely the workers' organizations by blurring their vision
of the real issues of the social revolution. To protect the workers from this
general 'epidemic' Stalin called upon the Social Democrats to unfurl their
banner of internationalism and to stress the unity and indivisibility of the
class struggle.(16)

Before commencing his attack on the Austrian Social Democrats, Stalin
elaborated the Marxist conception of nation. According to him, a nation
comprised four fundamental elements: (1) community of language, (2) community of territory, (3) community of economic life and (4) community
of psychological make-up. Only when *all* these four elements were present
there would be a nation which was defined by Stalin as 'a historically
evolved, stable community of language, territory, economic life and psychological make-up manifesting itself in a community of culture.'(17) The
nation being a historical phenomenon was naturally subject to the law of
change and has its history, its beginning and end.(18) Having thus established the Marxian conception of nation, Stalin proceeded to criticize the
Austrian Social Democrats' views. Springer's definition that 'a nation is a
union of similarly thinking and similarly speaking persons—a cultural
community of modern people no longer tied to the soil' and Bauer's
definition that 'a nation is the aggregate of people bound into a community
of character by a community of fate' were rejected by Stalin as ignoring
the objective character of nationhood and the changing historical and
economic conditions which produced it.(19)

There were other traits of nationhood which, in Stalin's opinion, the
theoreticians of Austrian social democracy had ignored. The nation was
not only a historical category but a historical category belonging to the
epoch of rising capitalism. The development of capitalism was everywhere
accompanied by the growth of national movements seeking to establish
national states. These national movements were spearheaded by the bourgeoisie and *in its essence* the national movement was always a bourgeois

crats is to promote the international culture of the proletariat of the entire
world." See *KPSS,* n. 6, 346.

16. Stalin, n. 5, 4.

17. *Ibid.,* 8.

18. In an article entitled "The Social Democratic View of the National
Question" published as early as 1904, Stalin had written "everything
changes . . . social life changes, and with it the 'national question' changes
too. At different periods different classes enter the arena, and every class
has its own view of the 'national question.' Consequently, in different
periods the 'national question' serves different interests and assumes different
shades, according to which class raises it and when." See Stalin, *Collected
Works* (Moscow) I, 31.

19. Stalin, n 5, 9-12; also see Carr, n. 8, 421.

struggle, one that was chiefly favourable to the bourgeoisie.(20) Other essential attributes of the nation, according to Stalin, were sovereignty and equality of all nations. Sovereignty by implication carried with it the right of self-determination, i.e., the right of a nation to political separation from an existing multi-national unit and to form its own independent national state. The assertion of sovereignty and equality of all nations cut at the root of the Austrian thesis which had sought to restrict their rights merely to the cultural sphere and thereby perpetuate the multi-national structure of the Austro-Hungarian empire.(21)

But the important question to which many Social Democrats in Russia, Poland and elsewhere wanted to have an answer was why Lenin and his associates, being adherents of socialism and internationalists in outlook, were preoccupied with advocating the right of nations to self-determination and with 'organizing nations.' They could not understand why socialists should concern themselves with mere nationalistic claims knowing fully well that nationalism was the very antithesis of internationalism and was a great hindrance to achieving socialism. Lenin also admitted these questions as pertinent and he even stated:

> Marxism is irreconcilable with nationalism, even if it is the 'fairest,' 'purest' most refined and civilized nationalism. Marxism advocates internationalism in place of nationalism of any kind, advances the amalgamation of all nations in the higher unity that is growing under our eyes with every *verst* of railway, with every international trust, with every workers' association that is international in its economic activities and also in its ideas and aims.(22)

But this basic Marxist hostility to nationalism which he also shared with other Social Democrats did not prevent Lenin from recognizing the historical legitimacy of national movements. He asked the critics of the nationalities policy of the RSDRP to ponder over the national question in Russia as it had existed at the beginning of the twentieth century. A correct understanding of the concrete specific features of this issue made clear that, of the innumerable nationalities living within the empire, only the Great Russian nationality had the opportunity to establish and consolidate its national state and that others were languishing under an oppressive régime which denied to them their legitimate national claims.

---

20. Stalin, n. 5, 13-17. Perhaps Stalin here was only expressing the already well-known views of Lenin on this question. Lenin had written that "throughout the world, the period of final victory of capitalism over feudalism has been linked up with national movements ... the tendency of every national movement is towards the formation of *national states,* under which the requirements of modern capitalism are best satisfied ... for the whole of Western Europe, nay, for the entire civilized world, the *typical,* normal state for the capitalist period is the national state." See Lenin, n. 7, 428.

21. Stalin, n. 5, 19, 22-3 and 26-8.
22. Lenin, n. 7, 145.

Confronted with such a situation, what were the Social Democrats and particularly, the Social Democrats belonging to the Great Russian nationality, expected to do? Could they remain totally unconcerned with it because it did not directly impinge upon the issues of social revolution and thereby, condone national oppression? 'The bourgeois nationalism of every oppressed nation,' wrote Lenin, 'has a general democratic content which is directed against oppression, and it is this content that we support unconditionally.'(23) Further, he declared that the only way of showing disapproval of Tsarist policy of national oppression was by recognizing the right of oppressed nations to complete political self-determination. If this right was not advocated and defended, Lenin argued, even the Russian Social Democrats became the accomplices of the despotism of the oppressing Great Russian nation.(24) Reasserting the Marxian dictum that no nation could be free if it oppressed other nations, Lenin called upon the Great Russian proletariat to emulate the example of the Swedish workers who, when Norway opted for secession from Sweden in 1905, demonstrated to the world that they were not infected by Swedish nationalism and readily recognized the right of the Norwegians to secede.(25) The policy of national oppression had to be combated for other reasons too. The limitation of freedom of movement, disfranchisement, suppression of language, restrictions on schools and other forms of repression perpetrated by Tsarism affected the workers no less if not more than the bourgeoisie. Therefore, the workers who opposed national oppression must champion the right of nations to self-determination.(26)

Such an advocacy of the right of nations to self-determination became obligatory, in Lenin's opinion, for the Great Russian members of the RSDRP even when the Social Democrats belonging to the oppressed nations on whom the right was conferred rejected it. (27) Lenin thought it was impossible to break away from the 'accursed history of Tsarism' in the national sphere without ensuring complete equality of all nations and making the recognition of the right of self-determination the cornerstone of the nationalities policy of the future socialist government of Russia. He firmly believed that more closely the democratic system of state approximated to complete freedom of secession, the rarer and weaker became the actual striving for secession in practice. (28) That the demand for self-determination did not contradict his basic centralist views was made clear by Lenin. He wrote:

> We demand the freedom of self-determination, i.e., independence, i.e., the freedom of secession for the oppressed nations, not because we dream of economic disintegration, or because we cherish the ideal of small

23. Lenin, n. 7, 440-1.
24. *Ibid.*, 440.
25. *Ibid.*, 453-4.
26. Stalin, n. 5, 17-18.
27. Lenin, n. 7, 454-5, 473-4.
28. Lenin, *Sochineniia* (2nd edition, Moscow, 1935) XIX, 39-40.

states, but, on the contrary, because we are in favour of large states and
the closer unity and even the fusion of nations, but on a truly democratic,
truly international basis which is inconceivable without the freedom of
secession. (29)

These pronouncements on the right to self-determination should not
mislead us to the belief that the Bolshevik and the liberal approaches to
it were identical. The spirit of dialectical relativism with which Marxists
analysed all questions including the national question, convinced the
Bolsheviks that the national question was a part of the general question
of social revolution. "If ... a dialectical approach to a question is required
anywhere" wrote Stalin, "it is required...in the national question." (30) The
dialectical method of reasoning which subordinates that which exists
relatively to that which exists absolutely, clearly subordinated the transient
and ephemeral national question to the interests of proletarian dictatorship.
The fleeting character of the national question as against the absolute
permanency of socialism became clear from Marx's well-known assertion
that "national differences and antagonisms between peoples are daily more
and more vanishing and the supremacy of the proletariat will cause them
to vanish still further." (31) The implicit faith of Lenin and other Bolsheviks
in the truth of this statement led them to oppose all attempts which sought
to make the right of nations to self-determination an absolute and eternally
valid doctrine. (32) Its temporary and conditional validity is the key to a
correct understanding of the Bolshevik thinking on the national question.

Just as Marx in his time had supported or opposed the national
movements of various European peoples on the basis of the objective role
they played in helping the cause of democracy and socialism, the Bolsheviks also argued that their support or opposition to the exercise of the
right of self-determination in any given case depended on certain factors.
Firstly, it depended on what stage of social development the nation
seeking political separation had reached, and secondly, which of its
various classes expressed its will. (33) The invocation of this "class-historical

---

29. Lenin, *Sochineniia* (2nd edition, Moscow, 1935) XVIII, 328.

30. Stalin, n. 5, 21.

31. *Ibid.* 33.

32. Lenin, *Sochineniia* (2nd edition, Moscow, 1935) XVI, 510; Plekhanov,
Sochineniia (Moscow, 1926) XIII, 265-8; D. L. Zlatopol'skii, *Obrazovanie
i razvitie SSSR kak soiuznogo gosudarstva* (Moscow, 1954) 18.

33. According to Lenin, the national question in any state fell into one
or another of the two distinct stages of the development of capitalism.
The first stage in which capitalism began to grow in the womb of an
essentially feudal society was also the period of the awakening of national
consciousness of the people, the birth of national movements and the
struggle for the establishment of national states. The second stage witnessed the breaking of national barriers, the growth of international unity
of capital, of economic life etc. Both these tendencies were the universal
law of capitalism, the first being the dominant feature at the beginning

viewpoint" not only helped in resolving the contradiction apparent in generally proclaiming the right to self-determination on the one hand and denying commitment to it in particular cases on the other, but also gave an impression that the Bolsheviks themselves were wholly neutral in the struggle of rival bourgeois groups in the national sphere. Lenin's clarification of the Bolshevik stand on this question was ingenious. He argued that just as the advocacy of the right to divorce generally did not involve a vote for divorce in a particular case, the advocacy of the right of self-determination did not commit the RSDRP to support every claim to political separation. (34)

An authoritative Party pronouncement on the national question was contained in the resolution adopted in the Poronin Conference of the Central Committee of the Party in 1913. It consisted of five main items:

1. That national peace under capitalist conditions would be possible only under a fully democratic republican form of government which would guarantee to all nations the right to use freely their native language in their social life and in schools, and by including in the constitution a provision which would do away with all class privileges on the one hand, and would protect the rights of national minorities on the other. In particular, there is need for a wide measure of regional autonomy and full democratic local self-government; the demarcation of the boundaries of these regional

---

of its development and the second characterizing developed capitalism which was nearer to socialist transformation. The Bolsheviks advocated the right of self-determination for nations which were in the first stage and the application of the principle of internationalism for states which had already reached the second stage. See Lenin, n. 7, 139-40.

34. Lenin, n. 7, 119. The practical implications of advocating the right of nations to self-determination by the RSDRP seem to have troubled Stalin more than they troubled Lenin. This becomes clear from his speeches and writings which are replete with hesitations, qualifications, hedgings and vacillations. In his well-known essay he posed the awkward question "What should the Social Democrats do when the Transcaucasian Tatars, for instance, as a nation assembled in their Diet and under the influence of their *mullahs* decided to restore the old order of things and to secede from Russia?" Though he never disputed the right of the Tatars to exercise the right to self-determination, Stalin under such circumstances never wanted the Social Democrats to remain indifferent to what happened to the toiling strata of the Tatar nation. He was inclined in favour of the Social Democrats' intervening in the matter to influence the will of that nation in a particular manner favourable to the toiling class. See Stalin, n. 5, 20. Such misgivings on the right to self-determination in Stalin's mind persisted for a long time. Though ultimately he veered round to the stand taken by Lenin on this question, nevertheless, at crucial moments he was inclined to reject the Leninist interpretation of the right.

autonomies and self-governing units must be undertaken by the local populations themselves in conformity with their economic and ethnic distinctions and national composition etc.;

2. separate national school administration within a given state is absolutely harmful from the point of view of democracy in general and the interests of class struggle in particular. The plan of the so-called 'cultural national autonomy' or 'the creation of institutions guaranteeing the freedom of national development' adopted in Russia by the bourgeois parties of the Jews and others correspond to such a division;

3. the interest of the working class demands the union of workers of all nationalities of a given state in proletarian organizations;

4. the Party supports the right of the oppressed nations of the Tsarist monarchy to self-determination, i.e., to secession and formation of independent states;

5. The question of the right of nations to self-determination must not be confused with the question of expediency of separation of any given nation. This issue must be dealt with by the Party separately in each individual case from the point of view of the whole social development and the interests of the class struggle of the proletariat for socialism. (35)

The fact that the above resolution on the national question specifically referred only to capitalist conditions and remained silent on what the Party's attitude would be towards the right of self-determination under socialism was a clear enough indication that the Central Committee of the Party did not think that socialism could be established in the near future in Russia. The outbreak of World War I, however, was to change that view. To Lenin the outbreak of the war symbolised that the contradictions within the capitalist system had developed to the breaking-point and that imperialism had caused capital to outgrow the boundaries of national states thereby creating the objective prerequisites for the establishment of socialism. (36)

In view of the brightening of prospects for the establishment of socialism in the near future, a need arose to reorient the Bolshevik approach to the doctrine of self-determination. Most of the Bolsheviks, including Stalin, Pyatakov, Bukharin and others, treated the right of self-determination as a doctrine valid only for capitalist conditions and considered that it had no place under socialism. The Polish Social Democrats had not given up their opposition to it in spite of the definite qualification prescribed by the Poronin Conference of the Central Committee to the exercise of the right of self-determination. They now started arguing that imperialism had rendered the right of self-determination 'infeasible' and 'illusory' as was evident from the destruction of so many national frontiers in Europe.

---

35. *KPSS*, n. 6, 315-16.
36. Lenin, n. 27, 37.

Further, they opposed the restoration of these national frontiers by Social Democrats under the slogan of right of nations to self-determination. (37) Such criticisms spurred Lenin to action. In his reply to the critics he defended the right of nations to self-determination both under imperialism as well as under the initial stages of socialism. In the process of preparing his reply Lenin developed a working formula for the application of the right to self-determination by the future socialist government of Russia.

The onset of imperialism, Lenin conceded, had no doubt, dimmed the prospects for a fuller and complete realization of all democratic rights including the right to self-determination. But this was not the same as rendering the latter either infeasible or illusory. Its realization was still possible although in an incomplete or mutilated form as was evident from the secession of Norway from Sweden. Lenin strongly condemned the view that Social Democrats should cease their advocacy of the right of self-determination. He asserted

> the fact that the struggle for national liberation against one imperialist power may under certain circumstances be utilized by another 'Great' power in its equally imperialist interests should have no weight in inducing social democracy to renounce its recognition of the right of nations to self-determination. (38)

On the contrary, he argued, that it had become essential to formulate the right of self-determination and other democratic rights and advocate them in order to draw a wider stratum of population both within the East European states and in the colonies into the revolutionary struggle. (39) This sudden emergence of the colonies within the orbit of the Bolshevik doctrine of self-determination was indicative of two important developments in Lenin's thinking on this issue. Firstly, the emergence of imperialism as a universal phenomenon had necessitated the organization of struggle against it on an equally universal basis. Secondly, an effective basis could be laid for collaboration between the progressive nationalism of Eastern European countries and of the colonies in a common fight against imperialism by voicing the demand of the latter to complete political self-determination. (40) How much faith Lenin had come to place in such a partnership becomes clear from his indignant outburst against Karl Radek's description of the Irish rebellion as a 'putsch.' He wrote:

> To image that a social revolution is conceivable without revolts by the small nations in the colonies and in Europe, without the revolutionary outbursts of a section of the petty bourgeoisie with all its prejudices, without the movement of non-class-conscious proletarian and semi-proletarian masses against the oppression of the landlords, the

---

37. *Ibid.*, 48, 245-6, 255.
38. *Ibid.*, 41.
39. *Ibid.*, 39.
40. *Ibid.*, 39.

church, the monarchy, the foreign nations, etc., to imagine this means repudiating social revolution. (41)

If the critics of the right of nations to self-determination were wrong in arguing that it had become illusory under imperialism, Lenin argued, they were neither right in denying its validity under the initial stages of socialism. He categorically asserted that

the necessity of proclaiming and granting freedom to *all* oppressed nations (i.e., their right to self-determination) will be as urgent in the socialist revolution as it was urgent for the victory of the bourgeois-democratic revolution, for example, in Germany in 1848, or in Russia in 1905. (42)

But this did not mean that Lenin like Otto Bauer thought that socialism would perpetuate nationalism for all time. On the contrary, he firmly believed that socialism would not only abolish the present division of mankind into small national states but would ultimately merge them; (43) but he did not think that this was a practical proposition in the period immediately following the establishment of socialism. He was too well aware that imperialism would leave its successor, socialism, a heritage of less democratic boundaries, a number of annexations in Europe and in other parts of the globe (44) and that "national antipathies will not disappear so quickly: the hatred—and perfectly legitimate hatred—of an oppressed nation for its oppressor will continue for a while; it will evaporate only after the victory of socialism and after the final establishment of completely democratic relations between nations." (45) Further,

by transforming capitalism into socialism, the proletariat creates the *possibility* for complete abolition of national oppression; this possibility will become *reality* "only"—"only"—when complete democracy is introduced in all spheres, including the fixing of state boundaries in accordance with the "sympathies" of the population, and including complete freedom of secession... (46)

The foregoing analysis of the evolution of the doctrine of national self-determination in the platform of the RSDRP in the pre-revolutionary

41. *Ibid.*, 269.

42. *Ibid.*, 45. Lenin stated that socialism as soon as it was victorious must not only declare the complete equality of all nations but also the right of nations to free and complete self-determination. Further he charged that socialist parties which failed to achieve these two things would be committing treachery against socialism. See *ibid.*, 37.

43. *Ibid.*, 40.

44. *Ibid.*, 244.

45. *Ibid.*, 267. Expressing the same view in the form of a principle, Lenin stated that "just as mankind can achieve the abolition of classes only by passing through the transition period of the dictatorship of the oppressed class, so mankind can achieve the inevitable merging of nations only by passing through the transition period of complete liberation of all oppressed nations i.e., their freedom to secede." *Ibid.*, 40.

46. Lenin, n. 35, 245.

period brings into sharp relief two divergent trends which influenced Bolshevik thinking on the national question. Firstly, opposition to the Tsarist policy of national oppression, and the need to draw wider stratum of the population of all nationalities into the revolutionary movement, induced the RSDRP to proclaim the right of all nationalities inhabiting Russia to free self-determination. Secondly, the achievement of socialism for which the RSDRP was fighting required a closer union of all workers irrespective of their national affiliations in a single, international workers' organization. The recognition accorded to the claims of nationalism in the platform of the RSDRP indicated the appreciation of the legitimacy of national claims in Russia where the remnants of feudalism continued to survive even in the twentieth century. But this did not prevent the Bolsheviks from proclaiming the primacy of the claims of socialism over the claims of nationalism and subordinating the right of self-determination to the right of the working class to achieve a socialist order, whenever a conflict arose between the two divergent ideologies. But this did not lead to the repudiation of the right of self-determination altogether. On the contrary, its validity under capitalism, imperialism and even under the initial stages of socialism, as we have seen, was admitted. But the stipulation of the qualifications which were incorporated into the clause on self-determination in the Party's programme in the Poronin Conference of the Party's Central Committee had rendered the exercise of the right possible only in certain circumstances on a relative and conditional basis. In deciding the feasibility or otherwise of the exercise of the right in any given case "the class historical viewpoint" was to be the sole determining factor. (47) The stipulation of this somewhat vague qualification for the exercise of the right of self-determination by any nation, in effect, took away much of the force of Lenin's earlier assertion that "the right to secession presupposed the settlement of the question . . . by the parliament (diet, referendum etc.) of the seceding state." (48)

In the Seventh Congress of the Party held in April 1917, some of the Bolshevik stalwarts like Stalin, Pyatakov and others turned against the Leninist interpretation of the right of self-determination. The drafting commission of the Congress under their influence adopted a resolution which declared that the national question could only be solved by "the

---

47. The stipulation of the "class-historical viewpoint" as the sole criterion for deciding any issue of actual separation was not clearly stated in the resolution adopted in the Poronin Conference. In view of the fresh controversies that arose on the right of self-determination after 1917, the Eighth Congress of the Russian Communist Party which met in March 1919, restated in clearest terms that "on the question who is to express the will of the nation to separation, the Russian Communist Party stands on the historical-class point of view, taking into account the stage of historical development of the given nation : whether it is evolving from medievalism to bourgeois democracy or from bourgeois democracy to Soviet or proletarian democracy etc." See *KPSS*, n. 6, 417.

48. Lenin, n. 7, 71.

method of socialist revolution under the slogan 'away with frontiers,'"
and rejected the solution of "splitting of great state formations into small
national states," and branded the right of self-determination as "simply
a phrase without definite content." (49) The adoption of this resolution
angered Lenin very much. In a fighting speech before the Congress, he
denounced the resolution as being an expression of chauvinism. In particular, Pyatakov came in for a severe drubbing. Lenin termed the latter's
slogan "down with frontiers" a mere "hodge-podge." Defending the right
of nations to self-determination once again, Lenin declared that there was
nothing bad if Finland, Poland and the Ukraine broke away from Russia
and branded those who opposed their right to such a separation as
chauvinists. Impatient over the eruption of defiance once again among
the Party members on this question, Lenin said, "we have been arguing
so much about this question, ever since 1903, that it is difficult to say
much about it now. Go where you please ... He who does not accept
this point of view is an annexationist, a chauvinist." (50) As a result of this
personal intervention of Lenin, the Pyatakov draft was rejected and the
Congress by a substantial majority adopted a resolution on the national
question which declared

> All nations composing Russia must have full right freely to separate
> and to form independent states. Denial of such a right, and failure to
> take measures that guarantee its practical realization, are tantamount to
> supporting the policy of seizures and annexations. (51)

For nations not desiring to separate from Russia, i.e., not desiring to
exercise their right to self-determination, the Congress recommended

> far-going regional autonomy; abolition of control from above; abolition
> of compulsory state language; drawing of boundary lines of the self-
> governing and autonomous regions on the basis of consideration by the
> local population itself of economic and ethnic conditions, of the
> national composition of the population, etc. (52)

Such was the form into which the Soviet nationalities policy had
crystallized in the twenty years' period of its evolution in the platform
of the RSDRP. It did not undergo any further change before October
1917 when the Bolsheviks seized power in Petrograd. One of the first
acts of the new Soviet Government consisted in the issue of a series of
proclamations which outlined the principles that were to guide the work
of its organs. Notable among them was the document entitled the "Rights
of the Peoples of Russia." The rights composed (1) the equality and
sovereignty of the peoples of Russia; (2) the rights of the peoples of
Russia to free self-determination even to the point of separation and for-

---

49. *Sed'maia* *("Aprel'skaia")* *Vserossiiskaia i Petrogradskaia obshche-*
gorodskaia konferentsiia RSDRP(B) (1934) 194, 269-71. Cited in Carr,
n. 8, 262.

50. Lenin, *Sochineniia* (2nd edition, Moscow, 1935) XX, 276-8.

51. *KPSS*, n. 6, 234.

52. *Ibid.*, 346.

mation of independent states; (3) the abolition of all kinds of national
and national-religious privileges and limitations and (4) the free development of the national minorities and ethnic groups inhabiting the territory
of Russia. (53) Shortly afterwards, the Soviet Government addressed a
special appeal to "All Toiling Mussalmans of Russia and the East" in
which it stated

> Moslems of Russia, Tatars of Volga and Crimea, Kirgiz and Sarts of
> Siberia and Turkestan, Turks and Tatars of Transcaucasia, Chechens
> and Mountaineers of the Caucasus, all those whose mosques and
> churches have been destroyed and whose customs have been trampled
> by the Tsars and oppressors of Russia!

> From now on all your beliefs and customs, your national and cultural
> institutions are declared free and inviolable. Build your national life
> freely and unhindered. You have the right to do so. Know that your
> rights as well as the rights of all the peoples of Russia will be protect-
> ed by the entire might of the Revolution and its organs, the Soviets of
> Workers', Soldiers' and Peasants' Deputies. (54)

Yet another concession made to the non-Russian nationalities was the
acceptance of the federal scheme. Before 1917 both Lenin and Stalin had
been implacable opponents of federalism and had favoured the establishment of a highly centralized unitary state structure in Russia. But towards
the beginning of 1918 when they were confronted with the task of building the new multi-national Soviet state structure their former hostility to
federalism underwent a radical change. They now recognized that the
adoption of a federal constitution was "a step forward" in the work of
merging the workers of different nationalities and in unifying their economic resources for building socialism. (55) In the declaration of the "Rights
of the Toiling and Exploited Peoples" adopted by the Third All-Russian
Congress of Soviets on 25 (12) January 1918, it was stated that "the
Soviet Russian Republic is established on the basis of a free union of
free nations as a federation of Soviet national republics." (56)

For implementing its nationalities policy the Soviet Government created
a special organ, the People's Commissariat for Nationality Affairs
(*Narkomnats*). On 26 October 1917 (O.S.) Stalin was appointed its Chairman. (57) At first the functions of the *Narkomnats* were ill-defined and it
carried on its work among the different nationalities of Russia through
several national commissariats and national sections created within itself

---

53. *Politika Sovetskoi vlasti po natsional'nym delam za tri goda 1917-
1920* (Moscow, 1920) 7. (Cited hereafter as *PSVND*).

54. *Ibid.*, 78.

55. S. L. Ronin, "Stalinskoe uchenie o natsii i o mnogonatsional'nom
Sovetskom gosudarstve," *Sovetskoe gosudarstvo i pravo* (Moscow) 2 (1950)
5.

56. *Istoriia Sovetskoi konstitutsii 1917-1956 v dokumentakh* (Moscow,
1957) 66. (Cited hereafter as *ISK*).

57. I. Deutscher, *Stalin: A Political Biography* (London, 1949) 176-7.

from time to time. The *Narkomnats* took care to see that these national commissariats and sections were staffed by persons who hailed from the nationalities concerned and were well acquainted with the life, languages, culture, etc., of those nationalities. During 1918 the number of these national commissariats and sections multiplied to such an extent as to give the *Narkomnats* the outward appearance of a miniature parliament of nationalities. (58) Towards the end of 1918 the organs of the *Narkomnats* were established within the various autonomous territories also. (59) A "Statute of the Peoples Commissariat for Nationality Affairs" issued considerably later charged the *Narkomnats* with the following functions:

(a) to secure the peaceful co-existence and fraternal co-operation of all nationalities and tribes of the RSFSR, and of the friendly Soviet Republics which were linked with it by treaty;

(b) to promote their material and spiritual development, in conformity with the peculiarities of their conditions of life, state of culture and economic position;

(c) to supervise the application of the nationalities policy of the Soviet régime. (60)

Thus, soon after the establishment of their régime, the Bolsheviks were equipped with both a policy and the machinery for carrying out the momentous task of building a supra-national state. In place of the policy of the national state pursued by the Tsarist régime in the multi-national Russian Empire, the Soviet Government put into practice a policy which aimed at building a number of republics which in proportion to the size of their territory, population and economic resources, were given an appropriate degree of internal autonomy. The expression "national in form but socialist in content" aptly describes the reconciliation effected by the Bolsheviks in their nationalities policy between the rival claims of nationalism and socialism.

No

---

58. In 1918 there functioned within the *Narkomnats* the Armenian, Byelorussian, Jewish, Lettish, Lithuanian, Moslem and Polish national commissariats, and national sections on the Caucasian Mountaineers, Maris, Kazakhs, Ukrainians, Chuvash, Esthonians etc. See I. Tsemerian, *Sovetskoe mnogonatsional'noe gosudarstvo, ego osobennosti i puti razvitiia* (Moscow, 1958) 94.

59. These local organs of the *Narkomnats* were charged with the work of (a) implementing the principles of the Soviet régime in the mother tongue of the nationality concerned; (b) implementing all the decrees' of the *Narkomnats;* (c) adopting all measures for raising the cultural level and the class consciousness of the working masses of the nationalities inhabiting the territory; (d) fighting the counter-revolution in its 'national' manifestations (the struggle against the national bourgeois governments etc.). See *PSVND,* n. 52, 145.

60. Rudolf Schlesinger, ed., *The Nationalities Problem And Soviet Administration:* Select Readings on the Development of the Soviet Nationalities Policies (London, 1956) 35.

APPENDI

Table Showing the Oblast-Uezd-wise Distribution

(The figures are base

Oblasts and uezds	Uzbeks	Kazakhs	Kirgiz	Tadjiks	Turkmens	Kara-Kalmala
1. The Amu-Daria Oblast'						
Chimbai uezd	5,637	15,751	—	4	3	58,61
	7.0%	19.4%	—	0.0%	0.0%	72.4
Sarakhan uezd	43,145	19,817	—	487	5,653	4,16
	54.3%	24.9%	—	0.6%	7.1%	5.2
Total for Amu-Daria	48,782	35,568	—	491	5,656	62,77
Oblast'	30.4%	22.1%	—	0.3%	3.5%	39.1
2. Semirechie Oblast'						
Alma-Ata uezd	3,729	128,313	2,096	2	—	
	1.6%	54.9%	0.9%	0.0%	—	
Dzharkent uezd	376	52,804	1,065	4	—	
	0.4%	62.6%	1.3%	0.0%	—	
Kara-kol' uezd	3,200	2,062	48,408	—	—	
	3.5%	2.3%	52.9%	—	—	
Lepsinsk uezd	113	74,789	585	3	—	
	0.0%	57.7%	0.5%	0.0%	—	
Naryn uezd	779	1,127	47,353	1	—	
	1.6%	2.3%	94.7%	0.0%	—	
Pishpek uezd	6,055	47,651	72,791	58	—	
	2.9%	23.2%	35.4%	0.0%	—	
Taldy-Kurgan uezd	810	123,584	498	19	—	
	0.5%	75.1%	0.3%	0.0%	—	
Total for Semirechie	15,062	430,330	172,796	87	—	
Oblast'	1.6%	44.8%	18.0%	0.0%	—	

3

the National Groups of the Turkestan ASSR

on the 1920 census)

Kurama	Taranchi	Kipchaks	Jews	Russians	Persians	Tatars	Armenians	Dungans	Others
—	—	—	—	755	21	199	—	—	8
—	—	—	—	0.9%	0.2%	0.1%	—	—	0.0%
—	—	—	—	5,034	861	321	—	—	123
—	—	—	—	6.3%	1.1%	0.4%	—	—	0.1%
—	—	—	—	5,789	882	520	—	—	131
—	—	—	—	3.6%	0.5%	0.3%	—	—	0.2%
—	24,728	—	—	68,255	—	3,292	—	1,491	1,784
—	10.6%	—	—	29.2%	—	1.4%	—	0.6%	0.8%
—	20,101	—	—	8,495	—	554	—	841	162
—	23.8%	—	—	10.1%	—	0.6%	—	1.0%	0.2%
—	74	—	—	34,027	—	1,153	—	43	2,577
—	0.1%	—	—	37.2%	—	1.2%	—	0.0%	2.8%
—	—	—	—	51,312	—	2,113	—	—	732
—	—	—	—	39.6%	—	1.6%	—	—	0.6%
—	1	—	—	464	—	150	—	103	16
—	0.0%	—	—	0.9%	—	0.3%	—	0.2%	0.0%
—	42	—	—	68,972	—	1.150	—	7,825	1,245
—	0.0%	—	—	33.5%	—	0.6%	—	3.8%	0.5%
—	43	—	—	37,137	—	2,152	—	—	311
—	0.0%	—	—	22.0%	—	1.3%	—	—	0.2%
—	44,989	—	—	268,662	—	10,564	—	10,303	6,827
—	4.7%	—	—	28.0%	—	1.1%	—	1.1%	0.7%

Oblasts and uezds	*Uzbeks*	*Kazakhs*	*Kirgiz*	*Tadjiks*	*Turkmens*	*Kara-Kalpaks*
3. Samarkand Oblast'						
Dzhizak uezd	89,520	11,438	—	832	—	—
	86.7%	11.1%	—	0.8%	—	—
Katta-Kurgan uezd	121,146	89	—	251	—	—
	97.1%	0.1%	—	0.2%	—	—
Samarkand uezd	199,854	561	—	120,361	—	—
	55.0%	0.2%	—	33.1%	—	—
Khodzhent uezd	61,482	10,397	14,063	113,023	—	—
	31.4%	5.2%	7.0%	56.0%	—	—
Total for the Samarkand Oblast'	472,002	22,485	14,063	234,467	—	—
	59.5%	2.8%	1.8%	29.6%	—	—
4. Syr-Daria Oblast'						
Ak-Mechet uezd	1,065	92,740	194	198	—	—
	1.0%	90.2%	0.2%	0.2%	—	—
Aulie-Ata uezd	12,985	110,013	47,295	617	—	—
	6.1%	51.3%	22.0%	0.3%	—	—
Kazalinsk uezd	445	73,436	779	259	—	—
	0.5%	84.7%	0.9%	0.3%	—	—
Mirzachul' uezd	12,527	9,218	—	2,490	—	—
	33.4%	24.6%	—	6.6%	—	—
Tashkent uezd	267,924	151,443	8,295	11,788	—	4,314
	45.7%	25.8%	1.4%	2.0%	—	0.7%
Turkestan uezd	32,850	44,214	1,185	9	—	—
	40.1%	53.9%	1.5%	0.0%	—	—
Chimkent uezd	42,370	124,951	93	6	—	—
	21.6%	63.7%	0.0%	0.0%	—	—
Total for the Syr-Daria Oblast'	370,166	606,015	57,841	15,367	—	4,314
	28.4%	46.4%	4.4%	1.2%	—	0.3%

Kurama	Taranchi	Kipchaks	Jews	Russians	Persians	Tatars	Armenians	Dungans	Others
—	—	—	—	1,343	33	—	42	—	89
—	—	—	—	1.3%	0.1%	—	0.0%	—	0.1%
—	—	—	951	1,614	12	—	146	—	459
—	—	—	0.8%	1.3%	0.0%	—	0.1%	—	0.4%
—	—	—	7,392	15,812	12,227	—	2,361	—	4,381
—	—	—	2.0%	4.4%	3.4%	—	0.7%	—	1.2%
—	—	—	111	2,367	—	—	31	—	261
—	—	—	0.1%	1.2%	—	—	0.0%	—	0.1%
—	—	—	8,454	21,136	12,272	—	2,580	—	5,190
—	—	—	0.1%	2.7%	1.5%	—	0.3%	—	0.7%
—	—	—	52	7,429	42	582	51	—	419
—	—	—	0.1%	7.2%	0.0%	0.6%	0.1%	—	0.4%
—	—	—	3	38,922	10	1,155	126	668	2,796
—	—	—	0.0%	18.1%	—	0.5%	0.1%	0.3%	1.3%
—	—	—	130	10,029	5	1,010	8	—	608
—	—	—	0.1%	11.6%	0.0%	1.2%	0.0%	—	0.7%
—	—	—	—	12,158	144	94	171	—	653
—	—	—	—	32.5%	0.4%	0.3%	0.5%	—	1.7%
,697	—	—	1,648	68,151	1,138	4,710	2,593	—	14,383
8.5%	—	—	0.3%	11.6%	0.2%	0.8%	0.5%	—	2.5%
—	—	—	149	2,848	9	263	32	—	405
—	—	—	0.2%	3.5%	0.0%	0.3%	0.0%	—	0.5%
—	—	—	313	27,549	20	240	95	—	620
—	—	—	0.2%	14.0%	0.0%	0.1%	0.1%	—	0.3%
697	—	—	2,295	167,086	1,368	8,054	3,076	668	19,884
3.8%	—	—	0.2%	12.8%	0.1%	0.6%	0.2%	0.1%	1.5%

Oblasts and uezds	*Uzbeks*	*Kazakhs*	*Kirgiz*	*Tadjiks*	*Turkmens*	*Kara-Kalpaks*
5. Turkmen Oblast'						
Krasnovodsk uezd	7	2,304	—	—	25,434	—
	0.0%	6.4%	—	—	71.0%	
Merv uezd	1,236	813	—	—	125,023	—
	0.8%	0.6%	—	—	82.7%	
Poltoratsk uezd	57	150	—	—	62,083	—
	0.1%	0.1%	—	—	65.4%	
Tedzhen uezd	11	12	—	—	48,476	—
	0.0%	0.0%	—	—	93.4%	
Total for the Turkmen Oblast'	1,311	3,279	—	—	261,016	—
	0.4%	1.0%	—	—	78.2%	
6. Fergana Oblast'						
Andizhan uezd	308,046	—	107,866	3,508	—	7,7
	65.2%	—	22.9%	0.7%	—	1.
Kokand uezd	419,148	—	16,472	67,945	—	9
	79.1%	—	3.1%	12.8%	—	0.
Namangan uezd	254,926	—	54,643	58,228	—	1,9
	65.9%	—	14.1%	15.1%	—	0.
Osh uezd	116,818	—	126,801	929	—	
	46.7%	—	50.6%	0.4%	—	
Fergana uezd	234,124	—	54,376	37,276	—	
	75.8%	—	12.1%	8.3%	—	
The Pamir Area	29	—	2,693	19,397	—	
	0.1%	—	12.2%	87.7%	—	
Total for the Fergana Oblast'	1,440,168	—	362,851	187,244	—	10,7
	68.2%	—	17.2%	8.9%	—	0.
Total for the Turkestan ASSR	2,347,491	1,098,677	607,551	437,656	266,672	77,8
	41.4%	19.4%	10.7%	7.7%	4.7%	1.

Source : RSFSR, Tsentral'noe statisticheskoe Upravlenie Turkrespubli

Kurama	Taranchi	Kipchaks	Jews	Russians	Persians	Tatars	Armenians	Dungans	Others
—	—	—	1	4,211	2,621	—	867	—	382
—	—	—	0.0%	11.8%	7.3%	—	2.4%	—	1.1%
—	—	—	750	9,839	4,424	—	4,199	—	4,844
—	—	—	0.5%	6.5%	2.9%	—	2.8%	—	3.2%
—	—	—	18	14,294	10,130	—	5,836	—	2,357
—	—	—	0.0%	15.1%	10.7%	—	6.1%	—	2.5%
—	—	—	—	1,610	1,236	—	294	—	274
—	—	—	—	3.1%	2.4%	—	0.6%	—	0.5%
—	—	—	769	29,954	18,411	—	11,196	—	7,857
—	—	—	0.2%	9.0%	5.5%	—	3.4%	—	2.3%
—	—	29,407	644	10,604	1,090	601	675	—	1,999
—	—	6.2%	0.1%	1.3%	0.2%	0.1%	0.2%	—	0.4%
—	—	413	1.179	16,977	911	813	1,697	—	3,596
—	—	0.1%	0.2%	3.2%	0.2%	0.1%	0.3%	—	0.7%
—	—	11,415	534	3,269	315	1,023	345	—	318
—	—	2.9%	0.1%	0.8%	0.1%	0.3%	0.1%	—	0.1%
—	—	—	2	5,326	5	102	24	—	367
—	—	—	0.0%	2.1%	0.0%	0.0%	0.0%	—	0.2%
—	—	1,214	1,588	11,869	42	149	293	—	2,151
—	—	0.3%	0.3%	2.6%	—	—	0.1%	—	0.5%
—	—	—	—	2	—	—	—	—	9
—	—	—	—	0.0%	—	—	—	—	0.0%
—	—	42,449	3,947	48,047	2,363	2,688	3,034	—	8,440
—	—	2.0%	0.2%	2.3%	0.1%	0.1%	0.1%	—	0.4%
9,697	44,989	42,449	15,465	540,674	35,296	21,826	19,886	10,971	48,329
1.1%	0.8%	0.7%	0.3%	9.5%	0.6%	0.4%	0.3%	0.2%	0.8%

tisticheskii ezhegodnik 1917-1923 gg (Tashkent, 1924) I, pt. 3, 45-8.

Table Showing the Vilaiet-wise Distribution of the

Vilaiets	Uzbeks	Tadjiks	Turkmens	Arabs
Baisun	19,064	16,864	—	6
	53,0%	46.9%	—	0.0%
Bek-budi	63,525	9,038	3,020	7,321
	76.0%	10.8%	3.6%	8.8%
Bukhara	284,753	39,044	12,773	31,511
	72.5%	9.9%	3.2%	8.0%
Garm	—	173,488	—	—
	—	95.6%	—	—
Guzar	37,405	—	—	—
	100%	—	—	—
Diushambe	24,710	82,998	401	—
	22.8%	76.6%	0.4%	—
Kerki	3,204	48	71,841	3
	4.2%	0.1%	94.4%	—
Kermin	76,991	390	—	6,326
	83.3%	0.4%	—	6.9%
Kuliab	28,703	102,763	—	400
	21.8%	77.9%	—	0.3%
Kurgan-tube	8,445	2,735	3,705	75
	54.7%	17.7%	24.0%	0.5%
Leninsk (Chardzhui)	34,782	13	68,791	1.255
	30.5%	0.0%	60.3%	1.1%
Nur-Ata	10,271	3,048	—	—
	45.6%	13.5%	—	—
Sary-Asi	55,844	26,977	165	150
	66.7%	32.3%	0.2%	0.2%
Shakhrisiabz	85,529	11,400	132	—
	87.2%	11.6%	0.1%	—
Shirabad	44,542	6,783	4,165	132
	78.8%	12.0%	7.4%	0.2%
Total for Bukhara Republic	777,768	475,589	164,993	47,179
	50.7%	31.1%	10.3%	3.1%

Source: *Materialy po raionirovaniiu Srednei Azii: territoriia i naseleniia*

C

National Groups of the Former Bukhara Republic

Kazakhs	Kara-Kalpaks	Kirgiz	Bukharan Jews	Other immigrant nationals	Total
—	—	—	36	—	35,970
—	—	—	0.1%	—	100%
730	—	—	—	—	83,634
0.8%	—	—	—	—	100%
9,473	70	—	3,308	12,416	393,348
2.4%	—	—	0.8%	3.2%	100%
—	—	8,030	—	—	181,518
—	—	4.4%	—	—	100%
—	—	—	—	—	37,405
—	—	—	—	—	100%
—	—	—	—	300	108,409
—	—	—	—	0.2%	100%
—	—	—	300	743	76,139
—	—	—	0.4%	0.9%	100%
4,245	2,025	—	1,694	769	92,440
4.6%	2.2%	—	1.8%	· 0.8%	100%
—	—	—	—	3	131,869
—	—	—	—	0.0%	100%
490	—	—	—	—	15,450
3.1%	—	—	—	—	100%
26	—	—	493	8.711	114,071
0.0%	—	—	0.4%	7.7%	100%
9,200	—	—	—	—	22,519
40.9%	—	—	—	—	100%
80	—	185	—	228	86,629
0.1%	—	0.2%	—	0.3%	100%
—	—	—	1,011	—	98,072
—	—	—	1.1%	—	100%
24	—	—	—	896	56,512
0.0%	—	—	—	1.6%	100%
24,268	2,095	8,215	6,842	24,066	1,531,015
1.6%	0.1%	0.5%	0.4%	1.7%	100%

Bukhary i Khorezma (Tashkent, 1926) I, Pt. 1, (Bukhara), 165-6.

APPENDIX D

Table Showing the Oblast'-wise Distribution of the National Groups of the Former Khorezmian Republic

National groups	*Kazakho-Kara-Kalpak oblast'*	*Novo-Urgench oblast'*	*Tashauz oblast'*	*Khiva Area*	*Total*
Uzbeks	16,236	188,476	62,278	97,414	364,404
	32.5%	97.0%	54.0%	96.0%	79.0%
Kazakhs	17,357	1,933	247	101	19,638
	35.8%	1.0%	0.2%	0.1%	4.3%
Kara-Kalpaks	4,116	100	—	46	4,262
	8.3%	0.0%	—	0.0%	0.9%
Turkmens	11,724	1,496	52,710	1,501	67,431
	23.5%	0.8%	45.8%	1.5%	14.6%
Persians	—	163	—	1,341	1,504
	—	0.1%	—	1.3%	0.3%
Tatars	451	345	—	394	1,190
	0.9%	0.2%	—	0.4%	0.3%
Russians	—	381	—	449	830
	—	0.2%	—	0.4%	0.2%
Arabs	—	1,248	—	—	1,248
	—	0.7%	—	—	0.3%
Others	—	76	—	322	398
	—	0.0%	—	0.3%	0.1%
Total	49,884	194,218	115,235	101,568	460,905

Source: *Materialy po raionirovaniiu Srednei Azii: territoriia i naselenie Bukhary i Khorezma* (Tashkent, 1926) II, Pt. 2, (Khorezm) 90.

BIBLIOGRAPHY

Primary Sources

"Administrativnoe delenie Turkestana v proshlom i nastoiashchem," in *Materialy po raionirovaniiu Turkestana*, Tashkent, 1922.

Biulleten' narodnogo komissariata zemledeliia Turkrespubliki : perspektivy narkomzema v sviazi s natsional'nym razmezhevaniem, Tashkent, 10-11 (Oktiabr'-Noiabr', 1924).

Biulleten' tsentral'nogo statisticheskogo upravleniia Turkmenskoi soiuznoi SSR, no. 3, Poltoratsk, 1925.

Biulleten' tsentral'nogo statisticheskogo upravleniia Uzbekistana, no. 1, Tashkent, 1925.

Dimanshtein, S. M., ed., *Revoliutsiia i natsional'nyi vopros: dokumenty i materialy*, Vol. III, Moscow, 1930.

Eudin, X. J., and Robert C. North, *Soviet Russia and the East 1920-1927: A Documentary Survey*, Stanford, 1957.

Frunze, M. V., *Izbrannye proizvedeniia*, Vol. I, Moscow, 1957.

Kalinin, M. I., *Rechi i stat'i 1919-1935*, Moscow, 1936.

Khronologischeskoe sobranie zakonov Turkmenskoi SSR, ukazov Prezidiuma Verkhovnogo Soveta, postanovlenii i rasporiazhenii pravitel'stva Turkmenskoi SSR, Vol. I, 1925-1944, Ashkhabad, 1960.

Kommunisticheskaia Partiia Sovetskogo Soiuza v rezoliutsiiakh i resheniiakh s'ezdov, konferentsii i plenumov TsK, pt. 1, 1898-1925, Moscow, 1953.

Kratkii obzor Sovetskogo stroitel'stva i narodnogo khoziaistva Kirgizii: materialy k dokladu Ispolkoma KAO 3-ti sessii VTsIK's RSFSR XII sozyva, Frunze, 1926.

Lenin, V. I., *Sochineniia*, Vols. XV, XVI, XVII, XVIII, XIX and XX, second edition, Moscow, 1935.

Lenin i Stalin, *Stat'i i rechi o Srednei Azii i Uzbekistana*, sbornik, Tashkent, 1940.

Leninskii sbornik, Vols. XXIV and XXXIV.

Materialy po raionirovaniiu Srednei Azii : proekt administrativnokhoziaistvennogo deleniia TSSR, Vypusk II, Tashkent, 1924.

Materialy po raionirovaniiu Srednei Azii : territoriia i naselenie Bukhary i Khorezma, Book I, Pt. I, (Bukhara), Book II, Pt. 2 (Khorezm), Tashkent, 1926.

Materialy Vserossiiskikh perepisei 1920 goda, perepis' naseleniia v Turkestanskoi Respublike, Pt. 1, vypusk 2, Tashkent, 1924.

M. V. Frunze na frontakh grazhdanskoi voiny : sbornik dokumentov, Moscow, 1941.

I s'ezd Kommunisticheskoi Partii (Bolshevikov) Uzbekistana : stenograficheskii otchët, Tashkent, 1925.

"Obrashchenie narodnogo komissariata po delam natsional'nostei Soveta Kazani, Ufy, Orenburga, Ekaterinburga, Sovnarkomu Turkestanskogo Kraia, chrezvychainomy komissaru Turgaiskoi oblasti, Vernenskomy Sovetu i drugim, 7 Aprelia 1918 goda," in V. Bystrianskii and M. Mishin, eds., *Leninizm*, Moscow, 1933.

Otchët o rabote pravitel'stva Kirgizskoi ASSR za 2 goda (*Mart 1927 g-Aprel' 1929g.*), Frunze, 1929.

Otchët Syr-Dar'inskogo oblastkogo ekonomicheskogo soveshcheniia za 1921-1922 khoziaistvennyi god, Tashkent, 1923.

Otchët 2-oi ekonomicheskoi konferentsii Turkestanskoi Respubliki, Tashkent, 1923.

Otchët tsentral'nogo komiteta kommunisticheskoi partii Turkestana za period s VII do VIII s'ezda 1923-1924, Tashkent, 1925.

Otchët Turkmenskogo oblastkogo ekonomicheskogo soveshcheniia, Poltoratsk, 1922.

Perepis' naseleniia v Turkestanskoi respublike, vypusk 5, Tashkent, 1924.

Pervyi vseuzbekskii s'ezd Sovetov rabochikh, dekhanskikh i Krasnoarmeiskikh deputatov Uzbekskoi sovetskoi sotsialisticheskoi respubliki: stenograficheskii otchët, Tashkent, 1925.

Piaskovskii, A. V., ed., *Vosstanie 1916 goda v Srednei Azii i Kazakhstane, sbornik dokumentov*, Moscow, 1960.

Plekhanov, G. V., *Sochineniia*, Vols. XII and XIII, Moscow and Leningrad, 1926.

Pobeda velikoi Oktiabr'skoi sotsialisticheskoi revoliutsii v Turkestane, sbornik dokumentov, Tashkent, 1947.

Pokrovski, S. N., ed., *Obrazovanie Kazakhskoi ASSR: sbornik dokumentov i materialov*, Alma-Ata, 1957.

Politika Sovetskoi vlasti po natsional'nym delam za tri goda 1917-1920, Moscow, 1920.

Sbornik dekretov, rasporiazhenii i postanovlenii tsentral'nogo ispol'nitel'nogo komiteta Sovetov Turkestanskoi Respubliki, 9 sessii, Tashkent, 1921.

Sbornik dekretov, postanovlenii i rasporiazhenii pravitel'stva TASSR za 1924g, Tashkent, 1924.

Sbornik vazhneishikh dekretov, postanovlenii i rasporiazhenii pravitel'stva TASSR za 1917-1922, Tashkent, 1923.

Schlesinger, Rudolf, ed., *The Nationalities Problem and the Soviet Administration: Select Readings on the Development of Soviet Nationalities Policies*, London, 1956.

S'ezdy Sovetov SSSR v postanovleniiakh i rezoliutsiiakh, Moscow, 1939.

Shest' let natsional'noi politiki Sovetskoi vlasti i Narkomnats, Moscow, 1924.

Sovetskaia politika za 10 let po natsional'nomu voprosu v RSFSR: sistematicheskii sbornik deistvuiushchikh aktov Pravitel'stv Soiuza SSR i RSFSR po delam natsional'nostei RSFSR (Oktiabr' 1917g.-Noiabr' 1927g.)

Spravochnik narodnogo komissariata po delam natsional'nostei, Moscow, 1921.

Sredne-Aziatskii ekonomicheskii raion, sbornik, Tashkent, 1922.

Stalin, J. V., *Marxism and the National and Colonial Question,* London, (n.d.).

Stalin, I., "Nasha zadacha na vostoke," *Bol'shevik Kazakhstana,* 9-10 (1920).

Stalin, I., "Natsional'nye momenty v partiinom i gosudarstvennom stroitel'stve," *Zhizn' natsional'nostei,* 3-4 (1923).

Stalin, J., *Problems of Leninism,* Moscow, 1947.

Stalin, I., "Sovdepam i partiinym organizatsiiam Turkestana, *Zhizn' natsional'nostei,* 7 (1919).

Statisticheskii ezhegodnik 1917-1924gg, Tashkent, 1924.

Statisticheskii spravochnik Turkmenskoi oblasti 1920-1924, Poltoratsk, 1924.

Stenograficheskii otchët. 3-ti chrezvychainoi sessii TurkTsIK, 15-16 Sentiabria 1924g, Tashkent, 1924.

Studenikin, S. S., ed., *Istoriia sovetskoi konstitutsii (v dokumentakh) 1917-1956,* Moscow, 1957.

Turkmeniia v period inostrannoi voennoi interventsii i grazhdanskoi voiny (1918-1920g), sbornik dokumentov, Ashkhabad, 1957.

"Vremennoe polozhenie. o revoliutsionnom komitete po upravleniiu Kirgizskim kraem: dekret narodnykh komissarov 17 iiulia 1919g," *Bol'shevik Kazakhstana,* 9-10 (1920).

Vserossiiskii tsentral'nyi ispolnitel'nyi komitet XI sozyva : vtoraia sessiia : stenograficheskii otchët, Moscow, 1924.

Vsesoiuznaia perepis' naseleniia 1926g, Vol. XV, Moscow, 1928.

Vsesoiuznaia perepis' naseleniia 17 dekabria 1926 goda : kratkie svodki : narodnost' i rodnoi iazyk naseleniia SSSR, vypusk 3, Moscow, 1928.

Vsia Sredniaia Aziia : spravochnaia kniga na 1926 khoziaistvennyi god, Tashkent, 1926.

Vyshinskov, A. Ia., ed., *S'ezdv Sovetov RSFSR v postanovleniiakh i rezoliutsiiakh,* sbornik dokumentov, Moscow, 1939.

"Zasedanie vtoroi sessii TsIK SSSR 24 Oktiabria 1924 goda: doklad Tov. Faizulla-Khodzhaeva," *Narodnoe khoziaistvo Srednei Azii,* 4 (November 1924).

Zhantuarov, S. B., ed., *Velikaia oktiabr'skaia sotsialisticheskaia revoliutsiia i grazhdanskaia voina v Kirgizii (1917-1920gg),* sbornik dokumentov, Frunze, 1957.

Secondary Sources

A. BOOKS

Abdullaev, M., *Obrazovanie Khorezmskoi Sovetskoi narodnoi respubliki i osnovnye etapy eë razvitiia 1920-1924,* Avtoreferat, Tashkent, 1950.

Agzamkhodzhaev, A. and Sh. Z. Urazaev, *Razvitie sovetskoi gosudarstvennosti v Uzbekistane,* Moscow, 1960.

Aleskerov, Iu., *Interventsiia i grazhdanskaia voina v Srednei Azii,* Tashkent, 1959.

Alkin, Ilias, *Sredniaia Aziia*: *ekonomiko-geograficheskii ocherk Kara-Kalpakstana, Kirgizstana, Tadzhikistana, Turkmenistana i Uzbekistana*, Vol. I, Moscow, 1931.

Aminov, A. M., *Ekonomicheskoe razvitie Srednei Azii*, Tashkent, 1959.

Antropov, P., *Chto i kak chitat' po istorii revoliutsionnogo dvizhenia i partii v Srednei Azii*, Samarkand, 1929.

Arsharuni, A. and Kh. Gabidullin, *Ocherki panislamizma i panturkizma v Rossii*, Moscow, 1931.

Artykov, A. K., *Promyshlennost' Turkmenskoi SSR za 25 let*, Ashkhabad, 1950.

Aziatskaia Rossiia, 3 vols. St. Petersburg, 1914.

Babakhodzhaev, A. Kh., *Proval angliiskoi politiki v Srednei Azii i na Srednem Vostoke v period priznaniia Sovetskogo gosudarstva de-fakto i de-iure (1921-1924 gg.)*, Tashkent, 1957.

Bailey, F. M., *Mission to Tashkent*, London, 1946.

Bartol'd, V.V., *Istoriia kul'turnoi zhizni Turkestana*, Leningrad, 1927.

Bartol'd, V. V., *Kirgizy*: *istoricheskii ocherk*, Frunze, 1927.

Bartol'd, V. V., *Sovremennoe sostoianie i blizhaishie zadachi izucheniia istoriia Turetskikh narodnostei*, Baku, 1926.

Baskakov, N. A., *Tiurkskie iazyki*, Moscow, 1960.

Bates, E. S., *Soviet Asia — Progress and Problems*, London, 1942.

Batsell, W. R., *Soviet Rule in Russia*, London, 1929.

Bekmakhanov, E. B., *Prisoedinenie Kazakhstana k Rossii*, Moscow, 1957.

Belotskii, M., *Kirgizskaia respublika*, Moscow, 1936.

Bennigsen, Alexandre and Chantal Quelquejay, *The Evolution of the Moslem Nationalities of the U.S.S.R. and their Linguistic Problems*, (Translated from the French by Geoffrey Wheeler), London, 1961.

Boersner, Demetrio, *The Bolsheviks and the National and the Colonial Question 1917-1928*, Geneva and Paris, 1957.

Boulger, Demetrius Charles, *England and Russia in Central Asia*, Vol. 1, London, 1879.

Burn, Capt. A. H., *Troublous Times*: *Experiences in Bolshevik Russia and Turkestan*, London, 1931.

Caroe, Olaf, *The Soviet Empire*: *The Turks of Central Asia and Stalinism*, London, 1953.

Carr, Edward Hallet, *The Bolshevik Revolution 1917-1923*, Vol. 1, London, 1950.

Cherdantsev, G., *Sredne-Aziatskie respubliki*, Moscow, 1928.

Chernov, K. I., *Obrazovanie i razvitie Tadzhikskogo sovetskogo sotsialisticheskogo gosudarstva v pervoi faze sovetskogo gosudarstva*, Avtoreferat, Tashkent, 1955.

Czaplicka, M. A., *The Turks of Central Asia in History and the Present Day*, Oxford, 1918.

Degtiarenko, N. D., *Razvitie sovetskoi gosudarstvennosti v Tadzhikistane*, Moscow, 1960.z

Deutscher, I., *Stalin*: *A Political Biography*, London, 1949.

Dodonov, I. K., *Ob istoricheskikh predposylkakh obrazovaniia Uzbekskoi SSR*, Tashkent, 1949.

Dusumov, Ia. M., *Ocherki istorii Kara-Kalpakskoi ASSR 1917-1927*, Tashkent, 1960.

Dzhunusov, M., *K voprosu o formirovanii Kirgizskoi sotsialisticheskoi natsii*, Frunze, 1952.

Etherton, P. T., *In the Heart of Asia*, London, 1925.

Fedorov, E., ed., *Materialy po revoliutsionnomu dvizheniiu Turkmenii 1904-1919*, Tashkent, 1924.

Filippov, S. T., *Frunze i Kuibyshev — organizatory pobedy na frontakh Srednei Azii (1918-1920)*, Ashkhabad, 1940.

Formirovanie i razvitie Kirgizskoi sotsialisticheskoi natsii, Frunze, 1957.

Fraser-Tytler, W. K., *Afghanistan: A Study in Political Developments in Central and Southern Asia*, second edition, London, 1953.

Gafurov, B. G., *Istoriia Tadzhikskogo naroda*, Vol. I, Moscow, 1949.

Gafurov, B. G., ed., *Materialy k istorii Tadzhikskogo naroda v Sovetskii period*, sbornik statei, Stalinabad, 1954.

Gafurov, B., and N. Prokhorov, *Tadzhikskii narod v bor'be za svobodu i nezavisimost' svoei rodiny*, Stalinabad, 1944.

Galuzo, P. G., *Kto takie byli Dzhadidy*, Tashkent, 1926.

Galuzo, P. G., *Turkestan — koloniia: ocherki istorii kolonial'noi politiki Russkogo tsarizma v Srednei Azii*, Tashkent, 1935.

Gordienko, A. A., *Sozdanie narodno-sovetskogo gosudarstva i prava i ikh revoliutsionno-preobrazuiushchaia rol' v Khorezme i Bukhare*, Tashkent, 1959.

Gordienko, A. A., *Sozdanie sovetskoi natsional'noi gosudarstvennosti v Srednei Azii*, Moscow, 1959.

Gordienko, A. A., *Tvorcheskaia rol' sovetskogo gosudarstva i prava v sotsialisticheskom preobrazovanii Turkestana*, Tashkent, 1958.

Hostler, C. W., *Turkism and the Soviets*, London, 1957.

Hayit, Baymirza, *Turkestan im XX Jahrhundert*, Darmstadt, 1956.

Iakubovskii, A. Iu., *K voprosu ob etnogeneze Uzbekskogo naroda*, Tashkent, 1941.

Inoiatov, Kh. Sh., *Oktiabr'skaia revoliutsiia v Uzbekistane*, Moscow, 1958.

Irkaev, M., and others, *Ocherk istorii sovetskogo Tadzhikistana (1917-1957 gg)*, Stalinabad, 1957.

Iskakov, Iu. I., *Razvitie khlopkovodstva v Uzbekistane*, Tashkent, 1960.

Istoriia Kazakhskoi SSR, Alma-ata, 1957.

Istoriia Kirgizii, Vols. 1 and 2, Frunze, 1956.

Istoria Kirgizii: uchebnoe posobie dlia srednei shkoly, Frunge, 1957.

Istoriia narodov Uzbekistana, Vol. 2, Tashkent, 1947.

Istoriia Uzbekskoi SSR, Vol. 1, pts. I and II, Tashkent, 1955.

Istoriia Uzbekskoi SSR, Vol. 2, Tashkent, 1957.

Karpov, G. I., *Vosstanie Tedzhenskikh Turkmeny v 1916 g*, Ashkhabad, 1935.

Khalfin, N. A., *Politika Rossii v Srednei Azii (1857-1868)*, Moscow, 1960.

Khodzhaev, Faizulla, *K istorii revoliutsii v Bukhare*, Tashkent, 1926.

Khodzhaev, Faizulla and others, *Ocherki revoliutsionnogo dvizheniia v Srednei Azii*, sbornik statei, Moscow, 1926.

Kisliakov, N. A., *Sem'ia i brak u Tadzhikov*, Moscow, 1959.

Kohn, Hans, *Nationalism in the Soviet Union*, New York, 1953.

Kovalev, P. A., *Mobilizatsiia na tylovye raboty naseleniia Turkestana i vosstaniia 1916 g*, Tashkent, 1957.

Kuliev, K. M., *Bor'ba kommunisticheskoi partii za ukreplenie sovetskoi vlasti i osushchestvlenie natsional'noi politiki v Srednei Azii 1917-1925 gg*, Ashkhabad, (n.d.).

Lamont, C., *The Peoples of the Soviet Union*, New York, 1946.

Lenskii, A., *Tadzhikskaia SSR*, Moscow, 1957.

Liashchenko, P. I., *Istoriia narodnogo khoziaistva SSSR*, Vol. 2, 4th edn., Moscow, 1956.

Lobanov-Rostovsky, A., *Russia and Asia*, Michigan, 1951.

Lorimer, Frank, *The Population of the Soviet Union : History and Prospects*, Geneva, 1946.

Mandel, W., *Soviet Far East and Central Asia*, New York, 1944.

Mansurov, G., *Za kul'turnoe stroitel'stvo natsional'nostei*, Moscow, 1927.

Manzhara, D. I., *Revoliutsionnoe dvizhenie v Srednei Azii 1905-1920 : vospominaniia*, Tashkent, 1934.

Materialy po istorii Kara-Kalpakov : trudy instituta vostokovedneiia akademii nauk, Vol. 7, Moscow, 1935.

Maynard, John, *Russia in Flux*, New York, 1948.

Mikhailov, N., *The Land of the Soviets*, New York, 1939.

Mukhammedberdyev, K., *Kommunisticheskaia partiia v bor'be za pobedu narodnoi sovetskoi revoliutsii v Khorezme*, Ashkhabad, 1959.

Murzaev, E. M., ed., *Sredniaia Aziia : fiziko-geograficheskaia kharakteristika*, Moscow, 1958.

Muraveiskii, S., *Ocherki po istorii revoliutsionnogo dvizheniia v Srednei Azii*, Tashkent, 1926.

Nepomnin, V. Ia., *Istoricheskii opyt stroitel'stva sotsializma v Uzbekistane (1917-1937)*, Tashkent, 1960.

Nepomnin V. Ia., *Ocherki istorii sotsialisticheskogo stroitel'stva v Uzbekistane (1917-1937)*, Tashkent, 1957.

Nusupbekov, A., *Ob'edinenie Kazakhskikh zemel' v Kazakhskoi sovetskoi sotsialisticheskoi respublike*, Alma-Ata, 1953.

Ocherki istorii kommunisticheskikh partii Turkestana, Bukhary i Khorezma v period natsional'no-gosudarstvennogo razmezhevaniia v Srednei Azii, Tashkent, 1959.

Ocherki istorii kommunisticheskoi partii Turkestana : sotsial-demokraticheskie organizatsii Turkestana v dooktiabr'skii period (1903-Mart 1917)g, Vol. I, Tashkent, 1958.

Ocherki istorii kommunisticheskoi partii Turkestana : Bol'sheviki Turkestana v period podgotovki i pobedy velikoi oktiabr'skoi sotsialisticheskoi revoliutsii i uprocheniia sovetskoi vlasti, Vol. 2, Tashkent, 1959.

Park, Alexander G., *Bolshevism in Turkestan 1917-1927*, New York, 1957.

Piaskovskii, A. V., *Revoliutsiia 1905-1907 godov v Turkestane*, Moscow, 1958.

Pierce, Richard, A., *Russian Central Asia 1867-1917 : A Study in Colonial Rule*, Berkeley and Los Angeles, 1960.

Pipes, Richard, *The Formation of the Soviet Union : Communism and Nationalism 1917-1923*, Cambridge (Mass.), 1954.

Radzhabov, S., *Tadzhikskaia SSR — suverennoe Sovetskoe gosudarstvo*, Stalinabad, 1957.

Rashidov, G., *Obrazovanie Turkestanskoi sovetskoi avtonomii*, Tashkent, 1954.

Rashidov, G., *Sozdanie sovetskogo gosudarstvennogo apparata v Turkestane (XI-1917-IV-1918)*, Tashkent, 1955.

Revoliutsiia 1905-1907 gg v Uzbekistane : sbornik statei i vospominanii, Tashkent, 1955.

Rizaev, G., *Sel'skoe khoziaistvo Uzbekistana za 40 let*, Tashkent, 1957.

Riazantsev, S. N., and V. F. Pavlenko, *Kirgizskaia SSR*, Moscow, 1960.

Ryskulov, T. R., *Kirgizstan*, Moscow, 1935.

Saakian, A., *25 let Turkmenskoi sovetskoi sotsialisticheskoi Respubliki*, Ashkhabad, 1950.

Safarov, Georgi., *Kolonial'naia revoliutsiia : opyt Turkestana*, Moscow, 1921.

Schuyler, Eugene, *Turkestan : Notes of a Journey in Russian Turkestan, Kokand, Bukhara and Kuldja*, 2 vols., London, 1876.

Shaw, Robert, *Visits to High Tartary, Yarkand and Kashgar*, London, 1871.

Shikmuradov, O., *Torzhestvo Leninskoi natsional'noi politiki v Turkmenistane*, Ashkhabad, 1958.

Shteinberg, E., *Ocherki istorii Turkmenii*, Moscow and Leningrad, 1934.

Shmelev, D., *Kirgizskaia SSR*, Moscow, 1957.

Sulaimanova, Kh. S., and A. I. Ishanov, eds., *Materialy k istorii sovetskogo gosudarstva i prava Uzbekistana*, Tashkent, 1958.

Tolstov, S. P., and others, eds., *Ocherki obshehei etnografii : Aziatskaia chast' SSSR*, Moscow, 1960.

Trainin, I., *Velikoe sotrudnichestvo narodov SSSR*, Moscow, 1946.

Tsamerian, I., *Sovetskoe mnogonatsional'noe gosudarstvo, ego osobennosti i puti razvitiia*, Moscow, 1958.

Tsamerian, I., *Velikaia epokha formirovaniia i razvitiia sotsialisticheskikh natsii v SSSR*, Moscow, 1951.

Turkmenskaia SSR : Administrativno-territorial'noe delenie na I Aprelia 1940 goda, Ashkhabad, 1940.

Tursunov, Kh. T., *Obrazovanie Uzbekskoi sovetskoi sotsialisticheskoi respubliki*, Tashkent, 1957.

Tursunov, Kh. T., *O natsional'no-gosudarstvennom razmeshevanii Shrednei Azii*, Tashkent, 1957.

Urazaev, Sh. Z., *Turkestanskaia ASSR i ee gosudarstvenno-pravovye osobennosti*, Tashkent, 1958.

Uzbekistan: ekonomiko-geograficheskaia kharakteristika, Tashkent, 1960.

Uzbekistan za 15 let: statisticheskii sbornik, Tashkent, 1939.

Vakhabov, M., *Formirovanie Uzbekskoi sotsialisticheskoi natsii*, Tashkent, 1961.

Vakhabov, M., *Tashkent v period trëkh revoliutsii*, Tashkent, 1957.

Vambery, Arminius, *Sketches of Central Asia*, London, 1868.

Voskoboinikov, E., and A. Zevelev, *Turkkomissiia VTsIK i SNK RSFSR i Turkbiuro TsK RKP(B) v bor'be za ukreplenie sovetskoi vlasti v Turkestane*, Tashkent, 1951.

Wheeler, Geoffrey, *Racial Problems in Soviet Muslim Asia*, 2nd edn., London, 1962.

Winner, Thomas G., *The Oral Art and Literature of the Kazakhs of Russian Central Asia*, Durham, N.C., 1958.

Yarmolinsky, Avrahm, *The Jews and other Minor Nationalities under the Soviets*, New York, 1928.

Zarubin, I. I., "Spisok narodnosti Turkestanskogo Kraia," *Trudy komissii po izucheniiu plemennogo sostava naseleniia Rossii i sopredel'nykh stran*, Leningrad, 1925.

Zenkovsky, Serge A., *Pan-Turkism and Islam in Russia*, Cambridge (Mass.), 1960.

Zevelev, A. I., *Iz istorii grazhdanskoi voiny v Uzbekistane*, Tashkent, 1959.

Zhdanko, T. A., ed., *Materialy i issledovaniia po etnografii Kara-Kalpakov (trudy Khorezmskoi arkheologo-etnograficheskoi ekspeditsii)*, Moscow, 1958.

Zhitov, K., and V. Nepomnin, *Ot kolonial'nogo rabstva k sotsializmu*, Tashkent, 1939.

Zhitov, K. E., *Pobeda velikoi oktiabr'skoi sotsialisticheskoi revoliutsii v Uzbekistane*, Tashkent, 1957.

Zlatopol'skii, D. L., *Obrazovanie i razvitie SSSR kak soiuznogo gosudarstva*, Moscow, 1954.

B. Articles

Aitakov, N., "Obrazovanie Turkmenistana," *Narodnoe khoziaistvo Srednei Azii* (Tashkent), 2-3 (1924).

Alekseenov, P., "Natsional'naia politika vremennogo pravitel'stva v Turkestane v 1917g," *Proletarskaia revoliutsiia* (Moscow), 79 (1928).

Aleskerov, Iu. N., "Pervaia Russkaia revoliutsiia i osvoboditel'naia bor'ba narodov Srednei Azii," in *Trudy Tadzhikskogo uchitel'skogo instituta imeni S.S. Aini*, Vol. 3, Samarkand, 1955.

Alkin, Ilias, "Natsional'no-gosudarstvennoe razmezhevanie Srednei Azii i VII s'ezd sovetov SSSR," *Revoliutsionnyi vostok* (Moscow), 6 (1934).

Alymov, A. and S. Studenikin, "Sovetskii federalizm i demokraticheskii tsentralizm," *Sovetskoe gosudarstvo* (Moscow), 1-2 (1933).

Aminov, Kh. A., "Iz istorii bor'by za osushchestvlenie Leninskoi natsional'-noi politiki v Turkestane (Noiabr' 1917g Iiun 1918g)," in *Trudy Uzbek-skogo gosudarstvennogo universiteta im. Alishera Navoi*, vypusk 83 (novaia seriia), Samarkand, 1958.

Ananov, I. N., "K preobrazovaniiu Sredne-Aziatskikh respublik," *Sovet-skoe pravo* (Moscow), 4 (1925).

Andreev, M. S., "Po etnografii Tadzhikov," in *Tadzhikistan*, Tashkent, 1925.

Arkhipov, K., "Bukharskaia narodnaia sovetskaia respublika—obzor kon-stitutsii," *Sovetskoe pravo*, 1 (1923).

Azuzian, A. K., "I. V., Stalin o vozniknovenii i razvitii sotsialisticheskikh natsii v SSSR," *Voprosy istorii* (Moscow), 9 (1952).

Azuzian, A. K., "Sotsialisticheskoe preobrazovanie natsii sovetskogo vos-toka," *Sovetskoe vostokovedenie* (Moscow), 5 (1957).

Bartol'd, V. V., "Ocherk istorii Turkmenskogo naroda," in *Turkmeniia*, Vol. 1, Leningrad, 1929.

Bartol'd, V. V., "Tadzhiki: istoricheskii ocherk," in N. L. Korzhenskii, ed., *Tadzhikistan*, sbornik statei, Tashkent, 1925.

Berkovich, M. Ia., "K voprosu o vozniknovenii Tadzhikskoi natsional'-nosti," in *Izvestiia Tadzhikskogo filiala akademii nauk SSSR*, 12 (Istoriia, iazyk i literatura) Stalinabad, 1946.

Bernshtam, A., "K voprosu o proiskhozhdenii Kirgizskogo naroda," *Sovet-skaia etnografiia* (Moscow), 2 (1955).

"Bor'ba za nezavisimost' Turkmenistana," *Turkmenskaia iskra* (Ashkh-abad), 29 (6 February 1925).

Broido, G. I., "Nasha Turkestanskaia politika i angliiskaia zhurnalistika," *Novyi vostok* (Moscow), 2(1922).

"Bukharskie Turkmeny," *Turkmenskaia iskra*, 20 (2 October 1924).

Burov, M., "Ekonomicheskaia storona problemy natsional'nogo razmezhev-aniia Srednei Azii," *Narodnoe khoziaistvo Srednei Azii*, 2-3 (1924).

Chekalin, N., "Sobytiia v Khorezmskoi Respublike," *Voennaia mysl'* (Moscow), 1 (1921).

Cherdantsev, G. N., "Raionirovania Sredniaia Aziia," *Planovoe khoziai-stovo* (Moscow), 7 (1927).

Chistiakov, O. I., "Obrazovanie Rossiiskoi federatsii 1917-1918," *Sovetskoe gosudarstvo i pravo* (Moscow), 10 (1957).

Chokaiev, M., "Fifteen years of Bolshevik Rule in Turkestan," *Journal of Royal Central Asian Society* (London), 20 (1933).

Chokaiev, M., "Turkestan and the Soviet Régime," *Journal of the Royal Central Asian Society*, 28 (1931).

Dasnazarov, "K desiatiletiiu Kara-Kalpakskoi ASSR," *Revoliutsionnyi vostok*, 6 (1934).

Degtiarenko, N. D., "Sozdanie i razvitie Tadzhikskoi sovetskoi sotsialis-Degtiarenko, N. D., "Sozdanie i razvitie Tadzhikskoi sovetskoi sotsia-listicheskoi gosudarstvennosti," in *Uchenye zapiski Tashkentskogo iuridi-cheskogo instituta*, vypusk I, Tashkent, 1955.

Dervish, "Bukharskaia sovetskaia narodnaia respublika," *Zhizn' natsional'nostei* (Moscow), 1 (1923).

Dodonov, I., "Burzhuazno-demokraticheskaia revoliutsiia 1917 goda v Turkestane," *Pravda vostoka* (Tashkent), 66 (7194) 1 April 1947.

E. M., "Razmezhevanie Srednei Azii," *Vlast' sovetov* (Moscow), 1 (1925).

Fami-Rusal', "Narodnoe prosveshchenie v Turkestane," *Zhizn' natsional'nostei,* 3-4 (1923).

Findeisen, Hans A., "A History of the Kazakh-Russian Relations," *Studies on the Soviet Union* (Munich), 4 (1960).

Frechtling, Louis, E., "Anglo-Russian Rivalry in Eastern Turkestan 1863-1881," *Journal of Royal Central Asian Society,* 26 (1939).

Galuzo, P. G., "Dva etapa natsional'no-osvoboditel'nogo dvizheniia v Srednei Azii," *Pravda vostoka,* 172, 30 July 1928.

Golubeva, R., "Velikaia Oktiabr'skaia revoliutsiia v Uzbekistane," *Istoricheskii zhurnal* (Moscow), II (1939).

Gordienko, A. A., "Obrazovanie i razvitie Turkmenskoi SSR," in *Uchenye zapiski iuridicheskogo fakul'teta SAGU,* vypusk II, Tashkent, 1956.

Granberg, V. G., "Obrazovanie Tadzhikskoi avtonomnoi sovetskoi sotsialisticheskoi respubliki," *trudy iuridicheskogo fakul'teta Tadzhikskogo gosudarstvennogo universiteta,* Vol. 8, Stalinabad, 1955.

Gurvich, G., "Printsipy avtonomizma i federalizma v sovetskoi sisteme," *Sovetskoe pravo,* 3 (1924).

Iakubovskaia, S. I., "Likvidatsiia fakticheskogo neravenstva natsii na primere istorii narodov Srednei Azii i Kazakhstana," in A. L. Sidorov, ed., *Istoricheskie zapiski,* 48, Moscow, 1954.

Ignat'ev V., "Natsional'nyi moment v raionirovanii," *Sovetskoe stroitel'-stvo* (Moscow), 10 (1929).

Inoiatov, Kh. Sh., "V. I. Lenin i stroitel'stvo natsional'noi gosudarstvennosti narodov Srednei Azii," *Istoriia SSSR* (Moscow), 2 (1960).

Iomudskii, K., "Istreblenie Turkmeny vo imia spaseniia chelovechestva," *Turkmenovedenie* (Ashkhabad), 10-11 (1927).

Ishanov, A.I., "Bukharskaia narodnaia sovetskaia respublika (1920-1924)," in *Uchenye zapiski Tashkentskogo iuridicheskogo instituta,* vypusk I, Tashkent, 1955.

Ivanov, P. P., "Kara-Kalpaki," *Sovetskaia etnografiia,* 4 (1940).

Ivanov, P. P., "Naselenie: kratkii statistiko-etnograficheskii ocherk," in *Vsia Sredniaia Aziia,* Tashkent, 1926.

Ivanov, P. P., "Ocherk istorii Karakalpakov," *Materialy po istorii Kara-Kalpakov* (Trudy Instituta vostokovedeniia akademiia nauk SSSR), Vol. 7, Moscow-Leningrad, 1935.

Kantor, E., "Sovetskoe stroitel'stvo i natsional'nye men'shinstva v RSFSR," *Sovetskoe stroitel'stvo,* 225 (1925).

Karklin, O., "Natsional'noe razmezhevanie Sredne-aziatskikh respublik," *Narodnoe khoziaistvo Srednei Azii,* 1 (1924).

Karklin, O., "Pod znamenem SSSR," *Turkestanskaia pravda* (Tashkent) 148, 6 July 1924.

Karpov, G., "Natsional'nye men'shinstva TSSR: kratkie svedeniia o chislennom sostave i istoricheskom proshlom," *Turkmenovedenie,* 3-4 (1931).

Karpov, G., "Turkmeniia i Turkmeny," *Turkmenovedenie,* 10-11 (1929).

Karpych, V., "K istorii vozniknoveniia Turkmenskoi SSR," *Turkmenovedenie,* 10-11 (1928).

Khodorov, A. E., "Lenin i natsional'nyi vopros," *Novyi vostok,* 5 (1924).

Khodorov, I., "K probleme raionirovaniia promyshlennosti Srednei Azii," *Planovoe khoziaistvo,* 1 (1927).

Khodorov, I., "Natsional'noe razmezhevanie Srednei Azii," *Novyi vostok,* 8-9 (1925).

Khodzhaev, Faizulla, "O Mlado-Bukhartsakh," *Istorik marksist* (Moscow), 1 (1926).

Khodzhibaev, A., "Sovetskii Tadzhikistan," *Sovetskoe stroitel'stvo,* 11 (1929).

"Khorezmskaia sovetskaia narodnaia respublika," *Zhizn' natsional'nostei,* 1 (1923).

Kondrashov, S. K., "Sredne-Aziatskoe razmezhevanie," *Planovoe khoziaistvo,* 4 (1925).

Konovalov, V., "Kara-Kalpakskaia avtonomnaia oblast'," *Sovetskoe stroitel'stvo,* 1 (1932).

Korablev, P. V., "Razrabotka Leninym i Stalinym osnovnykh printsipov sovetskogo mnogonatsional'nogo gosudarstva," *Voprosy istorii,* 3 (1954).

Korbe, "Sovety Srednei Azii," *Revoliutsiia i natsional'nosti* (Moscow), 12 (1934).

Kosbergenov, R., "Polozhenie Kara-Kalpakskogo naseleniia v Khivinskom khanstve v kontse XIX nachale XX vv," in *Kratkie soobshcheniia instituta etnografii* (Moscow), 20 (1954).

Kotliarevskii, S. A., "Pravovoe polozhenie avtonomnykh respublik, *Sovetskoe pravo,* 6 (1925).

Krylov, S. B., "Istoricheskii protsess razvitiia sovetskogo federalizma," *Sovetskoe pravo,* 5 (1924).

Kryl'tsov, I. I., "Gosudarstvennoe razmezhevanie Sredne-aziatskikh sovetskikh respublik: publichno-pravovye predposylki i posledstviia razmezhevaniia," *Vestnik iustitsii Uzbekistana* (Tashkent), 1 (1925).

Kryl'tsov, I. I., "O· printsipakh ekonomicheskogo razmezhevaniia Sredne-aziatskikh respublik," *Narodnoe khoziaistvo Srednei Azii,* 8-9 (1926).

Kryl'tsov, I. I., "Pravovoe oformlenie natsional'nykh respublik Srednei Azii: Turkmenistan," *Vestnik iustitsii Uzbekistana,* 6-8 (1926).

Kryl'tsov, I. I., "Zakonodatel'stvo Sredne-aziatskikh sovetskikh respublik," *Sovetskoe pravo,* 5 (1927).

Ksenofontov, F., "Natsional'noe razmezhevanie Srednei Azii," in *Vsia Sredniaia Aziia,* Tashkent, 1926.

Kul'besherov, B., "Sovetskoe stroitel'stvo v Srednei Azii i ego zadacha k 10-letiiu oktiabr'skoi revoliutsii," *Novyi vostok,* 19 (1927).

Kuliev, K. M., "Natsional'naia poliitka kommunisticheskoi partii v Srednei Azii v gody grazhdanskoi voiny i inostrannoi interventsii," in *Trudy instituta istorii, arkhaeologii i etnografii*, Vol. 1, Ashkhabad, 1956.

Landa, L. M., "Sozdanie narodnogo komissariata po natsional'nym delam Turkestanskoi ASSR i ego deiatel'nost' v 1918-1919," in *Iz istorii sovetskogo Uzbekistana* (sbornik statei) Tashkent, 1956.

Levin, I. D., "Sredniaia Aziia — primer konsolidatsii natsii v usloviiakh diktatury proletariata," *Sovetskoe gosudarstvo*, 6 (1934).

Lobanoff-Rostovsky, "The Soviet Muslim Republics in Central Asia," *Journal of Royal Institute of International Affairs* (London), 7 (1928).

Malleson, Maj. Gen. Sir Wilford, "British Military Mission to Turkestan 1918-1920," *Journal of Royal Central Asian Soviety*, 9 (1922).

Manelis, B. L., "Sozdanie sovetskoi gosudarstvennosti v Turkestane," in *Uchenye zapiski iurfaka SAGU, vypusk* 3, Tashkent, 1957.

Mukhamed'iarov, Sh. F., "K istorii provedeniia natsional'no-gosudartvennogo razmezhevaniia Srednei Azii v 1924 g," *Sovetskoe vostokovedenie*, 1 (1955).

Mumin-Khodzhaev, "Sed'maia soiuznaia," *Sovetskaia Aziia* (Moscow), 3-4 (1930).

Narimanov, N., "Lenin i vostok," *Novyi vostok*, 5 (1924).

Nazar, Begzhan, "Natsional'nye otnosheniia v Khorezme," *Narodnoe khoziaistvo Srednei Azii*, 2-3 (1924).

Nemchenko, M., "Natsional'noe razmezhevanie Srednei Azii," *Mezhdunarodnaia zhizn'* (Moscow), 4-5 (1924).

Nepesov, G., "Voznikhovenie i razvitie Turkmenskoi sovetskoi sotsialisticheskoi respubliki," *Voprosy istorii*, 2 (1950).

Nikolaeva, V. P., "Turkkomissiia kak polnomochenyi organ TsK RKP(B)," *Voprosy istorii KPSS* (Moscow), 2 (1958).

"Novoe torzhestvo Leninskoi natsional'noi politiki," *Pravda vostoka*, 117, 23 May 1932.

Novoselov, K., and Mel'kumov, "K voprosu o natsional'no-gosudarstvennom razmezhevanii Srednei Azii," *Kommunist Turkmenistana* (Ashkhabad), 6 (1957).

Nurbekov, K. N., "Obrazovanie Kirgizskoi suverennoi sovetskoi sotsialisticheskoi respubliki," *Sovetskoe gosudarstvo i pravo*, 9 (1958).

Pankov, A., "Naselenie Tadzhikistana: demograficheskii ocherk," in *Tadzhikistan*, Tashkent, 1925.

Pankov, A., "Polozhenie, granitsy, sostav i administrativnoe delenie Tadzhikistana," in *Tadzhikistan*, Tashkent, 1925.

Potseluevskii, A., "Razvitie Turkmenskogo iazyka," *Turkmenovedenie*, 10-11 (1929).

Radzhabov, S., "Etapy razvitiia sovetskogo gosudarstvennogo stroia v Srednei Azii," *Sovetskoe gosudarstvo i pravo*, II (1948).

Radzhabov, S. A., "Natsional'no-gosudarstvennoe razmezhevanie v Srednei Azii i ego znachenie dlia obrazovaniia Tadzhikskoi sovetskoi sotsialisticheskoi respubliki," *Materialy k istorii Tadzhikskogo naroda v sovetskii period*, Stalinabad, 1954.

Rastsvetaev, M., "Tadzhikskaia SSR," *Nasha strana* (Moscow), 12 (1938).

Rasulev, A., "Ocherki po istorii sovetskogo suda v Uzbekistane," in *Uchenye zapiski iuridicheskogo fakul'teta SAGU,* vypusk 2, Tashkent, 1956.

"Razmezhevanie Srednei Azii," *Turkmenskaia iskra,* 10 (20 November 1924).

Ronin, S. L., "Stalinskoe uchenie o natsii i o mnogonatsional'nom sovetskom gosudarstve," *Sovetskoe gosudarstvo i pravo,* 2 (1950).

Samoilovich, A. N., "Ocherki po istorii Turkmenskoi literatury," in *Turkmeniia,* Vol. 1, Leningrad, 1929.

Semenov, A. A., "K probleme natsional'nogo razmezhevaniia Srednei Azii: istoriko-etnograficheskii ocherk," *Narodnoe khoziaistvo Srednei Azii,* 2-3 (1924).

Shumilin, V. N., "Puti razvitiia narodnogo khoziaistva Tadzhikistana," *Novyi vostok,* 29 (1930).

Shutemov, Andrei, "Iz istorii natsrazmezhevaniia Srednei Azii," *Turkmenskaia iskra,* 1 (1924).

Skalov, G., "Ekonomicheskoe ob'edinenie Sredne-aziatskikh respublik kak faktor natsional'noi politiki," *Zhizn' natsional'nostei,* 5 (1923).

Skalov, G., "Khivinskaia revoliutsiia 1920 goda," *Novyi vostok,* 3 (1923).

Skalov, G., "Sotsial'naia priroda Basmachestva v Turkestane," *Zhizn' natsional'nostei* 3-4 (1923).

Soloveichik, D., "Revoliutsionnaia Bukhara," *Novyi vostok,* 2 (1922).

Stasevich, "Natsional'nyi sostav naseleniia RSFSR," *Zhizn' natsional'nostei,* 1 (1924).

Tiruriakulov, "O Kokandskoi avtonomii," in *Tri goda sovetskoi vlasti,* Tashkent, 1920.

Tiuriakulov, N., "Turkestanskaia avtonomnaia respublika," *Zhizn' natsional'nostei,* 1 (1923).

Tolstov, S. P., "K voprosu o proiskhozhdenii Kara-Kalpakskogo naroda," *Kratkie soobsheheniia instituta etnografii,* 2 (1947).

Tolstov, S. P., "Osnovnye problemy etnogeneza narodov Srednei Azii," *Sovetskaia etnografiia, sbornik statei,* 7-8 (1947).

Tolstov, S. P., "Velikaia pobeda Leninsko-Stalinskoi natsional'noi politiki (k dvadtsatitriletiiu natsional'nogo razmezhevaniia v Srednei Azii)," *Sovetskaia etnografiia,* 1 (1950).

Trainin, I., "Postanovka natsional'nogo voprosa," *Vlast' sovetov,* 5 (1923).

Tursunov, Kh. T., "Natsional'noe razmezhevanie Srednei Azii i obrazovanie Uzbekskoi SSR," *Voprosy istorii,* 10 (1964).

Ul'ianov, G., "K voprosu o podgotovke uchitel'stva natsional'nykh men'shinstv," *Narodnoe prosveshchenie* (Moscow), 11-12 (1924).

Urazaev, Sh. Z., "K voprosu o roli komissii VTsIK i SNK RSFSR po delam Turkestana v ukreplenii sovetskoi vlasti v Turkestane," in *Uchenye zapiski iurfaka SAGU,* vypusk III, Tashkent, 1957.

Usenbaev, K., "K voprosu ob obshchnosti territorii Kirgizskogo naroda v dorevoliutsionnyi period," in *Trudy instituta istorii,* vypusk 2, Frunze, 1956.

Vakhabov, M. G., "K voprosu o formirovanii Uzbekskoi burzhuaznoi natsii," in *Materialy nauchnoi sessii posviashchennoi istorii Srednei Azii i Kazakhstana v dooktiabr'skii period*, Tashkent, 1955.

Vasilevskii, "Fazy Basmacheskogo dvizheniia v Srednei Azii," *Novyi vostok*, 29 (1930).

Vikulin, K., "Kara-Kalpakskaia avtonomnaia SSR," *Sovetskoe stroitel'stvo*, 5 (1932).

Wheeler, G. E., "Cultural Developments in Soviet Central Asia," *Journal of Royal Central Asian Society*, 41 (1954).

Zelenski, I., "Natsional'no-gosudarstvennoe razmezhevanie v Srednei Azii," *Turkestanskaia pravda*, 20 (11 November 1924).

Zorin, A., "10 let sovetskoi Kirgizii," *Revoliutsionnyi vostok*, 6 (1934).

C. *Journals and Newspapers*

Central Asian Review
Istoricheskii zhurnal
Istoriia SSR
Istorik marksist
Journal of Royal Central Asian Society
Journal of Royal Institute of International Affairs
Kommunist Kazakhstana
Kommunist Turkmenistana
Kratkie soobshcheniia instituta etnografii
Mezhdunarodnaia zhizn'
Narodnoe khoziaistvo Srednei Azii
Narodnoe prosveshchenie
Nasha strana
Novyi vostok
Planovoe khoziaistvo
Pravda vostoka
Proletarskaia revoliutsiia

Revoloitsiia i natsional'nosti
Revoliutsionnyi vostok
Sovetskaia Aziia
Sovetskaia etnografiia
Sovetskoe gosudarstvo
Sovetskoe gosudarstve i pravo
Sovetskoe pravo
Sovetskoe stroitel'stvo
Sovetskoe vostokovedenie
Studies on the Soviet Union
Turkestanskaia pravda
Turkmenovedenie
Turkmenskaia iskra
Vestnik iustitsii Uzbekistana
Vlast' sovetov
Voennaia mysl'
Voprosy istorii
Voprosy istorii KPSS
Zhizn' natsional'nostei

Index